2 —

Reviews of Note
from colleagues and professionals

"THE CONTRIBUTORS BRING THE TRADITIONAL TOOLS OF ETHICS AND POLITICAL PHILOSOPHY TO BEAR IN A CLEAR AND FORCEFUL WAY ON ISSUES SURROUNDING THE RIGHTS OF HOMO-SEXUALS. The case they make . . . is so convincing that anyone reading this would be led to wonder how homophobia can continue to be so prevalent among those members of our society who claim to be rational. . . . Obviously appropriate for courses in gay studies, it could also be used as a primary text in any introductory course in ethics or political philosophy."
—David L. Hull, Dressler Professor in the Humanities, Department of Philosophy, Northwestern University

"SHOULD BE READ BY ANYONE WITH MORE THAN A PASSING INTEREST IN ETHICAL ISSUES INVOLVED IN GAY, LESBIAN, AND BISEXUAL LIFE IN THE U.S. TODAY. . . . An extremely valuable book for readers who want clear, careful, mostly jargon-free analyses of a number of ethical issues. . . . Contributes to the moral discussion of outing directly pursued in this collection's first section."
—Susan C. Hale, PhD, Assistant Professor, Department of Philosophy, California State University

D1711234

"PROVIDES AN IMPORTANT LOOK AT ETHICAL
ISSUES CENTRAL TO GAY AND LESBIAN ACTIVISM
IN THE NINETIES. Using a range of ethical theories, the authors show how ethical analysis can
challenge discriminatory practices and promote
gay and lesbian civil rights. Murphy has brought
together an impressive variety of essays by philosophers and legal scholars that clearly
illustrates the vital links between ethics, politics,
and activism. . . . Particularly compelling are
discussions of outing and the closet which analyze
not only the merits and limits of privacy rights
but also the complexities of truth-telling."**
—Julien S. Murphy, PhD, Associate Professor of Philosophy,
University of Southern Maine

Gay Ethics:
Controversies in Outing, Civil Rights, and Sexual Science

Gay Ethics:
Controversies in Outing, Civil Rights, and Sexual Science

Timothy F. Murphy, PhD
Editor

Gay Ethics: Controversies in Outing, Civil Rights, and Sexual Science, edited by Timothy F. Murphy, was simultaneously issued by The Haworth Press, Inc., under the same title, as a special issue of *Journal of Homosexuality*, Volume 27, Numbers 3/4, 1994. John P. De Cecco, Editor.

Harrington Park Press
An Imprint of
The Haworth Press, Inc.
New York • London • Norwood (Australia)

ISBN 1-56023-056-8

Published by

Harrington Park Press, 10 Alice Street, Binghamton, NY 13904-1580

Harrington Park Press is an Imprint of the Haworth Press, Inc., 10 Alice Street, Binghamton, Ny 13904-1580 USA.

Gay Ethics: Controversies in Outing, Civil Rights, and Sexual Science has also been published as
Journal of Homosexuality, Volume 27, Numbers 3/4, 1994.

The Haworth Press, Inc., 10 Alice Street, Binghamton, NY 13904-1580 USA

Library of Congress Cataloging-in-Publication Data

Gay ethics : Controversies in outing, civil rights, and sexual science / Timothy F. Murphy, editor.
     p.   cm.
    Includes bibliographical references and index.
    ISBN 1-56024-671-5 (acid-free paper).–ISBN 1-56023-056-8 (pbk. : acid-free paper)
    1. Homosexuality–Moral and ethical aspects–United States. 2. Coming out (Sexual orienta-
tion)–United States. 3. Outing (Sexual orientation)–United States. 4. Civil rights–United States.
5. Homosexuality–Physiological aspects. I. Murphy, Timothy F., 1955- .
HQ76.25.G415 1994
305.9′0664–dc20
                                    94-14155
                                       CIP

INDEXING & ABSTRACTING

Contributions to this publication are selectively indexed or abstracted in print, electronic, online, or CD-ROM version(s) of the reference tools and information services listed below. This list is current as of the copyright date of this publication. See the end of this section for additional notes.

- *Abstracts in Anthropology*, Baywood Publishing Company, 26 Austin Avenue, P.O. Box 337, Amityville, NY 11701

- *Abstracts of Research in Pastoral Care & Counseling*, Loyola College, 7135 Minstrel Way, Suite 101, Columbia, MD 21045

- *Academic Abstracts/CD-ROM*, EBSCO Publishing, P.O. Box 2250 Peabody, MA 01960-7250

- *Applied Social Sciences Index & Abstracts (ASSIA)*, Bowker-Saur Limited, Maypole House, Maypole Road, East Grinstead, West Sussex RH19 1HH England

- *Book Review Index,* Gale Research, Inc., P.O. Box 2867, Detroit, MI 48231

- *Cambridge Scientific Abstracts*, *Risk Abstracts*, Cambridge Information Group, 7200 Wisconsin Avenue, #601, Bethesda, MD 20814

- *Criminal Justice Abstracts*, Willow Tree Press, 15 Washington Street, 4th Floor, Newark NJ 07102

- *Criminology, Penology and Police Science Abstracts*, Kugler Publications, P.O. Box 11188, 1001 GD-Amsterdam, The Netherlands

- *Current Contents/Social & Behavioral Sciences*, Institute for Scientific Information, 3501 Market Street, Philadelphia, PA 19104-3302

- *Digest of Neurology and Psychiatry*, The Institute of Living, 400 Washington Street, Hartford, CT 06106

(continued)

- *Excerpta Medica/Electronic Publishing Division*, Elsevier Science Publishers, 655 Avenue of the Americas, New York, NY 10010

- *Expanded Academic Index*, Information Access Company, 362 Lakeside Drive, Forest City, CA 94404

- *Family Life Educator "Abstracts Section"* ETR Associates, P.O. Box 1830, Santa Cruz, CA 95061-1830

- *Family Violence & Sexual Assault Bulletin*, Family Violence & Sexual Assault Institute, 1310 Clinic Drive, Tyler, TX 75701

- *Index Medicus/MEDLINE*, National Library of Medicine, 8600 Rockville Pike, Bethesda, MD 20894

- *Index to Periodical Articles Related to Law*, University of Texas, 727 East 26th Street, Austin, TX 78705

- *Inventory of Marriage and Family Literature (online and hard copy)*, National Council on Family Relations, 3989 Central Avenue NE, Suite 550, Minneapolis, MN 55421

- *Leeds Medical Information,* University of Leeds, Leeds LS2 9JT, United Kingdom

- *Mental Health Abstracts (online through DIALOG)*, IFI/Plenum Data Company, 3202 Kirkwood Highway, Wilmington, DE 19808

- *PASCAL International Bibliography T205: Sciences de l'information Documentation*, INIST/CNRS-Service Gestion des Documents Primaires, 2, allée du Parc de Brabois, F-54514 Vandoeuvre-les-Nancy, Cedex, France

- *Periodical Abstracts, Research 1* (general and basic reference indexing and abstracting data-base from University Microfilms International (UMI), 300 North Zeeb Road, P.O. Box 1346, Ann Arbor, MI 48106-1346), UMI Data Courier, P.O. Box 32770, Louisville, KY 40232-2770

(continued)

- *Periodical Abstracts, Research 2* (broad coverage indexing and abstracting data-base from University Microfilms International (UMI), 300 North Zeeb Road, P.O. Box 1346, Ann Arbor, MI 48106-1346), UMI Data Courier, P.O. Box 32770, Louisville, KY 40232-2770

- *PsychNet*, PsychNet Inc., P.O. Box 470250 Aurora, CO 80047-0250

- *Psychological Abstracts (PsycINFO)*, American Psychological Association, P.O. Box 91600, Washington, DC 20090-1600

- *Public Affairs Information Bulletin (PAIS)*, Public Affairs Information Service Inc., 521 West 43rd Street, New York, NY 10036-4396

- *Religion Index One: Periodicals*, American Theological Library Association, 820 Church Street, 3rd Floor, Evanston, IL 60201

- *Sage Family Studies Abstracts (SFSA)*, Sage Publications, Inc., 2455 Teller Road, Newbury Park, CA 91320

- *Social Planning/Policy & Development Abstracts (SOPODA)*, Sociological Abstracts, Inc., P.O. Box 22206, San Diego, CA 92192-0206

- *Social Sciences Citation Index*, Institute for Scientific Information, 3501 Market Street, Philadelphia, PA 19104

- *Social Sciences Index*, The H.W. Wilson Company, 950 University Avenue, Bronx, NY 10452

- *Social Work Abstracts*, National Association of Social Workers, 750 First Street NW, 8th Floor, Washington, DC 20002

- *Sociological Abstracts (SA)*, Sociological Abstracts, Inc., P.O. Box 22206, San Diego, CA 92192-0206

- *Studies on Women Abstracts*, Carfax Publishing Company, P.O. Box 25, Abingdon, Oxfordshire OXI4 3UE, United Kingdom

Book reviews are selectively excerpted by the Guide to Professional Literature of the Journal of Academic Librarianship.

SPECIAL BIBLIOGRAPHIC NOTES

related to special journal issues (separates)
and indexing/abstracting

☐ indexing/abstracting services in this list will also cover material in the "separate" that is co-published simultaneously with Haworth's special thematic journal issue or DocuSerial. Indexing/abstracting usually covers material at the article/chapter level.

☐ monographic co-editions are intended for either non-subscribers or libraries which intend to purchase a second copy for their circulating collections.

☐ monographic co-editions are reported to all jobbers/wholesalers/approval plans. The source journal is listed as the "series" to assist the prevention of duplicate purchasing in the same manner utilized for books-in-series.

☐ to facilitate user/access services all indexing/abstracting services are encouraged to utilize the co-indexing entry note indicated at the bottom of the first page of each article/chapter/contribution.

☐ this is intended to assist a library user of any reference tool (whether print, electronic, online, or CD-ROM) to locate the monographic version if the library has purchased this version but not a subscription to the source journal.

☐ individual articles/chapters in any Haworth publication are also available through the Haworth Document Delivery Services (HDDS).

Gay Ethics:
Controversies in Outing,
Civil Rights, and Sexual Science

ABOUT THE EDITOR

Timothy F. Murphy holds a doctorate in philosophy from Boston College and is Assistant Professor of Philosophy in the Biomedical Sciences. He teaches in the Medical Humanities Program at the University of Illinois College of Medicine at Chicago. He is the coeditor of both *Writing AIDS: Gay Literature, Language, and Analysis* (Columbia University Press, 1993) and *Justice and the Human Genome Project* (University of California Press, 1994). He is also the author of *Ethics in an Epidemic: AIDS, Morality, and Culture* (forthcoming from the University of California Press) and is writing a book on the ethics of sexual reorientation therapy.

CONTENTS

Gay Ethics:
Controversies in Outing, Civil Rights, and Sexual Science

PART I.
STARTING POINTS

Introduction

The essays gathered here suggest how ethics have come to countenance gay and lesbian sexualities and identities in ways that move
beyond conventional philosophical analyses that focused exclusively on the morality of specific kinds of sexual acts, the nature of
perversion, or the cogency of scientific accounts of the origins of
homoeroticism. To the extent that questions about the ethics of gay
sexuality have been framed as questions about its sexual events or
origins, they have eclipsed other, more important questions about
the standing and treatment of gay men and lesbians in society generally. Made possible through years of activism and increasing
scholarly attention, the essays here raise questions that are not confined to the nature of perversion or the order of nature. Though they
often taken various forms and may begin in discussions of privacy
or biology, more often than not the questions raised here are questions of social justice.

In the opening essay, I offer a discussion which confronts the
notion that homosex is something set apart in the order of human

[Haworth co-indexing entry note]: "Introduction." Murphy, Timothy F. Co-published simulta-
neously in the *Journal of Homosexuality* (The Haworth Press, Inc.) Vol. 27, No. 3/4, 1994, pp. 1-7; and:
Gay Ethics: Controversies in Outing, Civil Rights, and Sexual Science (ed: Timothy F. Murphy) The
Haworth Press, Inc., 1994, pp. 1-7. Multiple copies of this article/chapter may be purchased from The
Haworth Document Delivery Center [1-800-3-HAWORTH; 9:00 a.m. - 5:00 p.m. (EST)].

1

sexuality. Resisting such a notion, I situate homosex alongside heterosex as its moral confederate, not as its alleged antagonist. I argue
that the morality of homosex is not reducible to questions of body
parts but instead that homosex is better and more accurately understood as a medium of human expression. Thus understood, the
moral meaning of homoeroticism is not confined to derogatory
analyses that depend on contentious and limiting assumptions about
the "nature" of human sexual interactions. On the contrary, homoeroticism thereby emerges as a valuable and important medium
in and through which persons express moral meanings that would
not be otherwise possible. It is not even obvious that homosex
requires any special moral justification. Thus construed, the ethics
that govern the practice of homosex are, then, merely the ethics that
govern human actions elsewhere.

If homoeroticism does not by itself require any special moral
justification, then ethical questions rightly focus on the way in
which gay and lesbian sexuality is socially and intellectually accommodated. The morality of outing has taken a central role in gay
ethics at this time when society and politics are in flux with regard
not only to the control of information generally but also the public
treatment of gay men and lesbians. The essays addressing outing–and being out–offer and defend a wide range of views. Jeremiah McCarthy offers an account that represents outing as an important repudiation of the evils of the closet, though he does not
conclude that outing is always moral. By contrast, David J. Mayo
and Martin Gunderson describe reasons they think outing should
usually be resisted, reasons that are rooted in respect for privacy
and self-determination. Mark Chekola acknowledges that the closet
serves a shielding function in homophobic society, but he also underlines the ways in which it signifies shame. He describes a
number of situations in which pursuit of one's interests justifies
outing, and he ultimately rejects the notion that there can be a
general rule against outing. The focus of the essay by Steven Barbone and Lee Rice is not so much outing per se as the question of
"being out." They note the ways in which personal identity is better
served by a focus on an individualistic ethic; they thus conclude that
there exists no general obligation to be out–though they do not deny
the value of being out. Instead, for them the better question is not

whether one should be out (or be outed) but whether being out serves one's interests or not. Whatever else separates these essays, taken together they offer formidable reasons to think that there is neither an absolute rule justifying or forbidding outing in all cases.

Certain perennial civil rights questions are also addressed in this volume. The question of gay marriage has returned to prominence for a number of reasons, reasons having to do with both the emergence of anti-discrimination laws and social interest in securing access to economic and social benefits that attend marriage and formalized domestic partnership. These questions emerge, too, at a time when courts around the country are coming to disparate and competing conclusions about rights in, for example, adoption, childbearing, and partner benefits. Craig Dean, who, with his partner Patrick Gill, has been fighting for the right to marry in the nation's capital, offers a brief on how anti-discrimination laws in the District of Columbia–and other supporting moral considerations–frame a convincing legal case for the option of gay marriage. A storm of media attention and public debate ensued President Bill Clinton's early 1993 statement of intention to rescind the ban on the presence of openly gay men and lesbians in the military. Having taken up the issue before Clinton's election, Claudia Card is well situated to analyze the way in which universities have moral obligations to resist discrimination. Her essay focuses on the discriminatory policies of the Reserve Officer Training Corps (ROTC), but its arguments extend to the military as a whole. She rightly insists that in addition to their important economic waste, policies of exclusion are the cause and consequence of the defamation of lesbians and gay men. She describes in detail the psychological, intellectual, and moral corruption that are fostered and rewarded by discriminatory policies. She makes it clear that the closeting required by lesbians and gay men in order to succeed in ROTC programs and the military generally are not choices lesbians and gay men would otherwise make except in response to a homophobic environment. She also makes clear the detriments of exclusionary policies to society's larger moral fabric.

Vincent J. Samar turns his attention to the question of anti-discrimination laws and finds that Western ethical traditions offer considerable and credible justification in favor of such laws. Far from being a bulwark of moral objection to gay and lesbian persons, Western moral traditions offer formidable–if conveniently over-looked–reasons why anti-discriminatory policies ought to be the rule rather than the exception in respect to employment, housing, and public accommodations. So that such laws will not be dismissed out of hand as unenforceable, Samar also details some of the practical ways in which such laws could be in fact reasonably and effectively carried out. In turn, Joseph Sartorelli argues that because such anti-discriminatory policies would fail to countenance many of the social evils endured by gay men and lesbians, affirmative action policies are justified as well. Looking at the way in which affirmative action policies are justified, Sartorelli finds that the social disadvantages suffered by gay men and lesbians–especially while young–constitute grave assaults on self-esteem and the potential for development. These indignities not only hamper the ability to flourish and enforce a servility of temperament, they are at least equivalent in force and significance to those morally undesirable circumstances that elsewhere justify affirmative action policies. Sartorelli finds, therefore, that the chief goal and message of affirmative action efforts should be to effect openness for gay people, given the importance of that openness for personal and political development. These efforts should have, too, important social benefits elsewhere and escape some of the objections raised to existing affirmative action efforts.

Science and medicine also continue to turn their attention to the question of homoeroticism, especially in an age of increasingly advanced biomedical research methods. Frederick Suppe surveys a number of accounts that have been offered to explain the causes of homosexuality, including recent studies about comparative brain structure size and the sexual orientation of twins. He finds that these accounts are typically beset by methodological flaws–including fundamental concepts underlying the research–and are therefore unconvincing in their claims of causality. More important than identifying the flaws of any particular account, he goes on to argue that the question of the origins of sexual orientation is of interest only against a set of objectionable normative assumptions about the nature of human sexuality generally and that it is an inadequately justified scientific question that ought to be abandoned.

Edward Stein, by contrast, grants the legitimacy of inquiry into the origins of sexual orientation but objects to the ways in which such science is used as a prop in arguments on behalf of and sometimes against gay and lesbian civil rights. He argues that empirical questions about the origins of sexual orientation are largely irrelevant to questions about whether and what kind of civic entitlements gay men and lesbians should have. He thinks that purely moral arguments should suffice to establish the rights of gay men and lesbians in society and the law. Arguments for gay and lesbian rights, that is, should not be based in particular accounts that sexual orientation is, for example, genetic in origin. In this sense the question of the origins of homoerotic orientations is morally moot.

Because of their continuing importance in the field, Michael Ferguson considers the notions of fixation and regression in psychoanalytic accounts of the origin of homosexuality. He finds that the use of these notions—especially by those analysts who declare homosexuality to be pathological—cannot be justified on the evidence offered on their behalf. He finds, specifically, that analysts' biases about the goals and norms of psychosexual development shape the way in which homosexuality has been declared pathologically fixated or regressive. He notes, that is, the intrusion of moral values about human sexuality into putatively value-free, scientific accounts.

In the concluding essay, Abby Wilkerson takes up the question of homophobia in medicine today. She rightly understands that such a question is not reducible to whether medicine does or does not formally declare homoeroticism to be a pathology. Indeed, she discovers that there are many ways in which medicine functions homophobically, and evidence for such homophobia may be found in the way in which people with HIV-related disease are treated by health care professionals, in the way in which medicine is used as an authority in the interpretation of AIDS, and in the representations of people with AIDS. She also is adept in pointing out how certain ways of framing questions about health care ethics, especially the presumption of "objectivity," can function homophobically in masking the legitimate health interests of gay men and lesbians.

While these questions are all significant to contemporary debates, they certainly do not exhaust the topics that properly fall under a consideration of gay ethics. In this regard, a note on the history of the volume is in order. I originally intended the collection to address questions of both gay and lesbian ethics. In fact, because of the way in which the essays here range over topics of interest to both gay men and lesbians, that intention has been met in a number of significant ways. But the collection has in fact addressed issues mostly from the perspective of men because–and only because–more men came forward in response to my search for contributors than did women. In their accounts, many of the essays here do speak of both gay men and lesbians, and even where they do not many of the arguments would apply without much modification equally to men and women. There is, though, certainly room for an anthology of lesbian ethics that collects essays mostly by women who will have their own perspectives about the way in which questions of ethics should be framed and answered.

It is also inevitable in these times, it is worth observing, that an editor runs up against hard questions of terminology. This collection has been assembled under the rubric "gay ethics." I do not intend that title in the literal definition of rubric as signifying a custom or form wholly established and settled by social authority. Indeed, this rubric will seem to some a mistake for a number of reasons, especially as it might be interpreted as conflating the interests and identities of men and women. It also fails to capture the interests of some who assume more self-consciously provocative labels or who aspire to more inclusive terminology. Certainly, all homoerotic behavior, identities, and politics do not transpire under the labels of gay or lesbian. Nevertheless, the terminology of gay ethics seems to me to have a useful function in identifying the nature and scope of the essays gathered here, and I have chosen that terminology in order to stress the continuities of these essays with the moral and political efforts that preceded them. This is only to say that there is abundant room, too, for other anthologies, for example, an anthology of "queer ethics" and the questions such perspectives make possible in regard to matters of language, identities, politics, and tactics.

That so much remains possible to do, moreover, is instructive in its own right. There are many ways in which the history of ethics has failed to use its rich resources and powerful tools in identifying, resisting, and proposing amends for the evils suffered by gay men and lesbians. Its failures in this regard have been committed both by act and omission. The essays gathered here do not recover all the ways in which the moral traditions might be used as resources for the ethical critiques made possible through gay and lesbian perspectives. Neither do these essays identify all the issues of moral interest in contemporary politics, law, religion, and society. These essays do, however, raise durable questions about the meaning of sexuality for private and public life, civics, and science. They pose challenges to enduring forms of social oppression in the military, civil rights, and even in the social conventions observed among gay men and lesbians themselves. They contest the agenda and moral interpretation of science. They also challenge the healing arts to attain a higher standard of ethics than they otherwise now have. And in so doing, they all make evident the ways in which ethics may and should be reclaimed to pursue the moral good for gay men and lesbians.

Timothy F. Murphy

Homosex/Ethics

Timothy F. Murphy, PhD

University of Illinois College of Medicine at Chicago

SUMMARY. Against the view that homoeroticism requires any special justification or consideration, this essay argues that homoeroticism is morally unproblematic in itself and that its genuine moral significance resides in illuminating the nature and meaning of human relations. Seen as a form of language, homosex shares common moral justification with heterosex as a bearer of human meanings and intentions. Thus understood, homosex is an important moral good as a language that expresses human meanings in ways that are not otherwise possible.

Though it might by now have become utterly ordinary, homosex continues to vex private conscience and public opinion. There are perennial questions (why is there homoeroticism?), and there are questions unique to our time (can openly gay men serve as Boy Scout leaders as their closeted counterparts in fact already do?). Discussion about the morality of homosex often trades in moral and

Timothy F. Murphy is Assistant Professor, Department of Medical Education m/c 591, 808 S. Wood St., University of Illinois College of Medicine, Chicago, IL 60612-7309. He is the coeditor of both *Writing AIDS: Gay Literature, Language, and Analysis* (Columbia University Press, 1993) and *Justice and the Human Genome Project* (University of California Press, 1994). He is also the author of *Ethics in an Epidemic: AIDS, Morality, and Culture* (University of California Press, 1994), and he is writing a book on the ethics of sexual reorientation therapy.

[Haworth co-indexing entry note]: "Homosex/Ethics." Murphy, Timothy F. Co-published simultaneously in the *Journal of Homosexuality* (The Haworth Press, Inc.) Vol. 27, No. 3/4, 1994, pp. 9-25; and: *Gay Ethics: Controversies in Outing, Civil Rights, and Sexual Science* (ed: Timothy F. Murphy) The Haworth Press, Inc., 1994, pp. 9-25. Multiple copies of this article/chapter may be purchased from The Haworth Document Delivery Center [1-800-3-HAWORTH; 9:00 a.m. - 5:00 p.m. (EST)].

religious clichés, this on all sides, and it is sometimes hard to avoid the conclusion that not only does moral philosophy not offer any pathway to a unified theory of human judgment, neither can it propose any definitive conclusion about the morality of homosex.

While it does seem to me that the moral arguments on behalf of homosex do carry the day against their competition, I do not want to rehearse here the usual arguments about pathology, normalcy, nature, or religion in order to defend the morality of homosex. Instead, I will argue that homosex stands on its own as sex because, like heterosex, it is a rich and fertile language for discovering and articulating the meanings of human life. Homosex, to say the least, permits capacities for strength, erotic possibilities, and moral meanings that are not otherwise available. Because homosex is not especially opposed to heterosex, both sexualities share many physical and conceptual continuities, and as I will try to show, moral continuities as well. In many regards, therefore, questions about the genitalia of bedroom partners are ultimately beside the moral point. Homosex and heterosex are divided only in the way that English and French are divided, and the differences are not in themselves morally significant except as they offer the opportunity to raise ultimately more significant moral questions about the relations between power and sexuality and about the meaning of difference.

FOREPLAY

In an essay called "Heterosex," Robert Solomon rightly argues that sexual desire is not a discrete, independently subsiding trait in persons, one that could be excised at will, leaving an otherwise intact person behind.[1] On the contrary, and he is right about this as well, a complex of human desires and activities becomes "sexual" mostly through the workings of custom and ritual. One may underline his thesis by noting that orgasm in infants does not, for example, carry the "sexual" meanings adults find in it.[2] What counts as "sexual" expression differs widely among cultures and even among generations within the same culture. One need only think of differences in dressing habits on beaches around the world to understand the variable meanings of sexuality. Sex is indeed more than the sum of anatomical parts and physiological processes. An adequate understanding of sexuality is possible and complete only through an appreciation of the functional meanings of sexuality in our personal and social lives. Just as human *nature* ultimately signifies not what is biologically, socially, or metaphysically given in human life but what can be *summoned* from human beings, the "nature" of our sexuality depends not only on what "parts" are involved but also on what others and our society call forth from us and on how we respond.

Thus does Solomon rightly believe that a recovery of the joys of heterosex (the ostensible goal of his essay) depends on an improved understanding of the poetry of sex and not on an increasingly exact analysis of bodily function: "Heterosex is first of all a kind of poetry, and there is no clear limit to richness of interpersonal feelings that it can express, given an adequate vocabulary and what we might call, tongue in cheek, sexual literacy" (223). To be sure, sexual literacy depends on behaviors, but these behaviors are fully intelligible only as bearers of intentions, emotions, and meanings. In that way, they are like written texts: literally meaningless without a reader.

Solomon's analysis may be extended by observing how facetious it would be to judge the written word merely as a composition in letters of the alphabet, its final worth decided in terms of, for example, spelling or typeface. Literary efforts should not be judged according to the number of times they use, for example, the letter "t." No work is distinguished merely because it avails itself of words, clauses, or techniques of anastrophe, caesura, hendiadys, or zeugma. Rather it is the way in which these elements and constructions are used–and received–that decide the fate and the meaning of a text. It is possible to see sexuality in the same way. It is neither parts nor acts by themselves that decide the significance of sexual relations but their *meanings* as constructs of their parts, behaviors, intentions, and interpretations.

Sexuality thus construed, it is hard to see why homosex should not be interpreted in the same way as heterosex. If there is no independently abiding desire in humans that is a priori (hetero)sexual, if sexuality is primarily a matter of definitions and meanings, then not only is there no reason to think of homoeroticism as anything but sex, there is also no reason to give heterosex any kind of priority in having greater claim to being the "essence" or "nature" of sex any more than there would be reason to assert that Latin or German were the "nature" of language itself and all other tongues merely a falling off from those culturolinguistic paradigms. On the contrary, homosex would seem to be conceptually continuous with heterosex insofar as it represents a similar range of intentions, desires, and definitions in the manner, if not in the same configurations. No less than heterosex, homosex represents fields of attraction, culturally defined, with expressive purposes, some of them more acrobatic than others, but bearers of meanings very often little or no different from those of heterosex.

Both homosex and heterosex would share, for example, common forms in pursuit of interpersonal and social goals and means of expression. And this would remain true whether the origins of homosex belong in–as the speculations about its origins go–fetal hormone deprivation, in unhappy family dynamics, genetic heritage, prideful revolt against the order of God, or merely in the lottery of unaccountable and serendipitous human difference. Homosex is as much about the contact between bodies as heterosex.[3] As much as heterosex, the expressions of homosex may after all be an adventure in discovery, an act of vengeance, a cold manipulation, an experiment in pleasure, a flirtation, an act of cowardice, an expression of sympathy, an act of theater, a passing fancy, an act of trust, a thoughtless relief, a defiance, a bored obligation, a willful expression of difference, a cozy evening at home, a fiery crash in the night, a rescue, and a way of belonging. By grounding the intelligibility of sexuality in its meanings rather than acts it is possible to see how the meanings of homosex are as rich, varied, and as open to invention as those of heterosex.

But there remains nevertheless a culturally abiding sense that homosex is somehow at odds with heterosex. Solomon himself, for example, prefaces his 1987 essay by expressing disappointment that homosex has eclipsed the joys of heterosex. Indeed, he speaks as if homosex were a threat to heterosex: "In the excitement, confusion, liberation, oral and moral indignation inspired by the rediscovery of homosexual love and legitimacy, heterosex has been somewhat left behind. Adam and Eve have become a tired paradigm, a fashion too established and too familiar to inspire philosophical speculation and excitement" (205). It is not clear, however, that Solomon needs the opposition of homosex and heterosex in order to achieve the recovery of the joys of heterosex. Kinsey's studies, and the Bell and Weinberg studies after, made it clear that homoeroticism is to be found as part of a great many lives which also happily accommodate heteroerotic relations.[4] Public visibility of self-identified gay men and lesbians does not wrest away from men, women, or children what sexual inclinations they otherwise have, and certainly homosex appears to be no threat at all to the displacement of heterosex from its privileged place as both cultural presumption and *force majeure* of contemporary social ideals and discourse. Indeed, if the appearance of gay men and lesbians in the entertainment media (such as television, cinema, and pornography) are any guide, not only is homosex no threat to heterosex but *stereotyping* homosex even appears to be one of the comforts of heterosex! That is, the appearance of homosex in public is often controlled by representation forms that tame its potential antagonism with heterosex. Moreover, even if there has been some eclipse of the joys of heterosex, it is not clear why increased public visibility of the joys of homosex is to blame any more than, say, cultural trends against sexuality generally.

Homosex is a "sexual" language that may appear, to be sure, foreign and unintelligible to those unfamiliar with it, but it is a language nonetheless that makes certain relations and meanings possible. Homosex is its own *lingua franca*, spoken by adherents across the world who each contribute to it, change it, define it, make themselves understood through it. It is in many regards, however, no more impervious to understanding than another spoken language. Much of its "vocabulary" and meanings can be "translated" into heterosex especially as homosex relations echo heterosex relations. But certainly all forms of translation eventually run up against structures, meanings, and concepts that find no exact equivalent in moving from one language to another. And so too will homosex have meanings that cannot be duplicated in heterosex. But it is not clear that the lack of complete conceptual or sexual equivalency between homosex and heterosex damages either sexuality any more than differences between spoken languages invite moral judgment on their comparative worth.

An understanding of sexuality that focuses on its meanings rather than its acts, moreover, makes it difficult to posit any moral superiority of heterosex per se to homosex per se. Both sexualities may be "spoken" in better or worse variants. Both forms of expression are also open to the venalities of human weakness and willful machination. No less than homosex, heterosex may involve serious moral impropriety. Heterosex may, for example, involve rape when its partners do not equally consent to intercourse. Heterosex is not beyond moral suspicion when tied to motives of manipulation and degradation, when it presupposes and perpetuates immoral social practices. Heterosex may recapitulate (and perpetuate) social phylogeny insofar as it bears the marks of objectionable inequality between sexes or other social injustices. To say that sex is merely heteroerotic is in the end to say very little about its morality. Homosex, moreover, bears the capacities for vice (and virtue) to be found in heterosex. But it is not clear that these vices are amplified in kind by being a matter of same-sex relations. The ostensible differences of gender involved in heterosex would not significantly alter this conclusion for reasons that will be discussed below.

Sexual morality, therefore, whether involving homosex or heterosex, belongs more ultimately to matters of meaning rather than to matters of genitalia or acts. It is worth saying too that the bodily expressions of homosex (and heterosex) are in an important way epiphenomenal to erotic attraction; they are a function of what biology makes possible. If men and women had body structures different from those they have now, it is likely that they would still find ways to love one another. It is Eros that invents the pleasures of bodies, not body parts that determine the predilections of Eros.

THE WILD THING

If what I have said above is correct, the morality of homosex per se would ultimately depend on its actual meanings in a particular context, in a particular relationship. Nevertheless, objections to homosex per se continue to endure: that it is unnatural, that it poses threats to family and society, that it is irreligious, that it is abnormal, and so on. Certain of these arguments have, to my mind, already been dispatched elsewhere, and I do not want to revisit them here.[5]

I do, however, want to discuss one argument that is used in various ways against homosex: that homosex is inferior sexuality because it fails to unite, as heterosex does, opposite genders.

It is this "unifying" feature of heterosex that led Solomon to pronounce heterosex as sex itself. "The central paradigm," he says, "which provides us with the 'natural' continuity with most of the animal kingdom and even a small minority of plants, is heterosexual intercourse." It is "the prototype for every alternative form of sexuality, from bestial to masturbatory. Heterosex is—sex" (206). On such a view, homosex would not appear to be sex at all, any more than talking to oneself could be called conversation. In his account of the erotic, Michael Scruton suggests that the superior nature of heterosex might be put this way: "In the heterosexual act, it might be said, I move out *from* my body *towards* the other, whose flesh is unknown to me; while in the homosexual act I remain locked within my body, narcissistically contemplating in the other an excitement that is the mirror of my own."[6] In its union of genders, heterosex is believed to offer the opportunities for reaching across differences to construct a relationship with another unlike one's self, to reach a complementarity that is not otherwise possible and whose benefits are set at the center of human rewards. Heterosex is therefore the occasion of courage, of adventure, of conquest, of exploration, and, finally, blessed union.

Compared to heterosex, homosex might appear to be a cowardly thing, an atavistic recoiling from difference. Indeed, some psychological accounts insist on the phobic nature of all homosex.[7] Same-sex love has been characterized as an immurement in the idolatry of self,[8] and its same-sex character invites the judgment that it is also narcissism. Thus are to be understood views that homosex is counterfeit sex, that male homosexuals are simply, unconsciously frightened fugitives from women, fleeing in their panic to one another,[9] locked in love with their own images in the way Narcissus was punished—as Ovid told the tale—for spurning the love of Echo.

Against a facile understanding that heterosex represents a union of differences unparalleled in homosex, it is worth observing the many ways in which heterosex does and does not unite "opposite" sexes. After all, its unions may be as transient as those in homosex.

Moreover, heterosex does not merge bodily, psychological, or chromosomal identities. Heterosex does not by definition unite disparate social roles of men and women; indeed many heterosex relations seem to be structured by profound divisions and differences between both the sexual identities and the gender roles of men and women; these divisions and differences may say more about the nature of power in these relations than they do about the differences of "male" and "female." Complementarity in sexual relations may have less to do with differences between male and female than with differences between the controller and the controlled.[10]

Eve Kosofsky Sedgwick has observed how few ways we actually have to express all the differences that exist between persons, how a few rough-edged distinctions are forced to bear the brunt of individuation.[11] But the same might also be said of the few ways we have for expressing *similarity* between persons. Men and women are alike in ways that defy expression, ways that bind them biologically, emotionally, morally, culturally, even geographically. What "differences" there are between men and women in heterosex may not loom especially large against the plethora of background traits they often share. In practice and in general, individual heterosexual partners typically share significant similarities in age, social standing, health, intelligence, emotions, political views, cultural views, standards of tolerance, hobbies, food and entertainment preferences, and so on. Sexual partners, therefore, are sometimes more united by their similarities than they are divided by their anatomical differences. Hence it is not surprising that heterosex personal ads lay out often stringent criteria of similarity as the *sine qua non* of acquaintance and what comes after. It may not be the conquest of difference that stokes sexual engines in heterosex so much as the lure of the familiar. Insofar as men and women share the same language, cultural background, religion, social class, and so on, differences of anatomy in heterosex may appear vanishingly small and their conquest a minor, maybe an inevitable achievement in a culture whose sexual orthodoxy presupposes heterosex as the virtual destiny of human nature. Given the magnitude of the social, familial, and conceptual forces that impel men and women toward one another, heterosex hardly seems a venture into the unknown; on the contrary, heterosex may appear as inevitable as the working of gravity. Given all the ways in which heterosex presupposes shared traits, anatomical differences seem almost beside the point, mere ripples in the fleshy mirrors in which we contemplate ourselves. Men and women are, after all, *exactly the same* as regards kingdom, phylum, class, order, family, genus, and species, this regardless of their gender or sexual habits.

It is also not clear that heterosex by definition represents strength in ways that homosex cannot, represents venturesomeness that homosex evades. Indeed, homosex can represent opportunities for growth and adaptation that are otherwise unavailable. It is well to remember that most gay men and lesbians are minorities *even in their own families.* They do not, that is, have the familial opportunity to model their sexual lives on someone with erotic attractions like theirs in kind. While growing up, many gay men and lesbians believe themselves, wrongly, to be the only one of their kind or they believe themselves to be destined to fates inferred from stereotyped representations in schoolyard jokes, fiction, and the movies. They lack in this regard all the support, models, counsel, and understanding that are freely, fully, and unconsciously available to heterosexually-destined children. Indeed, not only do they lack such models, they will be daily confronted with models antagonistic to their own experience. Boys will be teased about would-be girlfriends when in fact their sights are set on their classmates lingering in the locker room shower, and girls will be teased about husbands when in fact their wistful imaginations are occupied with the shy new girl who just transferred from the school across town. Images of gay men in the media will conjure up fates beset by mass murderers or inexorable deaths with AIDS, and images of lesbians will not fail either to evoke problematic futures. Beyond familial dynamics, moreover, there is an enormous influence of social influences that raise the standard of heterosex before all children, all amounting to an avalanche of heterosex symbolism and affirmation. Where mentioned at all, homosex will often be encountered as a matter of condemnation, scorn, and ridicule, as a way of marking difference and inferiority. Gay men and lesbians do not have available to them either preformed language for expression of their sexuality or preformed social opportunities for the pursuit of erotic lives (though in some places this diminishment is abating for some).

They do not ordinarily have the benefits of parental and social expectation to guide them. They find themselves at the mercy of public discourse and symbolism in education, media, and religion that presuppose heterosex as the order of human nature. When they go to the libraries for information, they find discussions of pathology, they find their books stacked alongside tomes about pornography and prostitution, and the newspaper indexes will refer parties interested in homosex to the subject-heading of AIDS.

Given these significant familial and culturally pervasive barriers to self-esteem and growth, gay and lesbian young people face challenges that offer them plenty of opportunity for the development of personal skills and capacities. It also requires of them risks and undertakings without analogue in heterosex. Far from being a matter of sheer cowardice, homosex brings opportunities for strength and heroism that are unparalleled in heterosex. Gay men and lesbians must typically find their own way in the world with little of the supportive cues and emotional parallels that are available, in regard to heterosex, in family dynamics, public behavior, and public culture. They must make a language of their own in order to express themselves. They must make their own way in finding social opportunities, seeking civic benefits and protections, and creating their own symbolism, imagery, and culture. They must, in short, make choices in kind that others do not have to make. And thus is coming out central to adult gay men and lesbians. Whatever else it is, coming out is a rejection of a culturally imposed ideal that heterosex is the nature and destiny of all persons. It is a declaration that one will speak henceforth from one's own experience and not be defined by and confined by public mythology. Thus construed, there is nothing about the possible social and personal meanings of homosex that require an a priori understanding of homoeroticism as inimical to human strength and courage or as a kind of sexual solipsism. On the contrary, as Richard Mohr has observed, "Gays might even have a thing or two to teach others about the divisions of labor, the relation of sexuality to intimacy, and the stages of development in love relationships."[12] This is to say that the pursuit of homosex is often by its very nature an adventure in invention and self-creation. It is not clear why this kind of courage should not be seen as equivalent in value to the kind of "heroism" that suppos-

edly leads men to women and women to men. Indeed, it even seems
fair to say that in certain circumstances, homosex requires *more* not
less strength than heterosex when it overcomes a hostile and indifferent world in order to find ways to share a sense of discovery,
touch, and intimacy.

Homosex, moreover, not only shares the capacity for strength
thought to typify heterosex, it also makes possible some meanings
of sexuality that could *not otherwise* occur. For example, homosex
can imply a defiance of public ideals, religious views, and sexual
conformity, this in ways unavailable to heterosex. It can be an act of
self-assertion without parallel in heteroeroticism given the ways in
which heterosex, as expected and nourished, does not invite confrontation with publicly professed sexual ideals and identities. And
thus are to be understood views like those of novelist John Rechy,
who in *The Sexual Outlaw* portrays homosex as revolutionary despite the fact that his protagonists live under cover of darkness and
screw one another entirely out of public view.[13] Such a sexual
revolution is not one that destroys the dominance of heterosex; it is
a revolution that person by person rejects the hegemony of heterosex by refusing to be controlled by socially defined gender roles,
as these have been formed by what Adrienne Rich has called "compulsory heterosexuality."

It is the sameness of genders in homosex that perhaps drives the
view—commonalities in heterosex notwithstanding—that homosex is
nothing more than masturbation writ large, that its "sterility" is
emotional and psychological as well as reproductive, that its "sterility" is both the cause and effect of homosex, that its uncomple-
mentary nature is inalterably narcissistic. There are, though, many
ways in which homo-eroticism does not deserve its etymology,
ways in which it is indeed not homo-erotic but allo-erotic. In his
essay "Homo-Narcissism; or, Heterosexuality," Michael Warner
has, for example, criticized the narcissistic view of homosex,[14]
arguing, first of all, that Freud's own analysis does not show homosex to be any kind of developmental regression because homosex is, after all, not merely pursuit of one's *own* image. Beyond
this specific analysis, Warner also holds that the view of homosex
as narcissism is itself a form of narcissism peculiar to modern
heterosex. It is a narcissism insofar as heterosex requires all sex to

reflect its own configuration in which there is an antagonistic Self-and-Other relationship, a relationship that permits and even requires forms of domination. This kind of analysis makes it clear that what is found "objectionable" in homosex is not the presence of certain behaviors so much as the absence of the traits around which identity, authority, and community have been traditionally defined. It is hard to see, therefore, in what ways the label of narcissism generates a significant objection to homosex if, in fact, the concept functions to advance its own ideology about the structure of interpersonal relations. *Even if* narcissism were the pursuit of one's own image, given the extent to which heterosex relations themselves presuppose and seek similarity, they too would be implicated in narcissism. It is not clear, that is, why similarity of body parts between partners should be seen as more indicative of narcissism than similarity of, say, deeply-held religious or political views.

Like the moral worth of heterosex, then, the moral worth of homosex ultimately depends not on questions of narcissism but on the people involved and the context of their lives. And it is here in looking at the social context of homosex that one finds moral questions worth raising, but these questions are not about the use of body parts and their "fit" or the intentions of nature.

AS IF AFTER SEX

If we adopt Solomon's approach to sexuality, that it is a kind of poetry, then the question of complementarity of genders or body parts does not define the ethics or poetics of sexuality. On the contrary, if we understand sexuality as a system of meanings and languages, there is no defensible reason to impose a single paradigm on the whole gamut of possible sexual relationships. The question of the complementarity of genders is only one question among many that might be asked about the "nature" of sexuality, and there is no reason to think it is the most pressing question either. The ethical questions relevant to homosex are the questions that apply elsewhere: does it enrich or debase, does it recapitulate objectionable domination, does it leave its partners dreaming on their pillows?

Other questions may be more important, too, about the ethics of homosex. These questions include inquiries about how homosex came to be culturally and morally problematic and how this "problematization" continues despite changing views in medicine and the law, despite evidence contrary to the supposed dangers of homosex. It is not only the specific conclusions of a moral argument against homosex that we must henceforth consider, it is the presuppositions and values of that argument that should be analyzed as well. The "morality" of homosex will be decided only to the extent that we analyze why a society can believe that homosex is a worse evil than violence inflicted against gay men, lesbians, and even those children who transiently exhibit homoerotic behavior. Why is it, such inquiry wants to know, that homosex is publicly disclaimed and declaimed but in fact widely practiced and tolerated by persons of every age, in every social stratum, in every religion, in every corner of the planet? How can homosex be what it is: the open secret of this society?[15] How is it that societies can be this profoundly and inexorably hypocritical?

Questions about the morality of homosex will not be much illuminated by looking at what two men do in bed for an evening or by studying how two women share household chores across a lifetime. Homosex should not be seen either as a question affecting only homoerotic partners. Homosex should be seen, if these analyses are going to work, as a reflection of the nature of moral and cultural history. Homosex is more illuminating when seen as a battlefield for the control of morality rather than as an adventure in anatomy. Homosex is more revealing when considered in terms of social power and labelling rather than as a case study in psychofamilial dynamics. Homosex is more revealing for the perspectives it offers about the nature of moral judgment than as an example of moral degradation to be listed alongside child abuse, prostitution, and drug use. Questions that probe into the conditions of the possibility of moral condemnation of homosex will not, of course, presuppose that there will be easy answers in the form of identifiably absent fathers and smothering mothers behind the judgments that constitute homosex as reified trait, evil, and disorder. Rightly pursued, however, as questions of moral archeology, they should reveal the conflicts and dominations that have brought us to where we are today and identify those moral ideologies which in framing an issue prejudice our conclusions.

Answers to these kinds of questions will lead, I expect, into analyses of the struggles for power that lie (not deep) beneath the surface of all human relations. Before there was Michel Foucault, Friedrich Nietzsche observed that every argument is a strategy, every opinion a confession, every morality an agenda for survival and domination.[16] Every morality, that is, has its genealogy not in the order of nature but in the order of human struggles to dominate and define the world. By focusing on specific acts and rules and not their more ultimate origins and preconditions, moral philosophy loses the opportunity to consider why, for example, out of all the possible differences in the catalogue of human variability it is homosex that elicits moral interest, conflict, condemnation, and debate.

To be sure, homosex itself remains morally problematic as far as its *practice* is concerned: whether any promised fidelity has been observed, whether relationships are beneficial and beneficent, whether equality in relations is preserved. And in these times, disclosures in sexual relations about disease and infection also take on moral significance. But these questions are *not* magnified in moral importance merely because partners do (as in heterosex) or do not (as in homosex) differ as to the presence of Y chromosomes. These questions are relevant to all sexual relations, regardless of differences or similarities in age, anatomy, race, class, or physical aesthetics. As Alan H. Goldman has observed, the rules governing sex are the rules that apply elsewhere.[17] The meanings of sexuality, both virtuous and vicious, may belong to sexual partners regardless of their sexual identities.

Because homosex meets a felt need of persons, because it is a rich means of expressing what it is to be a human being, because it illuminates the nature of sexuality, because it makes possible questions about the nature of social relations that could not otherwise be asked, because its absence would diminish the richness of being, it does not appear that homosex stands in need of any special moral justification. On the contrary, homosex appears to be a highly desirable form of human sexuality without which individual lives and our cultural and moral life would be significantly impoverished. At the very least, the loss of homosex would parallel the loss of a language and its capacity to describe the world and to offer a bridge between persons. It is worth observing that in many ways the declassification of homosex as a psychological disorder by the American Psychiatric Association[18] and other professional organizations did not rescue homosex from all the evils attributed to it. Religious bodies continue to condemn homosex.[19] The occurrence of AIDS in gay men has been taken as evidence of the immorality of homosex.[20] The Supreme Court of the United States still found a way to permit states to criminalize homosex should they so choose.[21] The U.S. military still finds gay men and lesbians a threat to the very existence of competent armed forces.[22] And glaring headlines about homosex ("Hitler was Gay!") still sell tabloids galore.

A seventeenth-century counsel warned that homosex would bring "Earthquakes, famine, pestilence, Saracens, floods, and very fat, voracious field mice."[23] By contrast, the dangers of homosex today are ordinarily cast in terms of threats to children, family, military *esprit de corps*, and religion. But in fact the "threats" to be found in homosex are often of an altogether different order. Homosex threatens the authority claimed in religion, government, and medicine to pronounce on and regulate the sexual lives and loves of all persons. Homosex threatens socially institutionalized hypocrisy which would rather permit and perpetuate injustice than honestly face the lives that people do in fact have. It threatens the status quo in matters of justice and equality. Homosex threatens, too, moral philosophy which can only see the naked individual before it, an individual without history or culture, an individual left thus exposed to the mercy of stark moral premises. Rightly considered, however, analysis of these "threats" of homosex should make it possible to ask with a new self-awareness why homosex should not take its place alongside heterosex as a vehicle of human hope, happiness, and love. And in making such inquiry, it will be possible, I think, to show how homosex is an irreplaceable human good for its benefits between men, between women, for its significance as a difference that illuminates the structure of human relations, for its significance as a spur to justice, and as a unique tongue in which the meaning of human lives are told. This is not to say that homosex cannot be used badly–any sex can; it is merely to say that in homosex there are unions whose complementarity literally fleshes out the plenitude of sexual being.

NOTES

1. Robert Solomon, "Heterosex," in Earl Shelp, ed., *Sexuality and Medicine*, Vol. 1 (Dordrecht: D. Reidel, 1987), pp. 205-224. Where they are contextually clear, further references to this title will be given in the text.

2. See Kenneth Plummer, "Understanding Childhood Sexualities," *Journal of Homosexuality* 20(1/2) (1990): 231-249.

3. See Alan H. Goldman, "Plain Sex," *Philosophy and Public Affairs* 9 (1976/77): 267-287.

4. See Alfred C. Kinsey, Wardell B. Pomeroy, and Clyde E. Martin, *Sexual Behavior in the Human Male* (Philadelphia: W. B. Saunders, 1948); Alfred C. Kinsey, Wardell B. Pomeroy, Clyde E. Martin, and Paul H. Gebhard, *Sexual Behavior in the Human Female* (Philadelphia, 1953: W. B. Saunders); and Alan P. Bell and Martin S. Weinberg, *Homosexualities: A Study of Diversity among Men and Women* (New York: Simon and Schuster, 1978).

5. See Richard Mohr, "Gay Basics: Some Questions, Facts and Values," in Christine Pierce and Donald VanDeVeer, eds., *AIDS, Ethics and Public Policy* (Belmont, CA: Wadsworth, 1988), pp. 193-205; Timothy F. Murphy, "Homosexuality and Nature: Happiness and the Law at Stake," *Journal of Applied Philosophy* 4 (1987): 195-204; Timothy F. Murphy, "Is AIDS A Just Punishment?" *Journal of Medical Ethics* 14 (1988): 154-160; and Michael Ruse, *Homosexuality: A Philosophical Inquiry* (New York: Blackwell, 1988).

6. Roger Scruton, *Sexual Desire* (New York: Free Press, 1986), p. 310. It is worth wondering whether Scruton's argument is not open to a reductio ad absurdum by considering whether the chasms that separate humans from plants and other animals might not also be breached in the name of the repudiation of narcissism he sees in homosex. Solomon also gives such a view credence when he says that the blending of differences and confusions is what "properly keeps" heterosex center stage (Solomon, p. 206).

7. I. Bieber, J. J. Dain, P. R. Dince, M. G. Drellich, H. G. Grand, R. H. Bundlach, M. W. Kremer, A. H. Rifkin, C. B. Wilbert, and T. B. Bieber, *Homosexuality: A Psychoanalytic Study* (New York: Jason Aronson, 1962), pp. 309, 318.

8. Karl Barth, "Church Dogmatics," in Edward Batchelor, ed., *Homosexuality and Ethics* (New York: Pilgrim Press, 1980), pp. 48-51.

9. Edmund Bergler, *Counterfeit Sex*, 2nd ed. (New York: Grune & Stratton, 1982).

10. Rosemary R. Ruether, "From Machismo to Mutuality," in *Homosexuality and Ethics*, pp. 28-32.

11. Eve Kosofsky Sedgwick, *The Epistemology of the Closet* (Berkeley: University of California Press, 1991), p. 22.

12. Richard D. Mohr, *Gays/Justice: A Study in Society, Ethics, and Law* (New York: Columbia University Press, 1988), p. 44.

13. John Rechy, *The Sexual Outlaw* (New York: Grove Press, 1977).

14. Michael Warner, "Homo-Narcissism; or, Heterosexuality," in Joseph A. Boone and Michael Cadden, eds., *Engendering Men* (New York: Routledge, 1990), pp. 190-206.

15. Sedgwick, p. 22.

16. Friedrich Nietzsche, *On the Genealogy of Morals* (New York: Random House, 1967).

17. Goldman, p. 283.

18. See Ronald Bayer, *Homosexuality and American Psychiatry*, 2nd ed. (Princeton: Princeton University Press, 1987).

19. Sacred Congregation for the Doctrine of the Faith, *Letter to the Bishops of the Catholic Church on the Pastoral Care of Homosexual Persons* (Washington, DC: United States Catholic Conference, 1986).

20. James L. Fletcher, "Homosexuality: Kick and Kickback," *Southern Medical Journal* 77 (1984): 149-150.

21. *Bowers v. Hardwick*, 106 S.Ct. 2841 (1986).

22. See Randy Shilts, *Conduct Unbecoming: Lesbians and Gays in the U.S. Military, Vietnam to the Persian Gulf* (New York: St. Martin's Press, 1993).

23. Helmut Thielicke, *The Ethics of Sex* (New York: Harper and Row, 1964), p. 276.

PART II.
OUTING AND THE CLOSET

The Closet and the Ethics of Outing

Jeremiah McCarthy, PhD

Brooklyn, New York

SUMMARY. Because social circumstances have changed, the question of outing has assumed an importance unknown in a time when homosexuality was a guarded secret. This essay describes the evils of the closet in terms of its affronts to the worth of gay men and lesbians. While outing might appear as a repudiation of the closet, this essay argues that not all outing is justified. On the other hand, the article also rejects those arguments that criticize outing as a

Jeremiah McCarthy holds a PhD in Philosophy from the University of North Carolina at Chapel Hill where he wrote a dissertation on Charles Peirce. He has held teaching posts at the University of Missouri-Rolla, Rutgers University, and the College of Staten Island and has written on pragmatism, semiotics, metaphysics, and sexuality.

Correspondence may be addressed to the author c/o Timothy F. Murphy, Department of Medical Education m/c 591, University of Illinois College of Medicine, 808 S. Wood St., Chicago, IL 60612-7309.

[Haworth co-indexing entry note]: "The Closet and the Ethics of Outing." McCarthy, Jeremiah. Co-published simultaneously in the *Journal of Homosexuality* (The Haworth Press, Inc.) Vol. 27, No. 3/4, 1994, pp. 27-45; and: *Gay Ethics: Controversies in Outing, Civil Rights, and Sexual Science* (ed: Timothy F. Murphy) The Haworth Press, Inc., 1994, pp. 27-45. Multiple copies of this article/chapter may be purchased from The Haworth Document Delivery Center [1-800-3-HAWORTH; 9:00 a.m. - 5:00 p.m. (EST)].

violation of privacy as well as arguments that defend outing as no violation of others' rights.

Malcolm Forbes, cultural icon and public heterosexual, was known to the readers of supermarket tabloids and gossip columns as Elizabeth Taylor's escort and presumed lover before his death in 1990. At the same time it was no secret with many members of New York's gay community that Forbes was a homosexual using Taylor as a beard. When Forbes died, *OutWeek* magazine quickly ran a story on his secret life as a gay man.[1] Thus began the "outing" debate: whether it is ever permissible to expose a person as homosexual who wishes to keep that fact a secret.

Outing has become an issue because the conditions of life for gays and lesbians are not what they were twenty or thirty years ago. Social relations form the basis of obligations. When social relations change, obligations may alter as well. In this paper, I will offer the strongest defense I can for the position that outing usually violates a right to privacy. I will nevertheless go on to argue that this defense fails because the conventions that the alleged right depends upon define the closet. I offer in this regard an analysis of the closet as an institution of oppression, arguing that the alleged privacy right would often be a right to oppress oneself and others. I will then go on to argue that outing can sometimes be justified as a tactic for eliminating enemies, destroying the closet, and asserting gay dignity, but that the practice is subject nevertheless to some restrictions.

PRIVACY

The privacy argument typically used against outing might be put in syllogistic form as follows.

1. It is better in general that people's rights to privacy be respected.
2. Outing violates the subject's right to privacy.
3. Therefore, outing is, in general, wrong.

Despite the broad nature of this argument, almost everyone who endorses it recognizes an exception to privacy in the case of closeted reactionary homophobes who pose a danger to the gay community. Such people may be outed because it will discredit them with their supporters and thus render them powerless. They are, moreover, only being treated according to principles that they have themselves endorsed by classing homosexuals as moral inferiors not deserving of the same rights as other people.[2] But for all other persons both public and private, it is said, outing is unjustified. The success of this argument depends on whether the right to privacy it invokes is real.

It might be objected that outing does not really involve a privacy right. Sexual privacy rights amount to the right not to be spied on and the right not to have others dictate the arrangements of one's sex life. What is counted as *privacy* for the homosexual here would be *secrecy* for the heterosexual, the right never to have information divulged that one is straight.[3] But no such right in the realm of heterosexuality is claimed or recognized. It is hard to see, therefore, that there is any such privacy right.

This position depends on the assumption that privacy rights in the realm of sex cannot be asymmetrical in the case of gay and straight. That idea might seem suspect, but it is not clearly wrong. Indeed, Vincent Samar's book on privacy, *The Right to Privacy: Gays, Lesbians, and the Constitution*, gives a way of defending the asymmetry and the anti-outing position.[4] The idea behind the defense is that privacy is an important value because it preserves and promotes autonomy. This is not particularly contentious and would likely be agreed to by people on both sides of the outing argument. Although Samar intended his theory to apply to the law, it can be adapted to clarify the privacy issue in outing.

In articulating his theory, Samar attempts to give an improved account of acts which John Stuart Mill classified as "self-regarding." An *act* is said to be *private* with reference to a class of agents when the consequences of the act, in the first instance, impinge on the basic interests of the actor, but not on the basic interests of the other agents (68). Basic interests are distinguished from derivative interests. *Basic interests* presuppose no social conventions or particular conceptions of facts (67-68). An interest in sexual relations would presumably be basic since it is independent of particular conceptions of facts and of social conventions (that is, one needs no particular conception of the world and no particular social arrangements to want to have sex). Basic interests fall into two categories: *freedom* and *well-being*. Examples of the first are freedom of expression and worship;[5] examples of the second are life and physical integrity. *Derivative interests* do presuppose social conventions or particular conceptions of facts. An interest in marriage would be a derivative interest since marriage depends on certain conventions (68). An interest in not having one's child taught by a homosexual would also be a derivative interest if it depended on the parent's idea that homosexuals are child-molesters, since that would involve a particular conception of homosexuals.

To *impinge* on an interest is to affect it adversely, as to ignore, deny, or restrict it (67). An act impinges on the basic interests of others *in the first instance* if the mere description of the act "without the inclusion of any additional facts or causal theories" entails that it impinges on another's basic interests (67). Thus, if Jack and Jill wish to have sexual relations with each other, the resulting act would count as a private act. The description of the act alone entails nothing that impinges on the freedom or well-being of agents other than the actors. But if Jack wishes to rape Jill, then we have an act that is not private since Jack, the actor, impinges, in the first instance, on basic interests of Jill.

A private state of affairs is defined with reference to private acts. A *state of affairs* is *private* with reference to a group of agents when "there is a convention, recognized by the members of the group, that defines, protects, preserves, or guards that state of affairs for the performance of private acts" (73). A privacy claim may be overridden if the claim will adversely affect another's capacity for autonomous action (70). Since autonomy provides the rationale for privacy, privacy may be limited in favor of autonomy.

It becomes clear quickly, when Samar's protocol is applied, that gay sex is private since in the first instance the act impinges on the basic interests of nobody but the actors. The important issue for outing concerns not sex acts, however, but the privacy claim concerning sexual orientation. Here is where a case can be made for the asymmetry of privacy rights between gay and straight. Among gays there has prevailed historically a well-understood convention of keeping the sexual orientation of other gays a secret. The information may be passed around among gays but may not be revealed to others, or at least not without the permission of the affected party.[6] The purpose of this convention is to protect and promote private acts. Specifically, it protects gay sex and the establishment of intimacy–private acts–from hostile forces which would otherwise disrupt the lives of gays by harassment, loss of jobs and housing, and imprisonment. Therefore, a privacy right concerning information about sexual orientation seems to exist for gays. There is, however, no analogous right for straights since they do not require concealment of sexual orientation in order to protect their private acts. In this sense, outing really does violate a privacy right, and if this were the sole ground on which the ethics of outing was to be decided, then there would exist a prima facie case against outing.

To the extent that one wants to protect sexual orientation as a non-disclosable trait of a person, as private, one has to argue as well, however, that honoring the closet promotes autonomy. *Autonomy* is understood as the ability to discover and pursue those purposes which are congenial to one's self. To *respect autonomy* is, at a minimum, not to interfere in its exercise. A *congenial purpose* is one which would be found to be such on the basis of sufficient reflection and experience. *Dignity* is one's worth as a moral agent, specifically, as an agent whose purposes and efforts to pursue them have the same claim to respect as anyone else's.

The notion that a rule against outing also promotes autonomy and dignity is, however, vulnerable to the criticism that the privacy right does not really promote autonomy. Logically, if autonomy is not advanced by conventions of non-disclosure, then the privacy argument fails. The convention of secrecy involved in the privacy claim is suspect in this regard. The secrecy convention is nothing but an essential mechanism of the closet, the institution that keeps gays invisible, a class of non-persons. Since, then, the privacy issue will turn on the nature of the closet, let us make a close and careful examination of that institution.

THE CLOSET

In the view of columnist Murray Kempton, "The closet happens to be the single human invention whose consequences have been universally benevolent."[7] In such a statement, Kempton voices the sentiments of many conservatives who see the closet merely as a way for homosexuals to avoid discrimination, a position consistent with the idea that anti-gay discrimination cannot be compared to other sorts of discrimination because it is avoidable through closeting. It can hardly be disputed that the closet has been an often welcome shield between people and the legal and social forces that aim to crush them—to kill them outright, to drive them to suicide, at the very least to destroy such happiness as they can achieve. But its shielding effects hardly make it wholly benign or even a means by which discrimination can be escaped. In fact, the closet is a radical assault on gay dignity, on the moral worth of gays as subjects of equal respect.

To understand the closet as an institution of degradation, I will take a look at an institution that may, at first, seem to have nothing to do with the closet. What Vaclav Havel calls the "post-totalitarian system" is the institution by which people are controlled in societies like the former Communist Czechoslovakia.[8] The post-totalitarian system works by rewarding people for compliance with itself in maintaining what Havel calls the "panorama" or "milieu"–a system of appearances exhibiting and reinforcing certain values endorsed by the regime (51-52). The regime's values are at odds with the "real aims of life" (65). Pursuing the latter, which are multiform, requires resisting official manipulation since the aims of life involve working for the interests of one's authentic self and not those of the phoney identity that the regime defines and thrusts upon one. In pursuing the real aims of life–living in the truth, as Havel calls it–one "breaks the rules of the game" and thereby discovers one's "suppressed identity and dignity" (55). Once the act of rebellion occurs, the system will mete out various punishments ranging from petty harassment to dismissal from jobs, loss of housing, arrest, trial, imprisonment, and reduction to a non-person.

To understand the relation between the post-totalitarian system and the closet, we need the concept of the *heterosexual panorama*. This is the backdrop of daily life in which everyone is assumed to be straight. It reminds people of what is expected in regard to gender propriety, of what everyone else does, of what they too must do in order to have success, respect, and love. Against the heterosexual panorama, gay sexuality is suppressed. Its existence is not just denied. That would involve a reference to its existence. Rather it is obliterated from people's consciousness. Gays are allowed to exist only by blending into the background. The price of survival—of having some life of one's own and decent means of support and even mere physical safety—is to surrender one's own identity and assume a specious one that the system of heterosexual domination assigns. In order to live, gays and lesbians become co-opted by the system that oppresses them. They strive after the aims of life that are their own, but the price of doing that is to join the forces that strive against them. They become the victim *and* the victimizer, the prisoner *and* the guard. The act of rebellion—the assertion of one's authentic self in the face of the system—subjects gays to a range of punishments from petty harassment to murder for breaking the rules of the game and claiming their true identity and dignity. The closet not only denies gay dignity, equal respect for the worth of gays as autonomous beings, but also has the uncommonly repellent quality of requiring gays to participate in the denial of their own worth.

I began with the idea that the closet is a protective device. Consider for a moment how it would be used to maximize protection, what life one would lead in order to take maximum advantage of its benefits in order to be as safe as possible. In fact, the closet protects only through invisibility. It rules out any defense that compels one to become visible. Gays can't prosecute queer-bashers even when the police will cooperate because a trial will expose them and may result in further harassment, loss of jobs, and loss of housing. They also cannot engage in any sort of public political activity to advance specifically gay political aims. And anybody who really wants to be safe had better not write out a check to ACT UP—you never can tell who might see the canceled check at the local bank. Thus the closet effectively closes off certain uses of the courts and political activities, depriving gays of full civil and political rights.[9] The closet also requires isolation. People in the closet risk exposure by living with a lover or by congregating with others of their own kind. Such isolation can lead to the type of impersonal and anonymous sex that is part of the male homosexual stereotype. But even furtiveness does not insure protection. The closet door may be torn off at any moment by the police raid of a tea room.

These reflections lead to what one might think of as the homophobe's ideal queer. He or she is a person so deeply closeted as never to give any overt symptom of homosexuality. In this case, the individual would be maximally protected by the closet, but the price would be a complete capitulation to the system of heterosexual domination, the thoroughgoing assumption of a false identity, the renunciation of the human ties which make life worth living–in short, a general self-degradation.

The inescapable conclusion is that the closet is no more than an accommodation to the denial of dignity on the part of a socially devalued and–until recently–a politically powerless group. It is an attempt to salvage some degree of autonomy and happiness. But it protects in about the same sense that hiding in the forests of Poland protected Jews being hunted down by Nazis. We might give that situation a name and refer to it as an institution, but I do not know what moral or intellectual pathology would lead anyone to think of it as a benevolent protector of autonomy even though it spares some persons from harm.

PRIVACY REVISITED

Let us re-examine the privacy claim in the light of the convention of the closet. Keeping the sexual orientation of gay and lesbian friends and acquaintances secret under some circumstances will promote the performance of private acts. But other privacy conventions–closing doors, drawing curtains, sealing envelopes, circulating medical information only with the patient's consent or only to those deemed to have a medical need to know–lack the double nature of the closet. It is a convention with two opposed effects. The most obvious one is that it prevents the system of morally indefensible social penalties for homosexuality from being brought to bear–morally indefensible because they aim to suppress private acts without justification. But at the same time, complying with the closet interferes with myriad private acts and with the autonomy of people in the closet. For example, on Samar's understanding of privacy, living as openly gay or lesbian is a private matter. What is private need not be secret. The knowledge of one's sexual orientation impinges, in the first instance, on no basic interest of another and so the act of living openly must be private.

As an instrument of degradation, the closet has, as its natural consequence, the maiming of autonomy in all the ways that I have described. That is its purpose. It is nothing more than the situation set up by the system of heterosexual domination, just as the Jew in hiding is a part of the situation set up by Nazi anti-Semitism. To suppose that in either case we have an autonomy-promoting situation is bizarre to the last degree. We have only a situation in which autonomy is not destroyed as utterly as it might be. Therefore, the closet, as a privacy convention (a) does not mainly protect private acts but functions to interfere with them, (b) in that respect fails to promote autonomy, and (c) does not promote autonomy in a way that compensates for interference in private matters. Consequently, the privacy argument, as a general defense against outing, fails.

REACTIONARY CLOSET CASES

The exception to the rule of non-disclosure that is almost universally agreed upon has to do with bigoted closet cases who pose a danger to the gay and lesbian community. The category includes, but is not limited to, politicians. For example, Terry Dolan, the late head of the National Conservative Political Action Committee, pursued a reactionary political agenda with several customary anti-gay elements but was, as his political buddies would say, a practicing homosexual. Revealing the truth about people like Dolan to their bigoted constituency will tend to discredit them with their supporters and render them powerless.

In view of the argument so far, one may look at homophobic closet cases simply in terms of their threat to the autonomy of others. Such politicians and other influential public figures maintain a system of oppression that infringes autonomy and that cannot be justified. To carry on their work, they have to invoke a privacy right that allows them to keep their sexual orientation secret. But the purpose of privacy rights is to promote autonomy. Consequently, there is no invoking of a privacy right to facilitate violations of autonomy. Hence, outing closeted homophobes is a justifiable exception even if one acknowledges a right to privacy regarding sexual orientation.[10]

Anybody using his power or influence to promote a hate-agenda would be subject to being exposed, according to my argument, whether known nationally or only locally, e.g., a parish priest who actively promotes intolerance. Whether the strategy of exposure would work in promoting larger goals of social tolerance or not is a different issue. The point here is only that such an exposure would not be ruled out on grounds of privacy.

An objection to outing even in these cases has to do with encouraging bigotry. The public exercise of inflaming anti-gay bigotry involved in bringing down the target, one might object, is worse than letting him continue to operate. But this argument is implausible. Destroying a powerful agent of bigotry weakens that bigotry by depriving it of an important resource. Consequently, I do not see any general moral objection to outing in this type of case.

RADICAL OUTING

Other cases of outing are more contentious. The question of where to draw lines may be approached by considering what, if anything, is wrong with radical outing involved in living in the truth in the most thoroughgoing way possible. The radical outer will not cooperate with the closet in any way. He will never, therefore, take any pains to cover up anybody's sexual orientation, though he will not go out of his way to reveal it either. He will simply treat the topic of gay sexuality in the same way he treats the topic of straight sexuality. The same privacy rights apply to both and the only such right involving information is the right not to be spied on and, perhaps, the right not to have the details of one's sex life made a topic of discussion even when the information is rightfully obtained.

Nobody advocates radical outing in this completely unrestricted form, but Richard D. Mohr comes close. The only constraints for Mohr are that outing should not violate a right of the person outed or, if it does, that the gain in dignity involved in living morally and destroying the closet should be greater than the indignity suffered as a consequence of being outed.[11] To return to dignity for a moment, the basis of an agent's dignity is his moral autonomy. Dignity is merely autonomy considered as an end. To respect someone's dignity is to treat the protection and promotion of his autonomy as equal in importance to the protection and promotion of one's own.

Next, to advance the discussion, I will imagine an example. Suppose that I am asked, concerning a female friend, who her constant–female–companion is. If the true and non-evasive answer to the question is "Her lover," Mohr's position requires me to treat the case just as I would if the question were about a male companion and the answer were the same. I should not cooperate with the closet, which cooperation is not only self-degrading but which also perpetuates the closet. I should tell the truth. Let us suppose, in addition, that I know my questioner is likely to pass on what I say to the principal of the school where my friend teaches and that if that happens she will likely be dismissed. Mohr would still say that I should tell the truth.[12]

Mohr has two ways of defending his position. First, he would say that there is no conflict of rights in the case, so I have not violated any right of my friend's in outing her. That is, the friend does not have a right not to be outed that would be violated by my honest answer. There may well be a right against arbitrary dismissal from a job, and her termination would violate that right. It is, however, the principal or the school board that does the violating of the woman's rights, not the outer. Outing provides only one among many necessary conditions for violation and to do so is not necessarily to violate a right.[13] So in this case, my right against self-degradation does not conflict with my friend's right against arbitrary dismissal.

One has the feeling that something has gone wrong with the analysis here, a feeling that is confirmed by looking at an analogous case where a crime has been committed. My right to distribute my property may not ordinarily conflict with someone else's right not to be killed. But if I give ammunition to someone in the expectation that he will use it to commit a murder, and he does so, I am an accessory before the fact. Consequently, the fact that an action does not violate a right and is of a type that is usually right, does not make it morally unproblematic.[14]

Mohr's second line of defense relates to cases where there is a conflict of rights. Even if it can be shown that there is a conflict of rights in my example, so that the outing involves the violation of a right–whether a right against arbitrary dismissal, against being set up for violations of rights, against invasion of privacy, or whatever–the outer does wrong only if the indignity of the possible violation outweighs the indignity of lying to protect the closet. But according to Mohr, the indignity of upholding the closet will almost always be worse than the indignity inflicted by the outing. The only exception that Mohr mentions is lying to thwart a government's efforts to kill gays (34).

To discuss this issue I need a procedure for judging the seriousness of a rights violation. Since the value at issue is autonomy, the degree of disruption of the agent's autonomy is that measure. So, for example, physical injury and deprivation of property are both wrongs and infringements of autonomy. Stealing every penny I own is a worse wrong than stealing my paper clips. One hobbles my ability to pursue my purposes, the other scarcely affects it. A wrong that confers a benefit, however, is still a wrong. If an employer fires me because I am gay–though I had intended to quit anyway–I would receive unemployment compensation that I would not have gotten otherwise. The wrong is not serious, but that is merely accidental.

Now I will analyze the weaknesses in Mohr's position. In the course of my discussion, an alternative policy will emerge that can be defended as a general guide regarding the morality of outing. First, because of a certain unclarity of exposition, Mohr seems to have missed the point that the indignity resulting from truthfulness will frequently be worse than that resulting from lying. It is true that the indignity of living a partly covert existence to keep a job may be greater than the indignity of being unjustly deprived of it by bigots. But the question has to do with the relative seriousness of each of a pair of rights violations, supposing, *contra* Mohr, that there is a conflict of rights in my imagined case. One of the rights in play is that against self-degradation, the other against arbitrary dismissal. So understood, the evils that result from outing in the case I have described appear to outweigh the goods, where the values are gains and losses in autonomy.

Mohr would, of course, dispute this point as it applies to my imaginary case because there is, according to him, no conflict of rights. If so, there is also no conflict in the case he mentions where it is permissible to cover up. Mohr says no one should give information that would help an extermination campaign against gays even if that reticence would mean supporting the closet. But why not? If violations of rights consequent on my acts are not relevant to the moral evaluation of my acts, then this rule must be true invariably. Murder cannot be logically an exception. For Mohr to carry through his position consistently, he might take cooperating with the closet to be *malum in se*. Like taking innocent life and misusing reproductive powers from the perspective of natural law ethics, it would be an act always wrong and never to be done. The other possibility is to find some device that permits assessment of rights-violating consequences to be taken account of in assessing the morality of outing. It appears that this latter option is, in fact, preferable to a position that declares protecting the closet invariably to be immoral.

I believe that no right against outing can be established when the consequences involve less than a violation of another's rights. Compliance with the closet is self-degradation, a denial of one's equal worth as a person. Hence, one cannot be required to comply in order to confer a benefit on someone or to prevent a loss, absent the violation of some important right. Thus, the demand of many people that we should "casually support their closet in the small ways we are often expected to do so" is frequently to be rejected.[15] Nothing will justify such collusion with the closet except a danger of rights-violating reprisals so ubiquitous as always to require extreme caution. Changing social conditions have, however, removed this danger in many places in contemporary society.

To my mind it is not outing in everyday circumstances that is problematic but outing where there are certain actual or probable dangers to the target. These include loss of life or physical injury, loss of employment, loss of child custody, loss of housing, and obstruction in consolidating a gay identity. The first two harms are illegal. The next three, inflicted by reason of sexual orientation, are illegal in some jurisdictions and candidates for that status in others. In each case, the legal right reflects a moral right. That there is a moral right not to be harmed in the last way is beyond argument. Hence, the evil consequences of outing in these cases will involve rights violations. For each type of harm it will usually be true that the loss of dignity to somebody involved in protecting the closet is less than the loss involved in consequence of outing. Yet for Mohr, since there is not a conflict of rights between outer and outed, outing would not be wrong.

The device that would allow rights-violating consequences of outing to be taken into account is, of course, a privacy right that requires the outed party's secret to be protected. According to Samar's theory of privacy rights, a right to privacy in these cases would be grounded by the fact that severe infringements of autonomy are likely without it. In this restricted class of cases, a privacy convention will promote autonomy more than no convention.

Mohr would object that the right is questionable since, unlike most rights, it requires some positive action–i.e., it is not just an immunity against coercion but a demand claim–and normally such rights are established only by agreement (18-21). According to Mohr, there is usually no agreement to maintain another's closet and, therefore, no right.

Persons with whom one associates, it must be acknowledged, have the right to decide the terms of that association. People may withdraw from the company of those who do not meet their terms. An expectation among gays has been that each would keep the secrets of the others safe from straights. The practice of mutual protection was no cause for remark but was certainly in the nature of an agreement. The custom was perfectly capable of being enforced by social pressure: "If you blab about me, I won't have anything to do with you and neither will anybody else." This was a well-known condition of association and, consequently, one implicitly agreed to.

My answer to the objection does not, however, commit me to the closet in all its force. The fact is that the expectation of absolute silence is weakening because society is changing. When the rational basis for a practice is weakened and when it has very bad effects that become avoidable, one at least has an argument for changing one's commitment to it. The fact that the outing debate is going on at all shows that gay morals are in flux in this respect and the nature of the commitment is up for debate.

As to the fact that the demand-claim involves deception and is therefore objectionable, I will only say that the burden of proof is on the person who thinks that deception to avoid persecution is wrong.

Another objection to my position is that the outing strategy that maximizes autonomy would be to out in all but cases of extreme peril. This would allow for the maximum promotion of autonomy by speedily destroying the closet. Recognizing even a restricted privacy right is not as autonomy-promoting, ultimately, as not recognizing such a right. Thus the rationale for the privacy right fails. To understand how the objection goes wrong, consider the best policy to minimize sexual transmission of HIV. The best policy is: no sex. If one wants to leave room for technologically unassisted procreation, then the best policy is: no sex except for procreation and then only between partners who have tested HIV negative. That policy would quickly reduce the sexual transmission of the virus almost to nil. The trouble with such a policy is that people won't follow it. Hence, it is not as good as a policy of encouraging no-risk and low-risk sex.

Whatever the reasons, people will not engage in any approximation to radical outing. Hence, sporadic attempts at it would not have much influence on the closet but would cause a good deal of indignity through rights-violating effects. Rightly posed questions of ethics are never questions about how people should live in some world in which they do not live, but how they should live in this world. Consequently, the policy to be adopted is the one which will in fact minimize cooperation with the closet and maximize dignity, the policy I propose, not radical outing or an approximation to it.

Yet another objection from Mohr might focus on the fact that the privacy right I propose would cover an illicit invocation of rights. For example, I may not invoke the right against being arbitrarily deprived of my children at the price of being closeted (34). The indignity involved in exercising the right is worse than that involved in its violation.[16] This example, which is Mohr's, is perhaps a bad one–many people would rank loss of children just below death–but the example does not affect the principle. A right is self-defeating when I lose more autonomy through its exercise than by waiving it. Thus, the privacy right I propose would protect choices which undermine the rationale for the right. The question is not, however, about the nature of these choices alone, but whether a policy of protecting them will promote autonomy more than the alternatives. Relative to what people are likely to do, allowing the illegitimate resort to the right is more autonomy-promoting. The alternative, again, is some approximation to radical outing, a policy that cannot be implemented.

THE CELEBRITY CLOSET

The celebrity closet presents a special case of outing in part because it involves the element of the journalistic double standard. According to common practice and the law, any aspect of the lives of celebrities is fair game for reporting. The one customary exception is homosexuality. The exception is maintained by lapses in journalistic ethics, suppression of the news or even its falsification. The Forbes story is instructive as an example. One can't deny that it is news when it turns out that Malcolm Forbes, one of America's most famous millionaires, was leading a double life, squiring Elizabeth Taylor amid the camera flashes but getting it on in his office with this or that cute guy of the moment. After *OutWeek* broke the story,[17] the mainstream media cowered, leaving it to the supermarket tabloids.[18] At the extreme, the *New York Times* ran a column by Randy Shilts dealing with the Forbes case and related issues.[19] Apparently through a combination of homophobia and class solidarity on the part of the editors, Forbes—by then widely known to have been in the closet—was referred to in that piece only as "a famous, deceased millionaire." If Forbes's imaginary liaison with Taylor had been the subject it would not have been necessary so ostentatiously to protect the family from shame and keep filth off the editorial page. The *Times*'s treatment of the column is an example of the very homophobia to which Shilts attributes the double standard.

The other aspect of the double standard is the falsification of the news. Because many closeted celebrities are out to a large number of people, those who do stories about them often know that they are gay or lesbian. These reporters are complicit with the celebrities and their publicists in writing stories giving the impression that the celebrities are straight when the reporters believe or know that the impression is false.[20] It is hard to imagine how the Malcolm Forbes-Elizabeth Taylor story could have been other than fraudulent when so many members of New York's gay community knew the truth about Forbes.

The sole privacy convention about reporting on the lives of celebrities relates to homosexuality and is an element of the closet. It helps protect the heterosexual panorama from being shown up for the phoney appearance that it is, and the convention certainly does not promote autonomy as much as its destruction would. The people reported on are high-profile elements of the heterosexual panorama, so a successful outing would make some significant difference in it, a gain for autonomy. Celebrities are also generally in a position to protect themselves against the rights violations that may be a consequence of outing, so celebrity outing need not be a great loss of autonomy for the target. Consequently, there is no reason based on dignity to respect the celebrity closet. The only way to get rid of that is to encourage honest reporting, a policy which is morally unobjectionable, or at least less objectionable than the present arrangement, which is its only real alternative.

CONCLUSIONS

The outing controversy has arisen because of changing social conditions that in many ways have undermined the rationale for the rule of non-disclosure. On a plausible understanding of privacy rights as preserving autonomy, the rule cannot be supported as a privacy convention. Maintaining privacy in regard to sexual orientation functions as an essential element in maintaining the closet. The latter is an insupportable institution dedicated to maiming gay autonomy and assaulting gay dignity especially as the closet forces gays to be the agents of their own degradation. A privacy right may only be invoked when doing so will promote autonomy, so, under present conditions, there is no general privacy right to have one's closet protected. However, such a right may be invoked when certain rights violations will otherwise occur. Recognizing this restricted right against outing is the most autonomy-promoting strategy at the present time and is more autonomy-promoting than no right at all.

NOTES

1. Michelangelo Signorile, "The Other Side of Malcolm," *OutWeek*, Mar. 18, 1990, pp. 40-45.

2. Randy Shilts, "Is 'Outing' Gays Ethical?" *New York Times*, Apr. 12, 1990.

3. Richard D. Mohr, *Gays/Justice: A Study in Society, Ethics, and Law* (New York: Columbia University Press, 1988), pp. 98-100.

4. Vincent J. Samar, *The Right to Privacy: Gays, Lesbians, and the Constitution* (Philadelphia: Temple University Press, 1991). In spite of the title, the book is a general treatment of privacy rights with applications to issues involving gays and lesbians as well as other issues. Where they are contextually clear, further references to this title will be given in the text.

5. Given these examples, which are Samar's, the definition of "basic interests" should probably be "interests independent of *particular* social conventions and particular conceptions of facts."

6. This convention has been formulated as an explicit rule by William Hanson and Wes Muchmore in this way: "You do not identify anybody as homosexual to any person who is heterosexual." See *Coming Out Right: A Handbook for the Gay Male* (Boston: Alyson Publications, 1982), p. 20.

7. Quoted by Richard Goldstein, "The Art of Outing," *Village Voice*, May 1, 1990, p. 35.

8. Vaclav Havel, "The Power of the Powerless," in Jan Vladislav, ed., *Living the Truth* (London: Faber and Faber, 1989), p. 40. The description of the post-totalitarian system is given mostly on pp. 41-67. Where they are contextually clear, further references to this title will be given in the text.

9. For an extensive discussion of civil and political disabilities, see Mohr, *Gays/Justice*, pp. 164-181.

10. Samar, p. 111, gives a somewhat similar treatment. Since he connects autonomy with democracy as a value needed for the proper functioning of democratic governments, he connects the outing issue with making citizens better voters. This I cannot agree with. The constituents who support bigots will likely not vote for them if they are found to be gay. But this seems to be an irrational response. The correct principle for intolerant constituents would seem to be "What matters the color of the cat as long as it catches mice?"

11. Richard D. Mohr, "The Outing Controversy: Privacy and Dignity in Gay Ethics," in *Gay Ideas: Outing and Other Controversies* (Boston: Beacon Press, 1992), pp. 33-34. Where they are contextually clear, further references to this title will be given in the text.

12. Mohr, personal communication.

13. Mohr, *Gay Ideas*, pp. 33-34.

14. The notion of conflict of rights that Mohr appears to be working with involves a kind of separability. There is a conflict of rights if the exercise of a right cannot exist without the existence of the violation of another right. Thus I can out my friend without thereby bringing on her termination, and I can give the murderer my ammunition without thereby killing his victim. By contrast, it is not pos-

sible to kill someone in self-defense without killing him. In the latter case, there would be a conflict between a right to kill in self-defense and a right not to be killed.

15. Mark Chekola, "Outing and the Closet: Some Moral Issues," Society for Gay and Lesbian Philosophy, New York, Dec. 29, 1991. A revised version of this address appears in this volume.

16. Apparently this accounts for Mohr's exceptional case. I must not out at the risk of life because this is the only case in which invoking a right at the cost of sustaining the closet is less than the price of not doing so, viz., death. But then how does the target get to invoke this right against the outer? The outer is merely exercising his right, not to say duty, to live in the truth and is not thereby violating the other's right not to be killed.

17. Michelangelo Signorile, "The Other Side of Malcolm," *OutWeek*, Mar. 18, 1990, pp. 44-45.

18. Michelangelo Signorile, "Gaystyles of the Rich and Famous," *Village Voice*, Apr. 3, 1990, pp. 23-24.

19. Shilts, "Is 'Outing' Gays Ethical?"

20. Steve Beery, "Liz Smith Mon Amour," *OutWeek*, May 16, 1990, pp. 44-46.

Privacy and the Ethics of Outing

David J. Mayo, PhD

University of Minnesota, Duluth

Martin Gunderson, PhD, JD

Macalester College

SUMMARY. This essay argues that, in the absence of a compelling justification, outing is immoral as a violation of privacy. Reasons for respecting privacy involve fundamental interests which encompass information about gay and lesbian sexual orientation. Utilitarian defenses of outing are criticized, as is Richard Mohr's analysis of privacy and defense of outing in the name of dignity. Mohr's claim that gay or lesbian sexual orientation does not fall within the scope of the right to privacy is rejected.

Outing is not a new phenomenon. For years, children have taunted others (gay and straight) with schoolyard accusations that they are "queer." What is new is that this practice has recently

David J. Mayo is Professor in the Department of Philosophy at the University of Minnesota, 10 University Drive, Duluth, MN 55812-2496. He specializes in applied ethics, specifically euthanasia and suicide, and privacy issues.

Martin Gunderson is Associate Professor, Department of Philosophy, Macalester College, 1600 Grand Ave., St. Paul, MN 55105-1899. He is also an attorney and specializes in bioethics.

The authors coauthored, with Frank S. Rhame, *AIDS: Testing and Privacy* (University of Utah Press, 1989).

[Haworth co-indexing entry note]: "Privacy and the Ethics of Outing." Mayo, David J. and Martin Gunderson. Co-published simultaneously in the *Journal of Homosexuality* (The Haworth Press, Inc.) Vol. 27, No. 3/4, 1994, pp. 47-65; and: *Gay Ethics: Controversies in Outing, Civil Rights, and Sexual Science* (ed: Timothy F. Murphy) The Haworth Press, Inc., 1994, pp. 47-65. Multiple copies of this article/chapter may be purchased from The Haworth Document Delivery Center [1-800-3-HAWORTH; 9:00 a.m. - 5:00 p.m. (EST)].

found serious advocates among gay rights activists and gay studies scholars. Legitimate publications, both straight and gay, have begun outing, beginning with the posthumous outings of Rock Hudson, Liberace, and Malcolm Forbes, and continuing more recently with those of Pentagon spokesman, Peter Williams, following Desert Storm, and Phyllis Schlafly's son, John, following the 1992 Republican national convention. Suddenly we find ourselves confronted not merely with the practice of outing but with a serious debate about its ethics, with advocates providing arguments which appeal to both utilitarian and non-utilitarian considerations. The defense of outing finds perhaps its most eloquent and persuasive advocate in Richard Mohr, whose widely-circulated essay, "The Outing Controversy: Privacy and Dignity in Gay Ethics," eventually appeared as the lead essay in *Gay Ideas: Outing and Other Controversies.*[1]

In what follows we wish to argue that outing is a *prima facie* wrong[2] because it ordinarily violates a person's right to privacy. A definitive argument that we have a right to privacy would require a complete theory of rights, which is beyond our present scope. We thus begin by assuming a right to privacy (even Mohr grants that people have a right to keep some information private) and then review three of the reasons usually put forward for holding that there is such a right. We then argue that these general reasons establish that the sexual orientation of a gay or lesbian person clearly falls within the scope of such a right. We then turn to both utilitarian and non-utilitarian arguments that have been offered in defense of outing. We specifically look at three arguments Mohr offers in his critique of the view that outing violates a person's right to privacy. We conclude that Mohr fails to refute the claim that outing violates a person's right to privacy.

THE CASE FOR THE RIGHT TO PRIVACY

Most people, including Mohr, concur that people have a moral right to privacy regarding certain personal information. As we have argued elsewhere, three primary considerations have been advanced in the literature on privacy to suggest this intuition is correct.[3] The first involves the place of privacy in discourse about rights. That is, we not only *assert* such a right to privacy, but we also speak of someone *exercising*, *waiving*, or *forfeiting* a right to privacy, and speak of others *violating* our privacy (or our right to privacy). It is difficult to see how this way of talking could be accounted for if we had no right to privacy. Moreover, we *act* as if we have such a right, for instance by leaving personal correspondence open on our desks but trusting that others will not read it. Secondly, the law articulates such a right in a number of circumstances, and legal rights are frequently an indicator of moral rights. Thirdly, we have certain interests in privacy which are central enough to be characterized as fundamental, and fundamental interests are often understood to generate moral rights.

We call attention to two such interests that are especially relevant to privacy regarding sexual orientation. The first of these is that, human nature being what it is, privacy is essential for the nurturing of autonomy and individuality.[4] According to this argument, the development of an autonomous individual involves a tension between the need to explore different ideas, ideals, and ways of living on the one hand, and strong and inevitable social pressures to conform on the other. All of us fear condemnation by others: this is especially true of young persons just beginning to explore values and develop their own ideals and standards of behavior which may differ from those of their peers or elders. Privacy is valuable because as we develop into individuals it provides each of us some insulation from social pressures and hence with room to investigate and try out ideas we might be reluctant to try out if we felt the scrutiny of others. As Ruth Gavison remarks, if we could keep nothing private, not even our thoughts:

> we would try to erase from our minds everything we would not be willing to publish, and we would not try to do anything that would make us likely to be feared, ridiculed, or harmed. There is a terrible flatness in the person who could succeed in these attempts.[5]

Whereas the first fundamental interest addresses the development of an autonomous individual, the second addresses the survival of such an individual in a pluralistic society. It holds that privacy protects us from the ignorance, intolerance, prejudice, and malice of others.[6] Many of us are uncomfortable around people who we know are fundamentally different from ourselves, whose beliefs, ideals, and values differ from our own. At the same time that we recognize this, we are committed at a theoretical level to the desirability of individuality, and hence to creating an atmosphere in which differences can develop and flourish. Respect for privacy is a mechanism we adopt to facilitate tolerance to help ease this tension. Privacy protects all of us from prejudice and malice we might experience–and practice–if we knew how different we are from each other.

SEXUAL ORIENTATION AS PRIVATE INFORMATION

The foregoing considerations support the intuition that people have a moral right to privacy. Consensus about privacy and its importance to fundamental human interests suggest, we maintain, that a person's gay or lesbian sexual orientation falls within the scope of a person's moral right to privacy. Even Mohr grants that both gays and straights generally presume this is private information (11-12). The law is largely silent on this question, but even if–as we shall argue–this information is private, the silence of the law in this regard should come as no surprise. Partly *because* gays have remained largely invisible, the law has been notoriously slow to respond to their fundamental interests, including those they have by virtue of living in a homophobic society. The law's failure to recognize privacy of sexual orientation may be related more to its neglect of the topic than to any principled judgment on the matter. And, more generally, we have many moral rights which are not echoed in legal rights. Thus, we cannot assume that the absence of legal judgments in favor of a right to privacy in regard to sexual orientation defines the morality of outing.

The arguments for a fundamental interest in privacy have special force in connection with sexuality generally and with sexual orientation in a homophobic society in particular. There may be no area in which privacy is more essential than sexuality. Sex is emotionally charged and subject to competing ideologies. Some groups are utterly opposed to sexual activity of any kind outside of marriage. Other groups are opposed variously to masturbation, birth control, sexual fantasizing, oral or anal sex, sex outside of marriage, or sex for any purpose but procreation. Many people are, of course, deeply homophobic and embrace attitudes and ideologies which vehemently oppose not only gay and lesbian sexual relations but any form of homoeroticism. Moreover, competing ideas about what constitutes appropriate sexuality and sexual conduct can give rise to harshly judgmental attitudes. It is not surprising, then, in such a context that even for heterosexual adolescents, sexual feelings probably trigger more shame, guilt, and general consternation than any others. Respect for privacy first creates a sphere in which people can better chart their own course in sexual matters while taking account of their own deepest needs, desires, and values. It can also protect each of us from the judgments, intolerance, and malice of others.

All of these concerns are even more urgent for gay and lesbian young people who face extra hazards as they begin to come to grips with their sexual orientations and chart a course for themselves in our homophobic world. The process of coming out, of course, typically proceeds in stages, beginning with an agonizing, alienating realization that one is "different" from one's peers, in a way that is widely viewed as quite terrible and which must be kept secret. This realization gives way to self-acceptance, and then proceeds through the decision to integrate one's gay or lesbian sexual orientation into one's life more or less completely (e.g., "coming out" into and entering the gay community) and more or less openly (coming out to others). Especially in the early stages of this process, there always lurks the terror of discovery or exposure and then the disgrace and humiliation one imagines this will entail.

A critical early stage in coming out is the person's discovery of and introduction to the gay community. Suddenly, a person coming out discovers that there are others who have preceded him or her through the same doubts and anxieties and who share his or her concerns. Moreover, such a person discovers there are real elements of *community* in the gay community. It is not merely a group of people defined by the accident of common sexuality but rather a group of people who are bound together by common desires, aspirations, concerns, and loyalties. Specifically, people entering the gay community are often startled when they finally realize the obvious— that other gays and lesbians they meet share (or at least at one time shared) their concerns about exposure, and that as a result they are highly respectful of their privacy. At *that* point the closeted gay or lesbian's sense of alienation begins to dissolve in the realization that there is a loyal brotherhood or sisterhood that understands, perhaps even shares, and certainly respects, concerns of privacy in regard to sexuality.

The need for this sometimes painful secretiveness would of course be unnecessary in a world in which there were no homophobia. Unfortunately, ours is not such a world. Given the world as it is, we believe a gay or lesbian person's interest in privacy with respect to his or her sexual identity is important enough to qualify as a fundamental interest and hence that this information is included within the scope of that person's right to privacy. Indeed, a person who is just coming to terms with his or her sexuality seems to provide a paradigm case of a person who needs the protection afforded by a right to privacy.

UTILITARIAN ARGUMENTS IN DEFENSE OF OUTING

Most arguments given in defense of outing begin with the claim that the closet is an evil because it ultimately is a mechanism by which gays and lesbians are oppressed. This oppression depends on heterosexual homophobia, which in turn requires the myth that gays and lesbians are *different*. This can be maintained only so long as gays and lesbians remain largely invisible: the closet is the mechanism that hides gays and lesbians from view and thereby maintains the myth. Steve Berry writes: "There's a reason we're the most despised minority on the planet. Too many people, of all ages, in all walks of life, still don't know of anyone who's gay."[7]

One utilitarian argument offered in defense of outing is that outing is one way to discredit myths about gay men and lesbians by confronting heterosexual homophobes with the fact that gays and lesbians are not rare, weird, alien "others" but are their ever-present parents, children, sisters, waiters, car mechanics, movie stars, educators, doctors, and fellow soldiers who are people just like everyone else. More specifically, it is argued that outing prominent and respected public figures is justified because it can force heterosexuals to reassess stereotypes and prejudices which form the basis of homophobia and its attendant evils.

We grant that homophobes should be forced to confront the myths upon which their fears and prejudices are based and even grant, moreover, that important goals like these provide gays and lesbians with a very good reason for coming out. However, such a goal no more justifies violating a person's right to privacy than the social desirability of large donations to charity justifies stealing from the rich to give to the poor. As Ronald Dworkin has noted, whatever the proper interpretation of rights, at the very least they trump considerations of utility, especially such diffuse utilitarian considerations as those invoked in this kind of argument for outing.[8] The violation of privacy involved in outing someone is—or at least is very much like—theft. It is theft from that person of control of private information. When someone loses control of that information, he or she may very well suffer serious harms, especially if that information triggers responses of prejudice, intolerance, and malice in others. Moreover, unlike most thefts, it may be irreversible.

A second utilitarian defense of outing addresses the internalized homophobia of self-hating closeted gays and lesbians. Internalized homophobia has various causes, including the prevalence of homophobia in our culture generally and the absence of gay and lesbian role models. While prominent and successful gays and lesbians may have good self-interested reasons to remain closeted, in doing so they contribute to the perpetuation of the myths underlying homophobia in the minds of gay and lesbian youth, as well as those in the minds of homophobic straights. According to this argument, young persons would find it easier to come to terms with their own sexuality if more gays and lesbians were out because they would be provided with positive role models. Thus Victoria A. Brownworth writes "at the heart of outing is a refutation of internalized homophobia."[9]

We recognize and concede that the public identification of positive role models represents an additional reason for gays and lesbians to come out. But such a consideration is not sufficient to override the right to privacy of gays and lesbians. *If* gays and lesbians quit regarding each other's gayness as privileged information and outing becomes commonplace, we believe that the net utility for gays and lesbians first coming to grips with their gayness would almost always be negative, and not positive, so long as society as a whole remains homophobic. Should they, for example, enter a gay bar their fear of exposure–which is currently irrational in most cases–would instead become well-founded.

A second consideration appeals not only to utility but also to dignity. Coming out is important not simply because one *is out* at the end of the process but also–and perhaps primarily–because one has been the primary agent of this self-affirming development. We believe that for many gays and lesbians, the successive acts of coming out–of acknowledging that one is gay or lesbian, first to oneself, then to progressively more people–represent an important exercise in self-development. These can be the acts by which the once-homophobic, closeted gay or lesbian seizes control of his or her own life, authors his or her self-identity, and ultimately replaces homophobic self-hatred with dignity and self-respect. This process is a critical exercise in self-authorship and the development of an *autonomous* self–a self freely setting the terms of its own existence instead of having them dictated by others who claim to know better. This consideration actually provides an additional argument for holding a closeted gay or lesbian has a fundamental interest in privacy: privacy here is important because it gives one control over the terms of one's own existence in this regard. And this is important not only as a matter of happiness but as a matter of dignity as well.[10]

DIGNITY AND THE CLOSET

According to Mohr, the closet is an institution which is so evil and insidious that the moral individual, as a matter of dignity, cannot participate in its existence or continuation. Mohr's non-utilitarian defense of outing involves rich and complex arguments which we cannot treat fully here. Instead, we will isolate several important threads of his defense of outing in order to assess their success.

Mohr agrees with utilitarian critics that the closet is the primary mechanism by which gays and lesbians are oppressed. Moreover,

Mohr grants that gays within the gay community do generally recognize a code of secrecy regarding sexual orientation. He refers to this code or convention of honoring each other's secrecy as 'The Secret'. Indeed, Mohr sees The Secret as "*the* gay social convention . . . the structuring element, the DNA, the constitutive convention of the gay community" (29-30). The closet and The Secret are especially insidious, he thinks, for two reasons. Borrowing from the account offered by Jeremiah McCarthy in this volume, Mohr insists that the closet doesn't merely oppress gays. Through the convention of The Secret, it also recruits them as willing agents of their own oppression. This dual tyranny is possible only so long as they cooperate and respect The Secret. The second reason is that the gay person who respects The Secret "accept[s] insult so that one avoids harm" (31), and in so doing "commits to the view of gays that the convention presupposes: that gays are loathsome and disgusting, to be kept from sight, nauseating if touched or seen, filth always to be flushed away" (33). Mohr views this as "a complete capitulation to the general social belief that the only good gay is a nonexistent one" (30). Any gay respecting The Secret, regarding himself or another, "commit[s] his life to the very values that keep him oppressed" (31). Mohr concludes that *as a matter of dignity* gays must renounce The Secret, neither remaining closeted themselves, nor participating in the closet on behalf of others.

We take exception to two of these claims. The first is that those who respect The Secret not only pay lip service to the values which oppress them but actually share, embrace, and even "commit their lives" to them. While some persons doubtless remain in the closet out of a sense of shame, it simply doesn't follow that *any* gay or lesbian who remains closeted shares or accepts homophobic values. This is true even if one acknowledges he is indirectly contributing to homophobia. Shame is not the only possible motivation for remaining closeted. Concern for either individual welfare or individual rights might also provide such motivation. For instance, a gay man may believe that remaining closeted himself, or not outing a lesbian, will reduce the risk of very real harms in a homophobic world. But even if he believes a closeted lesbian's fears are irrational and she would be better off if she were out, he may keep The Secret out of obligation, knowing that another had revealed herself to him in light of the convention and expected benefits of The Secret: trusting others to keep her sexual orientation confidential. He *might* even keep The Secret (again for himself or another) out of love or compassion for a homophobic straight. Imagine a gay man who is comfortable with himself, who loves a frail, elderly parent who is of another age and homophobic. In the abstract, it is easy enough to claim that we shouldn't humor others' hateful prejudices. However, there *are* competing values, and it seems either dogmatic or naive to insist in advance that there are *never* circumstances in which competing values should prevail. Mohr quotes Steve Berry approvingly: "The principle is really very simple. Either being gay is OK or it isn't" (37). But for most of us things really *aren't* that simple.

Second, we take issue with Mohr's claim that consideration of dignity alone should dictate the morality of actions, and that happiness (for oneself or others) is irrelevant to the morality of outing. Having grounded his case for outing squarely in considerations of dignity, Mohr is willing to let the utilitarian chips fall where they may: "It is not one's happiness that one is seeking through outing–it is the avoidance of being an instrument of insult to one's own dignity, the avoidance of complicity in one's own degradation" (43). He does acknowledge that many gays remain closeted for economic reasons or even to retain custody of their children, but he finds this morally irrelevant: "the closet case . . . barter[s] away his self-respect, his worthiness for respect, his dignity, for happiness, regard, and non-respectful love . . . accepts insult to avoid harm . . . [and thus] becomes a simulacrum–a deceptive substitute . . . of a person" (31-32). Moreover, the indignity is not confined merely to the closeted person alone. The openly gay person who keeps The Secret for others commits himself "to a similar vision of gay people and so commit[s] him[self] to give up his own dignity for the happiness of the closeted gay person. To do that," Mohr adds, "is the very inversion of the moral life" (33). At one point, Mohr acknowledges "*if* it were the case . . . that the government was shooting gays, I would morally be expected to suspend my dignity temporarily. . . . " But he then goes on to insist that even this would not be a matter of the protection of happiness but done "so that the current and prospective dignity of others is made possible" (34).

We believe Mohr is simply mistaken in holding that dignity simply outweighs all other values here–that "a dignity may outweigh a dignity, as a pleasure or measure of happiness may not" (34). We would hope, moreover, that Mohr would lie not only to save another's life but that he would be willing to do so simply as a matter of compassion, without having to reconstruct it as a matter of dignity.[11] Again, life is not as simple as Steve Berry suggests it is. In any event, it is not simple enough that one can always put dignity first. Life is morally complicated: along with dignity, we believe morality sometimes requires us to take account of both human welfare and individual rights.

OUTING AS A VIOLATION OF THE RIGHT TO PRIVACY

Mohr has attacked with gusto the claim that outing violates a right to privacy. In what follows we distinguish and consider critically three different objections Mohr brings to bear in this regard.

Objection 1: Those alleging a right to privacy confuse privacy with secrecy. In her book, *Secrets,* Sissela Bok proposes a distinction between *privacy* and *secrecy.* She defines *privacy* as controlled or limited access and *secrecy* as intentional concealment. Bok's contention is that while the two are related, they are not identical or even co-extensive: "Privacy need not hide; and secrecy hides far more than what is private."[12] Mohr endorses this distinction and argues that while there is a general right to privacy (or to control the access others have to us), this does not preclude outing, which is a question of secrecy. Mohr argues for special cases in which the right to privacy (or some other consideration) generates a right to keep certain information secret, but he also holds that there is no general right to secrecy and certainly none whose scope includes the information that one is gay.

We believe Bok's distinction is unhelpful, and even unclear, for several reasons. First, it is revisionary. There are long traditions, both within philosophical ethics and the law, which speak of a right to privacy in the sense we have been using the term.[13] Second, even using Bok's terminology it is often unclear whether what is at issue is privacy or secrecy, or, if both, how they relate. (Does, for example, the Fourth Amendment's protection against unreasonable searches and seizures protect our privacy or our secrecy? Does a woman who hides a key to her locked diary use privacy to achieve secrecy or vice versa?) Third, even if there is a clear distinction to be drawn, the point seems only terminological for present purposes. We have not argued for "a general right to secrecy." We only assert that people have a right to keep certain personal information about themselves private and that information about a person's sexual orientation provides a paradigm case of such information. The same point could have been made using the word "secret," and those who wish to follow Bok's analysis are invited to substitute the word "secret" wherever we have used the word "private."

Mohr feels this distinction is important because he believes we have a general "freestanding" right to sexual privacy, which encompasses a right to bodily integrity; a right to pursue central, personally-affecting values; and a right to the "sanctuary and repose" necessary for sex. By contrast, we have no general "freestanding" right to sexual secrecy but only a "derivative" right to sexual secrecy, which is "pendant from" the right to sexual privacy. This derivative right is the right against one's sex partner(s) that they keep secret the specifics of one's sexual behavior and performance but not sexual orientation itself.[14]

Many people, given a choice between "success in their unedited sex lives" on the one hand and on the other, economic security, custody of their children, and acceptance, freedom from fear, and happiness generally, might well choose the latter. It strikes us as peculiar to argue that a person is entitled to secrecy regarding sexual actions because it is a precondition of the sanctuary needed for "success in one's unedited sex life" but to deny the same privacy regarding the fact that someone is gay—even if, as is sometimes the case, such privacy is a condition of employment, custody of one's own children, acceptance, freedom from fear, or happiness generally. In other words, if the protection of sexual acts is necessary to ensure the repose of one's sex life, it is unclear why protection of sexual identity would not also be protected to the same extent it was necessary to achieve the repose of one's life generally.

One thread of our earlier argument that a gay or lesbian sexual identity falls within the scope of the right to privacy was that it so clearly instantiates the fundamental interest all of us have, as we develop into individuals, in some insulation from social pressures so we can investigate and try out ideas we might be reluctant to try if we felt the scrutiny of others. At one point, Mohr comes perilously close to offering virtually the same argument for the privacy of at least *some* information; he does so, however, in the language of secrecy:

> [S]ecrecy in one's thoughts and the inner dialogue such secrecy safeguards from harsh judgments of others are necessary to the development of the privacy of one's thoughts, to their truly being one's own. Even if the harsh judgments are not accompanied with actual invasions, say, with drugs and electrodes, and so do not violate bodily integrity, still the judgments must be blocked if personal thought is to be free. Thus, secrecy in our ideas is a precondition of one's very status as an autonomous moral agent–a person, that is, with ends of her own and the ability to revise those ends. (13-14)

He concludes that "Such secrecy is morally protected as a right not because of the nature of secrecy but because of the nature of privacy and personhood" (13-14). However, if sexual *identity* is construed as a matter of one's sexual preferences as distinguished from sexual *behavior* (as Mohr insists it should be) and if preferences, construed non-behavioristically, are interpreted as a matter of "one's thoughts and inner dialogues," it is difficult to see how Mohr can consistently claim that one has no right to secrecy regarding this information.

Objection 2: Outing typically reveals public, not private, information. Mohr notes that, generally, candidates for outing are persons who have participated publicly in the gay community. After pointing out that gay bars are "pubs"–that is, public accommodations–Mohr discusses the case of Oliver Sipple, the ex-Marine who thwarted an assassination attempt on Gerald Ford, and who was subsequently outed in the *San Francisco Chronicle*. Sipple lost a violation of privacy suit against the *Chronicle* on the grounds that it had reported only public events, including Sipple's attendance at gay bars, pageants, and parades.

In response, we would note first that Sipple's court loss here only indicates he had no *legal* right that this information be kept private.

We do not, however, claim that outing is illegal but that it is immoral. We have many moral rights for which there are no corresponding legal rights–for instance, the right to what friends promise us, or that strangers who see what's in our poker hand not reveal it to other players, or Mohr's own case of the right that our sex partners not discuss our sexual behaviors publicly.

Second, Mohr's objection seems to presume a tidy blanket dichotomy according to which any given piece of information is either private or public. According to this model, the cat is either in the bag or it is out and free, and once free remains at large. This model may be suitable to the legal notions of "public information" and "matters of public record," but we believe it is inadequate to capture the nuances of moral privacy. Specifically, we believe that moral violations of privacy are receiver-specific. What is at issue is not that a piece of information which is private *simpliciter* is revealed, but that private information about someone is revealed by a second party to a third to whom the first did *not* want it revealed. People of all ages, for instance, will share information with many other people who they expect will keep that same information from their parents. Imagine a young adult living far from home, who has an unsavory brush with the law which is a matter of "public record" in his new state but who wishes to keep this information from his parents. He has not been wronged if his parents happen to run across this information in the public record. But, he might well feel his privacy had been violated by a gossip who revealed the information to the parent, knowing he had wanted it kept private. Similarly, a woman with a listed phone number who stopped with a friend at a singles bar might justly feel her privacy had been violated if the friend gave her name and number without permission to a stranger who enquired after them. By the same token, while some gays and lesbians wish to remain closeted from the "straight world at large," and for that reason would not participate in a gay-lesbian parade, others are only concerned to remain closeted from certain persons (e.g., employers or specific family members).

This more complicated model of privacy implies that privacy is an issue more often than one might have thought. We believe so and wish to suggest that each of us moves socially and shares information within overlapping social groups, many of which are characterized by conventions of privacy. Setting aside for a moment the morally offensive features of The Secret, we nevertheless believe that The Secret's function within the gay community exemplifies certain complexities in this regard.

The conventions of secrecy governing various social relationships may be more or less formal and explicit. Sometimes, for instance in many professional-client relationships, they are spelled out explicitly by professional codes, and even receive legal acknowledgement. Social organizations such as fraternities and "secret societies" administer formal and explicit oaths of secrecy governing certain information, which may cover everything from secret ceremonies to membership, and even the very existence of the organization. Conventions of secrecy, however, also operate in less formally or clearly defined ways and within less clearly defined groups. Sensitive family matters are discussed typically only with family members, business matters only with business associates, and so on. Professors confide information to colleagues and assume they will have the good (moral) sense not to pass that information along to students or administrators. The Secret in the gay community also functions in such a way.

While conventions of secrecy serve to generate privacy rights, the sharing of restricted information which they make possible often also can serve to bond the individuals of the group together. Much as Mohr has suggested The Secret as the structuring and constitutive convention of the gay community, Charles Fried has argued that secrets are a precondition of friendship and intimacy because intimacy *consists in* the sharing of private information.[15] In any event, acceptance of and confidence in unspoken conventions governing privacy (such as The Secret) are typically a major element of trust and loyalty as they manifest themselves within any group in which they operate.

It should not surprise us that we frequently find ourselves in groups in which private information is shared and conventions of secrecy operate. Generally, while privacy is vitally important, it doesn't follow that more privacy is always better than less. (The same is true of food and sleep.) We value not only privacy but its opposite, social contact and sharing–including selective sharing of private information. In many aspects of our lives we value a balance between privacy and publicity and hence value control of that balance. All the reasons a person may have for wanting "private" information withheld from some parties may figure as reasons for wanting to share it with others. Out of fear and prejudice, a man may, for example, reveal to another he trusts that he is gay in an appeal for protection. Just as young persons beginning to explore values and struggling to develop their own ideals and standards of behavior value privacy because it provides them with some insulation from social pressures and hence with room to investigate and try out ideas they might be reluctant to try out if they felt the scrutiny and judgment of others, they seldom want *complete* privacy in this struggle. More often they want a close circle of trustworthy friends with whom to share their thoughts and who understand the "private" nature of what is being revealed to them. And again, the very process of sharing private information contributes to the formation of bonds of friendship.

Adults recognize the importance of these conventions in the formation of most social groups–particularly groups of friends–and teach them to their children at an early age as part of the virtues of loyalty and trustworthiness. A child moving to a new school, for whom it is difficult enough to break into an established circle of friends, will find it virtually impossible if he becomes known as a "tattle-tale." The concepts of a "fink," a "snitch," and a "rat" carry the same message. Sometimes, of course, a group member may have good reasons to violate the confidence and hence the privacy rights of another group member, for instance the teenager whose best friend has revealed in the confidence of friendship her heavy involvement with dangerous drugs. Cases of this sort can generate painful moral dilemmas in which privacy rights must be weighed against countervailing considerations. And sometimes conventions of secrecy may operate to serve ends of which we disapprove (e.g., Mafia or police codes of silence). The issues involved in "whistle-blowing" and "stool pigeons" represent other morally ambiguous cases.

Objection 3: The form of the alleged right to privacy is suspect. This objection to the claim that outing violates a person's right to privacy is perhaps the most subtle. Mohr argues that one person can have no right which generates a positive demand-claim on another in the form of a "gag-order" unless very specific circumstances are met. Mohr feels any such right, first of all, would violate free speech. But again, Mohr seems to be confusing law and morality. The guarantee of free speech is a legal guarantee that the government cannot restrict our speech. It doesn't guarantee there will be no moral restrictions, as are surely created by the conventions of silence within the groups we discussed above. A second thread of Mohr's objection is that the alleged right not to be outed isn't merely an "immunity right" against others but is a positive "demand-claim," in that it would impose a duty on others to do certain things (" . . . a complex web of actions and omissions, including lies, deceptions, and morally coerced silences") (20). Mohr claims that, except in extraordinary circumstances, no one can impose such an obligation on another without the other's consent. Once again, Mohr's thinking is shaped by the law, to which he is drawn for this single exception: "At common law, there is only one such involuntary duty between specifiable individuals, and it is telling. The duty is the duty of a parent to his own child" (20). Again, we must object that we are not arguing that outing is illegal, but that, absent extenuating circumstances, it is immoral. Mohr himself acknowledges that sex partners each have a right to privacy regarding their sexual behaviors; he apparently believes that the very act of having sex with someone imposes a "gag order" on the parties involved and creates a duty to which the sex partners never agreed (and, if locker room banter is any evidence, may never have crossed their minds). Moreover, Mohr's analysis of The Secret is that it is precisely the sort of convention that generates such moral rights and duties. By contrast, we have argued above that conventions like The Secret operate throughout our social lives to generate rights and duties of privacy.

CONCLUSIONS

Most advocates of outing argue passionately that the fears of harms which drive most people to remain closeted are largely unfounded. One remarkable feature of Mohr's advocacy of outing is that he readily concedes that being out, and being outed, sometimes costs gays and lesbians dearly in happiness. We share his view that the closet is insidious but are troubled by any argument which encourages one person to act in ways which put others at risk of serious harms they are unwilling to assume on their own. To put the point differently: we would have thought the fundamental argument of gay and lesbian activists against homophobes in whose judgment they are not living as they should, and who therefore take offense at how they do live and who would therefore try to forbid it, would be an appeal to liberal principles. Homophobes are entitled to any opinion whatsoever, but they are not entitled to dictate the terms of gay and lesbian existence. To do so would be an affront to their dignity. We are struck by the parallel: the advocates of outing hold closet cases are not living as they should and take offense at it. Here we would press the same reply: they are entitled to their opinions. They are even entitled to express their indignation and urge others to try and live as they—and for that matter we—feel they should. But they are not entitled to violate their trust and thereby dictate the terms of their existence. That would be no less an affront to their dignity.

NOTES

1. Richard D. Mohr, *Gay Ideas: Outing and Other Controversies* (Boston: Beacon Press, 1992). Where they are contextually clear, further references to this title will be given in the text.

2. By this assertion we mean it is presumptively wrong. However, it might be morally defensible in particular cases in which there are overriding considerations. Karen Thompson had to out her lover, Sharon Kowalski, in court in order to argue that she should be awarded custody of her following a serious accident. In this respect, outing is ethically on a par with the revelation of other private personal information, contrary to the will of the person involved.

3. Martin Gunderson, David J. Mayo, and Frank S. Rhame, *AIDS: Testing and Privacy* (Salt Lake City, UT: University of Utah Press, 1989). See chap. 3.

4. See Edward Bloustein, "Privacy as an Aspect of Human Dignity: An Answer to Dean Prosser," pp. 156-202, and Ruth Gavison, "Privacy and the Limits of Law," pp. 346-402, both in Ferdinand Schoeman, ed., *Philosophical Dimensions of Privacy: An Anthology* (Cambridge: Cambridge University Press, 1984).

5. See Gavison.

6. W. A. Parent, "Privacy, Morality, and the Law," in Joel Feinberg and Hyman Gross, eds., *Philosophy of Law* (Belmont, CA: Wadsworth, 1984), pp. 297-307.

7. Steve Berry, "Liz Smith, Mon Amour," *OutWeek*, May 16, 1990, p. 44.

8. Ronald Dworkin, *Taking Rights Seriously* (Cambridge, MA: Harvard University Press, 1977), p. xi.

9. Victoria A. Brownworth, "Campus Queer Query," *OutWeek*, May 16, 1990, p. 49.

10. As a counter-example to this argument, Mohr cites the case of outed Congressman Gerry Studds, who responded to being outed by publicly embracing his gayness and proclaiming "I've never felt better in my life." Mohr argues that what is crucial to a closeted gay taking control of his life is not that he *come* out, but that he embrace *being* out, " . . . as *his* coming out . . . in morally and psychologically important dimensions . . . " (Mohr, p. 42). Even if Mohr is correct here, the fact remains, however, that most gays find this more difficult if they are outed. Studds's case is exceptional in this regard.

11. To the extent that such a reconstruction is possible, opponents of outing could probably reconstruct as dignity the happiness that Mohr dismisses as irrelevant and, hence, argue that it comes down to weighing competing dignities after all.

12. Sissela Bok, *Secrets: On the Ethics of Concealment and Revelation* (New York: Pantheon Press, 1984), p. 11.

13. The Federal Privacy Act of 1974 and the Minnesota Government Data Privacy Act are only two pieces of legislation that address what Bok refers to as secrecy. Moreover, the right to privacy in the sense we are using the term is a central theme of the landmark *Philosophical Dimensions of Privacy: An Anthology.*

14. "The success of sex in our unedited lives presupposes the creation of sanctuary, a presumption that what one is doing is not being watched and subjected to judgment–even or especially through the indirect agency of one's partner himself. Therefore prospective secrecy–a presumption that what we are doing in our sexual fumblings will be kept just between us–is necessary for the privacy of sex. . . . A right to secrecy covering one's sexual actions derives from a right to privacy in sexual behavior." Mohr, p. 16.

15. Charles Fried, "Privacy: A Rational Context," in Richard Wasserstrom, ed., *Today's Moral Problems* (New York: Macmillan, 1979), pp. 365-377.

Outing, Truth-Telling, and the Shame of the Closet

Mark Chekola, PhD

Moorhead State University

SUMMARY. This essay examines the nature of being in the closet, coming out, and the practice of outing. It is argued that no general rule against outing can be maintained since outing others may be defensible as one pursues one's own legitimate legal and moral interests. Neither does privacy extend to all aspects of human life which someone may wish to keep secret, especially if information about sexual orientation is not obtained in any immoral way. Withholding information about sexual orientation may sometimes be justified but on grounds of secrecy and not in a way that always forbids outing. The shame and degradation of the closet are evils, but outing is not necessarily their solution, though any loss of "privacy" entailed by coming out of the closet can be more than compensated by the rewards of casting off implications of worthlessness.

Karen Thompson, a Physical Education professor at St. Cloud State University in Minnesota, was in 1991 denied guardianship of

Mark Chekola is Professor of Philosophy at Moorhead State University, Moorhead, MN 56563.

For helpful comments on earlier versions of this paper the author thanks his colleagues in the Philosophy Department at Moorhead State University, especially Sue Cataldi, and Richard Mayo, Jerry McCarthy, and Claudia Card. The present version benefited substantially from suggestions from Timothy Murphy.

[Haworth co-indexing entry note]: "Outing, Truth-Telling, and the Shame of the Closet." Chekola, Mark. Co-published simultaneously in the *Journal of Homosexuality* (The Haworth Press, Inc.) Vol. 27, No. 3/4, 1994, pp. 67-90; and: *Gay Ethics: Controversies in Outing, Civil Rights, and Sexual Science* (ed: Timothy F. Murphy) The Haworth Press, Inc., 1994, pp. 67-90. Multiple copies of this article/chapter may be purchased from The Haworth Document Delivery Center [1-800-3-HAWORTH; 9:00 a.m. - 5:00 p.m. (EST)].

her brain-damaged lover, Sharon Kowalski, after a five-year legal battle. This ruling was made despite Kowalski's indication that she wanted Thompson as her guardian. In a section of his ruling entitled "Outing," Judge Robert Campbell gave as a reason for his decision that "Thompson had violated Ms. Kowalski's privacy by disclosing her sexual orientation."[1] Kowalski appears to have come to terms with being a lesbian even though at the time of the accident she was deeply closeted, as Thompson had been. The judge's reasoning seems to be that revealing her partner's homosexuality prior to any actual consent was a serious enough violation of Kowalski's interests to evidence her unsuitability as guardian.

What was the reason for Thompson's outing Kowalski? She was Kowalski's committed partner, and she wanted to be involved in medical decision-making for and rehabilitation of Kowalski. *Not* outing Kowalski would have meant that Thompson would have had to abandon the relationship (which Kowalski's parents had difficulty accepting), gone away, and not pursued the legal battle for the right to take care of her life partner. Outing Kowalski was necessary to pursue what she regarded as her and Kowalski's rights. For Judge Campbell the duty to keep Kowalski's lesbianism secret was compelling enough to maintain even if it meant giving up her right to have the case heard in court. If Thompson cared enough about Kowalski to be suitable as her guardian, his reasoning implied, she would have respected a right to not have her homosexuality revealed. By the same reasoning, though, Thompson would be unable to reveal the relationship between the two which is the basis for her claim as guardian. On this line of thinking, whenever a legal dispute requires revealing the homosexuality of someone who cannot at that time give consent to the disclosure of that information, one would have to forgo any rights one might have in light of that disclosure. In other words, under those circumstances, gay and lesbian people would not have equal access to the judicial system.

This example is helpful in showing the complexity of the ethics of outing. This complexity has been hidden by too limited a focus in the media on the classic outing of celebrities and a failure to examine the moral issues raised by the phenomenon of "the closet." Many people vehemently oppose outing, finding it morally outrageous. Opposition is often automatic and so strong that it appears to be a clear item of common moral consciousness. The following comments in a letter to the editor that appeared in the *Los Angeles Times* in response to an article about outing are typical of reactions expressed in discussions about the issue: "I cannot condone the practice of 'outing'. What I do in private is no one's business but my own. It is my place, and no one else's, to tell people."[2] The columnist Anna Quindlen refers to outing as "a practice that I deplore."[3] Thomas Stoddard, head of Lambda Legal Defense and Education Fund, says outing "looks mean and nasty."[4] Hunter Madsen, a co-author of *After the Ball: How America Will Conquer Its Fear of Gays in the 90's*, says, "Coming out is the major trauma in every gay person's life. To raise the specter of a witch hunt by your own community only makes that process more difficult. Blackmail has long been used by straights against gays to get what they want. It's not surprising that blackmail should occur as a technique among the most radical gays."[5] Resorting to even stronger language, writer Fran Lebowitz claims, "It's damaging, it's immoral, it's McCarthyism, it's terrorism, it's cannibalism, it's beneath contempt. . . . To me this is a bunch of Jews lining up other Jews to go to a concentration camp."[6]

These reactions to outing imply a strong rule against outing. Violation of that rule seems as clearly morally wrong to the authors above as killing people because they are Jews or torturing people for fun. However, in the Thompson-Kowalski case, failure to out means failure to respect a relationship and to forfeit rights one believes one has. If that's so, then outing cannot be universally wrong. Other cases to be discussed later show, by contrast, that *not* outing is sometimes morally wrong, such as where it would involve hiding the real nature of a crime such as a gaybashing murder or where it would involve failing to obey a duty to a friend. A general rule against outing cannot be maintained. The issues are too complex and the ideals appealed to as condemnatory of outing, such as privacy, are less clear than the anti-outers think.[7] Since outing has to do with "opening the door of someone's closet" let us first consider the concept of the closet and what it means to "come out" of the closet.

THE CLOSET AND OUTING

"The closet" is an institution, a set of practices occurring within the context of a culturally or morally negative view about homosexuality, which has at least two functions. One is to provide a means of protection and survival; the other is to provide a means for hiding something about which one feels shame. First, it is a way of keeping secret information that, if known, might lead people to despise and perhaps do harm to someone. This function then is morally analogous to Jews in Nazi Germany not revealing they are Jewish or hiding in a secret attic. The second function, related to shame, can operate even without real dangers. Here the closet is a way of one's keeping hidden information concerning oneself about which one is ashamed and embarrassed.

"Coming out," short for "coming out of the closet," is a term that has come to be used to refer to the acknowledgement and disclosure of same-sex sexual orientation. There are degrees or levels of being in the closet and coming out. At the deepest level of being in the closet, one has not accepted one's homosexuality. When one realizes and acknowledges one's homosexuality, one comes out to oneself. This information may not yet be revealed to any other person (though often it is the case that some others may have surmised it before the individual did). Revealing one's sexuality to another person is a second level of coming out. Associating with other gay and lesbian people, dating, and perhaps entering into a sexual relationship with a person of the same sex is another level of coming out. The person might then share it with some close, non-gay friends. The levels continue, including coming out to family (for many an especially significant step), coming out to coworkers, and so on.

"Outing" is generally associated with revealing someone's homosexuality in the media. Discussions of outing, such as those quoted from earlier, often focus exclusively on the outing of celebrities and notables such as Malcolm Forbes[8] and Assistant Secretary of Defense Pete Williams.[9] However, Judge Campbell did not limit his reasoning to celebrities, for surely Thompson and Kowalski were not in any way celebrities at the time of Kowalski's accident. Neither will I limit outing's scope to celebrities in this essay.

While "outing" has been generally used to refer to disclosing homosexuality, the core of it is disclosing the truth about someone where that truth may draw attention to or cause difficulties which that person might not welcome. Thus, without stretching things very much we can speak of outing in areas other than sexual orientation: outing someone as a passing black, Jew, or, in some situations, a philosophy teacher. Furthermore, given the levels of the closet, there can also be different kinds of disclosure at the various levels. For example, in talking with a friend who I believe is gay, I might prod, attempting to get the person to admit his homosexuality. "I think you need to face the fact that you are gay" might at that point be uncomfortable information for that person. If, however, the person has been struggling with the issue and has been suffering from inertia, this outing of himself to himself is perhaps a valuable catalyst for personal growth.

Some of the reasons gay and lesbian persons have wanted to control carefully information about their sexual orientation are clear. Some have lost jobs, apartments, respect of the community, and have sometimes been assaulted and killed. Remaining hidden in such a context might be seen as a way of avoiding danger. However, sometimes the targets of discrimination have been closeted gay people whose sexual orientation has nevertheless been correctly guessed or figured out, so we might question how powerful this sort of control of information actually has been. In addition, openness about one's homosexuality in 1993 in the United States is not as problematic as it would have been in 1963 or even 1983. Some institutions and jurisdictions now protect certain rights in regard to sexual orientation. Many people are in situations such that, whether they clearly recognize it or not, the dangers of being open are not real or serious. Many accounts of individuals coming out include discussions of how liberating it has been and how fears that were felt were unwarranted. To be sure, there are some people who do face real dangers even in the United States. And in some other societies it would be very dangerous to reveal one's homosexuality. However, at present in the United States there are many for whom it would not be dangerous to be open. Insofar as such people remain closeted, we have to look at the second function of the closet, keeping the information hidden out of shame.

In "Shame and Gender," Sandra Bartky discusses the role of

shame in oppression. According to Bartky, shame can be preliminarily characterized as "a species of psychic distress occasioned by a self or a state of the self apprehended as inferior, defective, or in some way diminished."[10] While typical analyses of shame emphasize a belief component of shame (which presumably could then be assessed as being warranted or not), when it is shame connected with oppression, instead of a belief component there are "feelings" and "sensings" with regard to falling short of a norm which cannot be characterized as "belief." They are unclear and unarticulated and often not conscious. She focuses on shame experienced by some women about their gender, and sees it as "not a discrete occurrence, but a perpetual attunement, the pervasive affective taste of a life."[11] She further notes, "Not only does the revelatory character of shame not occur at the level of belief, but the corrosive character of shame and of similar sensings, their undermining effect and the peculiar helplessness women exhibit when in their power, lies in part in the very failure of these feelings to attain to the status of belief."[12]

This analysis is very helpful with regard to the oppression of gay and lesbian people. Shame does, in fact, often involve articulated beliefs, beliefs that gay people are unnatural, perverted, sick, or immoral. For gays the "other" before which they may feel shame may be society, God, or for those of a natural law bent, the universe. The coming out process often involves struggling with these beliefs. However, in addition to these overt beliefs there are also unarticulated sensings that remain in the consciousness of many even if they have dealt with articulated anti-homosexual views. This shame, "a perpetual attunement, the pervasive affective taste of a life," is much harder to deal with, but clearly is a powerful influence in the lives of many gay and lesbian people. If we take Bartky's gender example and alter it to a homosexual example, just as it is irrational for someone to think that her views are worthless or her paper awful because she is a woman, it will be irrational for a homosexual to believe that she is inferior or might lack worth because she is gay. In each of the cases the person might not articulate it that way, but in the end that turns out to be the only possible reason why she assesses her ideas or paper that way or doesn't want her sexuality to be known. These concepts are difficult to delineate, but they seem key to understanding oppression and especially self-oppression.

Bartky discusses how this sort of shame that many women face is one that black people have and do face as well. She makes a remark about these forms of oppression that is strikingly apt with regard to the homosexual closet: "The need for secrecy and concealment that figures so largely in the shame experience is disempowering . . . for it isolates the oppressed from one another and in this way works against the emergence of a sense of solidarity."[13]

How is this discussion relevant to the ethics of outing, the disclosure of someone's homosexuality? The notion of shame has yet to be appreciated in the ethics of outing, and the meaning of that shame may in fact have a role to play in assessing the moral significance of outing. Certainly, it may illuminate universal condemnation of outing. *Coming Out Right*, a 1982 handbook for people newly coming out, advises, "You do not identify anybody as a homosexual to a heterosexual."[14] But can this general anti-outing rule be held without exception? The Thompson-Kowalski case has been shown to be one counterexample. Let us consider some more cases. The discussion assumes the context of the present in the United States.

CASES AND THE CLOSET

It is clearly the case that some negative attitudes about homosexuals and acts of discrimination do continue to exist and are evil. Laws need to be changed before gay and lesbian people are treated with full justice and equality. However, we will focus on the issues of what moral problems there are with someone's homosexuality being revealed where he would rather that it not be revealed, and the corresponding issue of whether his remaining closeted may be morally problematic. It may be that the ease and general acceptance of the closet has actually delayed the quest for protective legislation. In that way, individual morality has a significant relationship to issues of public policy. Nevertheless our focus will be on issues of individual morality here, rather than on public policy or social morality. We will consider five actual cases, a possible case, and then go on to look at reasons offered on behalf of the rule against outing.

1. A newspaper article reported as accidental the death of a priest who, while attending a conference distant from his home, fell on the stairs at an adult bookstore and hit his head as he was coming up from the area for viewing gay porn movies, where "cruising" regularly takes place.[15] Details about accidental deaths are routinely reported, and in this case it resulted in the disclosure of the priest's very probably being gay.

2. The president of a conservative anti-gay Lutheran synod and his wife had some mysterious medical problems. They were eventually diagnosed with HIV infections. He then admitted to having had numerous homosexual relationships over a period of twenty years.[16] She died shortly afterward of AIDS-related complications. While this case does include the individual himself eventually admitting his sexual practices, still it was only his and his wife's illness related to accidental HIV infection which prompted the disclosure.

Even though these two cases do not involve celebrities who as such are understood to have waived entitlement to much privacy, they are, because of circumstances and the media's role in providing information to the public, "public figures for a season," and, at least in terms of the law, it would be difficult to claim that this kind of outing is an invasion of privacy.[17] Once they attain this status, it is difficult to claim that their sex lives should not in any way be reported. And no information reported in these cases was obtained in a covert, intrusive way. It should be noted that virtually anyone could through chance (by being a victim of a crime, a witness of a crime, or, like Oliver Sipple, someone who helps foil an attempt to assassinate a president) become a "public figure for a season." This is one of the ways in which the homosexual closet may involve a false sense of control. Our third case involves someone who is clearly a "public figure for a season." But, as we shall see, there are other issues related to privacy that arise with regard to this case as well.

3. A gay man was brutally murdered under circumstances which made it seem gaybashing was the likely motive.[18] When his homosexuality was revealed in the media, the person who was perceived as the source of the information was accused of "outing" him, and some claimed it was wrong to out someone even after death and even if the dead person was not especially closeted.[19] Victims of

murders and especially brutal murders do become "public figures for a season." Even if one were to claim that there are privacy rights of the dead, keeping this murder victim's homosexuality secret would have gotten in the way of seeking justice. The information is necessary as part of the quest to understand what might have happened. In addition, in gaybashing cases perpetrators often try to use a panic defense, claiming the victim made a sexual advance and it caused panic. Such a defense tactic has more power if the homosexuality of the victim is hidden until it comes up during a trial. Furthermore, given the fact that violence against gay people does occur, it is important that this be known by the public, in order to make clear the need for social change and protection. Thus a failure to bring the information about the victim's sexuality to light in a case such as this would be morally wrong.

4. A man who is a close friend of a married woman finds out accidentally from an acquaintance that the woman's husband frequents an adult bookstore where he picks up men for sex. The man who receives this information knows that the woman perceives her relationship to be sexually exclusive and also that she is extremely health conscious and concerned about health risks. He carefully checks to be sure the person giving the information has accurately identified the man in question and ascertains that he has.

While we may think that matters that relate to the relationships of others are generally not one's business, it would seem in this case that there might well be a duty arising out of the close friendship the man has with the woman to try to bring the husband's deceit to light given the jeopardy she might be in with regard to sexually communicable diseases. Acting on such a duty would be forcing the disclosure that her husband is engaging in sex with other men. There may be disagreement about what would be the best strategy (for example, whether to first confront the husband to insist that he be honest), but it is still the case that most options would involve disclosure that the husband would likely not welcome. Here a duty related to friendship seems to take priority and would make the disclosure justified.

5. A gay man, known to me, whom I will call John, experienced the following forced disclosures. John, age 53, a former clergyman, was working as a financial administrator in a regional office of his

church. A hostile former lover wrote a letter to the bishop who was in charge of the region, who happened to be anti-gay, disclosing his sexual relationship with John. The bishop insisted that John submit to an investigation and hearing. John instead resigned and took a job elsewhere. Two years later John, now in his mid-fifties, returned to the same community to serve as a financial administrator in a large medical institution. A month after he began work his superior received a letter and an anonymous phone call, both indicating that John was gay. He was fired; the reason given was fear that his lifestyle might interfere with fundraising for the institution.

This is the sort of case that people very much opposed to outing seem to have in mind, where someone experiences harm resulting from the revealing of information about the person's sexuality. And I think we can see that John was the victim of two morally reprehensible forced disclosures. The first, by the hostile former lover very much appears intended to cause harm to John, perhaps as an act of revenge. That his situation, being employed by a religious group, made him very vulnerable, is common knowledge. The second case was probably malicious gossip. The person who wrote the letter must have believed that the information would make a difference to the medical institution and might lead to his dismissal. Why else write the letter? John was clearly harmed by these forced disclosures, and the disclosers were morally wrong in what they did.[20] We should note, however, that in the discussions about outing this is not the standard sort of case that comes up. The wrongness of this case can be explained without resorting to a rule against outing.

Before going on to consider arguments against outing, let us consider a species of cases involving disclosure of homosexuality. Homosexuals who are open, "out," regularly face decisions about whether or not to be open about others who are gay or lesbian but closeted. Let us assume that I am out and that I have not made a specific promise to someone to conceal his homosexuality from others and I am not in a special relationship (such as counselor-client) with him that presumes confidentiality. I know Jones is gay because I've seen him at gay events, know him socially, or it is generally known that he is gay. Jones is closeted but faces no particular known danger should others find out he is gay. Let us say that in conversation someone asks me whether Jones is gay, or why

Jones has recently been so out of sorts. If I say that Jones is gay, or explain that the reason why Jones is out of sorts is that he has just broken up with a lover of ten years, I have "outed" Jones. But to avoid outing I would have to somehow evade the question or lie. I could say that I cannot answer the question (which very response suggests he is gay) or I could lie and say I don't know. In any case, I am put in a morally compromised position. I have to lie or evade on Jones's behalf. Knowing that someone is closeted but has no good reasons to remain in the closet is an unfortunately common phenomenon.

Following *Coming Out Right*'s advice, I would be enjoined in this last circumstance from being honest with the person with whom I am conversing. (We are assuming she is heterosexual. There is an interesting general practice of being more open with fellow homosexuals, perhaps implied by the book's advice, suggesting the practices of something like a secret society.) But why? There's no promise, no special relationship requiring confidentiality, and Jones is not clearly at risk. What seems to remain as the reason why Jones's closet should be respected is the shame function of the closet, discussed earlier. Jones would rather that people not know he is gay because it would be embarrassing, and perhaps they might think ill of him. If I, someone who is openly gay, lie or evade on Jones's behalf, then I have to accept shame as a compelling reason to support his closet. This amounts to self-degradation: supporting Jones's closet in this case involves not only lying or evading but also degrading myself.[21] Barring very special reasons, it would seem that being honest about Jones in this situation is morally justified rather than prohibited. But we need to look more closely at the arguments used to support a rule against outing to see if this is so.

THE CASE AGAINST OUTING EXAMINED

The most common objection to the kind of disclosure that falls under my definition of "outing" is that it violates a right to privacy. It will be argued that it is difficult to hold that one has such a right to privacy in this regard. Rather, objections to outing have to do with wanting to keep information, which is not by its nature private, *secret*. There seems to be general agreement that some matters are private, such as medical information, communication with counselors, and bank and phone card numbers. The consensus seems to be that we can choose to reveal such information ourselves but that others do not have a right to have access to that information. We are the gatekeepers here. There is cultural variability here, to be sure. This discussion will assume the context of practices in the United States.[22]

Information about marital status, whether one has children, whether one is dating someone is not thought of in general as private. Where there are "privacy laws" that make it illegal to ask about these things, their real function and meaning has to do with claiming this information is in certain situations *irrelevant* to a particular purpose–in considering someone for employment, for instance. If Merv Griffin is married, or has been living with a woman for a long time, saying that publicly would not be seen as a violation of privacy. If someone carefully avoids saying anything about dating someone or being married, evades it when asked, and is embarrassed and angry when it is disclosed, we would regard it as unusual, manifesting a strange shame or perhaps special situation that requires keeping that information secret. For example, if, while at a philosophy conference, I run into John in a bar where unbeknownst to me he is trying to pick up a woman, and I not only say "hello" when we meet, but ask him about his wife and children, the disclosure that he is married might upset him because it could railroad his attempt to spend the night with the woman he has met. However, it doesn't seem that his privacy has been violated.

Of course, social consensus here is bifurcated: with regard to heterosexual relationships, these topics are appropriate for conversation; with regard to homosexual relationships, silence is the "rule." Sexual orientation, when it is heterosexuality, is generally not regarded as private in the least. Moral consistency requires, however, that, barring special reasons to the contrary, sexual and emotional relationships should be treated similarly: either both homosexual and heterosexual relationships should be regarded as private matters or not as private matters. Since the general practice seems to be to regard such relationships as not being essentially private matters, it seems to me we cannot use an appeal to the *privacy* of relationships to claim that revealing homosexuality is morally wrong as a rule.

The concept of privacy has to do with accessibility. My thoughts are private. If I have thought I might be gay, but have not said so to anybody, then in that sense of "private," my thoughts are private. However, when we talk about a right to privacy we mean a moral sense of private: the information is not private in the sense that it is in my head and I have control over who finds out about it, but private in the sense that others don't have a right to access, unless I permit it. If I have written about my realization I am gay in my diary, and someone steals it and publishes it, my privacy has been clearly violated. Similarly if I have talked with a counselor, clergyperson, or physician about my sexuality, and that person reveals it to another without my consent, my privacy has been violated. More accurately, we might say a duty of *confidentiality* with regard to private information has been violated. If, however, I am out at the level of socially interacting with other gay and lesbian people or having a lover, then it is hard to see my wanting to remain closeted to others as a matter of privacy in a morally relevant sense. If I don't want people to know about these aspects of my life it seems to be instead a *secret*. This distinction between privacy and secrecy, which originates with Sissela Bok, has also been used by Richard Mohr in his recent discussion of the outing issue.[23]

Sissela Bok claims that *privacy* has to do with protection from *unwanted* access, while *secrecy* has to do with hiding: *intentional concealment*. The two overlap, but are nevertheless distinct. She notes: "Privacy need not hide; and secrecy hides far more than what is private. A private garden need not be a secret garden; a private life is rarely a secret life."[24] As was noted earlier in discussion of the shame function of the closet, secrecy is often used with regard to matters about which one feels shame. Douglas Shenson, a physician writing about dealing with AIDS in his practice, uses the privacy/secrecy distinction as well: "But secrecy will never be a successful strategy in coping with AIDS. The role of 'the secret'—as opposed to that of privacy, which functions to maintain the integrity of the individual in his relations with others—is always subversive. It distorts communication with loved ones—topics are avoided and worries are multiplied—and it reinforces a notion of unwarranted, solitary shame. Indeed solitude is the psychological and political snare of the stigmatized."[25]

There seems to be nothing essentially private with regard to information about sexual orientation as such. *Privacy* does not apply. Rather, in a context where one might be harmed or thought ill of with regard to it, or because one is ashamed of it, one might decide that one wants to keep it *secret*. The reasons for the secret can then be evaluated as justifiable or not. So, for example, in a country where there is a death penalty for homosexuality, keeping one's homosexuality secret would be seen as justified. Similarly, in the United States, if some skinheads ask someone if he's gay, it would seem that keeping it a secret in that circumstance is justified. In both of these cases the secret is justified because someone wishes the information to do unjustified harm to the person. It is legitimate self-protection that justifies withholding the information as a secret. *It is not that the information as such is private.* Of course, not all secrets that are in a person's interest are morally justified. If I'm stealing computers from the government or university, keeping that secret may be in my interest, but nevertheless, morally unjustified.

The outing issue has to do with whether or not keeping one's homosexuality secret is justified, rather than a general rule against outing. It is clear why in some situations or at some times people have wanted to conceal it. The idea of a collective practice of secret-keeping may have made sense in the past in American society where disclosure of sexual orientation might well have caused serious problems for gay men and lesbians. However, for many today those dangers are fortunately greatly reduced.

Those who appeal to privacy as an objection to outing have in mind the idea of a general right to be left alone, to not have attention drawn to one that one may not welcome. This justification is weaker than a right to privacy, given that quite often unwelcome attention can be drawn to one where no right seems to be violated: e.g., someone criticizing an idea one has expressed, someone staring at one, or someone trying to sell one something. *Rudeness* may be the proper concept to apply here rather than outing. But let us consider some ways in which the "right to be left alone" is seen as something stronger and related to privacy, and whether we can in this way bring the concept of privacy back to try to defend the position of the anti-outers.

In an influential analysis of privacy related to law, William Prosser claims, "The law of privacy comprises four distinct kinds of invasion of four different interests of the plaintiff, which are tied together by the common name, but otherwise have almost nothing in common except that each represents an interference with the right of the plaintiff, in the phrase coined by Judge Cooley, 'to be let alone.' "[26] The four different sorts of invasion of interests he distinguishes are intrusion (e.g., filming someone without their permission), embarrassment (drawing attention to someone other than a public figure in a way that causes embarrassment), false light (suggesting something false about someone, such as using someone's photograph in an article about prostitution when that person is not a prostitute), and appropriation (e.g., making money by using someone's name or photograph without permission). Let us see whether any of these categories will apply to outing.

Since I am considering situations where outing makes claims that are true, then clearly one cannot claim it casts a false light on someone. Since we are dealing with situations where the fact that someone is gay or lesbian is known at least by some persons because he or she attends gay social events or maintains a household with someone of the same gender, for example, it would be hard to appeal to its being an intrusion per se. So these two categories of a claimed right to privacy will not help here.

Appropriation might apply to cases of outing where someone outs another for money, such as the person reportedly paid $100,000 by the *National Enquirer* for revealing his sexual relationship with John Travolta.[27] This would require further consideration, since such appropriation is not quite like using someone's name to endorse a product or their photo without their consent. But if it will not count as appropriation with regard to the law related to privacy, where a main motive for the disclosure is to make money, it seems reprehensible. But this only shows this case of outing is morally wrong, not that all outing is wrong. And part of the reason this case of outing is wrong is that the money is to be made (the *National Enquirer* is willing to pay) because some will think it embarrassing or shameful that the celebrity is gay. The outer is sharing in the negative view of homosexuality in doing the outing and is not motivated simply to tell the truth or avoid lying where it would be self-degrading.

Embarrassment is the category that remains in Prosser's distinction of invasion of interests that are appealed to under the general term of "privacy." Certainly some people are embarrassed when their homosexuality becomes known. In Prosser's discussion he considers a famous case, "The Red Kimono Case," involving a former prostitute acquitted of murder who was living a new life with a new name. Seven years later her new identity was disclosed in a movie, and she filed suit. The court did rule that this was an invasion of a right to privacy.[28] But here someone had been acquitted in court, radically changed her life, and wanted to live a new, quiet life, and the movie drew significant, unwanted attention to her new life. The embarrassment that closeted homosexuals experience when their sexuality becomes known seems to be very different. It seems to be an embarrassment related to the shame function of the closet. Judge Campbell seemed to have this sort of embarrassment in mind in his ruling in the Thompson-Kowalski case. Thus, the various categories of not "leaving someone alone" that are used in legal cases that are grouped together loosely under "privacy" do not seem to give us a way of salvaging that concept as a support for a general rule against outing.

THE EVILS OF THE CLOSET

Earlier two functions of the closet were identified: protection from harm and protection related to shame. The general view of the closet held by the anti-outers, where the individual is seen as having the right to control all information about their sexual orientation implies that the closet, while it may be unfortunate, is not morally problematic. Heterosexuals as well as homosexuals should support it. That this defense of the closet is morally problematic may be seen by the following considerations.

First consider what the heterosexual counterpart of the closet would look like: it would involve hiding all feelings of being sexually attracted to someone and any information about dating, becoming engaged, and being married. In addition, one would have to conceal being pregnant or keep secret that one has children, since those states suggest heterosexuality. This degree of concealment seems utterly absurd, yet those who oppose all outing (except for perhaps very hypocritical public figures) treat the homosexual counterpart of this, the closet, as perfectly acceptable.

The closet has costs and involves moral problems. It requires doing things to keep "the secret" and brings self-degradation. Living with someone of the same sex and being together regularly in public might give the secret away, as would purchasing certain kinds of publications or attending certain events. In addition, the closet brings self-degradation. Jeremiah McCarthy has written elsewhere in this volume about the "heterosexual panorama," the background of everyday life in which it is assumed everyone is heterosexual. One is rewarded for compliance, but at the cost of giving up one's own real identity and assuming a false one. In doing this one becomes, as McCarthy has said, "the victim *and* the victimizer, the prisoner *and* the guard." This kind of self-degradation is a heavy cost of the closet though it may be warranted where it is very clearly the lesser of evils. The clear danger seems to outweigh the moral cost of leaving unchallenged the view of homosexuality as shameful by keeping one's homosexuality secret.

McCarthy adopts the term "heterosexual panorama" from Vaclav Havel's discussion of what Havel calls the "panorama" of the "post-totalitarian system" that existed, for example, in communist Czechoslovakia. The tactic for dealing with both sorts of oppressive panoramas is "living in the truth"–for gay people that means coming out, by which they "cease to be compliant in the system of heterosexual domination, kill the guard within, and, acting on their own principles, become free."[29]

Another way to see moral questions about the closet and outing is to consider the phenomenon of "passing." Imagine that a black person in his early forties is nominated for a position on the Supreme Court. Let us say that this person is light enough so he could "pass" as being white.[30] Investigation reveals that he passed as white in college, law school, and at first positions in law. Though at that time it was not impossible for black people to gain entrance into those schools or to be hired for such a position, this was done, the candidate claims, to make life simpler and avoid any potential hassles. What would happen to this person's nomination? Such a revelation would likely take the candidate out of the running. It would probably be argued that this person's denial of his identity is a cowardly form of lying and manifests shame about his race. While the advantage and the simplifying of things in one's life make the resorting to passing in some sense understandable, most would regard it as a low thing to do. Someone who would do that would be unsuitable for a position requiring integrity and the public trust.

Or consider the example of a woman, sufficiently androgynous in appearance, who passes as male to advance her career beyond glass ceilings, to earn a higher salary, and to be at less risk of sexual harassment or rape. What should our judgment be here? While we can understand the desire for a simpler life and advantages, I think we would be critical of her deception because it denies her true nature, seems at least partly based on shame, and the stakes are not sufficiently high. It would be different if this were done one hundred years ago.

Finally consider the example of a gay or lesbian person who passes as straight. Given the "heterosexual panorama" this is, of course, not at all difficult for most to do, and, as a matter of fact, is probably done by all gay and lesbian people at some times, and the majority of gay and lesbian people in this society a lot of the time. Is the closet as a form of passing morally justified?

The same criticisms of racial and gender passing would apply here. Unless the stakes are clearly sufficiently high, it is denying one's identity and lying, and it manifests shame about one's nature. It is in general easier for gay people to pass as straight than it is for most blacks to pass as white or women to pass as men. This is, however, no moral justification for it. While it is true that there is more legislation protecting racial minorities and women, they are still exposed to dangers and difficulties because of their race or gender. Therefore if it is morally wrong for them to pass, it would seem to be morally wrong for gay and lesbian people to pass. It might be argued that the closet is justified because while conditions for homosexuals might be generally good now, who knows what might happen in the future? But the same could be argued with regard to racial minorities. Again, where there is clear, demonstrable danger it would seem that keeping one's sexual orientation secret is warranted. But it is the need to protect oneself from the clear danger that justifies it, not any essential privacy about one's sexual orientation. Given the moral issues that arise, the casual tolerance and support of the closet, even where the person has no good reasons to defend it, is shocking.[31]

Although fear of harm is often cited as the motivation for the closet, we must remember its other function: dealing with shame. Given that many homosexuals remain closeted even where there is clearly no significant danger to them it would seem that it is the shame function that it is really serving, in a manner very similar to Bartky's description of the shame that many women feel about their gender. Insofar as this is the motivation for remaining closeted, albeit often not fully conscious, closeted homosexuals in failing to assert their worth are engaged in servility, accepting the view of their oppressors and doing exactly what their oppressors want them to do. Thomas Hill, Jr., has argued that a problem with servility is that the servile person fails to respect morality: "A person who fully respected a system of moral rights would be disposed to learn his proper place in it, to affirm it proudly, and not to tolerate abuses of it lightly."[32] Such a person is at risk of being unable to respect others fully. If these observations are true, it would seem that the closet should become a tool of last resort rather than a presumed way of life.

Shame is not only a motivation for many to remain closeted, it is the motive of many outings as well. Many of the ways the media operate with regard to homosexuality connect it with shame. This will give us a way of morally evaluating some of the ways the media "outs" or fails to out someone who is homosexual. To the extent tabloids run stories about the homosexuality of celebrities to boost sales, it would seem that they and their readers see homosexuality as titillating and embarrassing. So the media and the public are connecting homosexuality with shame in their use of it. But, once such stories appear, the quick and angry denial voiced by some celebrities who have been claimed to be lesbian or gay seems to be equally motivated by seeing homosexuality as shameful.

Some of the avoidance of outing does seem deeply rooted in this sort of negative view of homosexuality. Gabriel Rotello, editor of the now defunct *OutWeek*, the magazine that made Malcolm

Forbes's sexuality public, claims, "The major exception to all this celebrity openness is homosexuality. This creates the impression that homosexuality is, in effect, the worst thing in the world. After all, if you can write about extramarital affairs, abortion, a First Lady's drug problem, or a rock star's penchant for beating his wife, but you can't write about Malcolm Forbes's sexual orientation, what other implication could there be?"[33]

Another way in which the media seem to act on a view that connects homosexuality with shame is a phenomenon one writer, Lindsey Van Gelder, calls "inning"–"keeping gay people in the closet even when they have no desire to be there."[34] She cites refusal to list surviving life partners in obituaries as one example. Another has to do with the story of a lesbian whose partner was killed in a 1989 Santa Cruz earthquake. Photos of her pounding the earth were widely used in the media. In interviews she was open about her relationship and insisted it should be acknowledged, yet most reporters bypassed the issue.[35] This avoidance certainly goes further than the presupposition of heterosexuality; it is the denial of homosexuality even when it is openly admitted.

Insofar as accepting the view that homosexuality is shameful underlies some of these practices in the press, they share moral problems similar to the phenomenon of passing. They fail to respect the personhood and the moral rights of the people involved.

OUTING AND ETHICS

In an ideal world, gay and lesbian people would be honest and "out" themselves. What about this world? It has already been shown that a general rule prohibiting outing cannot be defended. The position of the anti-outers referred to at the beginning of the paper is too extreme; it does not allow for cases where not outing would be wrong. The way to evaluate cases of outing is to use already available moral principles, not any special rule against it. Barring special considerations (such as clear danger or having made a promise), an out gay person would be morally justified in revealing the sexuality of a closeted homosexual where to not do so would be to lie, evade, and engage in self-degradation. Note that the claim here is that such an outing would be justified, not that there is a duty to out.

Given that remaining closeted in situations where there aren't clear reasons justifying it involves diminished integrity (in terms of failing to be honest, not respecting oneself, being motivated by shame that involves a servility to certain societal views), there may be some situations where, given the role or position of a person, this failure of integrity warrants disclosure. Just as the black person passing for white might be unsuitable for the Supreme Court, the contemporary gay person passing as straight might be unsuitable for certain positions.

As an example here, let us consider college teachers, especially those who are tenured at colleges and universities or in jurisdictions where sexual orientation is protected, and who have no special reason to remain closeted. Do gay and lesbian faculty in such situations have a *duty* to come out such that by not doing so they are lacking in integrity? If we interpret the duties of teachers to focus simply on the teaching of their subject, we might say that whether to be open is a matter for individual conscience. However, it does seem that many also see teachers as having a general duty to serve as models for students and to help students in ways other than simply teaching them about the subject matter. Since often information about the sexual orientation of homosexual teachers becomes known and discussed among students anyway, being closeted does suggest to students that the individual feels there is some reason to try to hide that information. It could be argued that in this situation a kind of trust that is given to the person occupying the position has been violated by this lack of integrity. If so, being honest about the truth about persons where they should have been honest themselves would seem to be warranted. Note that the appeal here is not to the utility of their being good models but to the lack of integrity involved.

This line of reasoning should also apply to other positions where integrity and honesty are seen as being particularly important: counselor, judge, and clergy.[36] Public officials, whether elected or appointed, become public figures, and as such are seen to be in effect accepting some loss of privacy. But, in addition, it would seem that honesty and integrity are seen as critical to their role, and this might well justify honesty even where it might not be welcomed by the individual. So this line of argument might well justify outing an Assistant Secretary of Defense or a Senator.

In the case of public figures such as actors and actresses the integrity argument won't work. There just isn't the sort of "public trust" that exists with regard to teachers, clergy, or public officials. Nevertheless, they are public figures, and it is clear that things about their lives are regarded as newsworthy. So they can't appeal to a right to privacy to keep attention away from their sexuality.

The position being argued for here is controversial, and is, to be sure, one that may well anger some. However, it seems that it is where logic leads. With regard to sexual orientation we are in a time of transition, as we are with regard to some other issues, such as gender. That may mitigate some of the falling short of the sort of standard argued for here. But it does so only, I would argue, with the understanding that it is important to face the issues of the evils of the closet and the need to foster honesty and self-respect, not only socially but individually as well. In much of the discussion about the outing issue it is surprising how people have lost sight of the importance of the truth. If truth is valued, then there can be neither easy support of the closet nor blanket criticism of outing.

NOTES

1. Nadine Brozan, "Sides are Bypassed in Lesbian Case," *New York Times*, April 26, 1991. The Minnesota Supreme Court later reversed the district court decision, and Karen Thompson is now guardian of Sharon Kowalski.
2. "Letters in View: The Practice of 'Outing' Draws Fire," *Los Angeles Times*, April 1, 1990, p. E4. Letter quoted is that of G. L. Leyner.
3. Anna Quindlen, "Arthur Ashe Story Raises Tough Questions About Media's Role," *Forum* [Fargo, ND–Moorhead, MN], Apr. 15, 1992.
4. David Gelman, "'Outing': An Unexpected Assault on Sexual Privacy," *Newsweek*, Apr. 30, 1990, p. 66.
5. Beth Ann Krier, "Whose Sex Secret Is It?" *Los Angeles Times*, Jan. 22, 1990, p. E1.
6. Rebecca Lewin, "A Few Minutes With Fractious Fran," *The Advocate*, July 3, 1990, p. 63.
7. Randy Shilts ("Is 'Outing' Gays Ethical?" *New York Times*, April 12, 1990, p. A23) makes a similar claim. He claims a tension between his role as a journalist who does not want to reveal the homosexuality of anyone who is not a very hypocritical public official and his role as a gay person who is out during the

AIDS crisis. I would argue that the crisis of AIDS is not the only reason why the general rule cannot be held.

8. Outed by arch-outer Michelangelo Signorile in "The Other Side of Malcolm," *OutWeek*, Mar. 18, 1990, pp. 40-45.

9. Outed by Michelangelo Signorile in "The Outing of Assistant Secretary of Defense Pete Williams," *The Advocate*, Aug. 27, 1991, pp. 34-44.

10. Sandra Bartky, "Shame and Gender," in her *Femininity and Domination* (New York: Routledge, 1990), pp. 83-95; 85.

11. Bartky, p. 96.

12. Bartky, p. 95

13. Bartky, p. 97.

14. William Hanson and Wes Muchmore, *Coming Out Right: A Handbook for the Gay Male* (Boston: Alyson Publications, 1982), p. 20.

15. "Death of Priest at Adult Bookstore Ruled Accidental," *Forum* [Fargo, ND–Moorhead, MN], Nov. 4, 1988.

16. Tom Majeski, "Pastor with AIDS Quits Lutheran Post, Admits He Had Gay Sex for 20 Years," *St. Paul Pioneer Press-Dispatch*, Apr. 9, 1992.

17. William L. Prosser, "Privacy: A Legal Analysis," in Ferdinand Schoeman, ed., *Philosophical Dimensions of Privacy: An Anthology* (Cambridge: Cambridge University Press, 1984), p. 120. About "public figures for a season," Prosser cites *Restatement of Torts* (1939): "until they have reverted to the lawful and unexciting life led by the great bulk of the community, they are subject to the privileges which publishers have to satisfy the curiosity of the public as to their leaders, heroes, villains and victims."

18. The account of this murder may be found in the *Forum* [Fargo, ND–Moorhead, MN], April 9-14, 1991, in articles by Tom Pantera.

19. The author was interviewed for a television news report on Fargo, ND, WDAY-TV, Apr. 11, 1991. The interviewer knew from his research that the victim was gay and intended to reveal that, and interviewed the author to get reactions from the gay community to an apparent gaybashing murder. The news report was edited in such a way that the information that the victim was gay seemed to be given by the author during the interview with him. Reactions were reported to the author by various individuals.

20. John did threaten to sue the medical institution and received a settlement from them. That this happened was never made public in the community but only in the local and regional gay press. The settlement included an agreement to not discuss it. The fact that there had been some coverage in the gay press, however, made it possible to leak it to the other media. John, however, decided he didn't want it made public for fear of difficulties at his age in getting another job and because his former wife and children live in the community. The fact that many cases of discrimination are never publicized creates difficulties for seeking gay and lesbian rights protections since many do not think such discrimination occurs.

21. Richard Mohr also makes this point in "The Outing Controversy: Privacy and Dignity in Gay Ethics," in his *Gay Ideas: Outing and Other Controversies* (Boston: Beacon Press, 1992), pp. 30-31.

22. For example, the Turkish language has two different questions for asking one's name, one for one's first name and one for one's last name. In meeting someone casually it is thought of as snoopy or intrusive to ask someone's last name. There needs to be a special reason for it, or a closeness before it is appropriate. This is clearly different from American practice. The discussion in this essay, however, assumes the context of practices in the United States.

23. Mohr, pp. 11–48.

24. Sissela Bok, *Secrets: On the Ethics of Concealment and Revelation* (New York: Pantheon, 1982), p. 11.

25. Douglas Shenson, "When Fear Conquers: A Doctor Learns About AIDS from Leprosy," *New York Times Magazine*, Feb. 28, 1988, p. 48.

26. Prosser, p. 107.

27. Doug Brantley, "Look Who's Apologizing," *The Advocate*, Oct. 23, 1990, p. 56.

28. Prosser, p. 109.

29. See Jeremiah McCarthy's "The Closet and the Ethics of Outing" in this volume.

30. Richard Wasserstrom discusses the role of the concept of passing in racism in his essay "On Racism and Sexism," in Richard Wasserstrom, ed., *Today's Moral Problems*, 3rd ed. (New York: Macmillan, 1985), p. 3.

31. It should be noted that there is in society a presumption of heterosexuality: everyone is assumed to be heterosexual. The individual so presumed is not, of course, responsible for that assumption. However, when I write of a gay or lesbian person passing as straight I have in mind a person intentionally doing or not doing things to lead people to believe they are heterosexual. So, if I am in a same-sex relationship and respond, when asked if I am married, "No, I'm single," I am, of course, not being fully honest and am *intentionally* leading my questioner to believe I am heterosexual.

32. Thomas E. Hill, Jr., "Servility and Self-Respect," in Jane English, ed., *Sex Equality* (Englewood Cliffs, NJ: Prentice-Hall, Inc., 1977), p. 178.

33. Mitchell Hartman, "When to Say Someone is Gay," *The Quill* 78 (1990): 6.

34. Lindsey Van Gelder, "Straight or Gay, Stick to the Facts," *Columbia Journalism Review* 29 (1990): 53.

35. Van Gelder, p. 53.

36. This shows a moral outrageousness in the anti-homosexual policies of many religious groups. Their gay and lesbian clergy are forced into the diminished integrity of the closet.

Coming Out, Being Out, and Acts of Virtue

Steven Barbone, BS
Lee Rice, PhD

Marquette University

SUMMARY. We examine three philosophical models for (gay) self-identity: utilitarianism (exemplified by Eichberg), deontologism (Mohr), and individualism (Spinoza). The first two, we argue, overlook the personal and multi-faceted nature of social relations. We argue that the framework of methodological individualism is better suited to deal with the issues of self-identity as they affect questions of whether, when, and how to come out, and being out. This framework suggests that there is no moral principle which could apply universally in regard to being out and that there are common situations in which it is not morally appropriate to come out or to be out at all.

Coming out has been an omnipresent theme within gay literature, social criticism, and psychological studies of gay lifestyles.[1] The

Steven Barbone is a teaching assistant in Philosophy at Marquette University, Milwaukee, WI 53233, and may be reached at 5901barbones@vms.csd.mu.edu.

Lee Rice is Associate Professor of Philosophy at Marquette University and may be reached at 6802ricel@vms.csd.mu.edu.

The authors would like to thank Dr. Douglas Den Uyl, Bellarmine College, Louisville, and Dr. Timothy Murphy, University of Illinois at Chicago, for helpful comments on earlier drafts of this paper.

[Haworth co-indexing entry note]: "Coming Out, Being Out, and Acts of Virtue." Barbone, Steven and Lee Rice. Co-published simultaneously in the *Journal of Homosexuality* (The Haworth Press, Inc.) Vol. 27, No. 3/4, 1994, pp. 91-110; and: *Gay Ethics: Controversies in Outing, Civil Rights, and Sexual Science* (ed: Timothy F. Murphy) The Haworth Press, Inc., 1994, pp. 91-110. Multiple copies of this article/chapter may be purchased from The Haworth Document Delivery Center [1-800-3-HAWORTH; 9:00 a.m. - 5:00 p.m. (EST)].

phenomenon of outing, both as a political strategy and as a moral positioning, has more recently come up for debate, and has had both its supporters and its detractors,[2] in part because of its problematic relations to issues of privacy and self-determination.[3] We argue that in their focus on outing, such debates frequently bypass more important philosophical and moral questions which relate to underlying questions seldom made explicit about individual identity and the nature of human community.

Just as the concept of outing and one's moral attitude toward outing depend upon a particular attitude (often either unexplained or question-begging) toward being out, so we claim that the concept of *being out* itself cannot constitute the bedrock of any analysis relating to this cluster of questions; it in turn depends upon a particular attitude toward the individual and the nature of relationships within the social community. Quite obviously, if being out is morally preferable to the closet,[4] then that fact would constitute a *prima facie* moral argument for outing, even if such an argument were offset by considerations of privacy and self-determination. Discussions of being out versus being closeted, however, usually address problems of *coming out* rather than questions of *being out*. These discussions seem to fall into two broad categories. The first is psychological and emphasizes the debilitating aspects of closeted behavior at the individual level and of the gay ghetto at the community level.[5] While normative claims are often smuggled in the back door (the term "ghetto," for example, itself blurs the line between social description and normative prescription), they are seldom addressed directly, and it is seldom clear the extent to which the claims about the negative aspects of the closet are due to social contingencies (which themselves may be undesirable). The second category is, for want of a better phrase, that of "consciousness-raising," and Rob Eichberg's 1991 best-seller, *Coming Out: An Act of Love*, is as good an example as any of this approach. Primarily aimed at those in search of self-help devices, work of this kind not only targets readers' self-perceived inadequacies but seldom addresses underlying moral questions. Such work also typically suffers from the absence of empirical studies to support claims made regarding its efficacy.

It is our view that there are three basic models from which we can begin to understand "being out of the closet." The first of these is a rule-utilitarian model, and this is here represented by Eichberg and Dennis Altman; the second, more closely paralleling a Kantian deontological ethics, is typified here by Richard Mohr; the third model follows from a reading of the individualism of the seventeenth-century philosopher Benedict Spinoza. We believe that, once the more fundamental question of the normative value of self-identity—in this case, being out of the closet—is addressed, the moral importance of such issues as outing or even just coming out become matters of negligible importance which should be more sensibly examined in light of judgments made concerning identity in the first place.

We also argue that the first two approaches are collectivist or communitarian in nature—both in their original formulation by John Stuart Mill and Immanuel Kant and in their current incarnations in Eichberg and Mohr—and that, probably because of the limitations in such perspectives,[6] they both fail to address some central issues concerning (gay) self-identity. Our suggestion will be that some form of methodological individualism better addresses the issue of *whether* to come out and *how* to be out and also provides a more humane and moral perspective for resolving *personal* issues relating to the latter. The issue of *coming out,* we suggest, is overemphasized, since, on any account, its *telos* is that of being out, and the Kantian and utilitarian frameworks are too rigid and unyielding at the individual level to provide a framework for addressing these personal issues.

One of the functions of philosophical reflection is to jar one into looking at problems in a new way. Seventeenth-century German philosopher Kant had little to say about homosexuality beyond a few unconvincing words regarding its immorality and punishability (an issue sadly resurrected in the contemporary AIDS literature).[7] Nineteenth-century British philosopher Mill supported the legalization of homosexual acts without addressing their morality. It is safe to say that neither of these men thought through the issues deeply. Spinoza, on the other hand, has nothing whatsoever to say about homosexuality. Addressing the moral issues from within these three frameworks may be jarring, but it emphasizes a central point we wish to make: the sooner moralists within the gay tradition come to

realize that the underlying moral principles which must be brought
to bear on issues such as being out, coming out, and outing are *not*
in any way unique or indigenous to the gay experience or situation,
the more cogent will be the force of their arguments from a moral
perspective. If there were such a thing as "gay ethics," it would be
an application of more general (and not "gay") ethical principles to
the gay situation.

The form of methodological individualism which we advocate is
that of Spinoza, who, though he wrote nothing about gay issues, had
a great deal, and in our opinion, a great deal of worth, to say about
the relation between the individual and the community.[8] Our approach will not be historical but analytic; and we do not seek to
provide a genealogy leading from either Eichberg or Altman to
Mill, or from Mohr to Kant. We argue that the issues of being out
and of outing depend upon wider moral questions whose application is not limited to the gay experience.

BEING OUT AS SOCIAL BENEFICENCE

We begin, then, by examining the rule-utilitarian approach which
seems to underlie the rhetoric of empowerment found in the approach taken to coming out by Eichberg and others. Rule-util-
itarians adopt a principle for validating rules, rather than individual
acts (i.e., "tokens") falling under them, according to their production of human happiness (positive) or unhappiness (negative); the
utility value of a rule is defined simply as the balance of happiness
or satisfaction over unhappiness or pain produced by the acts falling
under it. Thus, if there were a rule or maxim which dictated that
gays should be out of the closet, and such a rule were shown to
produce greater utility than any alternative rule, such a rule would
be validated. The normative value of being in or out of the closet
becomes then merely a matter of moral arithmetic.[9]

Being out of the closet is often defined as an ongoing process of
coming out; such a definition is often used in National Gay Task
Force literature, for example.[10] There is assuredly a great deal of
slide between the two since the principled decision to be out requires a continuous stream of individual decisions concerning how
to come out in particular situations. But that fact in itself suggests

an important difference between the two. *Coming out* is a principled decision whereby one affirms his or her own identity, whereas *being out* refers to the aggregate of behavior which one pursues as a result of that decision. Once one makes the decision for self-disclosure, presumably on the basis of one or more general moral principles, the question of how to be out must be raised at a variety of levels of social intercourse. The upshot of our discussions of utilitarian, duty-based, and virtue-based principles, however, will be that these different principles for coming out dictate radically different answers to the context-relative questions which must be handled in everyday life.

Eichberg also recognizes that being out of the closet is not a once-and-for-all exodus from the closet and suggests that it is a cumulative progress which "may ultimately lead to a public phase where one is open and free to be exactly who she or he is" (40). Furthermore, according to such a rule, being "who one is" is a necessary component of happiness:

> *The only way to be happy is to be happy.* The only way to feel good about who you are is to feel good about who you are. You are who and what you are. (66)

Though these tautologies are often little more than catchy slogans, they help make clear Eichberg's underlying concept of gay self-identity. Being out is equated with being "who you are," and it is a necessary foundation for happiness. The moral *telos*, then, for Eichberg includes achieving the greatest possible level of happiness for the individual which means the greatest level of "being who you are" (self-identity).

There is obviously, as the National Gay Task Force pamphlet suggests, a continuum between coming out and being out, and Eichberg sometimes (but not always) uses them interchangeably. Where they are distinct, the former is a means to the latter. We can simplify things somewhat by viewing coming out as the adoption of a principle or maxim of openness regarding one's (sexual) identity and being out as the continuum of behavior which follows from the thoroughgoing adoption of such a principle. This is a minimalist interpretation. Being out may not require doing anything, but it at least involves passive non-concealment. Any criticism which we would offer using the minimalist interpretation would extend to any stronger norm which sees being out as requiring active disclosure.

Eichberg's approach to being out is, however, anecdotal rather than analytic, and he never clearly explicates what it is that he means. If we assume that "being who one is" entails being out (i.e., living the process of coming out), then we may wonder if this process has an end beyond the process itself or whether one is required constantly to keep coming out. Happiness in any but the most fragmentary or momentary form may not be achievable if we believe that it involves reaching a certain level of being out, but only in a never-ending process of coming out. This is probably what Eichberg means when he relates his own experiences of coming out to any and all whom fortune tosses onto his path:

> To draw from my own experience, I am very public about my sexuality. Not only do I share freely this information with others, but . . . each time I sit next to someone on an airplane, or talk to someone at a gym who does not know who I am, I come out privately with that person through sharing who I am and what I do professionally. Furthermore, each time I share myself with someone new I have a personal experience . . . *regardless of whether the issue you are coming out about is your sexuality or some other secret you have been carrying around with you, the process is basically the same.* It is a process of becoming comfortable with yourself and sharing yourself freely with others. (40-42)

The basic moral arithmetic involved in this principle is not too difficult to calculate. Happiness is being who one is, which in turn entails being (or coming) out of the closet, and the more out one is (or the greater number of people to whom one comes out?), the more one is oneself and thus the greater one's own likely happiness.

Such a moral stance might appear individualistic at first sight since it presupposes (probably wrongly) that acts of coming out are always felicific. For the utilitarian, however, if an action brings about one unit of happiness for the agent but even just two units of unhappiness for a bystander, then its utility value is negative. What needs to be examined, then, is the possible effects being out has on others to whom we are out, be they family, co-workers, friends, or even complete strangers, such as Eichberg's fellow airline passengers.

The utilitarian framework of the means by which coming out is said to contribute to one's "identity" and greater social value is not difficult to discern. Many (including Eichberg) suggest that those (presumably non-gay) people who have knowingly encountered gay people are more likely to be supportive of gays and "gay rights." In the pamphlet, mentioned above, designed for people considering coming out of the closet, the National Gay Task Force claims:

> Each time even one gay person *comes out* to such non-gay persons, their world view is challenged, their fears about homosexuality are confronted, and their level of understanding is raised. The awareness that a person one loves or respects *is gay* often has a profound impact on a non-gay individual's willingness to reexamine *his* or *her* ideas, attitudes, and feelings about *our* lives and *our* rights!

Being out is seen by Eichberg as an educational gift for the entire community, helping all people, gay or not, to understand better what it means to be gay, to replace stereotypes, to allow greater diversity and self expression, and to ensure gay people a less hostile world (17). Altman argues that such a coming out represents not just the rejection of sexual repression in the individual but that it has a causal role to play in the liberation of society itself from sex-negative modes of consciousness.[11]

Under such a communitarian conception, coming out not only contributes to individual self-identity but also has long-term, beneficent consequences for society as a whole. In this light it becomes not just a *right* for gays (insofar as no moral imperative commands concealment) but a *duty* to the community at large. The transition from right to duty marks the difference between what one *may do* based on individual perceived need and what one *must do* based on moral principle.

Such a transition is marked by Eichberg's claim that gayness is, by its nature, a political issue. "Most people consider their sexuality to be very personal, but being gay is a political issue whether we like it or not!" (59). Altman holds similar views: "L'oppression des homosexuels fait partie de la répression générale de la sexualité, et notre libération devra faire partie d'une révolution totale dans les attitudes sociales."[12] Furthermore, Eichberg notes:

> If we come out, openly and lovingly as who we are, we disabuse people of their stereotypic beliefs and lay the foundation for a broader view of what it means to be gay–and ultimately for a change in individual and social attitudes, understanding, and acceptance. If homosexuals were out openly and publicly, major gains would be made in legal, health, and social issues. . . . It is time to take responsibility for this situation. While there have always been many good reasons for coming out, I believe there are even more reasons now. (60)

This stance implies that even if there were negative utility for a particular person to be out of the closet, then the social calculations would still entail that person's being out: despite suffering the possibly unhappy consequences of being publicly known as homosexual, the total benefits to the community would nevertheless override. On this point, Eichberg agrees: "Bear in mind, I believe it is preferable to let people know you are gay, even if this creates a battle, than to remain in a state of denial." He also urges that even those who *already* feel good about themselves should come further out of the closet, even if it makes them uncomfortable or involves loss of their privacy (61).

Classical rule-utilitarianism, however, is more vulnerable to the facts and to the social context than Eichberg's anecdotal approach would suggest. One may ponder the question of the universality of Eichberg's principle. Is it addressed to Americans? An Iranian who came out might find that the negative utility of execution overrode any putative social utility of a brief public pronouncement of gayness; and, from chronicles closer to home, we wonder whether the situation for young people in some U.S. secondary schools or high schools would differ in more than degree. Certainly, the recent murder of U.S.S. *Belleau Wood* sailor Allen Schindler in Japan might argue against the utility of coming out. Eichberg's book, of course, arises from "The Experience" workshops he directs, so we may assume that his principle is directed at this market as its primary target: middle-class and reasonably educated adults who are protected and less vulnerable than, for instance, blue-collar workers or the young. Even with this limiting assumption, however, the rhetoric of individual and social empowerment is validated only with anecdotal data. Like the analogous problem of regression in psychotherapy, the authors writing in this tradition offer no follow-up data to examine, and the issue of sample bias cries for resolution. In the real world, the individual and social calculations may be bewilderingly more complex than authors like Eichberg suggest.

If the above points appear like sniping, there yet remains an underlying theoretical problem which is not addressed, and that is the problem of Eichberg's assumption that gay self-identity *requires* "being out." Note that this is a question of being out rather than of coming out. Eichberg clearly assumes that gays can only achieve "empowerment" for themselves (*qua* human beings) by being out, and that a community without individuals so empowered is debilitating for all of its members, gay and non-gay alike. We believe that this global assumption is unwarranted, though it may hold more or less true in some communities, notably those which are most sex-negative. In communities where sexual preference is not regarded as an issue fraught with cosmic consequences, the notions of "out" and "in" may lack social meaning entirely.

CLOSETS AND INTEGRITY

The Kantian perspective differs from the utilitarian in assessing the internal state of the agent as primary rather than the social consequences which flow from his or her actions. Despite the dissimilarity of the deontological model from the utilitarian one, we find that thinkers who argue from a Kantian perspective often arrive at a position similar to the utilitarian via a different reasoning process. From such a perspective, the morality of a rule depends upon its being autonomously willed for all people (the first formulation of Kant's "categorical imperative"). The duty ethicist will argue either that all people should be out of the closet or that all people should be in the closet. It is the integrity and universality of the "willing" (what Kant called a "maxim of conduct") which forms the criterion of right action here and not the consequences of the maxim *in foro externo*. Kantian ethics is thus an ethics of interiority or motivation.

The core of this issue is what "being out of the closet" means, and for Mohr that meaning can be reduced to "living in the truth" (37-39). Not to live truthfully is the greatest immorality and the standard by which moral living can be judged. Therefore, to understand the normative value of this "living in the truth," we need to know more about what it means to be in the closet. This semantic issue relates directly to the outing controversy as well. If it were true that, as Mohr says, "Outing is both morally permissible and an expected consequence of living morally" (12), we would need to examine whether being out of the closet ("living in the truth") is itself a moral demand made upon all agents (whether gay or non-gay) as a consequence of living morally. If–and indeed *only* if–being out of the closet were a moral imperative for all, then it would be an imperative for gays as well.

One way to consider someone's being in the closet is to imagine that person's "passing" as non-gay, that is, a closeted person who is not already perceived to be gay by other people. That other people do not note the closeted person's sexual orientation may not, however, be a function of the person's intentions. Mohr, however, defines passing as a form of lying (32-33). Note, however, that in this definition, to pass requires that the passer *actively* engage in deception since the passer would be the one "holding oneself out." "Holding oneself out," though, could also refer in a more general sense to one who *either* purposely lies or misrepresents him or herself *or* to one who says or does nothing to combat others' possible misconceptions about him or her. Either way, life in the closet, according to Mohr, is morally debasing, not only because it is "life as lie," but because, worse still, it also involves debasement of the personhood of the closet-case (and by extension, all people). It is this indignity added to the dishonesty of the passer which makes being in the closet especially loathsome.

The "devolution of the person as person" comes about because the closet is somehow forced on the passer. According to Mohr, it is not something that would otherwise be chosen (we are not told why) but is something coerced (26). The conditions which force the person into the closet may be economic–fear of employment penalties–or even attitudinal–since to allow others to acknowledge one's homosexual orientation is to allow them to view one as "scum" (26). The closet-case, then, not only intentionally deceives society by actively and passively presenting him or herself as non-gay, but the passer does so to achieve or to maintain certain material/economic ends and/or because the passer may believe that to be perceived as homosexual is bad, evil, and disgusting. Furthermore, the more people that remain in the closet, the more these debilitating ideas about gay people can be re-enforced, or at least not challenged. After all, according to Mohr's line of argument, since so many people actively work to conceal this aspect of their personalities, being gay must be thought to be bad (37). The cycle of a self-fulfilling prophecy is begun. Because being in the closet undermines by its deceitfulness the basis of honest and meaningful relationships among members of society, forces people to denigrate themselves, and helps to maintain erroneous and hurtful beliefs about gays, being in the closet is seen as an evil to be abhorred and avoided.

If it were true that the world of the closet is the worst of all possible worlds, then it would follow that each person universally would be morally better off leading a life free of any similar deceit, though "morally better off" here may not entail being materially better off ("happier"). Perhaps we are reading more into the phrase, "living in the truth," than should be read, but it seems offered as a general dictum of which non-concealment of sexual identity is derived as a special case. Mohr seems to be presupposing Kant's dictum that morality generates agents who are *worthy of happiness*, albeit not perhaps happy in fact. The categorical imperative is that each person should disavow the closet, not only for him or herself but for everyone as well. To "live in the truth" would then require not only no active deception but would demand that the gay person (or the wealthy person, or the intellectual, or the Roman Catholic) attempt to dispel any possible erroneous beliefs held by others about his or her sexual orientation (and income and intelligence and religion), insofar as not doing so would be tantamount to passing, which is not morally permissible. If integrity demands that sexual orientation should not be hidden but proclaimed, then consistency requires that all other group memberships also be brought to the surface.[13] Furthermore, not to identify oneself openly as a member of any category or group to which one belongs could be seen as self-denigrating, and thus it too would be an evil. Mohr is not clear on why it is that sexual orientation should itself alone require the kind of disclosure he advocates. Perhaps it is the fact that the group is socially denigrated which generates the imperative. For our purposes, the difference is moot, since we do not accept the claim that self-disclosure at any level (sexual identity or other) is a necessary component of human dignity.

Utilitarian thinkers such as Eichberg or Altman must presuppose certain factual consequences as following from hypothetical de-closeting, but can leave the exact nature of the closet modestly ambiguous. Deontological thinkers like Mohr, on the other hand, must impart a certain amount of conceptual baggage to the closet to begin with. If the closet is defined *behaviorally* in terms of people's unwillingness to make public their sexual orientations, then it becomes a *factual* question whether such behavior is denigrating and represents a loss of integrity (and we think that this question can frequently be answered in the negative). Mohr and others, however, seem to assume that the question is a *definitional* one, which means that they take *being closeted* and *lacking integrity* as coextensive. If that assumption is accepted, then it follows that no person could possess integrity without disclosing his or her sexual orientation. This seems an overbroad conclusion. Surely, a person could possess integrity but be simply indifferent to or without communication with others in his or her own community. Such a state would offer no reason, nor perhaps opportunity, for self-disclosure.

In short, on Mohr's account, the determination as to whether a person is closeted or not is *ipso facto* a moral decision. This is a feature of Kantian ethics in general and has nothing to do with closetedness per se. It is the *motives* for non-disclosure which determine the nature of the maxim—not the consequences of the maxim in the behavioral arena. This strikes us as a species of question-begging. Like Kant's examples of suicide, false promising, and the like, it has the advantage of simplicity (the moral rules are tidy, neat, and universal) but one cannot fail to suspect that the simplicity is in the mind of the moralist rather than in the real world of human relations.

We suggest that individual sexual identity is neither a public nor a political issue by its very nature, though it may become so under certain social contingencies. For this reason, we argue that it cannot be covered under any universal rule or norm. Communities are too diverse, and individual situations within them too complex to support any such principle. If the United States were a special case, then that case should be made; and if that special case were morally dilemmatic, then the alternatives under each horn of the dilemma would need to be spelled out. Mohr himself concedes that non-disclosure is often (but, for him, wrongly) supported by considerations of privacy, but he then goes on to treat privacy as essentially a matter of social or legal rights or obligations. More promising in our view is the conception of privacy in terms of a cluster of goals based upon complex social interaction, a view suggested by Thomson[14] and developed in an engineering context by Rachels.[15] Except in its narrowest legal sense, the concept of privacy is part and parcel of the larger cluster of concepts surrounding personal identity, and it is to those concepts that we now turn.

INDIVIDUALS, VIRTUE, AND SOCIAL RELATIONS

Under the view of the identity which we propose, there exists a close connection between our ability to control the levels of access which others have to us via information about us and our ability to create and maintain *different* kinds of social relationships with others. This underlines the jarring aspect of Eichberg's treating "coming out" as involving the same moral perspectives whether it be with a casual co-traveler or a parent. Surely the social relationships involved are vastly different. Our point here is *not* that different patterns of disclosure of behavior are appropriate to different relationships but rather that the different patterns of behavior *constitute*, at least in part, the defining criteria for the relationships themselves. This is a *descriptive* claim regarding human sociality, and we will examine some descriptive consequences shortly; but among some authors the descriptive claim is offered in such a way as to bring prescriptive features in through the back door.

One example we have already seen of packing prescriptive and descriptive components into a single concept is Mohr's definition of the closet in terms of moral debasement. The notion of coming out (*la sortie des placards*) almost always evokes humor or amazement among, for example, French gays with whom we have had the opportunity to discuss it at some length. For those with whom we have talked, coming out to the postman or the casual acquaintance in the locker room seems to suggest boorishness rather than some universal maxim proclaimed as the highest moral goal for all people. André Baudry's survey suggests a similar reaction.[16] Eichberg's assumption that such a *sortie* always has a positive utility value seems no less outrageous in this context than Mohr's assumption that failure to do so results from "living a lie." Their points may be culture-specific, and certainly French society is more pluralistic than American in terms of sexual lifestyles; but we wonder to what degree the normative claims in Mohr's definition even apply "across the board" to the U.S. situation.

Perhaps Mohr might go along with some of the above, by granting (as Eichberg clearly would not) that disclosure to casual passers-by is not a moral consequence of integrity but that active efforts to conceal one's sexual orientation would violate principles of integrity. But we can and should be able to conceal our sexual orientation from someone for the same reason we conceal our bank accounts, our lovers' tastes in food, or a myriad of other information: not because the *content* of the information is a source of shame (to us), but rather because our interlocutor does not enjoy a level of access which makes such information appropriate.

An exactly similar point is sometimes made within engineering ethics and in relationship to data base acquisition and distribution of information, especially transactional data.[17] What bothers many about computer data bases of this kind is not (or at least not necessarily) *what information* they contain; since very often the computer has no more information than was previously available from a myriad of other sources in any case. What bothers, rather, is the aggregate *quantity* of such information, combined with the fact that we lack control over the criteria of *relevance* for its distribution to others. The discomfort arises not in the perception that there is much information which others have about us (this was no less true before the dawn of computing), but rather in the perception that we do not *control* it.

We can now move from the *descriptive* to the *prescriptive* component of this thesis about the differentiality of relations. Human relations within a community, and indeed, the entire community, are a means by which the individual is able to grow and develop. Reducing the large number of such relations to a lowest common denominator, or attempting to treat all such relations as guided by the same set of norms, is morally self-stultifying. It is the community composed of its numerous relations which exists to support the individual, and not the other way around.

In a phenomenological way of making the same point, one might say that what Lee Rice or Steven Barbone *is*, is the sum total of information *about* him. While *he* may have access to that source of his own social identity, the possibility of *his* maintaining or sustaining a complex and multi-tiered set of social relations (whether to postman, to lover, or to parents) depends at least in part upon *his* determining to *whom* he is so related and *why*. It is not the possibility for the brute existence of such relations which depends upon their being under the individual's control, but rather it is the individual's ability to see those relations as a manner in which he or she *defines* himself or herself which is at issue. This is sometimes characterized as a principle of "autonomy."[18] It does not entail that the right to *make* the decisions always results in making the *right* decisions, but it does suggest that their rightness or wrongness must be made within the matrix of the individual person, and not in the interest of overall social utility (*pace* Eichberg) or universal principles of morality (*pace* Mohr).

This prescriptive principle returns us squarely to the claim made earlier: questions about being out, coming out, and outing do require some position on the relationship of individual to community and the moral status of the individual. The utilitarian and Kantian perspectives are communitarian in nature, and their failures can often be traced back to just this feature–the focus on either the effects of the individual's action upon the community (utility) or the individual's motives with respect to that community (deontology). The methodological individualism adumbrated by Spinoza is, we believe, free of some of the debilitating effects of such a communitarian ethic.

To present simply what we believe is the most useful model for living morally requires some insight into Spinoza's notion of virtue. It is that feature which enables us to maintain and to perfect our own respective individual natures or identities: "Virtue is the human power . . . which is defined only by the conational activity by which people strive to maintain their own beings (identities)."[19] The notion of virtue is linked to that of conational activity (*conatus*) which is always focused upon the individual "conator":

> By virtue and power I mean the same; that is, virtue, as related to the human being, is his or her very essence or nature, insofar as he or she has the power to bring about what can be understood through the laws of his or her *individual* nature.[20]

In an effort to better achieve this end, we enter into communities but only because being in community is better for us *as individuals*. "Just as each person seeks what is most useful to him or herself (*sibi utile quaerit*), to that extent are people most useful to one another (*sibi invicem utiles*)."[21] For the sake of the present argument, we here enumerate only the *consequences* of Spinoza's lengthy argument.

According to such a view, in a very concrete and direct way, any individual judges that he or she has a better chance of securing happiness (maintaining and developing his or her individual identity) by relating to a community of others which have something in common with him or her than he or she would have being completely alone. The virtuous person knows that the community exists for the individual–not the individual for the community. Mohr himself writes, "We ought to stick to the vision of the *Declaration of Independence* and believe that communities exist to guarantee rights of individuals and we should be very wary when the concept of community is used to generate obligations" (21). The virtuous life, then, is one wherein each person seeks his or her own ends and goals in the way that seems to him or her the most likely to secure them.

Some will object to an idea of virtue and ethics which on face value seems utterly self-serving and egoistic. But Spinoza is only a psychological egoist, and the thesis of self-interest relates to his view of human *natures* and does not logically preclude the possibility of ethical altruism. We use *natures* in the plural here because

Spinoza is a nominalist, and one great insight which he offers is that the Platonic myth of an all-embracing human *nature* lies at the heart of the communitarian ethic. We need not here argue that the individual *and* the community are both best served when each person pursues his or her own best interests.[22] We do, however, insist that virtue and common sense demand that any type of disclosure should be considered by an individual for each particular circumstance and relationship instead of falling under some universal moral imperative, no matter whether that imperative be sanctioned internally or by some abstract concept of the "good of the community."

To bring the discussion back to the question of being out of the closet, one must ask, at each opportunity, "What's in it for me?" Self-disclosure is and should be self-serving, and so it makes sense to examine each opportunity in order to determine if it truly does promote one's own identity interests. We may decide that disclosure of gayness to our parents best helps us by bringing to our relationships added information which will better aid us in defining ourselves to them. We may decide that sharing our orientation with fellow passengers, or the postman, or the boy bagging our groceries does not in any way enhance our relationships or bring about any benefits to us in any way (perhaps not with the grocery boy). It is at the point at which one decides to whom and when and how to disclose different things about one's self that one is really the most empowered and, consequently, virtuous.

Against the utilitarian claim, we say it is not best for the community that everyone should come out to everyone else and urge that this may be irresponsible not only for each person individually, but also to the community at large. As members of the "gay community," for example, we are not always well served by those who might seek to identify themselves with us merely by the accident of our mutually shared sexual orientation. Few would argue that society at large or the gay "community" itself was at all enhanced by mass murderer Jeffrey Dahmer's being publicly known as gay. The utilitarian may argue that there is strength in numbers, but this is true only to the extent that each person strives for a single end. The argument is senseless, however, if each person is striving to attain his or her own individual goals by building and maintaining *as he or she best sees fit* a variety of particularized relationships to other individuals in the community.

Against those who urge self-disclosure as a universal norm, we reply that what should be the universal norm is rather a hypothetical conditional: if it is in one's best interest to come out within particular relationships to others, then one ought to do so. To disregard this condition is to put oneself in the condemnable position of morally coercing others to be in a situation which they might not otherwise choose and for which there are no sound reasons for choosing. Paradoxically, this position is exactly what Mohr abhors and finds so denigrating about being in the closet in the first place since he incorrectly believes that the closet is *always* forced. The virtuous person is not forced to be in or out of the closet: he or she allows differential access to self in ways which serve his or her own interests. It could be in one's interest to nail the closet door closed, as it may have been in Nazi Germany and is in some contemporary communities still. If being out of the closet brings about pain or destruction with no consequent return on one's investment, then far from being liberating, it is both immoral and stupid.

It then follows that the questions of coming out and outing are secondary to larger questions of differential self-disclosure as a means of providing a varied network of social relations. Virtue demands that we each strive to flourish, and since we best do that in community, we create and maintain relationships that best serve our own respective needs. If a particular relationship would serve one better if one's sexual orientation were known, then one would act virtuously by being out in that context; if another relationship better suits one without any self-disclosure, then one acts more virtuously by not being out. If it affects one not a whit whether another person is closeted, then the question of outing does not even arise or make sense. If one perceives a gain from another's being outed, then in pursuing self-interest, one acts morally by outing that person. Actually, a case could be made for *not* outing the closeted politician who enacts anti-gay legislation if the threat of outing rather than actual outing better serves one's interests. If one's objective is to prevent or to reduce such enactments, then surely the *threat* of exposure would provide a more potent means of control or manipulation than would most conceivable after-effects of an actual exposure.[23]

By bringing the issue of disclosure to the level of the individual rather than that of the community, we believe that we offer a more humane and rational stance. Without dismissing the importance of "gay pride," we suggest that individual pride is foremost and that our communities are best served and, more importantly, best serve the individuals within them by fostering and supporting the conscious and self-directed growth of individuals.

NOTES

1. See Dennis Altman, *Homosexual: Oppression and Liberation* (New York: Avon, 1971); Dennis Altman, *The Homosexualization of America* (Boston: Beacon Press, 1982); Rob Eichberg, *Coming Out: An Act of Love* (Baltimore: Penguin, 1991); Martin Hoffman, *The Gay World* (New York: Basic Books, 1968); and Richard Mohr, *Gays/Justice: A Study of Ethics, Society, and Law* (New York: Columbia University Press, 1988). Where further references to the Eichberg volume are contextually clear, they will be given in the text.

2. Among its supporters are counted Richard Mohr, *Gay Ideas: Outing and Other Controversies* (Boston: Beacon Press, 1992), and among its detractors are Yvonne Zipter, "To Be or Not to Be Out: Gay and Lesbian Cops Debate," *In Step Magazine*, Nov. 6, 1991, pp. 64-65; Tom Vanden Brook, "Critics Decry Outing, But Some Gays Say: Get Used to It," *Milwaukee Journal*, Oct. 27, 1991, sect. J, pp. 1-6; and Gene Bland, "Quiet, Please: Marching Isn't the Answer–Being Is," *New York Native*, May 12, 1986, p. 29. Where further references to Mohr's *Gay Ideas* book are contextually clear, they will be given in the text.

3. W. A. Parent, "Privacy, Morality, and the Law," in D. G. Johnson and J. W. Snapper, eds., *Ethical Issues in the Use of Computers* (Belmont, CA: Wadsworth, 1985), pp. 201-215.

4. As argued by Mohr in *Gays/Justice* and Eichberg.

5. Thomas S. Weinberg, "On 'Doing and Being' Gay: Sexual Behavior and Male Self-Identity," *Journal of Homosexuality* 4 (1978): 123-142; Martin P. Levine, "Gay Ghetto," *Journal of Homosexuality* 4 (1979): 363-378.

6. Lee C. Rice, "Homosexualization and Collectivism," *Philosophy & Theology* 2 [disk supplement #1] (1988): 45-60; Steven Barbone, "Virtue and Sociality in Spinoza," *Iyyun [Jerusalem Philosophical Quarterly]* 42 (1993): 383-395.

7. Timothy F. Murphy, "Is AIDS a Just Punishment?" *Journal of Medical Ethics* 14 (1988): 154-160.

8. For a discussion of the sociological dispute concerning methodological individualism as it applies to Spinoza, see Lee C. Rice, "Individual and Community in Spinoza's Social Psychology," in Edwin Curley and Pierre-François Moreau, eds., *Spinoza: New Perspectives* (Leiden: E. J. Brill, 1990), pp. 271-285. One application of methodological individualism to the notion of gay identity is given by Rice in "Homosexualization and Collectivism." The correlative notion of "virtue" (*virtus*) is examined by Barbone in "Virtue and Sociality."

9. The matrix of calculations is not always a simple affair, however, since the problems of long-term and short-term consequences and the qualitative ranking of beneficent actions are indigenous to any utilitarian approach. For the purposes of this study, we ignore these deeper meta-theoretical problems.

10. National Gay Task Force, *Coming Out* [pamphlet] (New York: National Gay Task Force, 1987).

11. Dennis Altman, *Homosexuel(le): oppression et libération*, Claude Elsen, trans. (Paris: Fayard, 1976), pp. 88-94, 111-117. It is interesting to note that the translation of Altman into French involves not only a change of language but also of concepts. Many ideas which were not expressed in the English original come to the surface when the book is translated for an audience which experiences the world differently than we anglophones. On the particular point cited, see the translator's accompanying notes on "sex-negativity," a largely American or anglophone phenomenon.

12. Altman, 1976, p. 75.

13. For an interesting twist on this notion, see Greg Erlandson, "A Modest Proposal: 'Outing' Pro-Lifers," *Our Sunday Visitor* 85 (42) (1993): 23.

14. Judith Jarvis Thomson, "The Right to Privacy," *Philosophy & Public Affairs* 4 (1975): 295-314.

15. James Rachels, "Why Privacy Is Important," in D. G. Johnson and J. W. Snapper, eds., *Ethical Issues in the Use of Computers* (Belmont, CA: Wadsworth, 1985), pp. 194-201. See also Mike W. Martin and Roland Schinzinger, eds., *Ethics in Engineering* (New York: McGraw-Hill, 1989), pp. 233-235.

16. André Baudry, ed., *Les Français et l'homosexualité: Sondage réalisé par l'I.F.O.P.–Arcadie* 26 (no. 304) (1979).

17. David Burnham, *The Rise of the Computer State* (New York: Random House, 1983).

18. Vivienne C. Cass, "Homosexual Identity Formation: A Theoretical Model," *Journal of Homosexuality* 4 (1978): 219-235; 224. See also Martin Dannecker, *Theories of Homosexuality* (London: Gay Men's Press, 1981).

19. "Virtus est ipsa human potentia . . . quae solo conatu, quo homo in suo esse perseverare conatur, definitur." Spinoza, *Ethica*, Part IV, proposition 20, demonstration. Translations from the text of Spinoza are our own. The edition used is that of J. Van Vloten and J. P. Land, *Benedicti de Spinoza opera quotquot reperta sunt*, 3rd ed., 4 vols. (The Hague: M. Nijhoff, 1914). *Conatus* in Spinoza always refers to an individual's "drive-like" endeavoring or striving to flourish and to exist as that individual.

20. "Per virtutem et potentiam idem intelligo; hoc est, virtus, quatenus ad hominem refertus, est *ipsa hominis essentia seu natura*, quatenus potestatem habet quaedam efficiendi, quae per solas ipsius naturae leges possunt intelligi." (Emphasis added.) Spinoza, Part IV, definition 8.

21. Spinoza, Part IV, proposition 35, corollary 2.

22. On this point see Barbone, "Virtue and Sociality."

23. Pierre Fontanie, "Suicide et homosexualité," *Arcadie* 27 (1980): 108-113, 176-184.

PART III.
CIVIL RIGHTS AND SOCIAL JUSTICE

Gay Marriage:
A Civil Right

Craig R. Dean, JD

Washington, DC

SUMMARY. This article describes the author's efforts to secure marriage rights for same-sex couples in the District of Columbia. The importance of such rights are described in terms of their benefits to partners in areas such as inheritance, taxation, and benefit to society. It is argued that refusal to recognize same-sex marriages is not justified by statute and that discrimination on the basis of sex

Craig R. Dean is an attorney practicing in Washington, DC. He graduated from Georgetown University Law Center in 1989. Mr. Dean is the founder and Executive Director of the Equal Marriage Rights Fund. He and his lover of seven years, Patrick Gill, are suing the District of Columbia for the right to marry. Correspondence with the author and inquiries regarding the non-profit corporation which is funding Dean and Gill's legal battle may be addressed to: Equal Marriage Rights Fund, P.O. Box 18707, Washington, DC 20036.

[Haworth co-indexing entry note]: "Gay Marriage: A Civil Right." Dean, Craig R. Co-published simultaneously in the *Journal of Homosexuality* (The Haworth Press, Inc.) Vol. 27, No. 3/4, 1994, pp. 111-115; and: *Gay Ethics: Controversies in Outing, Civil Rights, and Sexual Science* (ed: Timothy F. Murphy) The Haworth Press, Inc., 1994, pp. 111-115. Multiple copies of this article/chapter may be purchased from The Haworth Document Delivery Center [1-800-3-HAWORTH; 9:00 a.m. - 5:00 p.m. (EST)].

111

violates the District's Human Rights Act. Certain prior court cases, moreover, affirm the moral logic for extending marriage rights to same-sex couples.

As one Washington, D. C., observer put it, "people dropped their teeth" when in November 1990 my lover, Patrick Gill, and I applied for a marriage license and then filed a lawsuit when the District of Columbia denied that application because we are Gay.[1] By refusing to give us the same legal recognition that is given to heterosexual couples, the District government has devalued and degraded our relationship as well as that of every other Gay and Lesbian couple.

At one time, interracial couples were not allowed to marry in the United States. Gays and Lesbians are still denied this most basic civil right not only here but around the world. Can you imagine the outcry if *any other* minority group were denied the right to marry legally today?

Marriage is more than a piece of paper. Marriage is an important civil right because it gives societal recognition and legal protection to a relationship and confers numerous benefits to spouses. In the District of Columbia alone, there are over one hundred automatic marriage-based rights.

In every state in the nation, married couples have the right to be on each others' health, disability, life insurance, and pension plans. Married couples receive special tax preferences for exemptions, deductions, and refunds. Married couples may jointly own real and personal property, an arrangement which protects their marital estate from each other's creditors. Spouses may automatically inherit property and have rights of survivorship that avoid inheritance tax. Though unmarried couples, both Gay and straight, with the help of lawyers may duplicate some of these rights, these rights are by no means guaranteed. For married couples, the spouse is legally the next of kin in case of death, medical emergency, or mental incapacity. In stark contrast, for same-sex couples, the family is considered next of kin, not the partner. In light of the AIDS crisis, the denial of marriage rights can be even more ominous.

Therefore, the denial of legal marriage to Gays and Lesbians is an incredible act of multiple discrimination. Patrick and I felt that we had no honorable alternative but to stand up and fight for our love right. We are now in a protracted and costly court battle with the District of Columbia and are alleging a two-fold discrimination.

First, in refusing the marriage application, the District violated its gender-neutral marriage law. Nowhere does its legal code state that a marriage must consist of a man and a woman or that a married couple may not be of the same sex. Secondly, the District violated its Human Rights Act. For Gays and Lesbians, this 1977 law is the strongest Human Rights Act in the nation because it explicitly prohibits discrimination based on sexual orientation. According to the Act, "every individual shall have an equal opportunity to participate in the economic, cultural and intellectual life of the District and have an *equal opportunity to participate in all aspects of life.*"[2]

The law is clearly on the side of gay and lesbian marriage. In fact, in 1987, the D. C. Court of Appeals, interpreting the D. C. Human Rights Act, held that "the eradication of sexual orientation discrimination is a compelling governmental interest."[3] Moreover, in the very same case, the Court elevated anti-Gay discrimination to the same level as racial and gender discrimination, holding that these three types of bigotry are equally morally repugnant to society.[4] The District of Columbia is, therefore, the only place in the United States where Gays and Lesbians receive some type of equal protection status.

As of this writing, our lawsuit is currently on appeal.[5] The litigation in the lower court ended in a dismissal in two decisions. The first decision, in January 1992, was on D. C. law. The court, unable to rely on statutes, cited three full pages of biblical scripture as to what society means by marriage and why homosexuals cannot fit this model. The second decision, which was on the constitutional issues, came in June 1992. The judge simply upheld his earlier dismissal, stating that homosexuals do not deserve the same constitutional protections as other minority groups.

Needless to say, we are glad to be out of the lower court and in the D. C. Court of Appeals. We are extremely hopeful of a victory there because unlike the lower court, the Court of Appeals has created perhaps the most forceful Gay rights language in any case in any jurisdiction in the United States.[6] We expect to have our first hearing in the Court of Appeals by the fall of 1993 and a decision sometime in 1994.

Even politicians have agreed about the rectitude of gay and lesbian marriage, at least when such agreement is convenient. D. C. Mayor Sharon Pratt Dixon stated that she favored legalizing same-sex marriage and that "the world is a changing place and we should accept it."[7] That was during her campaign. It is unfortunate that since her election the Mayor has been reluctant to make similar statements of support for equal marriage rights. It is even more unfortunate that, rather than attempt to apply the law fairly, Mayor Dixon is instead wasting taxpayer money to fight us in court.

Some argue that Gay marriage is too radical for society. We disagree. Actually, Gay marriage is pro-family. According to a 1988 study by the American Bar Association, eight to ten million children are currently being raised in three million Gay and Lesbian households.[8] Approximately, therefore, six percent of the U. S. population is made up of gay and lesbian families with children. Why should these families be denied the advantage and protections granted to other families. Does anyone seriously think that society is served by policies which disadvantage this many citizens?

Furthermore, Gay marriage is socially conservative because it would strengthen society. Few would deny that marriage is an important thread that weaves the fabric of society together. It has been estimated that approximately ten percent of a given population is Gay or Lesbian; if so, denial of marriage rights for Gay men and Lesbians weakens the fabric of society. Put another way, if one removed ten percent of the threads in one's suit coat, how strong would that suit coat be? Similarly, when the stability of relationships in an entire minority group is undermined, all of society gets hurt—witness the AIDS crises.

On the other hand, allowing gay marriage would help bring society together by increasing tolerance and assimilation. It is paradoxical that mainstream America stereotypes Gays and Lesbians as unable to maintain long-term relationships, while at the same time denying them the very institutions to stabilize such relationships.

Twenty-five years ago, one third of the United States did not allow interracial marriage. It took a Supreme Court decision in

1967, *Loving v. Virginia*, a case similar to ours, to strike down these discriminatory prohibitions and to redefine family and marriage.[9] Then, as now, those who argued against granting civil rights spoke of morality, social tensions, and protection of traditional family values. But now, as then, the real issue is justice versus oppression.

NOTES

1. Henry Mitchell, "Gays and the State of Matrimony," *The Washington Post*, Jan. 11, 1991, p. D2.

2. District of Columbia Code, Section 1-2511.

3. *Gay Rights Coalition v. Georgetown*, 536 A.2d (D.C. 1987).

4. *Id.*

5. *Dean and Gill v. The District of Columbia*, Superior Court of the District of Columbia, Civil Action No. 90-CA-13892, District of Columbia Court of Appeals, No. 92-CV-737. This article was sent to press in May 1993.

6. *Gay Rights Coalition v. Georgetown*, 536 A.2d at 35.

7. *Washington Times*, Sept. 14, 1990, p. A6.

8. *Developments in the Law: Sexual Orientation and the Law*, 102 Harvard Law Review 1508, 1629 (1989).

9. *Loving v. Virginia*, 388 U.S. 1 (1967).

The Military Ban and the ROTC:
A Study in Closeting

Claudia Card, PhD

University of Wisconsin, Madison

SUMMARY. This article examines reasons for university involvement in protesting ROTC policies discriminatory toward lesbians and gay men. The formal exclusion of lesbians and gay men from the military permits not only the abuses in selective enforcement of the policy and considerable economic costs to maintain it, but also contributes to the perpetuation of the closet. Closeting is not a phenomenon chosen by lesbians and gay men for reasons of their own, and it rewards deceit, penalizes honesty, blames lesbians and gays for the mistrust of others, and effects a psychological division ("doubling") of individual identity and corrupts individual responsibility. For these reasons, university educators, as committed to the advance of truth, have an obligation to protest ROTC compliance with discriminatory policies.

In May 1992 U.S. Representative Patricia Schroeder of Colorado introduced a bill into the House of Representatives that would lift the military ban on lesbians and gay men. Much has occurred since

Claudia Card is Professor in the Department of Philosophy, 600 N. Park St., University of Wisconsin, Madison, WI 53706. She is the author of "Lesbianism and Choice" (*Journal of Homosexuality* 23 [3] [1992]: 39-51) and many articles in feminist ethics and lesbian culture. This essay will be a chapter in her book, *Lesbian Choices* (Columbia University Press, forthcoming).

[Haworth co-indexing entry note]: "The Military Ban and the ROTC: A Study in Closeting." Card, Claudia. Co-published simultaneously in the *Journal of Homosexuality* (The Haworth Press, Inc.) Vol. 27, No. 3/4, 1994, pp. 117-146; and: *Gay Ethics: Controversies in Outing, Civil Rights, and Sexual Science* (ed: Timothy F. Murphy) The Haworth Press, Inc., 1994, pp. 117-146. Multiple copies of this article/chapter may be purchased from The Haworth Document Delivery Center [1-800-3-HAWORTH; 9:00 a.m. - 5:00 p.m. (EST)].

117

then: the election of President Clinton, who promised to lift the ban and has meanwhile ordered that questions concerning sexual orientation no longer be asked of entrants and that enforcement of the ban be suspended; the continued "comings out" of highly placed members of the armed services; the beating death in Japan apparently by shipmates of gay Seaman Allen Schindler; the ruling by Los Angeles Federal district court judge Terry Hatter in the case of Keith Meinhold of the Navy that the ban violated equal protection rights guaranteed by the Constitution.[1] At the present writing, President Clinton is working with the Defense Department on how to go about permanently lifting the ban and on drawing up new codes of sexual conduct for the armed services.

By the time this essay sees print, I hope the objective of Representative Schroeder's bill will be realized. It will not be enough, however, to lift the ban. A long history of misinformation and ignorance has created a need for remedial education about lesbians and gay men, especially at the level of officer training. Even were the Defense Department to take such measures, the ethical issues would not, unfortunately, be suddenly moot. For, lesbian and gay closeting and their attendant evils have analogues in many programs offering careers with hierarchies of authority in which people work primarily with others of the same sex, from athletic programs and nursing schools on university campuses to convents and other religious orders. The history, consequences, and ethics of the military ban will be instructive as long as such closeting exists and until remedial education has taken effect.

THE UNIVERSITY OF WISCONSIN AND THE ROTC PROGRAM

In December 1989 an all-faculty meeting–the first in nearly two decades–was held in the University of Wisconsin Stock Pavilion to discuss the Reserve Officer Training Corps (ROTC) program's violation of campus nondiscrimination policies in its exclusion of lesbians and gay men. The meeting was called in response to a petition circulated by an *ad hoc* committee of which I was a member. The protested ban against lesbians and gay men is a policy (not a piece of legislation passed by elected representatives) that originated in the Defense Department during World War II.[2] It extends throughout the uniformed military services, aiming to exclude from service both "persons who engage in homosexual conduct" and those "who, by their statements, demonstrate a propensity to engage in homosexual conduct."[3] Through this policy university students could be excluded from benefits (including scholarships) of a program offering courses for university credit, and they would be excluded in violation of the campus's policy against discrimination on the basis of sexual orientation. This was what made the ROTC program our specific target of protest.

The all-faculty meeting revolved around a motion from the *ad hoc* committee asking the University Board of Regents to terminate contracts with the ROTC if its discriminatory policy were not eliminated within four years. It is one thing to object to a policy and another to sever connections with the entire program. Favoring the latter presupposes that the policy is serious indeed and that severing connection would not produce a worse situation. The situation of the University of Wisconsin is complicated by its being a land grant institution.[4] Land grant funds are appropriated to colleges "where the leading object shall be, without excluding other scientific and classical studies and including military tactics, to teach such branches of learning as are related to agriculture and mechanical arts."[5] Thus, the university is presently obligated to offer instruction in military tactics. Were the ROTC program withdrawn from the campus, the university would have to do one of three things: (1) find another way to offer instruction in military tactics (as it did prior to the ROTC program), (2) persuade the U.S. Government to renegotiate its land grant agreement with respect to the nature of the public service instruction a university could offer to fulfill its obligations, or (3) cease to be a land grant institution. Setting aside the third possibility, my committee thought it worth looking into how "instruction in military tactics" might be uncoupled from induction into military service. More ambitiously, the university might negotiate with the Government to offer nonmilitary public service training–for example, in education, health care, or other social services–in nondiscriminatory programs with national service upon graduation as a condition of scholarship support, much as current

ROTC scholarship students are expected to return service to the Government.

The motion, with its ultimatum, passed 386-248 at the faculty meeting, but then was overturned on a written ballot distributed by campus mail, which included many voting who had not attended the meeting. The ROTC program is therefore still with us, while the university administration has pursued ways to stimulate change of the Defense Department's policy in Washington.

There seem obvious advantages, from a humanist perspective, to having military officers trained on college campuses (a policy, incidentally, not altogether popular with many military personnel). Some of these advantages are offset, however, by severe homophobia and heterosexism encouraged by present policy, counteracting attitudes of free inquiry that a liberal campus, such as Wisconsin's, tries to foster. My concern here is not basically with the advantages and disadvantages of the ROTC's presence on campus. My concern is with the general defamation of lesbians and gay men and consequent moral corruption, especially at the level of career officers, fostered by the Defense Department's policy. These concerns give members and friends of a land grant university reason to protest the Defense Department's policy vigorously, regardless how they otherwise feel about the ROTC or military service.

The faculty meeting was not just an attempt to determine the fate of a particular motion. It was also an attempt to arouse faculty from apathy. Many seemed to feel that although the ROTC exclusion is embarrassing to a liberal campus, it was not worth a fuss because many people find ways to get around it. For a few who had never thought about it, the question whether the ROTC exclusions *were* unjustified was a real one. Finally, some faculty apparently assumed that protesting a program's policies presupposes basically approving of the program itself, and they did not want to give the impression of approving of the ROTC program. And so, when my turn came to speak, I directed my statement not to the specifics of the motion but to some basic ethical issues. Speakers were chosen alternately for and against the motion and allotted two minutes each. This was my two minutes' worth:

A South Hall plaque, from the Class of 1955, says, "You shall know the truth, and the truth will make you free."[6]

It has been said that no lesbians or gays have actually been discriminated against by the ROTC on this campus.[7] This means that the ROTC has no records of those against whom it has discriminated. Because of the *closet* phenomenon, this is not surprising. Knowing the policy, most lesbians and gays don't waste time applying; some lie in response to the question, Are you homosexual? Others discover who they are after they are in and do not disclose it. There is a widespread view that if lesbians and gays would just keep quiet–stay in the closet–what others didn't know wouldn't hurt them, and everyone would be happy. This view grants that there is no sound basis for discrimination, that the problem is the reactions of others. But promoting closeting respects prejudice rather than minority rights. It is not an honorable response.

The ROTC policy rewards lesbian or gay students who lie and threatens to penalize those who would tell the truth. There is a parallel with seventeenth-century England when non-Christians were not permitted to testify in courts of law. Non-Christians willing to lie about their religion were permitted to testify, while those who were *honest* were excluded, on the ground that *their* testimony could not be trusted.

The ROTC's discrimination policy prevents us from knowing who and how many lesbian and gay students on this campus are excluded (or even *in*cluded). It says, in effect, if you are honest enough to tell us who you are, we will exclude you because we will then know you are unreliable.

A policy that encourages and rewards dishonesty about the things that are most important in our lives, whether our religious beliefs or our most intimate relationships, is disgraceful. I, personally, find the University's willingness to maintain contracts with a group who persists in such policies an insult. It would be a joke were it not an insult. It is not funny because it is so dishonorable. Tolerating such policies undermines the search at this university for the truths that are supposed to make us free.

I now think it misleading to suggest that few lesbians and gays waste time applying. It may be primarily those openly lesbian or gay who would find it a "waste of time." Others may routinely apply, drawn to opportunities to work closely with others of the same sex in an environment offering power and possible adventure, especially women bored by stereotypically feminine work and men bored by stereotypically gay professions.

THE EXPERIENCE OF U.S. LESBIANS
AND GAYS IN MILITARY SERVICE

According to a June 1992 *New York Times* article, countries permitting lesbian and gays to serve "with some restrictions" (not specified) include Austria, Belgium, Denmark, France, Finland, Germany, Italy, Japan, the Netherlands, and Spain.[8] Since then, Canada and Australia have joined their ranks. The United States is not the only country, however, whose military policy bans lesbians and gay men. Britain has such a ban also.[9]

The *New York Times* reported in 1990 that "according to Pentagon data, about 1,400 gay men and women are forcibly discharged [from all the Armed services] each year, with lesbians let go at three times the rate of gay men" and that Navy statistics from 1985 to 1989 "show lesbians were discharged at twice the rate of gay men."[10] According to a report released in June 1992 by the General Accounting Office, between 1980 and 1990, "the Pentagon discharged 16,919 enlisted personnel and officers for homosexuality or permitted them to resign."[11] No one knows how many escape being discharged or asked to resign. However, recent books by Allan Bérubé and Mary Ann Humphrey confirm in detail the common knowledge that a great many lesbians and gay men presently serve and always have.[12] Many interviewees freely confessed to having lied on their applications.

In addressing the university faculty I focused on the moral implications of closeting, in part because of the following, then recent, event. After a Faculty Senate meeting a few weeks before at which my committee's protest of the ROTC's discrimination was mentioned, I overheard two colleagues, one saying, "When I was in service during World War II, there were lots of gays. Everyone knew. Nobody cared as long as they kept quiet. Why can't they just keep quiet? Why do they have to make a fuss?" These professors seemed unaware of discharges and denials of reenlistment facing lesbians and gay men (whom "everyone knows") after the war, refusals to recommend them for promotions that might trigger expulsion, or the constant terror of exposure, should one fall from grace with whoever is currently not reporting one.

A romantic view of military lesbians and gay men protecting one another and being protected by sympathetic officers is also fostered among lesbians and gay men by such stories as the following from Johnny Phelps, awarded a purple heart "and several other combat medals from the Pacific" during World War II. She worked for General Eisenhower in Germany just after the war. She says:

> The General . . . gave me a direct order. "It's been reported to me that there are lesbians in the WAC battalion. I want you to find them and give me a list. We've got to get rid of them." And I . . . said, ". . . Sir, if the General pleases, I'll be happy to check into this and make you a list. But you've got to know, when you get the list back, my name's going to be first. . . ." His secretary at the time was standing right next to me. . . . She said, "Sir, if the General pleases, Sergeant Phelps will have to be second on the list because mine will be first. You see, I'm going to type it." He sat back in his chair and looked at us and then I said, "Sir, if the General pleases, there are some things I'd like to point out to you. You have the highest-ranking WAC battalion assembled anywhere in the world. Most decorated. If you want to get rid of your file clerks, typists, section commanders, and your most key personnel, then I'll make that list. But when I make the list, I want you to remember that we haven't had any illegal pregnancies, we do not have any venereal disease, we have never had any negative reports, and we have always served and done our duty. . . . Since this unit has been here, it has received Meritorious Commendations on a regular six-month basis. Now if you want me to get rid of these women, I'll get rid of them, but I'll go with them." He just looked at me and said, "Forget that order. Forget about it." That was the last we ever heard of it.

> There were almost nine hundred women in that battalion. I could honestly say that 95 per cent of them were lesbians.[13]

The ban was still new. The war was popular. Camaraderie led many to look past the policy. Yet, this kind of tale gives only a partial picture of practices the ban has fostered during the past fifty years. Since then, other officers, perhaps feeling outnumbered, have responded less honorably than Sgt. Phelps.

As Johnny Phelps's story reveals, because of officers' discretionary powers, not all lesbians and gays who serve are equally closeted. Covertness may be unnecessary for many in wartime. According to the *Wall Street Journal* in January 1991, lesbians and gay men who served in the Persian Gulf with their superiors' knowledge of their homosexuality and without actions brought against them were about to be discharged; in July of that year, the *Wall Street Journal* reported that discharge proceedings had begun on gay veterans of Operation Desert Storm.[14] Such hypocrisy calls to mind the well-known case of African American Perry Watkins, drafted and inducted into the Army during the Viet Nam war despite his affirmation of his gayness from the beginning. The Army even had him entertain troops in drag. They then denied him reenlistment because of the homosexuality he had always affirmed. He told Mary Ann Humphrey that he applied three times for discharge during the war on the grounds that he was a homosexual and was denied each time, although the white men he knew who made the same kind of application had theirs granted (248-257). When they found him useful, the Army found ways to keep him in; when they found him no longer anything but an embarrassment, they tried to keep him out. He appealed the Army's refusal of reenlistment, and in 1987 the Ninth Circuit Court of Appeals ruled 7-4 in his favor, although not on Constitutional grounds that would help others' cases.

When the content of a policy is so highly questionable that many of those charged with enforcing it (such as members of the widespread lesbian and gay officer networks referred to by Mary Ann Humphrey's interviewees) cannot be presumed to agree with its bases, they may exercise considerable "discretion" in enforcing it. In practice, this means that when the policy *is* enforced, the real reasons are often irrelevant to the content of the policy, which becomes a vehicle for the exercise of many kinds of prejudice, not just prejudice against lesbians and gays. This compounds abuse. When the policy is unjust to begin with, those against whom it is enforced suffer at least a double injustice. Such abuses are notorious also from the history of capital punishment. With respect to both capital punishment and the exclusionary policy regarding lesbians and gay men, those most liable to suffer have been those already most oppressed, those with the least power to mobilize protest. In the United States, it is often people of color, especially poor people of color. In this connection, it is not surprising that lesbians are forcibly discharged at many times the rate of gay men.

Miriam ben-Shalom, president of the Gay, Lesbian, and Bisexual Veterans of America, is another casualty of officer discretion who refused to leave quietly. She enlisted in the U.S. Army Reserve in 1974. During her second year, when there was a large number of discharges, she asked why she was not being kicked out with the others and says her commanding officer told her, "Oh, there's this regulation, but it's up to the discretion of the commander. Besides, you're really good at what you do. We have no arguments with you, so don't worry about it"–implying that if they had "arguments" insufficient for a discharge, they could trot out the policy against lesbians.[15]

In 1976, Miriam ben-Shalom was discharged when her commander recommended her for a commendation. Recommendation for a promotion or commendation is a way to initiate a discharge when a "flag" has been placed on the candidate's file. "A flag is placed on anyone's personnel file when some action is pending. In my case it had to do with my verbal statements about being a lesbian."[16] Perry Watkins reports also that because of his sexual orientation he was not given awards and decorations during his last enlistment: "they had to consider their 'image.'"[17]

It is often noted that most of those discharged have been enlistees, not officers.[18] Those responsible for discharging them can easily be lesbian or gay officers with an investment to protect against being outed by the indiscretions (or by the principles) of others. Army recruiter "Elizabeth Strong" (pseudonym) told Mary Ann Humphrey she never asked applicants "if they were gay" but would feel no compunction about denying admission to any who answered the application form's homosexuality questions affirmatively: "If he is stupid, stupid enough to admit it when everybody knows you can't do it and be in the military, then he's not smart enough to come into my Air Force, and that's how I feel" (246). Reports from lesbian and gay enlistees of their terror of lesbian and gay officers and lack of support from those quarters suggest that some lesbian and gay officers hunt down enlistees who they fear are insufficiently closeted. Closeted officers are in a prime position to manipulate lesbians or gay men under their authority. Some are said by Mary Ann Humphrey's interviewees to bargain with lesbians or gay men who agree to spy on others and turn in lists (218). Ironically, lesbian and gay officers who have the most power can have the strongest motives to maintain the closet, deferring to (if not internalizing) socially sanctioned fear and hatred and contributing to the oppression of those with the least power. Thus it is especially important to address discrimination in an officer training program, such as the ROTC. The evils of closeting can take root in especially pernicious ways at this level, a matter to which I will return.

The implication of the rhetorical question, "Why can't they just keep quiet?" that things are basically all right for those who just do their jobs well is thus a long way from the truth. Some of Mary Ann Humphrey's interviewees indicated that *after they became officers,* they were put in touch with a network of lesbian or gay officers in many cities. Yet informal networks, embodying social prejudices of the time, are not there for everyone. An African American lesbian in the Navy told Mary Ann Humphrey that she knew of groups in which one could be "totally out and practicing" but that because of racism she did not belong (157). But even officers with major commendations are discharged if they come forward as lesbian or gay, as in the widely-publicized cases of Leonard Matlovich (over ten years' Air Force service, Purple Heart, Bronze Star) and, more recently, Colonel Margarethe Cammermeyer of the National Guard (over 27 years of service, Bronze Star, Veterans Administration Nurse of the Year award) and Tracy Thorne, the Naval officer who came out in May 1992 on TV's "Nightline."[19]

An interesting implication of Johnny Phelps's Eisenhower story is that it would not be in the Defense Department's interest to enforce its anti-lesbian and anti-gay policies uniformly, because of the sheer numbers of outstanding and highly responsible personnel who would have to be to let go if it did. The military sounds like a political outer's paradise: how could the Defense Department continue to maintain its policy if all the lesbians and gays in positions of responsibility were outed? And yet it does maintain that policy despite already astounding costs of doing so. The cost of the Defense Department's discriminatory policies was estimated at $27 million in 1990 for the 1,000 lesbians and gays dismissed, based on an estimated $28,226 to replace an enlisted person and $120,772 to replace an officer.[20] The General Accounting Office estimates that from 1980 to 1990 it cost $498 million to recruit and train replacements for those discharged.[21] Ethically, these are not, however, the most important costs. The most important costs may be the corruption of lesbian and gay officers who are *not* booted out and who perpetuate the defamation of lesbians and gays by the policy they enforce.

WHAT'S WRONG WITH CLOSETING?

"Why can't they just keep quiet?" came from a university colleague knowledgeable in political thought and trained in argument, whose analytical skills and political sensitivities I have known and respected for more than two decades. I realized upon overhearing his remarks that to be taken seriously by faculty on the ROTC issue, I would have to address his question. Setting aside the erroneous assumption that keeping quiet is sufficient not to get one expelled (and the equally erroneous assumption that failure to "keep quiet" is sufficient for discharge), I focused on the assumption that living in a closet is not so bad, nor, consequently, is tolerating others' being made to do so.

My colleague's response is not peculiar to men who served in the military during World War II. Something like it turns up even among contemporary university students. Occasionally they write me notes protesting my "exhibitionism" if I identify myself during lecture as lesbian, which I sometimes have occasion to do, as my heterosexual colleagues often have occasion to refer to their spouses and children. Informal evidence suggests that the pro-closeting attitude is as common in college athletics as in the ROTC program, in nursing schools, in college dormitories, and generally in same-sex settings that bring members of the university into close physical proximity with one another. The very tone of the question, "Why can't they just keep quiet?" like the notes from students, shows how "closeting" is urged upon lesbians and gays, *not something we choose for reasons of our own.*

There are at least three pernicious aspects of a policy that inevitably fosters closeting. First, it rewards lying and penalizes honesty. For those committed long-term to an environment in which the deception initiated must be maintained, this is morally corrupting. If intimate relationships are among the most important parts of one's life and one is willing to lie systematically about them to protect one's standing or even to gain standing in the military, that raises the question of what else one may be willing to lie about to protect that standing. More importantly, having to enforce against others a policy that one knows applies equally to oneself may lead to psychological "solutions" involving serious abdications of responsibility, a matter to which I will return. Second, the policy demeans all lesbians and gay men by upholding a stance that would be justified only if lesbians and gay men were in truth responsible for the fear, disgust, or revulsion of others. In doing so, it encourages the false assumption that lesbians and gay men *are* responsible for those reactions. This is particularly unjust in a context in which lesbians and gay men have no way, even if they were moved to do so, to disabuse others of the ignorance on which their fears and hostilities are commonly based. One of the best ways to combat such ignorance is for lesbians and gay men with proven records of service and achievement to "come out." But, of course, those who come out are subject to expulsion, regardless of their records of service and achievement, and many of those discovered are offered an honorable discharge or the opportunity to resign in return for leaving quietly. The ban thus institutionalizes homophobia, insulating against criticism a derogatory image that reaches beyond the present into future generations. Third, the policy deters quests for self-knowledge and rewards closed-mindedness. It penalizes an open attitude regarding some of the most important aspects of our lives. Consequently, it confines and insults *all* students, not just those who presently identify as lesbian or gay. Such discrimination turns honest lesbian and gay students into second-class campus citizens (although they pay first-class tuition). It subjects dishonest ones to unchecked manipulation and extortion. And, as I will suggest in the next section, it makes potential monsters of career officers.

LIVING A LIE AND "DOUBLING"

For the sexually inexperienced and others who have not been visibly present in lesbian or gay communities, there is no effective check on answers to application form homosexuality questions; the applicant's word is all the military has had at that point. Some applicants, apparently, never dared disclose the truth to themselves. "Janice" (pseudonym) told Mary Ann Humphrey she got involved with an officer "who was so closeted—I can remember her saying to me, 'We're not like those other lesbians. We're not real lesbians. We just love each other' " (129-130). For those who lie to get in, or stay in after deciding that they are lesbian or gay, systematic deception becomes a way of life (an irony of referring to homosexuality as "an alternative lifestyle"). Under investigatory pressure after others were pushed to identify them, two of Mary Ann Humphrey's lesbian interviewees used marriage as a cover, one with a gay man who also needed a cover, the other with a heterosexual man who apparently was unaware of being used. Some simply got pregnant. Others, less drastically, restyled their hair, began wearing make-up, and flirted with male officers. Almost all said they dated men as a cover.

Why do they put up with living this way? Some do not; they quit voluntarily or come forward, forcing the hands of others, as in the cases of Leonard Matlovich, Margarethe Cammermeyer, and Tracy Thorne.[22] Yet others remain, retiring with full benefits. If their pretenses were literally survival tactics, they might take pride in their resourcefulness. But many enlisted voluntarily, some because it appeared their best route to an education and career training. They experienced the necessity for pretense as demeaning, not as a source of pride. In some cases, enlistment was their most promising route out of an abusive home, poverty, an intolerant small-town environment, or all three. Extortion and manipulation by superior officers was an upgrading from physical and sexual assault at home. If such a life compromises the moral character that education ideally develops, many of those so compromised may otherwise have received no education beyond high school (if that). Thus, the initial misfortunes of some make the evils of closeting seem a small price to pay for a way out. This makes such lesbians and gay men exploitable in the maintenance of institutionalized homophobia. Unlike Perry Watkins, who affirmed his gay identity and was thereby unmanipulable, those who succumb to closeting are used, in being abused, to perpetuate oppression and injustice against others.

Not all who live the heterosexual lie have the excuse of escaping a worse situation. Some are highly educated and come from economically privileged backgrounds (which, of course, does not rule out domestic abuse). Some have chosen to serve because of their own moral ideals. Others live out their parents' ambitions for them, rather than their own projects. One should be reminded of officers who became war criminals in Nazi Germany and of other highly educated persons who became complicit in genocide. Psychologist Robert Lifton's work on the Nazi doctors offers an interesting analysis of a certain psychological "solution" those living a double life may find to cope with intolerable stress. Inquiring into how physicians came to design and participate in Nazi medical experiments, using their skills to kill rather than to heal, Dr. Lifton proposes:

> The key to understanding how Nazi doctors came to do the work of Auschwitz is the psychological principle I call "doubling": the division of the self into two functioning wholes, so that a part-self acts as an entire self.[23]

The idea is that the self who lived inside the death camps divided, psychologically and yet as a functioning whole, from the self who was loving with spouse, children, and the dog at home. The division was not simply between skills called upon in different contexts but between incompatible values and emotional responses. Doubling, he argues, enabled the Nazi doctors to avoid intolerable stress, by avoiding the confrontation of contradictions in their own values and practices.

This hypothesis is offered as an *explanation*, not as an excuse.

Dr. Lifton's ethical view is that the doubler's responsibility "is in no way abrogated by the fact that much doubling takes place outside of awareness" (418); that "to live out the doubling and call forth the evil is a moral choice for which one is responsible, whatever the level of consciousness involved" (423-424). His investigation into doubling is intended as a "psychological probing on behalf of illuminating evil" (418). He does not explain, philosophically, how it is possible to be responsible for what takes place outside of awareness. However, there is both legal and moral precedent for his position. What enters awareness is often something over which we have, or can develop, considerable control. Reckless and negligent behavior are examples of conduct for which people are held responsible, both legally and morally, although the dangers and harms the agents failed to avoid were outside their awareness. What we attend to and what we ignore reveal as much about our character as what we do with what falls within our awareness. Arrogance is an example of a character trait of which its possessors are typically unaware, although habits of self-reflection can make one aware. If doubling has elements outside of awareness, it may still be within the agent's responsibility in the wider sense of what occurs through one's choices or failures to choose; it may even be potentially brought within the agent's awareness. In a narrower sense, one can choose not to, or simply fail to, *take* or *accept* responsibility with respect to what is, in the wider sense, within one's responsibility. It makes sense to hold people responsible for such choices and failures—for abdications of responsibility, for example. The way I read Dr. Lifton's analysis of what he calls doubling, it can involve an abdication of responsibility as a "solution" to the problem of stress produced by conflicts between one's own values and practices.

Dr. Lifton lists five characteristics of doubling: (1) "a dialectic between two selves in terms of autonomy and connection," (2) "a holistic principle," (3) "a life-death dimension," (4) "the avoidance of guilt," and (5) "both an unconscious dimension . . . and a significant change in moral consciousness" (419). By claiming that doubling is more "holistic," he distinguishes doubling from what Pierre Janet called "dissociation" and what psychoanalysts have called "splitting." Although he refers to "the mechanism" of doubling, the "mechanism" seems simply to *be* the systematic refusals to face value and emotional contradictions, especially as these refusals appear not to have been accompanied by amnestic barriers characteristic of multiple personalities, nor to appear as suddenly and spontaneously as multiple personalities (which, unlike doubling, appear early in childhood).

Most of Dr. Lifton's five characteristics of doubling seem to fit, or to be adaptable to, the double lives of lesbian and gay career officers. The guilt, or shame, they avoid is that of hypocrisy in enforcing against others a policy applying equally to themselves; some may also be avoiding self-hatred simply for being lesbian or gay. The only characteristic that may not obviously be routinely applicable is the "life-death dimension." Yet the recent beating death of gay Seaman Allen Schindler raises unanswered questions about the prevalence of even this dimension. Institutionalized homophobia and hostility provide major stress for lesbians and gay men in service. In the summer of 1991 it was reported that "Sgt. Timothy Miller, a 25-year-old officer, allegedly shot his lover, 20-year-old Spc. Terry Wayne Stephenson, days before Miller was to be court-martialed on three counts of sodomy and four counts of indecent conduct. . . . Miller apparently shot himself shortly after Stephenson's body was found."[24] One can only speculate how many cases are not reported with such details. For those who fear that lesbians or gay men might harass and rape them the way men have harassed and raped women, for those who think such behavior is a normal aspect of sexual attraction, the possible presence of lesbians or gay men in close physical proximity to them or in positions of power over them is easily a source of stress. The public does not know how often military lesbian or gay deaths are attributable, in whole or in part, to consequences of stress produced by such fears in others. For those who entered military service not to escape an even worse history of abuse but, say, to fulfill ethical ideals, a career of lesbian or gay passing may be made tolerable by the creation of a special military self, a shield from stresses that lead others to quit voluntarily, a shield from contradictions in one's own values and practices which becomes thereby at the same time a barrier to integrity and accountability. Dr. Lifton's hypothesis about how far "doubling" can enable one to go in departing from values one calls one's own makes it a terrifying prospect to contemplate, let alone encourage. Although he allows that doubling *can* be life-saving, "for a soldier in combat, for instance; or for a victim of brutality such as an Auschwitz inmate, who must also undergo a form of doubling in order to survive" (420), his examples of the Nazi doctors illustrate the potentiality for a disruption of integrity that involves an awesome abdication of moral responsibility. Thus, an officer training program that attracts lesbians or gay men who are willing systematically to lie and prove themselves by rooting out others in enforcing a ban that applies as much to themselves as to their victims, may be training potential moral monsters.

INSTITUTIONALIZED HATRED AND THE "MORALE" PROBLEM

The Defense Department's discrimination policy is no longer defended by claims that being lesbian or gay interferes with job performance. The official reason now given by the Defense Department for the ban is, rather, that the *presence* of lesbians and gay men "adversely affects the ability of the Military Services to maintain discipline, good order and morale; to foster mutual trust and confidence among service members, to ensure the integrity of rank and command; to facilitate assignment and worldwide deployment of service members who frequently must live and work under close conditions affording minimal privacy; to recruit and retain members of the Military services; to maintain the public acceptability of military service; and to prevent breaches of security."[25] The widespread presence of closeted lesbians and gay men in the military, however, suggests that it is not the *presence* but the *perception* of lesbians and gay men that has been thought to present a problem. This is an astute move on the part of the Defense Department. Lesbians and gay men must be closeted for the old fear of extortion to have even initial plausibility. If the *perception* of lesbians and gay men is said to provide a morale problem, closeting appears to be the "solution." Thus, the Defense Department seems to have all bases covered: lesbians and gay men who are "out" present a morale problem; those who are "in" present a security problem. Neither argument, however, withstands scrutiny.

There is no attempt by the Defense Department to defend the

bases of alleged morale problems, for such problems have their source in mythology, ignorance, inexperience, and irrationality. Such deference to prejudice, however, not only fosters horizontal abuse among lesbians and among gay men but also produces a self-reinforcing cycle of hatred toward lesbians and gay men by others. Discrimination, itself stigmatizing, reinforces the already existing stigma of being socially hated (which is then cited in defense of discrimination, etc., *ad infinitum*). Deference to what is commonly called "homophobia" *solidifies* it and *passes it along from one generation to the next*. In *respecting* such hostilities, it gives hatred a social sanction. To respect and sanction disfiguring hatreds rather than honesty about the most important things in our lives encourages values not worth defending.

In practical terms, the concern about "morale" comes down to fears of *noncooperation*, at best, and of *sexual harassment and rape*, at worst. Analogously to its prior resistance to racial integration, the military seems to fear that others will refuse to take orders from lesbian or gay officers out of a lack of respect for them. Yet it has also the disanalogous concern about consequences of heterosexuals' fears of sexual harassment or rape by lesbians or gay men. It is an interesting question to what extent the latter fear is actually rooted in the common toleration of sexually abusive behavior *of heterosexual men toward women*, such behavior as was exhibited, for example, by a number of male pilots of the Tailhook Association at their September 1991 convention in Las Vegas, when at least twenty-six women, half of them naval officers, reported that they were assaulted while they were "forced through a hotel corridor gantlet of drunken, groping pilots."[26] Legitimizing fears of either noncooperation or assault places responsibility on lesbians and gay men for the ignorance and (anticipated) insubordination of others. Rape and sexual harassment are evidently a serious problem of *heterosexual* men, and general rules against such behavior should be taken seriously, regardless of the perpetrator's sexual orientation. The "morale" argument, however, usually does not pretend that it is the fault of lesbians and gay men if others lack respect for them or even fear them. For an ROTC program on a university campus, appeals to problems created by ignorance should have no credibility whatever. The mythologies that perpetuate social hostility toward lesbians and gay men are exposed and examined critically in university courses.[27] If more such courses are needed, the university is in an excellent position to address that need. Faculty from coast to coast are presently agitating for lesbian and gay studies programs, which would address that need. In an academic environment, differences in politics and orientation should be productive rather than divisive, addressed through discussion and exchange of points of view, adding to the common fund of knowledge about human experience. The Netherlands offers an example of confronting prejudice with education. Its defense department has published a colorful eight-page brochure, *Homosexualiteit en defensie* ("Homosexuality and Defense"), which begins:

> Homosexuals in the military–is that possible? Of course it is. Furthermore, it is obvious. The military is a mirror of society. . . . We produced this brochure for homosexuals–to make it clear that they are welcome in the military–and for heterosexuals–to make them realize what kinds of problems their colleagues are facing.[28]

When educational efforts are unsuccessful, the military can require cooperation on pain of insubordination. Were it necessary to exclude anyone, proven perpetrators of assault (regardless of sexual orientation) and those refusing to cooperate in the presence of lesbians and gays could be excluded. The point about the locus of responsibility is analogous to that of the feminist response to those who would keep women off the streets in order to prevent rape: the way to make streets safe is not to keep women off the streets but to keep rapists off the streets. Likewise, the way to produce a healthier ROTC program and military is not to exclude lesbians and gay men but to exclude disrespect for lesbians and gays and to refuse to tolerate any sexual abuse.

The Ninth Circuit Court of Appeals in its judgment regarding lesbian Army Reserve Captain Dusty Pruitt has recognized the weight of the point about others' prejudices, as others did earlier with respect to analogous "morale" arguments used in defense of racial segregation in the armed forces (removed by President Truman's order in 1948) and barring women from military service.[29] On August 19, 1991, the Ninth Circuit Court ruled that the Army's policy requiring discharge of homosexuals should be subjected to "active rationality review" and in May 1992 upheld that ruling, rejecting the Defense Department's request for a rehearing. On December 7, 1992, the Supreme Court denied the government's appeal, which means the Army must come up with a new justification for the exclusionary policy or offer Dusty Pruitt a settlement.[30] What the requirement of "active" rational review means, basically, is that the Army cannot continue to rely on traditional arguments that anti-gay biases of other members of the Army would create problems. Judge Canby, of the Ninth Circuit Court, quoted from *Palmore*: "The Constitution cannot control such prejudices, but neither can it tolerate them. Private biases may be outside the reach of the law, but the law cannot, directly or indirectly, give them effect."[31] The implication is that the Army can no longer appeal to prejudice to justify excluding lesbians and gay men but must find something wrong with lesbian and gay job performance.

As judged by military standards, however, there is now public evidence that lesbians' and gay men's performance records are not inferior. In October 1989 openly gay Congressman Gerry Studds of Massachusetts received a Defense Department study, "Nonconforming Sexual Orientations and Military Suitability," by Dr. Ted Sarbin, a professor of psychology and criminology, and Dr. Ken Karols, a Navy flight surgeon, of the Defense Personnel Security Research and Education Center (PERESEC). A few months later, he received a second report, "Preservice Adjustment of Homosexual and Heterosexual Military Accessions: Implications for Security Clearance Suitability," by Michael McDaniel, also a Defense Department researcher, although this report had not been submitted to the Pentagon. Both reports (known as the PERESEC reports) were publicized by representatives Studds and Patricia Schroeder.[32] The first report concludes that "sexuality is unrelated to job performance in the same way as is being left- or right-handed."[33] The second report suggests that lesbians and gay men display military suitability "that is as good or better than the average heterosexual."[34] Decades ago, the Crittenden Report, commissioned by the Navy in 1957–which, according to Congressman Studds, it took twenty years and a court order to pry from Pentagon vaults[35]–had already concluded that "The number of cases of [extortion] as a

result of past investigations of homosexuals is negligible. No factual data exist to support the contention that homosexuals are a
greater risk than heterosexuals."[36] And in 1991 a Defense Department memo was anonymously leaked to the National Gay and
Lesbian Task Force, stating that "the same criteria should be used
for gays as for straights in deciding whether to grant security clear-
ances."[37]

While these reports destroy the Defense Department's traditional
arguments, they should offer cold comfort to lesbians and gay men.
For they also show how well lesbians and gay men can be made to
turn on one another. Our main reason for opposing the Defense
Department's ban should not be that *by military standards* we do
our jobs as well as if not better than others. More important for us is
that some of the jobs produced by the ban are morally corrupting for
lesbian and gay officers to have to perform and humiliating to all
lesbians and gay men who are not discharged. Our ability to pass
muster testifies to our ingenuity and cleverness, not to our character.

In view of the rampant deception, self-deception, hypocrisy,
lying, spying, manipulation, and extortion fostered by the current
anti-lesbian and anti-gay policy, the Defense Department's morale
argument is especially ironic. What could be more demoralizing
than such practices as these? How conducive to morale is an environment in which people known by their colleagues to be deserving
of commendations or promotions are passed over because recommending them might lead to their discharge? How conducive to
morale is an environment in which exclusionary policies are known
to be arbitrarily enforced? How conducive to morale is it to work in
an environment in which "nobody really trusted anybody" because
officers plant spies to draw up lists?[38] To work in an environment in
which anyone can accuse anyone, without evidence, and expose
them to intense investigation as a result? An environment in which
tight networks protect officers who violate regulations that they
enforce against others who are not skillful enough at deception and
lying? (And what else are these skills used to conceal?) One might
suspect that were present discriminatory policies eliminated and
remedial education instituted, military morale among reflective personnel would improve several hundred percent.

A STATE SEXUALITY?

Finally, it is incompatible with the goals of a state university to penalize students for inquiry regarding sexuality. The University of Wisconsin would not tolerate penalties for student inquiry into religious beliefs. If the military required a certain religious orientation, that would raise serious questions about supporting a state religion. But there should no more be a state sexuality than a state religion. One's dispositions to form, or not form, intimate partnerships are at least as central to the quality of one's life and one's moral integrity as the freedom to worship, or not worship, as one chooses. Before President Clinton ordered that questions about sexual orientation be dropped, students who were engaged in open inquiry with respect to sexuality who did not pretend to have answers from the outset would have been subject to exclusion from the ROTC, because many, if honest, would have had to give hesitant, qualified, or agnostic answers to such questions.

This line of reasoning does not presuppose that sexuality–any more than religion–should be exempted from moral evaluation. On the contrary, it presupposes that the freedom to inquire without prejudice is required for informed moral evaluation. If the military were truly concerned to screen out applicants who might engage in incontrovertibly immoral sexual behavior, it should seek to identify rapists and sadists. Rape crisis centers could be helpful in designing questions for application forms that would help identify those who cannot recognize when they are committing rape and those who do not care. Domestic violence workers might be likewise helpful in designing questions that would help identify sadists.

WHY RADICAL FEMINISTS SHOULD CARE

I have been asked why I, a committed feminist, bother with the ROTC. Why would I *want* lesbians *in*cluded? Isn't it contrary to feminist values to work for such inclusion? Or reformist, rather than revolutionary?

My response is complex. First, some questioners may be confusing femin*ism* with femin*inity*. Fighting against men is incompatible with popular ideals of *femininity* and widely (although not universally) held to be the prerogative of the *masculine*. (Fighting among women, on the other hand, is often encouraged by those adhering to the same ideals.) Such ideals are enforced most among women of white middle classes, who also use them to judge others. Feminists have long objected that "femininity," so understood, is a political construction of femaleness used to keep women subordinate and subservient to men.[39] During the past two decades, the women's self-defense movement has instituted in most major cities of the United States physical and attitudinal training programs, often cooperating with rape crisis centers, with the objective of enlarging women's options to include effectively fighting back against assailants.[40] Many women have aptitudes for physical activities from which we have been traditionally discouraged to keep us in our place–aptitudes for sports, for example, and for battle, as well. Lesbians have always been outstanding among athletes and warriors (though not always visible as lesbians). The Amazon tradition, although less popular than the Sapphic, is a major strand of lesbian culture, extending from the ancient Amazons through many "cross-dressers" of modern times to contemporary lesbians in U.S. and other military forces.[41] History documents amazons–formidable bands of women warriors–in every age, in every part of the globe.[42] Even if fighting against men were "unfeminine," it would not follow that it is either unfemale or unfeminist.

The second part of my response begins by pointing out that it is one thing to choose not to exercise an option and another not even to have the option. I want lesbians not to be excluded from the option, as long as we live in a society (or even a world) with major armed forces. My concern is not that of a reformer who sees opportunities for lesbian advancement in reformed military institutions. My concern is what exclusion means for who we are. To be excluded in advance from a public program for no good reason is demeaning to those excluded and to all who share the identity on the basis of which they are excluded. Such exclusions help to construct a disfiguring image of all who share the excluded identity. Thus, even were a student not interested in ROTC, it is still in the interest of that student for the option not to be foreclosed on grounds of sexual orientation. What is at stake is one's dignity in communities in which one lives daily, even one's very identity in those respects in which it is a social construction and not simply a reflection of one's individual psychology or family background.[43]

Nevertheless, those who have never considered seriously the opportunity for military training may not know how they would evaluate the option. Where military service is the *only* public service to which citizens may be obligated, those denied access to military service may become beholden to others for public defense and security. Although during wartime Rosie and other women previously slated for domestic service were welcomed as riveters and so forth, her services were not recognized as military. No veterans' benefits were attached to it. After the war, she was told to go home so returning soldiers could have their jobs back. The debt traditionally exacted from women who do not serve militarily has been feminine service. A feminist who acknowledges a debt to be honored might prefer to "pay her way" in military service, as many women did during World War II. The concept of "military service" might be radically transformed if service obligations were truly democratic and distributed in an egalitarian manner. In a war genuinely supported by the people, who would be home to defend but children, the old, and the ill? Caring for them might have to be recognized as wartime military service, with full benefits, awards, purple hearts, and the rest.[44]

If it is not obvious that a feminist would in principle oppose serving militarily, neither does it follow from rejecting "femininity" that she would embrace modern weapons or the values war has most often implemented. The uses of violence, military and otherwise, raise issues over which feminists, like others, are deeply divided. Many would agree with Professor Gerda Lerner, who argued passionately in a public campus address in 1991 that in modern warfare, it is too often the case that *there is no defense of women, children, and old people who are not soldiers themselves, that these are the people most likely to be killed in the event of war fought with modern technology.*[45]

I do not rest my case upon the value of actually exercising the option to become a member of the ROTC or any branch of military service. I emphasize, rather, the importance of not being excluded in advance from the possibility of honorable candidacy for such service. Feminist values do not obviously exclude absolutely the eligibility of such service. Exclusion by the Government is a denial of the normal options of citizenship. On a campus with an ROTC program, such exclusion becomes a denial of the normal options of students in good standing. Wrongful exclusions contribute to an unjust social construction of those excluded as dishonorable, abnormal, or somehow shameful, which affects them in all areas of their lives, not just in their choices of which courses to take.

It is sometimes objected that were it wrong to exclude lesbians and gay men through no fault of their own because such exclusions are demeaning, then it would also be wrong to exclude from military service those with such physical disabilities as blindness, deafness, or loss of the use of limbs. For, neither are such disabilities the fault of those who suffer them, and others might use such exclusions to support wrongful stigmatizing.

At least two things are wrong with this argument. First, citing the absence of fault is misleading. For, it suggests both that no choice is involved in becoming lesbian or gay or in incurring a disability, and that were such a choice possible, one would be at fault to make it. Yet a foreseeable disability may be incurred as a consequence of justifiable choices (as when one is injured in performing a meritorious act), the role of choice in becoming lesbian or gay is disputed among lesbians and gay men, and were it not for hardships imposed and inconveniences experienced by others, there might be nothing to regret about living a life as lesbian or gay or with any of many forms of disability.[46] Second, appealing to the predicament of those with disabilities is intended as a *reductio ad absurdum*, assuming without argument that it *is* justifiable to exclude from service those lacking ordinary physical abilities. However, the argument that wrongful exclusion from normal options of citizenship contributes to an unjust social construction of those excluded can also be heard as supporting the inclusion, as much as possible, of those with physical disabilities. Many today prefer to be recognized as differently abled; they are able to perform a wide range of services when others are open to the possibilities and cooperate.[47] There may also be services that can be well performed by some who have been dismissed in the past as mentally disabled.[48]

Finally, it is also true that if lesbians and gay men were not barred from military service, we would have access to veterans' educational programs and health services, and even to jobs that are presently available on a preferential basis to veterans. Preferential hiring is highly controversial among white men when its recipients are nonveteran women or people of color, but veterans have received preferential treatment for decades. The Veterans' Preference Act of 1944 specified that for certain jobs, no nonveteran was even to be considered unless no veterans were available.[49] This may be a good reformist argument for changing the Defense Department's policies regarding lesbians and gays. However, although I do not dispute the justice of this argument, it is not the consideration that motivates my concern.

CONCLUSIONS

What benefits can be expected from the abolition of the ROTC's policies of discrimination against lesbian and gay students? I have no special reason to expect lesbians and gay students to sign up in great numbers to contribute their talents to the ROTC, although perhaps they will. I will not be surprised, however, if many already in come out (I do not mean resign)–at least, if the military also takes seriously its duty to protect its lesbian and gay members against assault by others. Eliminating the stress of a double life with its terror of exposure, the associated manipulative powers of and over others, and barriers to deserved promotions and commendations can be expected to affect performance positively. Speaking from experience, coming out for me in my profession–which I did in the late 1970s–has had a very positive effect on my ability to work well. More importantly, removing the need for what Dr. Lifton calls "doubling" would improve the integrity and accountability of lesbian and gay officers in military service. Ethically, this is one of the two most important benefits.

The other is that removal of this discriminatory policy will strike a blow against institutionalized fear and hatred and the public disfigurement of lesbians and gay men not only on campus but in the larger world. Lesbians and gay men will be recognized to have the normal rights of citizens in good standing, whether or not they serve militarily. The next generation will inherit less public defamation than ours did. Diminishing the disfigurement of lesbians and gay men and penalizing instead those who refuse to respect us potentially will extend far beyond campus and military, as generations graduate and move out into the world or return to civilian life, taking with them attitudes developed on campuses and in military environments into communities everywhere. This is why, as a feminist lesbian who is also an educator, I care about this issue.

AUTHOR NOTE

The author is indebted to Joe Elder, Michael Olneck, and Jim Steakley and other members of the *ad hoc* Faculty Against Discrimination in University Programs Committee for long and helpful discussions, to Rick Villaseñor in response to whose invitation she agreed to lend her efforts to the battle against the campus ROTC discrimination, to Richard Mohr for his books, *Gays/Justice: A Study of Ethics, Society, and Law* (Columbia University Press, 1988) and *Gay Ideas: Outing and Other Controversies* (Beacon Press, 1992), as well as his constant encouragement and many helpful references, and to Tim Murphy for useful questions and comments and clippings from the *Windy City Times*.

NOTES

1. Most of this essay was written during the summer of 1992; it has been revised and updated to early March 1993.

2. However, in 1950 Congress created the Uniform Code of Military Justice, a code that prohibits both homosexual and heterosexual oral and anal sex. See Chris Bull, "And the Ban Played On," *The Advocate*, Mar. 9, 1993, p. 38, for this and other milestones in the history of the military ban.

3. From Defense Department policy quoted in Representative Gerry Studds's "Forward" to Kate Dyer, ed., *Gays in Uniform: The Pentagon's Secret Reports* (Boston: Alyson, 1990), p. xiv. The policy does not extend to non-uniformed advisers, such as Assistant Secretary of Defense Pete Williams, outed by Michelangelo Signorile in *The Advocate* (Aug. 27, 1991), pp. 34-44, to protest Defense Department hypocrisy.

4. Many other universities and colleges that are not land grant institutions have either refused to have an ROTC program on campus or have taken a position like that of my *ad hoc* committee's motion. According to the *Windy City Times*, Oct. 3, 1991, p. 10, Dartmouth College, for example, told the Defense Department that "it will discontinue the campus program if there is no change by April 1993."

5. 7 U.S.C. 304.

6. I attached no significance to the Biblical origin of the quotation about truth and freedom. Nor do students and faculty at this state university usually attach religious significance to it. It is commonly cited as though it applied to truths sought in university classrooms, laboratories, libraries.

7. Two state senators in a letter to the President of the Board of Regents (Dec. 6, 1989) maintained that "After checking, we are not aware of a single instance in which a homosexual who enrolled in ROTC courses was not commissioned by the program because of sexual preference."

8. Eric Schmitt, "Barring Homosexuals Called Costly to Military," *New York Times*, June 20, 1992.

9. According to the *Lesbian/Gay Law Notes* (Summer 1992, p. 54), Britain "will no longer prosecute military personnel for engaging in gay sex, but will continue to discharge all personnel discovered to be gay."

10. "Navy Is Urged to Root Out Lesbians Despite Abilities," *New York Times*, Sept. 2, 1990. Estimates since then have placed the figure for the discharge of lesbians as high as ten times the rate of gay men (Signorile).

11. John Gallagher, "GAO: Military Spent $500 Million Discharging Gays," *The Advocate*, July 30, 1992, p. 20.

12. Allen Bérubé, *Coming Out Under Fire: The History of Gay Men and Women in World War II* (New York: Free Press, 1990); Mary Ann Humphrey, *My Country, My Right to Serve: Experiences of Gay Men and Women in the Military, World War II to the Present* (New York: Harper Collins, 1990). Where they are contextually clear, further references to this title will be given in the text. Allan Bérubé spent ten years interviewing lesbian and gay veterans, unearthed hundreds of letters between gay GIs, and studied many newly declassified documents. Mary Ann Humphrey was moved to gather the interviews for her book (about a third published under pseudonyms) after she was booted out of the Army Reserve when a former male colleague outed her to satisfy a grudge. The just released *Conduct Unbecoming: Politics, Prejudice, and Homosexuality in the U.S. Military* (New York: St. Martin's Press, 1993), by Randy Shilts, draws on interviews with over 500 closeted gay servicepeople.

13. Humphrey, p. 40.

14. Signorile, p. 36.

15. Humphrey, p. 188.

16. Humphrey, p. 188.

17. Humphrey, p. 254.

18. "Officers seem to receive more lenient treatment. Only 227 officers were discharged or resigned because they are gay, 1% of the total figure of discharges," Gallagher, p. 21.

19. On Leonard Matlovich, see Humphrey, pp. 151-155. I take my information on Col. Margarethe Cammermeyer from a clipping from the *Windy City Times*, Sept. 26, 1991, p. 4, "Lesbian Colonel Booted After 27 Years of Service," and on Tracy Thorne, from the *Wisconsin State Journal*, Aug. 9, 1992, pp. F1-2.

20. Schmitt, "Barring Homosexuals."

21. Gallagher, p. 20.

22. At least one of Mary Ann Humphrey's interviewees quit quietly and voluntarily.

23. Robert Jay Lifton, *The Nazi Doctors: Medical Killing and the Psychology of Genocide* (New York: Basic Books, 1986), p. 418. Where they are contextually clear, further references to this title will be given in the text.

24. Signorile, 38.

25. Dyer, p. xiv, quoting from Defense Department policy.

26. "Running a Gantlet of Sexual Assault," *Newsweek*, June 1, 1992, p. 45. This incident was unusual in not being simply laughed off, although its being taken seriously seems to be setting a new precedent.

27. At the University of Wisconsin the Women's Studies Program has offered a course on lesbian culture since the late 1970s (which I taught, off and on, for a decade) and has also co-sponsored an interdisciplinary course on male homosexuality taught by male professors in German history, sociology, and biology. Other courses in Women's Studies, philosophy, sociology, and social work, for example, also address these issues.

28. *The Advocate*, July 30, 1992, pp. 32-33.

29. *Pruitt* v. *Cheney*, 57 E.P.D. (9th Cir. 1991).

30. *Lesbian/Gay Law Notes*, Jan. 1993, p. 1.

31. *Palmore* v. *Sidoti*, 466 U.S. 433 (1984). Quoted in *Lesbian/Gay Law Notes*, Sept. 1991, p. 55.

32. Both reports are contained in Dyer, and a selection from the first report is included as an appendix in Humphrey.

33. Dyer, p. ix.

34. Dyer, p. x.

35. Gerry Studds in his "Forward" to Humphrey, p. viii.

36. Dyer, p. xvi. The term used was "blackmail," which uses "black" as a metaphor for evil.

37. David Olson, "Memo Undermines Military's Ban on Gays," *Windy City Times*, Sept. 19, 1991.

38. Humphrey, p. 182.

39. See, for example, Sarah Lucia Hoagland, *Lesbian Ethics: Toward New Value* (Palo Alto, CA: Institute of Lesbian Studies, 1988), chap. 2, "The Feminine Virtues and Female Agency." An earlier classic is Kate Millett's *Sexual Politics* (Garden City, NY: Doubleday, 1970), chap. 2, pp. 23-58.

40. On women's self-defense, see Andra Medea and Kathleen Thompson, *Against Rape* (New York: Farrar, Straus, Giroux, 1974); Linda Tschirhart Sanford and Ann Fetter, *In Defense of Ourselves: A Rape Prevention Handbook for Women* (New York: Doubleday, 1979); and Denise Cagnon and Gail Groves, eds., *Her Wits about Her: Self-Defense Success Stories by Women* (New York: Harper & Row, 1987). The organization Men Stopping Rape is also committed to many of the goals of the women's self-defense movement and is taking responsibility for educating men about sex and gender oppression. Of interest to pro-feminist men is John Stoltenburg, *Refusing to Be a Man: Essays on Sex and Justice* (New York: Penguin, 1990).

41. On the ancient Amazons whom the Greeks claimed pride in defeating after an exhausting battle at Athens, see Abby Wettan Kleinbaum, *The War Against the*

Amazons (New York: McGraw Hill, 1983), pp. 5-38, and Susan Cavin, *Lesbian Origins* (San Francisco: Ism Press, 1985), chap. 3. Abby Kleinbaum does not contest the verdict of many academic historians that such Amazons never existed. Susan Cavin exposes the shallowness of arguments to this conclusion that have dominated the discussion since about the first century BCE. On "cross-dressers," see Julie Wheelwright, *Amazons and Military Maids: Women Who Dressed as Men in Pursuit of Life, Liberty and Happiness* (London: Pandora, 1989). The author seems uninterested in the likely lesbian identity of many of her subjects, although authors mentioned in her bibliography are. On twentieth-century women in military service, many lesbians, see Lillian Faderman, *Odd Girls and Twilight Lovers: A History of Lesbian Life in Twentieth Century America* (New York: Columbia University Press, 1991), pp. 118-38. Miriam ben-Shalom reports that she fought in the Israeli Army almost a year and a half before she enlisted in the U.S. Army Reserve (Humphrey, p. 187).

42. See, for example, Guy Rothery, *The Amazons in Antiquity and Modern Times* (London: Griffiths, 1910).

43. On gay dignity, see Mohr, *Gays/Justice*, chap. 14, "Dignity vs. Politics: Strategy when Justice Fails," pp. 315-37, and *Gay Ideas*, chap. 1, "The Outing Controversy: Privacy and Dignity in Gay Ethics," pp. 11-48.

44. Virginia Woolf proposed in *Three Guineas* (New York: Harcourt, Brace, & World, 1938) that motherhood be recognized and paid as a state service (p. 110) and, in her wonderful discussion of military uniforms and hierarchies, invited readers to imagine the responses to mothers wearing on their shoulders a tuft of horsehair for each child (pp. 20-21).

45. Public Lecture, State Historical Society Auditorium, Apr. 4, 1991, University of Wisconsin-Madison.

46. On roles of choice in becoming lesbian, see my "Lesbianism and Choice," *Journal of Homosexuality* 23(3) (1992): 39-51.

47. There is a growing body of literature on deaf culture, protesting the stigma of "disabled." See, for example, Carol Padden and Tom Humphries, eds., *Deaf in America: Voices from a Culture* (Cambridge, MA: Harvard University Press, 1988). There are also anthologies of political writings by those who are blind, paraplegic, epileptic, and subject to a variety of other disorders or disabilities. Two such feminist anthologies are Marsha Saxton and Florence Howe, eds., *With Wings: An Anthology of Literature by and about Women with Disabilities* (New York: Feminist Press, 1987), and Susan E. Browne, Debra Connors, and Nanci Stern, eds., *With the Power of Each Breath: A Disabled Women's Anthology* (Pittsburgh: Cleis Press, 1985).

48. On "ablemindism," see Carol Van Kirk, "Sarah Lucia Hoagland's *Lesbian Ethics: Toward New Value* and Ablemindism," *Hypatia* 5 (1990): 147-152.

49. 5 U.S.C. Sec. 3310 (1972). Cited by James Nickel, "Preferential Policies in Hiring and Admissions: A Jurisprudential Approach," *Columbia Law R.* 75 (1975): 534-558; reprinted in Richard A. Wasserstrom, ed., *Today's Moral Problems*, 2nd ed. (New York: Macmillan, 1979), p. 231, n. 5.

A Moral Justification for Gay and Lesbian Civil Rights Legislation

Vincent J. Samar, MPA, JD, PhD

Chicago, Illinois

SUMMARY. This essay explores, in two parts, the problems of justifying civil rights legislation for gays, lesbians, and bisexuals. Part I shows that discrimination against gays and lesbians at least in respect to employment, housing, and public accommodations is an evil unsupported by ethical traditions in utilitarianism, rights theory, and communitarianism. It also shows that two theories, Kantian theory and natural law theory, which do support such discrimination on the claim that homoerotic behavior is universally or objectively immoral only do so because of a failure to make precise the concept of "natural" which underlies those theories. Part II argues that anti-discrimination legislation is both an appropriate and effective means to promote the idea that discrimination against lesbians and gays in respect to most employment, housing, and public accommodations is sufficiently injurious to both individuals and society that it should not be tolerated. The section also explains how such legislation might succeed practically in eliminating discrimination in these areas.

Vincent J. Samar is Adjunct Professor of Philosophy at Loyola University of Chicago and Instructor of Law at Illinois Institute of Technology, Chicago/Kent College of Law. He is a practicing attorney and the author of *The Right to Privacy: Gays, Lesbians and the Constitution* (Temple University Press, 1991). Samar has run for local political office and been a long-time activist in Chicago's gay and lesbian communities. Correspondence may be addressed to the author at Philosophy Department, Loyola University, 820 N. Michigan Ave., Chicago, IL 60611.

[Haworth co-indexing entry note]: "A Moral Justification for Gay and Lesbian Civil Rights Legislation." Samar, Vincent J. Co-published simultaneously in the *Journal of Homosexuality* (The Haworth Press, Inc.) Vol. 27, No. 3/4, 1994, pp. 147-178; and: *Gay Ethics: Controversies in Outing, Civil Rights, and Sexual Science* (ed: Timothy F. Murphy) The Haworth Press, Inc., 1994, pp. 147-178. Multiple copies of this article/chapter may be purchased from The Haworth Document Delivery Center [1-800-3-HAWORTH; 9:00 a.m. - 5:00 p.m. (EST)].

147

The past ten years have seen dozens of municipalities and seven states pass civil rights legislation aimed at protecting gays and lesbians from discrimination in employment, housing, and places of public accommodation such as banks, hotels, mortgage companies, restaurants, retail establishments, and schools.[1] The past fifteen years have seen several federal bills introduced to protect lesbian and gay civil rights, including one currently pending in Congress.[2] President Bill Clinton has openly supported a federal civil rights bill to protect gays and lesbians.[3]

In part, the successes in enacting legislation in this area at the state and local levels and in garnering support at the federal level for such legislation have been due substantially to the willingness of gay men and lesbians to come out of the closet and to join with other ostracized or marginalized groups such as women, the disabled, and racial minorities in order to claim publicly equal rights of citizenship.[4] One consequence of this development has been to draw public attention to lesbian and gay contributions in various occupations that had been thought mistakenly to be exclusively heterosexual.[5] These successes may also have been due to increased public awareness of empirical studies suggesting that homosexuality is neither a chosen nor a learned response.[6] Finally, the American public has been made aware through various news reports of the prevalence of anti-gay and anti-lesbian discrimination.[7] All of this has led some politicians, military officials, the media, and various other groups in the United States to engage in a debate at the federal, state, and local levels about whether discrimination against lesbians and gays is morally justified, and, if not, whether laws should be enacted to prevent this form of discrimination.[8]

Any legislation that seeks to limit the freedom of private citizens to hire, house, or serve whom they want in their business establishments requires a moral justification. This is because a free society is predicated on the belief that individuals can choose to associate with whomever they wish. This does not mean that the existence of any restrictions necessarily renders a society unfree. What it does mean is that such restrictions must complement the freedom that the society holds dear under an applicable moral theory. Moreover, because at least some lesbians and gay men can avoid discrimination only by remaining in the closet, the justification for anti-discrimination legislation protecting this group must go beyond considerations of affiliative or affectional orientation to protect some homosexual behavior. In this sense, anti-discrimination legislation for gays and lesbians will depart from prior justifications involving racial, gender, ethnic, and age *statuses* by having to take into account statements or perceptions related to *conduct.* Consequently, the justification for such legislation does not run the easy mile of "they could not help what they are," for there is always the counter-argument that one does not have to act upon any desire one may have, as well as the counter-argument that society does not have to support any and all such desires.

In this essay, I will take up some of the typical arguments that have been used to try and justify discrimination against gays and lesbians in employment, housing, and public accommodations. I will, then, address them one by one, demonstrating that they are irrational or based on irrelevant information. In doing this, I will show how some of these arguments reflect ethical views under utilitarianism, rights theory, communitarianism, and natural law. Absent from this discussion will be analyses of purely religious texts and traditions since I am presupposing the existence of a society which values personal, ethical, and religious pluralism.[9] Without deciding among the theories to be discussed which is the right foundation for the structure of a democratic society, I will nevertheless show how each theory, on its own merits, would decide whether such discrimination is justified, and how together utilitarianism, rights theory, and communitarianism provide a minimal moral content that supports enacting statutes aimed at preventing discrimination.

GAY/LESBIAN DISCRIMINATION IS UNJUSTIFIED

Typical arguments proffered in favor of discrimination against gays and lesbians include the following:

1. In order to maintain social stability, society needs to exclude from the mainstream those groups that the majority deems to be too far different or "deviant."

2. At least in respect to the private sector, people have the right to hire, house, or serve in their business establishments whomever they want.
3. The overall good of society (as defined by its most dominant values) may be enhanced if discrimination is allowed.
4. Protecting gays and lesbians from discrimination undermines morality.
5. Protecting lesbians and gays encourages role models harmful to children.
6. Protecting gays and lesbians against discrimination opens the door to affirmative action programs for lesbians and gays.
7. The right to the free exercise of religion may conflict with the right to nondiscrimination.

Reasons one through five are theoretical. In particular, reasons one through four are purely normative in that they rely for their justification on one or another ethical theory. Reason one, for example, is usually offered in a utilitarian context whereas reason two presupposes a rights theory. Reason three tends to be asserted from a communitarian point of view, and reason four is most often asserted on the basis of natural law. Depending on how one interprets the claim, reason five is an admixture of ethical theory and causal psychology. By contrast, reasons six and seven are practical in that they question how (if at all) legislation could be structured to avoid a broader consequence than what a minimal justification for nondiscrimination would allow.

Clearly, some discrimination in employment such as favoring persons who are appropriately educated to practice law or medicine over those not so educated is justified while most discrimination based on race, religion, gender, or disability is not justified. (I am assuming here that the control of education—via controlling accreditation, curriculum or admissions policies—is neither designed nor has the effect of keeping power unfairly distributed only in the hands of one group of people.) So the question is: What is it that makes some kinds of discrimination justified but not other kinds? Obviously, context plays a role, as when the religion of the person is relevant to whether he or she becomes a member of a particular clergy. But exactly what role context plays must itself be justified.

Although it may seem like a truism to say that discrimination based on irrational prejudice or matters unrelated to the opportunity sought (called "invidious" discrimination) is unfair, it is nevertheless true. (From hereon in I will use "discrimination" to mean only the invidious sort.) And this truth can be seen to cut across boundaries of utilitarianism, rights theory, and communitarianism once we make clear what we mean by "irrational" and "irrelevant."

By "irrational" I mean that the claim cannot be proved either by reference to physical evidence or by deduction from a noncontroversial premise or at least one that is plausible. Belief that the stars control our activities is irrational because we cannot devise an astrological test that predicts the future with a degree of accuracy higher than would be expected by random chance. The reason for the requirement of a noncontroversial premise is to recognize that the theory adopted should apply in a society that approves of pluralism in personal values and religious beliefs. By "irrelevant" I mean that the evidence chosen does not support the claim at hand. That a person knows how to drive does not prove either that he or she is a good or bad driver. "Irrational" thus attaches to a claim while "irrelevant" goes to the evidence supporting the claim.

At this point, it should be noted that I am treating "rational" and "relevant" not as theory-specific but as ethical-area-specific—that is, what would be rational and relevant within a particular ethical tradition.[10] My rationale for doing this is not that individual theories within a particular area might not provide more specific criteria for what is rational and relevant. Rather, it is that across the areas considered there is enough certitude on (at least) the grosser interpretations of these concepts to suggest their overall application.

In the case of gay and lesbian discrimination in housing, employment, and public accommodations much of the debate turns on irrational claims (such as "homosexuality is an abomination to God")[11] or irrelevant evidence (such as gay sex is inferior because it cannot produce children).[12] The few allegedly rational and potentially relevant claims made (such as the charge that gay people are more inclined to molest children and spread disease) are easily refuted by available evidence.[13]

Applying the concepts of rationality and relevancy to the three ethical theories referred to above, we discover the grounds upon which lesbian and gay discrimination in employment, housing, and public accommodations is unjustified. We also begin to unpack some of the arguments that are often used against claims that the state has an obligation to avoid such discrimination. The affirmative argument for a state obligation to end discrimination in this area will be taken up in the next section.

From a utilitarian standpoint, discrimination would be justified if it serves to maximize utility (i.e., if it serves to aggregate utility by affording the greatest happiness to the greatest number).[14] Since utilitarianism specifies no preordained 'good' to be achieved, the greatest happiness principle is satisfied when, in light of the various competing goods that the members of society take to be important, there is more satisfaction to be obtained in meeting some particular social good (hopefully, in light of thought and reflection) than there is dissatisfaction from the loss of other competing goods. However, as will be argued, any form of discrimination is not to be tolerated. If the discrimination is *irrational* or *irrelevant*, then allowing the discrimination may create more unhappiness and less utility than would otherwise be the case. This is especially true where what is at stake is of central importance to the individual as is where one lives or how one earns a living.[15] Denying lesbians and gays access to housing, jobs, and places of public accommodation based on irrational prejudice or irrelevant evidence needlessly creates unhappiness for the persons whose desires are frustrated, and loss of benefits to the society from its gay and lesbian members.

First, it is economically inefficient for the society to limit anyone from buying property or participating in those professions to which they are most suited. Regarding this latter point, there may also be a loss of creativity from discriminatory barriers.

Second, being free of the fear that one might be discriminated against because they are gay encourages openness, which itself is positively beneficial both to the individual and to the society. It is positively beneficial to the individual when the person can feel good about him- or herself because he or she no longer has to suppress that central element of personal identity which is the basis for decisions about whom one might love, be with, or share a life with.[16] (In this same vein, coming out to parents and friends ensures that the love one feels—or, unfortunately, sometimes does not feel–from them is honest and not based on an artificial image of the self.)[17] It is positively beneficial to the society when large numbers of its members begin to accept gays and lesbians because the coming out decision has shortened the social and political distance that previously separated lesbians and gays from the rest of society.[18] Shortening the social and political distance may mean more attention to the battle over AIDS funding and related sex-education, which until recently has had a disproportionate impact on the gay male community.[19] It may also mean more attention to issues like gay-bashings.[20] No longer can we speak of "those people over there," for now we must also include "these people over here." This latter point is not only beneficial to the individual's need to overcome feelings of isolation but to society's interest in overcoming prejudicial and irrational fear. For the more lesbian and gay people come out in many different walks of life, the more will stereotypes be broken down and replaced with a more realistic view about the actual makeup of society. All of these potential gains are undermined, however, so long as discrimination may result in losing one's home, career, or other important public accommodations.

Still, it might be argued that adopting a policy of discrimination against gays and lesbians would provide the society with a needed scapegoat, especially at times of trouble. That is because ostracizing openly gay or lesbian persons is easier than ramming contrived accusations through a court. Moreover, the existence of such a policy would not be likely to cause non-gay members of society to become concerned that the policy might eventually be applied to them.

The problem with this attempt at justifying anti-gay/anti-lesbian discrimination is the level of abstraction at which the argument is offered. Discrimination against lesbians and gays is either irrational or irrelevant when there is no hard evidence that such persons *as a class* actually cause physical or mental harm to others. Consequently, a third utilitarian reason for not allowing such discrimination is that such discrimination may breed anxiety in society generally since no one will ever be certain that a similar prejudice will not evolve against them. That is to say, no one will ever be certain that they will not be made part of some class judged worthy of discrimination. Even if the presence of gays and lesbians in the minds of people is currently underestimated, given the efforts by many activists to obtain public forums on questions of rights, there is no reason to assume that this state of affairs will continue. Thus, if not now, certainly in the future, whenever one hears of someone being discriminated against, he or she will not know whether the discrimination was justified (in the sense that it was based on more than a *mere* perception of harm) or not. Consequently, it is difficult to detect any social utility in discriminating against gays and lesbians in employment, housing, and public accommodations, when such a practice encourages an atmosphere of paranoia and irrationality harmful to society as a whole.

It might also be argued that if Western society has allowed gay/lesbian discrimination for hundreds of years, why should it change now? This argument, however, ignores the fact that benefits are additive and that both society and the individual benefit more when the potential of each person is tapped to the maximum extent.[21] For example, racial separation was for a long time (and to a lesser but more insidious extent still is) practiced in the schools of this country.[22] One of the drawbacks of racial separation in the school is that the potential of most African-American youth is stifled by a poorer quality of education and lack of self-esteem vis-à-vis the broader society.[23] A similar response could be made to the military's policy of discharging openly gay and lesbian persons from the services in order to ensure the morale of the troops.[24] Surely, educating the troops about what homosexuality is, who gay people are, and what types of interpersonal conduct are appropriate while on duty could go a long way toward resolving morale problems (not only in respect to gays and lesbians but also indirectly in respect to military women) without having to engage in this form of discrimination. This is, indeed, what happened when the armed services were ordered racially integrated.[25]

Under rights theory, invidious discrimination is never justified because it undermines individual autonomy. However, not all cases of discrimination need be invidious. Consequently, cases in which people appear to be justified in discriminating against gays and lesbians are not really cases of invidious discrimination because the affectional orientation is relevant. An example would be a heterosexual male who chooses to marry a heterosexual female. Where rights theory becomes problematic is where there are two or more rights in conflict. For example, how should one resolve the conflict between a claim to manage one's business or housing as one pleases and the right not to be discriminated against? Here, the right to freedom should be tolerated unless autonomy generally (in the sense of each person to decide for him- or herself what is in his or her own interest) is better served by not allowing it than by allowing it.[26] This is because protecting liberty protects autonomy generally. More specifically, the right of freedom to do with one's business or housing as one chooses ought to win out over the right not to be discriminated against if the result would better promote overall individual autonomy for the society generally than not allowing it.[27] On the other hand, if allowing the right to freedom would inhibit or restrict more autonomy generally than not allowing it, then the right to freedom is not justified. Where the latter is true, the maximum allowance of interference with liberty is the minimum necessary to protect autonomy generally.[28] This appeal to maximal autonomy does not undercut any claim to a deontological basis for the right at stake. For the question here (unlike for the utilitarian) is not the good to be achieved, but affirmation of the underlying principle (in this case autonomy) that justifies the right in the first place. Thus, where the right to freedom is based in individual autonomy, a principle of equality (that seeks to further the promotion of autonomy generally) can limit exercise of that right.

Here it is important to distinguish two different extremes of rights theory: classical liberalism (or libertarianism) and egalitarian liberalism. Under the classical liberal or libertarian view, an individual's freedom to do what he or she wants with his or her own property (whether in their persons as to whom to associate with or other objects) is the most important value. The only limitation is that one cannot use his or her freedom so as to deprive another of a similar freedom. Consequently, under a libertarian rights theory, there is never a justification for limiting one individual's freedom to use his or her property merely for the sake of advancing the welfare of another. In contrast, the egalitarian liberal values equality above freedom. Consequently, the egalitarian liberal would support a scheme of civil liberties (as well as social and economic rights) that affords all persons the same opportunities. This difference between the two views can be seen in the different ways they would approach the question of discrimination. Because the libertarian wants to maximize individual freedom, the right not to be discriminated against (even if it is based on irrational or irrelevant criteria) is overridden in the private sector although not in the public sector. In contrast, for the egalitarian liberal, the right not to be discriminated against, when based on irrational and irrelevant criteria, always undercuts human dignity and respect for persons and, therefore, is not overridden by the right to freedom.

Both libertarians and egalitarian liberals alike would recognize that irrational discrimination or discrimination based on irrelevant evidence against openly gay or lesbian persons restricts the autonomy of this group by limiting its opportunities to compete for the essential goods of society on the same basis as society offers to its other members.[29] Such denial has two basic components. On the objective level, it denies lesbian and gay individuals the freedom to be openly gay and still participate in receiving the same benefits afforded other members of society. Such exclusion also has the effect of skewing occupational patterns of gay men who are unable or unwilling to hide their sexual orientation toward certain professions which are stereotypically viewed to have less immediate, direct impact on the important questions of life or the important value aspect of property and are often labeled "unmanly."[30] At the subjective level, irrational discrimination or discrimination based on irrelevant information denies some gay and lesbian individuals a means to express publicly their uniqueness in a way that is self-fulfilling and likely to promote their own happiness, while not threatening the objective interests of any other person. Furthermore, failing to allow open expression can lead to development of self-doubt, lost self-esteem, and self-hatred.[31]

Libertarians and more egalitarian liberals disagree over what should be done to correct such prejudice. Libertarians would say that laws cannot be used to restrict the use of private property or employment practices in the private sector whereas egalitarian theorists would allow the law to prevent discrimination (based on irrational or irrelevant views about sexual orientation). This seeming impasse between libertarians and egalitarian liberals should not lead one to the conclusion that rights theory can develop no firm position on this topic. If one separates out liberty (as a system of rights defining equal citizenship) from the worth of liberty (as the capacity to advance one's ends within a system of equal rights),[32] then one must endeavor to resolve the problem in terms of more basic principles–principles underlying both libertarian and egalitarian views–which rational persons would want guaranteed as a minimal condition for the advancement of the responsible pursuit of their ends.

Here two theories serve as possible bases for a solution. The intuitionist approach of John Rawls, for example, asks what persons would choose if they were in a position of not knowing anything about themselves but only in a position of knowing general economic and psychological facts about human beings.[33] Clearly, they would choose not to allow arbitrary discrimination, for they would be afraid of discovering that they were themselves the objects of discrimination once the veil of personal ignorance was lifted from them. A rationalist approach, as developed, for example, by Alan Gewirth, argues that every rational agent (a person who can act voluntarily for his or her own purposes) must logically accept on pain of contradiction that every other agent has the same rights as oneself to freedom and well-being because these are the proximate necessary conditions of human agency.[34] Here, arbitrary prejudice is avoided because such prejudice assumes that certain features (not in the definition of agency) are relevant when all that is at stake for the establishment of moral rights is that one be a moral agent. Thus, both of these theories would condemn arbitrary discrimination especially where individual well-being is threatened. However, both of these theories are controversial because they raise deep philosophical questions about the nature of moral-theory justification.[35] Pending an ultimate resolution of this controversy, one might tentatively (because it starts from a value-laden assumption) adopt the following approach toward solving the problem of discrimination.

It would seem that our democratic society generally accepts the idea that all persons should have the opportunity to discover, amidst numerous competing interests and compatible with a like freedom for all, what is in their own interests. If this is true, then gay and lesbian persons should have the same rights to discover what is in their interests as every other person at least where there is no rational and relevant reason for their being denied these rights. But clearly lesbians and gays are deterred from discovering who they are by the possibility of loss of job, housing, and other important public accommodations. If society believes that people ought to be allowed to discover what is in their own interests, then it must grant to gays and lesbians the level of autonomy (in the sense of freedom from arbitrary discrimination) that would allow this discovery to occur.

From a communitarian position, discrimination should be allowed only when it serves the interests of society treated as an organic whole. Here the individual is seen as constituted by society rather than as constituting society.[36] Discrimination is not allowed where denying someone full citizenship will produce, on balance, more of a detriment to society (perhaps in the form of a lost resource) than not. Thus, the question of whether one can discriminate from a communitarian standpoint (even as to essential elements of well-being) cannot be answered independent of a conception about the overall good of the society at stake.[37] In this sense, a communitarian view need be neither liberal nor conservative. Modern communitarians often differ from their classical forerunners (philosophers like Plato, Rousseau, and Marx) in that the "good" to be obtained is not something eternal or outside the society but is, rather, a constitutive element of the society in question. This does not mean that communitarians ignore at a fundamental level the influence of who holds power. Rather, they see the actions of those who hold power as often reflecting the society's deeper values. For example, certain forms of discrimination that may be allowed in a society of fundamentalist Christians may not be allowed in a more pluralistic society, especially one which values tolerance of differing personal moral and religious points of view.[38] The only exception to the latter would be discrimination necessary to support the very existence of the society, such as providing laws against murder, theft, and insurrection. On the other hand, why should anyone need to start from so narrow a premise in a society that avows personal religious and moral freedom? Clearly in a pluralistic society one should hope to avoid supporting such discriminatory claims.

Discrimination against gays and lesbians in employment, housing, and public accommodations can create an artificial image of a homogeneous society that is not true to life, thereby sowing the seeds of discontent which could in the long run undermine social stability. (An excellent example of this problem is Patrick Buchanan's homophobic denunciation at the 1992 Republican National Convention of "the" gay and lesbian "lifestyle" as inimical to traditional American "family values." That speech played a role in galvanizing many citizens to vote Democratic.) This is especially true if gay/lesbian discrimination becomes a testing ground (because of the unpopularity of the group) for a broader-based social/political agenda for society at large. Such a domino theory of moral views exhibits itself when justifications for discriminating against lesbians and gays are based on the view that these groups fail to engage in procreative sex (a view which in addition to its questionable claim to moral authority is not always even factual). From here, it is only a short step to a more generalized criticism of the rights of women to choose abortion or even to enter into nontraditional professions. Additionally, allowing this discrimination against gays and lesbians ignores the fact that at least part of this group's contribution to a pluralistic society might lie in setting examples for how persons of different sexual orientations (much like persons of different genders, races, and ethnic groups) can live and work together. At a more sophisticated level, the removal of sanctions against the acknowledgement and expression of affectionate emotional responses would contribute significantly toward "a repudiation of stereotypical gender roles" which feminists, and more recently proponents of male liberation, have advocated.[39]

Looking at the issue from an approach framed by natural law theory, discrimination is justified when it promotes the inherent (or divine) purpose of nature as discovered from nature's laws. According to Aquinas, for example, the inherent purpose of nature is discovered from the order of natural inclinations.[40] It is in this sense that natural law theory makes a claim to moral objectivity. Specifically, three inclinations provide, in the order stated, the basis for evaluating the morality of human acts. First, since everything in nature has substance (i.e., continues to exist over time), survival is the first and foremost tenet. Hence, we have laws against violence and murder, and a claim from some for laws prohibiting abortion.

Next, because human beings share with all other animals a desire to procreate and rear offspring, procreation becomes a second important inclination. Herein lies natural law's traditional prohibition against all forms of sexual expression/activity (especially homosexuality) which are not procreative. Finally, human beings have as part of their unique nature the desire to seek knowledge of God. This is natural law's claimed moral basis for freedom of worship.

Natural law theory, however, does not suffice to show that the homosexuality of a person is immoral per se. This is because the kinds of things that should count as relevant arguments in natural law theory are themselves problematic. First, acceptance of a divinely-ordered plan of nature is a controversial claim as indicated by the fact that modern science may proceed without any assumption about the teleological design of its objects of study. Second, what constitutes the 'natural' in natural law is not precise (at least) under Aquinas's formulation. For example, why is it natural to have heterosexual intercourse during an infertile period while it is unnatural to have intercourse using a contraceptive. Why is heterosexuality more natural than homosexuality? Is 'natural' just a substitute for 'statistically average,' in which case the question might be why one would want to be statistically average? Is natural supposed to mean, not found in nature other than in humans? If so, then it must be recognized that many of the actions that natural law is supposed to prohibit–such as homosexuality–are found in nature.[41] It is also unclear why the concept of the natural (when employed in moral theory) should embody any broader conception of nature than what is unique to human beings. Or is natural supposed to mean morally right, in which case, the concept of the natural begs the question of what is morally right?[42]

A similar criticism applies against Kant's view of homosexuality. Kant argued, from the second version of the categorical imperative ("Act so that you treat humanity, whether in your own person or that of another, always as an end and never as a means only"),[43] that homosexuality was universally wrong because it violates the end of humanity in respect of sexuality which is to preserve the species without debasing the person.[44] Kant thought that the homosexual self is degraded below the level of animals and, thus, degraded in itself. No violation of the second version of the categorical imperative occurs, however, once one drops the anti-natural thesis. The flaw in Kant's approach can be seen in the fact that gay and lesbian people fall in love with partners and, under any meaningful sense of that term, treat those persons as ends and not simply as means.[45]

Obviously, not every moral theory will succumb to the same sorts of criticism. Nevertheless, regardless of the theory one chooses, discrimination against lesbians and gays in housing, employment, and public accommodations, because it is usually based on either irrational or irrelevant grounds or on a loose use of concepts, causes serious suffering to the individuals involved and a detriment to the society that loses the benefits of the full and unfettered contributions of its lesbian and gay members. This, then, leads us to the minimal moral content, if morality (in the broad sense of the combined three traditions discussed above) is to be satisfied, that supports eradicating gay and lesbian prejudice. That content derives from a conjunction of values found in the three ethical traditions of utilitarianism, rights theory, and communitarianism. Conjunction is sought here in order to guarantee a level of agreement among the three ethical traditions on arbitrary discrimination. Thus, any form of discrimination which simultaneously restricts social utility, inhibits individual autonomy, and does not foster cooperative arrangements within a pluralistic society is morally unjustified and must be avoided. Since gay and lesbian discrimination most often involves these evils, it morally must not be allowed.

Finally, we take up an objection that seems more related to a misunderstanding of a psychological cause than the inappropriateness of a particular ethical theory. Here it might be objected that (at least) in respect to teaching in schools and supervising children at day-care centers, discrimination against gays and lesbians is necessary to offset a child's desire to take adults as role models.[46] However, this objection is too loose. If it means that children exposed to an openly gay and lesbian teacher or guidance counselor would likely adopt that person's sexual orientation, it is factually false. Much evidence points away from this means of how sexual orientation is acquired and toward either a biological or early developmental model which is not based in learning theory, let alone chance encounters with teachers of whatever sexual orientation.[47] If it means that a person who is on the borderline between being gay or straight might be encouraged to be gay, it conflates choice with discovery and ignores the fact that most of the people whom a child will have for role models will be straight.[48] If the objection means that a child should not be exposed to an "immoral lifestyle," then it once again begs the question. Obviously, all of these interpretations are too facile to provide even a psychological reason for believing that interaction with gays and lesbians is harmful to children.[49] More generally, what this objection shows is that irrationally-based prejudice against gays and lesbians is deeply ingrained in some of society's most fundamental biases.

A JUSTIFICATION FOR CIVIL RIGHTS LEGISLATION

Thus far, I have argued that discrimination against persons who are gay or lesbian (or, perhaps more to the point, 'who are perceived to be gay, lesbian, or bisexual') in employment, housing, and public accommodations is not ethically justified. But how far should society go to eliminate this kind of discrimination? Would society, for example, be justified in passing statutes that would make sexual orientation discrimination in these areas illegal, analogous to the 1964 Federal Civil Rights Act that made discrimination based on race, creed, and national origin illegal?[50] (Incidentally, such statutes would also have the effect of making discrimination against heterosexuals—perhaps by a disgruntled gay person—illegal in the same way they sanctioned discrimination against gays and lesbians.) How, moreover, would such statutes be enforced? How would one prove discrimination? Would there not have to be the defense "I did not act based on the fact that he/she was gay?" Clearly, if such statutes are to be useful, answers to all of these questions are necessary. Such answers bear, moreover, on the propriety of passing such legislation in the first place. For if a statute cannot be enforced or enforced fairly, then to enact it into law may undercut the value of law as a protection against social harm. Additionally, if such a statute could be enforced too easily (whenever the claimant turned out to be gay) without adequate allowance for the possibility of a defense (the employer may not in fact have acted against an employee on the basis of sexual orientation), then it could place the legal system in the position of unduly supporting the interests of one group over another. Obviously, we are led to question whether law is the best vehicle to avoid discrimination, even if gay/lesbian discrimination is wrong.

The law *is* indeed the best vehicle to protect the rights of gay, lesbian, and bisexual individuals for at least one reason. Law has the ability to help form social attitudes. That is, if one lives in a society where the belief is strong that what the law requires (at least in respect to interpersonal conduct) is what morality requires, then the fact that gay/lesbian discrimination is illegal is one reason to think that the probabilities favor it being immoral as well.[51] Moreover, the benefit of having such laws to attack the problem of social injustice that attends sexual orientation discrimination (as previously discussed) well offsets the (surmountable) enforcement problems just mentioned.

Law plays the role (in a society where the institutions of government are thought to operate with a modicum of justice) of setting the norms for social behavior that in the long run operate to correct social inequities by at least eliminating the most egregious forms of such inequities from institutions. Much of the derogatory language that used to be associated with racial minorities has fallen out of fashion because the varied institutions of society, including the law, and possibly because of it, have deemed such usage to be morally and sometimes legally unacceptable.[52] This does not mean, of course, that such discrimination does not occur under a more covert form of language and acts.[53] It does mean, however, that there is something wrong with the overt practice of discriminatory behavior. So law treats the evil of discrimination by driving it out of "nice" places where people can feel free to discriminate overtly.

What should a law look like that would protect against anti-gay, anti-lesbian discrimination? Because this essay has not sought a foundation for anti-gay, anti-lesbian discrimination in any particular ethical tradition but has considered several competing traditions, it can at most state the minimal moral content that such anti-discrimination laws must meet.

First, since much of the discrimination that occurs in this area is the result of perceptions rather than actual information about persons' sexual orientation, the law must prohibit discrimination against persons whose real *or perceived* affectional desire is hetero-sexual, homosexual, or bisexual.[54]

Second, such a law should apply to the private as well as the public sector since both areas have the same potential for affecting individual and social well-being.

Third, the best form for such a law would be a statute setting a blanket prohibition against discrimination in employment, housing, and public accommodations. Since the private sector is being included (there being no constitutional protections and only limited tort protections in this sector), a statute is necessary. The areas of employment, housing, and public accommodations are the ones most likely to affect persons' decisions to come out and to be free in the affectional expression of their sexual orientation.

Fourth, because many businesses operate in interstate commerce, there is a need for uniformity of enforcement across state lines. Thus, federal legislation is needed along with concurrent state and local protections. The rationale for the latter is first to set politically obtainable examples for how such legislation might work in order to advance a political climate where federal legislation is possible, and second to remove the full burden of enforcement from one level of government. This latter point also provides a check that discrimination will not be covertly allowed because any particular political view dominates one level of government at a given time.

Fifth, such a statute should provide for both criminal and civil penalties against individuals or companies. The rationale for providing criminal penalties of high fines (especially against companies) and possible imprisonment (against individuals) is to create a strong deterrent to persons engaging in harmful discriminatory acts. Moreover, stating society's strong disapproval for this form of discrimination by the use of criminal sanctions helps undermine the prejudice that gives rise to these acts. The rationale for allowing civil remedies is, first, that most cases of discrimination (especially covert discrimination) will probably not be provable beyond a reasonable doubt even though there may be a preponderance of evidence suggesting the discrimination and, second, to redress more directly the economic (as in lost wages) and emotional harms caused the victims of discrimination by a direct form of compensation. Thus it is sufficient in terms of meeting minimal moral content that legislation be passed prohibiting sexual orientation discrimination in employment, housing, and public accommodations in both the public and private sectors and placing the burden of proof on those who would seek to bring a charge of discrimination. However, the fact that such legislation might meet these minimal moral requirements should not be taken to prevent agencies of the government from imposing higher standards not specifically required by statute in contexts where benefits are being distributed (e.g., awarding of contracts or special incentives to firms practicing affirmative action, instituting educational programs aimed at dispelling homophobia, etc.). This follows from the duty government has to treat all persons without regard to irrational or irrelevant prejudice under all three moral traditions.

For example, to offset racial discrimination, federally insured institutions that take mortgage applications (like banks, savings and loans, and some other institutions) are required by the Treasury Department to ask the race of the applicant.[55] If the applicant refuses to answer, then the interviewer is supposed to put down what he or she believes the race to be and the reasons why.[56] By analogy, should an applicant for a mortgage loan be asked his or her sexual orientation? If the applicant refuses to answer, should the interviewer put down what he or she believes to be the sexual orientation? Surely it is reasonable to allow such a question to be on the application form provided that it is optional (like the race question) in order to discourage lenders from discriminating and to create a climate that encourages gay people to come out of the closet.

The question of whether interviewers should be required to put down what they believe to be the sexual orientation of the applicant is more problematic. This is because stereotyping according to "traits" (including racial traits) is both inaccurate and itself contributes to the social construction of discrimination. Indeed, the very selection of traits may carry with it the derogatory attitudes that create a climate of fear and oppression that is the cause of the oppression in the first place. In the case of sexual orientation, there is no certain means by which to link particular traits with specific affectional desire, let alone specific behavior. On the other hand, certain actions–such as two men applying for a loan on a one-bedroom condominium that they plan to hold as their primary residence–do suggest sexual orientation. The same may be said of a man and a woman. Consequently, while stereotyping should not generally be encouraged, one can easily imagine situations in which an interviewer could be asked to choose from a relatively limited set of statistically reliable options as a basis for identifying the applicant's sexual orientation. Given that this requirement would ensure the availability of mortgage loans to gay and lesbian persons without depriving anyone else of such loans, it is not morally objectionable.

Of course, nothing here is meant to suggest that stereotypical statements made about gay people should not play a role in proving discrimination elsewhere. In that instance, perception may be part of the discrimination itself; in the regulation area, however, reliance on perception is more difficult because one must avoid creating the very prejudice one is trying to eliminate.

Other federal departments and agencies may, of course, maintain compliance regulations in excess of basic protections in order to insure a true change in attitudes toward equality. For example, a contractor who receives a financial award from the Department of Transportation to perform some community service might be required to set aside twenty-five percent of its subcontracts for placement with minority-owned businesses and five percent with businesses owned by women.[57] What percentage of contract placements should be reserved for gay-, lesbian-, or bisexual-owned businesses is unclear. One approach would be to look at the total number of such businesses in the area to be served by the contractor and to base the percentage on that figure. This might have the effect of encouraging more gays and lesbians to come out of the closet in order to develop and be employed by such businesses.

Along a related line, the Internal Revenue Service requires any non-public educational institution (such as private colleges, universities, secondary and primary schools, and technical instruction schools) with a tax-exempt status to include in its student-recruitment advertisements, at least once a year, a non-discrimination statement listing the categories of race, color, creed, and national origin in a space of no less than three column inches in newspapers that are reasonably likely to be read by all racial segments of the community and in a section of the newspapers likely to be read by prospective students and their families.[58] Presumably, if anti-gay, anti-lesbian discrimination legislation were passed, then the IRS would probably amend its requirement to include "sexual orientation" among the other categories. This would be a relatively minor alteration to an already existing procedure.

It should be noted that absent from this analysis is an argument for affirmative action programs to *require* (independent of a receipt of a governmental benefit) employers and landlords to hire or rent apartments to proportionate numbers of gays and lesbians as exist in society. This is because the analysis is based only on minimal moral requirements that such antidiscrimination legislation must meet. Were discrimination to continue, however, then, as more and more gays and lesbians come out of the closet, such programs might become necessary.

The administration of mandatory affirmative action programs is likely to be costly both for the parties being regulated and the society which must do the regulation. Additionally, while particular private sector firms might find government incentives for affirmative action enticing, the possibility of a general consensus developing as to how much affirmative action is necessary to offset current discrimination is doubtful.[59] Consequently, the least intrusive solution for the private sector would be immediate anti-discrimination legislation so that the need for a more expansive moral argument favoring affirmative action policies would not have to be countenanced.

Finally, nothing in the kind of statute proposed here is meant to impose an unconstitutional burden on the free exercise of religion as protected by the first amendment. This is because, again, we are dealing only with minimal moral requirements, and certainly the first amendment is itself supported on moral grounds. Indeed, a rationale for protecting the free exercise of religion is that individual autonomy and social stability are best served where government does not step into matters so personally affecting individual conscience as is centrally displayed by religious institutions. A similar rationale for allowing in some instances infringement on religious exercise is that such measures are necessary as the *only* means available by which individual autonomy or social stability can be protected. Thus the first amendment has been interpreted to permit the government to regulate religious exercise in certain compelling circumstances.[60] Where such a compelling interest is shown, the maximum amount of intrusion on religious freedom is the minimum necessary to satisfy the state's interests. Certainly, from all that has been said above, the eradication of sexual orientation discrimination is a compelling interest of the state. So one must ask, what can the statute prescribe with respect to limiting religious freedom? Clearly, the statute cannot force an endorsement by a religious institution contrary to its values. But, insofar as the statute is applied to institutions like schools, hospitals, and universities that have mixed sectarian and religious purposes, it can require equal distribution of the facilities and services that would normally accompany a purely sectarian purpose.[61]

As to the matter of enforcement, we need to know whether a particular act was motivated by a discriminatory *intent* or not. Since, unlike being African-American, in which case racial statistics (such as who holds the better-paying jobs in a company) can be fairly conclusive evidence of discrimination, gay people who remain in the closet are not as readily identifiable as to their sexual orientation. In this sense, anti-gay/anti-lesbian discrimination is more analogous to discrimination based on religion than to racial or sex discrimination.[62] So the question arises: To what evidence can a judge or jury turn where the alleged discrimination is at least not overt? Usually, the employer will not say, for example, "We don't hire gays." The answer lies in the very feature that identifies one's sexual orientation–namely, the behavior that manifests the affectional desire to be with another person of the same sex rather than someone of the opposite sex. Discrimination based on affectional desire may manifest itself overtly in a company's policy against hiring or renting an apartment to gays or lesbians, or covertly in language, as when an interviewer asks, "Are you married or dating?" Overt discrimination arises in a housing context where the lease or condominium regulations provide a rule against renting an apartment to two persons of the same sex or to two persons not legally married, or where a mortgage company fails to approve a loan for the purchase of a single family dwelling by two or more persons because they are not related by blood or marriage. In the employment context, fear of discrimination can arise where a job application form asks the name of a person to contact in case of an emergency or the name of a beneficiary for the company's life insurance policy. It can also arise when one has to decide how to respond to a company invitation to a holiday party for employees and their spouses, or if one has to fear being seen walking down the street holding hands with another person of the same sex because the town in which they live is relatively small and everyone is well known. In the context of public accommodations, schools, restaurants, camp sites, and short-term housing establishments may have a policy not to serve perceived lesbian or gay persons or to allow persons of the same sex to share a bedroom. In some of these situations, the decision to discriminate may be made on very subtle criteria (a person's looks, style of dress) that are also not very precise. Even so, the object of the discrimination is the individual's freedom to express the same affectional behavior to another of the same sex that is expressed between opposite-sex couples and this behavior is very precise. Consequently, discovering *discriminatory* limits on the freedom to practice affectional behavior should be the key to discovering anti-gay and anti-lesbian discrimination.[63] Obviously, of course, not all forms of affectional behavior need be tolerated provided that the differences do not separate out gays and lesbians from heterosexual couples.

How might such discrimination be proved? In anti-gay discrimination cases, the means for making evidentiary determinations are very similar to the means currently employed in race, sex, and age discrimination cases except that the identifying criterion is a behavior and not just a trait.[64] For example, at the overt level, if the employer has a company manual, does it declare there is no discrimination based on sexual orientation or marital status? If there is a social function for employees and spouses, has the employer indicated that same-sex couples are invited? In companies in which there are a number of known gay employees and based on their years of employment, education, and training, do their numbers in the different ranks match what would be statistically expected if discrimination were not occurring? Has there been harassment on the job either by fellow employees of which management is aware but does nothing about, or is there harassment by management itself?

In preparing a defense, behavioral considerations should also play a key role. Does the employer regularly encourage openly gay and lesbian employees to play active roles in the social life of the company? If a company has a large number of openly lesbian and gay employees, are they in all ranks of management or are they statistically gathered at the bottom? Is disparaging and harassing language not only disapproved of but, when directed at specific employees, seriously sanctioned? If these conditions are met, then the employer should have a good defense against unjustified charges of sexual orientation discrimination.

At this point it might be questioned: Why should an employer have any affirmative duty to create an open environment for gays and lesbians? Why is it not sufficient that the employer simply not discriminate? The problem is in knowing whether discrimination has occurred. Since behavior is the determining factor and gay, lesbian, and bisexual behavior can be kept in a closet, there are few means to weed out this form of discrimination in any comprehensive way, other than by requiring positive efforts by an employer to create an open environment for analogous manifestations of such behavior that would be permitted to heterosexuals. Of course, there are limits to just how far an employer should have to go in order to create an open environment. Does an employer, for example, have to advertise jobs in a gay newspaper just because they are advertised in a newspaper of general circulation? Is there an educational issue here: employers learning openness to persons of different sexual orientation and gays and lesbians learning to trust certain employers not to discriminate if they come out of the closet? Is it sufficient that wherever the employer states its policy of nondiscrimination, it include among the several categories "sexual orientation?" The answer cannot be stated with precision because the discrimination alleged can be very insidious. What can be stated is that the complaining party should have the burden to prove the discrimination.

In civil cases, the claimant should bear the burden to prove the discrimination by a preponderance of the evidence because it is the claimant who asserts that the employer has not met the law's requirement not to engage in sexual orientation discrimination. Once this element is met, we would say that the claimant has established a *prima facie* case of discrimination. Next, the employer who claims not to have discriminated would respond in a way that would persuade a court that sexual orientation discrimination did not transpire. This is the second element of the discrimination test. At this point, what and how much evidence would be needed depends on what evidence was initially offered to prove discrimination and the context in which the discrimination was alleged to occur. Was the claimant fired after it became known that he or she was gay or lesbian? Was the claimant passed over for a promotion? Was the work environment hostile and harassing and was anything done to try to create a more peaceful employment situation? Since the questions here concern the evidence proffered, there is simply no absolute standard against which they can be judged independent of context. A similar approach applies in a criminal case except that the standard of proof is beyond a reasonable doubt and the complaining party is the state.

Similarly, in the case of housing or public accommodations, a *prima facie* case is established if there is a provision in a lease or condominium rules prohibiting same-sex households or a policy of a hotel or motel against providing a room to two persons of the same sex when they would do so for opposite-sex couples. It is also established by a school policy prohibiting admittance of gay students and by policies like that of the Boy Scouts of America prohibiting gay persons from becoming scouts. (The latter, however, may be protected on first amendment grounds if no state action or government money is involved.) But here too, such discrimination need not be so overt, and a *prima facie* case might be established if an informal screening process accomplishes the same end. In either case, the burden would shift to the landlord or owner or manager of the public accommodation to prove by a preponderance of the evidence that discrimination was not the driving element. In the case of rental housing at least where a large rental complex is concerned, a statistically significant number of rentals to same-sex couples would be some evidence to offset a claim of discrimination. In the case of mortgage or other lending companies, showing that an individual's financial status provides the reason for failing to grant the loan should help in overcoming a claim of discrimination. For some public accommodations like schools, hotels, and restaurants, the frequency and variety of persons accommodated should similarly refute an unjustified charge of discrimination. Obviously, each case will differ and evidentiary issues are acute. Nevertheless, resolving these issues is certainly not impracticable. And given the serious harm to individuals and society that discrimination creates, the benefits would seem to be well worth the effort.

CONCLUSIONS

This essay has argued that discrimination against gays, lesbians, and bisexuals in employment, housing, and public accommodations is not justified from utilitarian, rights theory, or communitarian points of view. It has also shown that traditional approaches of natural law theory and Kantian ethics to the topic are wrongheaded. Finally, it has demonstrated why legislation is an appropriate means for resolving the problem of such discrimination and has painted a general picture of what such legislation should look like and how it might be enforced. The essay has been thus attentive both to the theoretical issues and to the practical difficulties that are likely to attend legislation of this kind. In so doing, the essay has shown that a primary focus for such legislation must be the protection of affectional behavior on the same basis as is normally afforded to heterosexual persons. If this essay has succeeded in its fundamental goal, it demonstrates that legal protections for gays, lesbians, and bisexual persons are both morally obligatory and practically enforceable.

AUTHOR NOTE

Few people truly earn the appellation "friend." I dedicate this article to David, my friend.

Special thanks to Timothy Murphy, Bruce Barton, Ted Grippo, and Howard Kaplan for their editorial suggestions on an earlier draft of this article.

NOTES

1. Given that the next generation of gay and lesbian civil rights activists will aim their efforts primarily at the federal and state levels, it is worth noting that anti-discrimination laws covering (at least some) housing, employment, and public accommodations have already been passed in California, Connecticut, Hawaii, Massachusetts, New Jersey, Vermont, and Wisconsin.

2. Civil Rights Amendment Act of 1991, S. 574, 102 Cong., 1st Sess. (1991).

3. Bettina Boxall, "Gays Alter Dynamics of Politics; Homosexuals Have Become More Visible on the Campaign Trail–as Players and as Targets. From the Presidential Race to Local Contests, Views on Gay Rights Contrast Sharply," *Los Angeles Times*, Sept. 15, 1992, p. A1.

4. Recent referenda on ballots in Oregon and Colorado have sought to amend their state constitutions to allow anti-gay discrimination. The Oregon measure, which many think would have required schools to teach that homosexuality was a perversion and unnatural, went down to defeat; but the Colorado measure, which prohibited making gay persons a protected class, was passed. The latter (if not held unconstitutional) nullifies local civil rights ordinances such as exist in Denver. Bill Behrens, "Anti-Gay State Initiatives Mixed," *Windy City Times*, Nov. 5, 1992, p. 1.

5. " '*We are everywhere*' *is not just a catchy slogan, it is the truth!* By most estimates roughly 10 percent of the population is homosexual. In the United States this translates to over twenty-five million men and women. Whether this figure should be higher or lower is unimportant to me. What is significant is that lesbians and gay men are present in virtually every extended family, friendship circle, ethnic group, religion, organization, field of employment, political party, economic strata, town, city, state, and country." Rob Eichberg, *Coming Out: An Act of Love* (New York: Plume, 1990), pp. 156-157.

6. The evidence suggests that sexual orientation–viz., affectional/sexual desire toward a member of the same sex–is established either before birth or very shortly thereafter but *not* by any process of learning. See Sharon Kingman, "Science/Nature, not Nurture?" *The Independent: The Sunday Review Page*, Oct. 4, 1991, p. 56 ("Science may, it seems, be about to furnish proof that homosexuality has a biological basis, that it is part of the spectrum of normal human behavior, as common or garden [variety] as being extrovert or left-handed"); Janet Shibley Hyde, *Understanding Human Sexuality*, 3rd ed. (New York: McGraw-Hill, 1986), p. 425 (citing research indicating that homosexuality is not a learned response); A. Bell, M. Weinberg, and S. Hammersmith, *Sexual Preference–Its Development in Men and Women* (Bloomington, IN: Indiana University Press, 1981). Perhaps it is the fact that studies of these kinds have received increasing attention in the mainstream press that accounts in part for society's seemingly greater tolerance (if not acceptance) of lesbian and gay people, following Kant's 'ought implies can' principle.

7. In an employment survey of 386 gays and lesbians living or working in New York City, 61% reported it would be a problem if they were to become known as gay on the job; 39% said it was probable or very probable that they would have difficulty getting a promotion or transfer; 32% indicated it was unlikely that they would have the same level of job security as heterosexuals; and 21% said they had experienced an actual instance of job discrimination. See National Gay Task Force, *Employment Discrimination in New York City: A Survey of Gay Men and Women* (Washington, DC: National Gay and Lesbian Task Force, formerly National Gay Task Force, 1980). Also telling of the probability of dis-

crimination is a memorandum from the Office of the General Secretary to all U.S. Catholic Bishops, which included a statement from the Vatican Congregation for the Doctrine of the Faith, which stated in part that "There are areas in which it is not unjust discrimination to take sexual orientation into account, for example, in the consignment of children to adoption or foster care, in employment of teachers or coaches, and in military recruitment." See Congregation for the Doctrine of the Faith, "Some Considerations Concerning the Catholic Response to Legislative Proposals on the Non-Discrimination of Homosexual Persons," reprinted in *National Catholic Reporter*, July 31, 1992, p. 10.

Existing civil rights laws do not protect against sexual orientation discrimination. See *DeSantis v. Pacific Telephone and Telegraph Co., Inc.*, 608 F. 2d 328 (9th Cir. 1979), holding that Title VII of the Civil Rights Act of 1964, 42 U.S.C. § 2000e *et seq.* and 42 U.S.C. § 1985 (3) does not protect a person who is fired because of sexual orientation); see also Rhonda Rivera, "Queer Law: Sexual Orientation Law in the Mid-Eighties (Part II)," *University of Dayton Law Review* 11 (1986): 275; ibid., "(Part I)," *University of Dayton Law Review* 10 (1985): 459; R. Rivera, "Recent Developments in Sexual Preference Law," *Drake Law Review* 30 (1980-81): 311; R. Rivera, "Our Straight-Laced Judges: The Legal Position of Homosexual Persons in the United States," *Hastings Law Journal* 30 (1979): 799. See generally J. Katz, *Gay American History* (New York: Crowell, 1976) (showing that discrimination against gays and lesbians has existed throughout American history).

8. See generally, Boxall, "Gays Alter Dynamics of Politics."

9. Others have raised interpretive challenges and historical criticism to Jewish and Christian ethical views hostile to homosexuality. See, e.g., John Boswell, *Christianity, Social Tolerance, and Homosexuality* (Chicago: University of Chicago Press, 1980), and Michael Ruse, *Homosexuality: A Philosophical Inquiry* (New York: Blackwell, 1988).

10. As for the question of adjudicating among ethical areas, issues of rationality and relevance are no longer as certain. However, I need not venture into this area of metaethics since by and large most metaethical systems would seek to justify one of the four areas I do discuss.

11. Leviticus 18:22, 21:3.

12. *Summae Theologica, The Basic Writings of Saint Thomas Aquinas*, Anton C. Pegis, ed. (New York: Random House, 1945), Vol. II, Q. 94, AA. 2.

13. See Hyde, *Understanding Human Sexuality*, p. 425, indicating that most child molesting is done by heterosexual men with young women. In particular with respect to the spread of disease, in which the greatest concern centers on AIDS: it is now known that HIV cannot be spread by casual contact (John G. Bartlett and Ann K. Finkbeiner, *The Guide to Living with HIV Infection* [Baltimore: Johns Hopkins University Press, 1991], p. 10) and that the gay community has been in the forefront in seeking to halt the spread of this disease through education. See Dick Thompson, "A Losing Battle with AIDS; On the Streets of San Francisco, Victims Cry for Attention and Help," *Time*, June 2, 1990, p. 42; cf. Michael M. Phillips, *States News Service*, June 27, 1990 ("Health officials at Centers

for Disease Control, hoping to immunize the agency against attacks from congressional conservatives, have adopted new rules limiting how explicit federally-funded-AIDS education materials can be"). As for other sexually communicable diseases, they can also be protected against through education, and most are treatable, though some are virulent and some have no cure.

14. The issues under discussion apply whether one is an act utilitarian like Jeremy Bentham, rule utilitarian like Stephen E. Toulmin, or an ideal utilitarian like John Stuart Mill.

15. See Richard Mohr, *Gays/Justice: A Study of Ethics, Society, and Law* (New York: Columbia University Press, 1988), p. 145.

16. Sigmund Freud pointed out that civilization has always caused human beings to repress their sexual desires which are a constitutive part of their personality. See *Civilization and Its Discontents* (New York: Norton, 1961).

17. See Eichberg, *Coming Out*, pp. 156-157.

18. Although sometimes himself giving in to stereotypes, Richard A. Posner, in *Sex and Reason* (Cambridge, MA: Harvard University Press, 1992), pp. 301-302, nevertheless makes an important point in explaining how stereotypical traits such as "effeminacy" tend to get exaggerated in intolerant societies.

19. Christine Woolsey, "Employers Ill-Prepared for AIDS," *Business Insurance*, Oct. 7, 1991, p. 1.

20. Richard Lacavo, "Jack and Jack and Jill and Jill: In the Quest to Instill Tolerance, Schools are Increasingly Instructing Children about Homosexuality; What Should They Be Taught and When?" *Time*, Dec. 14, 1992, p. 52.

21. Here I follow Plato in the *Republic* (4.433a) when he states that the city is just when "each one man must perform one social service in the state for which his nature was best adapted."

22. Plessy v. Ferguson, 163 U.S. 537 (1896), established the principle that separate but equal education for the races was constitutional.

23. Brown v. Board of Education, 347 U.S. 483 (1954), declared "separate but equal education" to be inherently unequal and unconstitutional.

24. See Ben-Shalom v. Marsh, 881 F. 2d 454 (7th Cir. 1989). See also recently released study produced by the Rand Corporation (1993).

25. See Guido Calabresi, "The Supreme Court, 1990 Term: Forward: Antidiscrimination and Constitutional Accountability (What the Bork-Brennan Debate Ignores)," *Harvard Law Review* 105 (1990): 80.

26. For example, the freedom to discriminate cannot be allowed to undermine the state's obligation to equalize the right to well-being which is essential to the very freedom at issue. See Alan Gewirth, *Reason and Morality* (Chicago: University of Chicago Press, 1978), pp. 324-325.

27. For an example of how this approach might resolve conflicts of rights where one of the rights is to privacy, see Vincent J. Samar, *The Right to Privacy: Gays, Lesbians and the Constitution* (Philadelphia: Temple University Press, 1991), pp. 104-112.

28. Samar, *Right to Privacy*, pp. 112-117.

29. Mohr, *Gays/Justice*, pp. 140-141.

30. Posner, *Sex and Reason*, p. 302.

31. See Eichberg, *Coming Out*, pp. 46-47.

32. John Rawls, *A Theory of Justice* (Cambridge, MA: Harvard University Press, 1971), pp. 204-205.

33. Rawls, *Theory of Justice*, pp. 136-142.

34. Gewirth, *Reason and Morality*, p. 133.

35. See, e.g., ibid., pp. 19-20, 108-109, 340-341 (criticizing Rawls); Norman Daniels, ed., *Reading Rawls: Critical Studies of a Theory of Justice* (New York: Basic Books, 1975); *Gewirth's Ethical Rationalism: Critical Essays with a Reply by Alan Gewirth*, Edward Regis, Jr., ed. (Chicago: University of Chicago Press, 1984) (presenting various objections to the Gewirthian model); Deryck Beyleveld, *The Dialectical Necessity of Morality: An Analysis and Defense of Alan Gewirth's Argument to the Principle of Generic Consistency* (Chicago: University of Chicago Press, 1991) (arguing in favor of Gewirth's position and against his critics).

36. See Alan Gewirth, *Political Philosophy* (London: Macmillan, 1965), p. 10.

37. See, e.g., Michael J. Sandel, *Liberalism and the Limits of Justice* (Cambridge: Cambridge University Press, 1982), chap. 4 (arguing that a theory of justice must be connected to a theory of the good).

38. See, e.g., Jeb Rubenfeld, "The Right to Privacy," *Harvard Law Review* 102 (1989): 765 (noting that "the intolerant heterosexual can claim, on personhood's own logic, that crucial to *his* identity is not only his heterosexuality but also his decision to live in a homogeneously heterosexual community").

39. David E. Greenberg, *The Construction of Homosexuality* (Chicago: University of Chicago Press, 1988), p. 470 (stating why conservatives fear efforts to liberalize society's attitudes on homosexuality).

40. *Summa Theologica*, vol. II, Q. 94, AA. 2.

41. Michael Ruse, *Homosexuality*, pp. 188-192 (arguing against a number of unnatural theses including that homosexuality is unique to human beings and is not found in nature generally and homosexuality is contrary to human evolution); see also Hyde, *Understanding Human Sexuality*, p. 20 (referencing studies indicating that homosexual behavior is exhibited by animals other than humans).

42. Mohr, *Gays/Justice*, pp. 37-38, n. 30. In Aquinas's formulation of natural law, there are internal inconsistencies. On the one hand, Aquinas says that the precept that one must not kill is a derivation from the natural law precept that one should do no harm to anyone (*Summa Theologica*, vol. II, Q. 95, AA.4.). On the other hand, one specification of the natural law allows for capital punishment. Since Aquinas has no way to distinguish between these two outcomes on the basis of his theory, the theory is internally inconsistent. See Gewirth, *Reason and Morality*, pp. 279-280.

43. Immanuel Kant, *Foundations of the Metaphysics of Morals*, Lewis W. Beck, trans. (Indianapolis: Bobbs-Merrill, 1959), p. 47.

44. Immanuel Kant, *Lectures on Ethics*, Louis Infield, trans. (Indianapolis: Hackett, 1963), p. 170.

45. Ruse, *Homosexuality*, pp. 193-194.

46. Despite evidence that homosexuality is not a learned response (see note 5 above), schools continue to discriminate against *known* gays and lesbians. See Rowland v. Mad River Local School District, Montgomery County, Ohio, 730 F. 2d 1272 (10th Cir. 1984) (upholding constitutionality of statute permitting a teacher to be fired for engaging in public homosexual activity–i.e., committed with a person of the same sex and indiscreet and not practiced in private); Gaylord v. Tacoma School District No. 10, 88 Wash. 2d 286, 559 P. 2d 1340 (1977) (allowing dismissal of a male teacher when he admitted he was gay).

47. See note 5 above.

48. The famous "Kinsey Studies" show that most persons are neither exclusively heterosexual nor exclusively homosexual but fall across a scale of variations in sexual directedness. See Alfred C. Kinsey, Wardell B. Pomeroy, and Clyde E. Martin, *Sexual Behavior in the Human Male* (Philadelphia: W. B. Saunders, 1948); Alfred C. Kinsey, Wardell B. Pomeroy, Clyde E. Martin, and Paul H. Gebhard, *Sexual Behavior in the Human Female* (Philadelphia: W. B. Saunders, 1953).

49. A similar argument can be made in the area of gay and lesbian parenting. However, because this article is focused primarily on employment, housing, and public accommodation discrimination, I do not treat this issue here. For a discussion of the privacy dimensions to gay and lesbian parenting see Samar, *The Right to Privacy*, pp. 148-152.

50. Civil Rights Act of 1964, P.L. 88-352, 78 Stat. 241, 28 U.S.C. § 1447, 42 U.S.C. § § 1971, 1975a-1975d, 2000a-2000h-6 (1964).

51. See Joel Feinberg, "Civil Disobedience in the Modern World," in Joel Feinberg and Hyman Gross, eds., *Philosophy of Law*, 4th ed. (Belmont, CA: Wadsworth, 1991), p. 131.

52. Mohr, *Gays/Justice*, p. 25.

53. See Mohr, *Gays/Justice*, p. 24; see also Tom L. Beauchamp, "The Justification of Reverse Discrimination," in W. T. Blackstone and Robert Heslep, eds., *Social Justice and Preferential Treatment* (Athens, GA: University of Georgia Press, 1976) (showing how metaphorical associations and even choice of active or passive verbs can be used to degrade women).

54. See Janet Halley, "Politics of the Closet," *University of California at Los Angeles Law Review* 1989 (36): 915, 946-947.

55. See, e.g., 12 C.F.R. § 27.3 (1992); 12 C.F.R. § 338.7 (1992).

56. Ibid.

57. See 49 C.F.R. pt. 23, subpt. D, app. A. It should be noted that in *Richmond v. Croson Co.*, 488 U.S. 469 (1989), the U.S. Supreme Court held unconstitutional, as violative of the fourteenth amendment's equal protection clause, a city's set-aside program for construction contracts for racial minorities where there was no proof of actual discrimination by the city's construction industry. However, three of the five justices who voted to overturn the local set-aside program indicated that Congress may have the right to create such programs under the fourteenth amendment's enforcement provision.

58. Rev. Proc. 75-50, 1975-2 C.B. 587.

59. One of the counterarguments to affirmative action programs involving race has been that there is no general consensus as to when adequate reparations will have been made for past discrimination. See Lisa H. Newton, "Reverse Discrimination as Unjustified," *Ethics* 85 (1973): 308-312.

60. Gay Rights Coalition v. Georgetown University, 536 A. 2d 1, 31 (D.C. App. 1987).

61. Ibid., p. 38.

62. It should be noted that I am focusing on human freedom rather than persons because the nature of this form of discrimination is such that it can force one into a closet in which one retains the face of a person while truly being denied expression of a substantial, fundamental, and unique aspect of personality and a right to be one's self.

63. Title VII of the Civil Rights Act of 1964 prohibits discrimination in employment practices based on "race, color, religion, sex, or national origin" if the employer is "engaged in an industry affecting commerce" and has twenty-five or more employees. The phrase "industry affecting commerce" is defined as "any activity, business, or industry in commerce or in which a labor dispute would hinder or obstruct commerce or the free flow of commerce." 21 U.S.C § § 2000-2000e-2 (1964).

64. Even in government employment, where there are due process protections, there is a substantive need for direct, equal protection of homosexual conduct. This is shown by the dismissal of an Equal Employment Opportunity Commission typist when it was discovered that prior to his being hired, he publicly hugged and kissed a male by the elevator in the building in which he worked, and that since being hired, he had applied for a marriage license for a same-sex relationship, helped organize the Seattle Gay Alliance and, as a result, was the subject of extensive television, magazine, and newspaper publicity. Singer v. United States Civil Service Commission, 530 F. 2d 247 (9th Cir. 1976) (holding that whatever protection there might be for a gay civil service employee under *Norton*, that protection ceases when his or her conduct becomes notorious); Childers v. Dallas Police Department, 513 F. Supp. 136 (N.D. Tex. 1969) (known gay man was denied transfer/promotion to "shopkeeper" in police department despite satisfactory job record and high test score); cf. Norton v. Macy, 477 F. 2d 1161 (D.C. Cir. 1969) (mere possibility of embarrassment from private homosexual activity is insufficient to support a dismissal from government employment). Military regulations that require separation from the service for gays and lesbians will identify the individual according to whether or not he or she engages in, desires to engage in, or intends to engage in bodily contact between members of the same sex for the purpose of satisfying sexual desires. See, e.g., U.S. Army Reg. 135-175, § § 2-36 through 2-39 (1992).

Gay Rights and Affirmative Action

Joseph Sartorelli, DPhil, MS

Arkansas State University

SUMMARY. While affirmative action programs exist for a number of groups, little serious consideration has been given to the establishment of such programs for gay men and lesbians. This essay argues that many of the conditions that justify current affirmative action programs would also justify their extension to gay people, both in terms of compensation for injuries suffered and in terms of benefit to both individuals and society generally. It is argued that anti-discrimination policies are hard to enforce and in any case would be inadequate to redress many of the wrongs suffered by gays and lesbians. It is concluded that programs favoring gay visibility are morally justified.

Within recent years in the United States and some other countries, there has been a realization that certain groups of individuals have suffered much hardship at the hands of the majority of people (or the majority of people in power). At times, and sometimes for long periods, this hardship has been aided and abetted, if not substantially caused, by the institutions of the state itself. With this

Joseph Sartorelli has a doctorate in Philosophy from Oxford University and is presently Assistant Professor of Philosophy at Arkansas State University and Visiting Scholar at Harvard University, where he has also been Visiting Assistant Professor. He also holds an MS in computer science. Correspondence may be addressed to him at the Department of Philosophy, Arkansas State University, State University, AR 72467, or at jsart@quapaw.astate.edu.

[Haworth co-indexing entry note]: "Gay Rights and Affirmative Action." Sartorelli, Joseph. Co-published simultaneously in the *Journal of Homosexuality* (The Haworth Press, Inc.) Vol. 27, No. 3/4, 1994, pp. 179-222; and: *Gay Ethics: Controversies in Outing, Civil Rights, and Sexual Science* (ed: Timothy F. Murphy) The Haworth Press, Inc., 1994, pp. 179-222. Multiple copies of this article/chapter may be purchased from The Haworth Document Delivery Center [1-800-3-HAWORTH; 9:00 a.m. - 5:00 p.m. (EST)].

179

realization has come a feeling of obligation to make amends for the wrongs done to these groups, an obligation eventually transfigured into policy at the very highest levels of the land. In the United States, blacks, women, Hispanics, and Native Americans have been focused upon for the making of amends. But there is, of course, no reason to limit consideration to these groups alone. The driving force behind the selection of these groups has been a general principle of rectification of a bad situation; and an obligation should be felt in any case in which this general principle applies.

The general policy of rectification has come to be known as the policy of affirmative action. I shall understand affirmative action, on the broad conception, to be a policy of distributing benefits to, or reducing hardships for, a particular group of people that does not apply to all, and which has a certain *affirmative* aspect.[1] On this understanding, then, there are at least two separable facets of affirmative action: the particular sort of distribution of benefits or reduction of hardships (the distributive result desired), and the message to be sent. Both of these together might be thought of as the ends to be achieved. Now a particular affirmative action program is a particular means intended to achieve those ends. As such, it may or may not in fact achieve the intended ends. A final element in the general picture of affirmative action is the justification given for the policy.

The affirmative action programs that are most familiar are ones that involve job benefits. But job benefits are not the only kind of benefits that might be involved in an affirmative action program.[2] Indeed, even job benefits could figure into an affirmative action program, if at all, in at least two ways: at the level of ends themselves, or at the level of means to some other ends.

Now, one group of people who have seldom been seriously considered as recipients of affirmative action benefits are gay people. (For the sake of brevity, I shall use the term "gay people" to apply to both gay men and lesbian women, as well as their younger counterparts who have sometimes adopted other terminology to describe themselves.) Aside from being mentioned as part of the scare tactics of right-wing homophobic pressure groups, the issue of affirmative action for gay people has seldom even been raised. More enlightened people, liberals among them, who at least oppose

such things as job discrimination against gays, stop short of favoring affirmative action, often either because they have simply not
thought about whether more work needs to be done to further the
civil rights of gay people beyond simple opposition to job and other
forms of discrimination, or because they quite blithely suppose that
once anti-discrimination laws are in effect, gay people will by that
very fact become endowed with the full rights and benefits of citizenship, equal to those enjoyed by their heterosexual brothers and
sisters. This second rather sanguine view seems to be the one held
by Michael Ruse.[3] I believe that going only to the point of anti-discrimination laws without serious consideration of affirmative action
is a grave oversight and indicates great insensitivity to the plight of
gay people in modern societies. Moreover, I think that if, in general,
affirmative action can be justified for the traditional groups for
which such policy is presently in force in this country, then it can be
justified for gay people. In the remainder of this essay I shall devote
myself to that task.[4]

JUSTIFICATIONS FOR AFFIRMATIVE ACTION

The justifications that have been given for affirmative action
generally seem to divide roughly into three categories–instrumental
justifications, backward-looking justifications, and forward-looking
justifications.[5]

Instrumental justifications are those which justify the use of affirmative action as an instrument for ensuring fairness in the application of non-discrimination laws. Anti-discrimination laws may be
difficult to enforce in many circumstances against the forces of
prejudice, both conscious and unconscious, and especially if it is of
a secondary nature.[6] It is easier to verify that affirmative action
steps have been taken than that no discrimination has taken place
and such steps are likely to have effects similar to those of anti-discrimination laws ideally enforced.

Backward-looking justifications, as the name suggests, accord
significance to what has happened in the past. Such arguments for
affirmative action advert to past wrongs that have been done to a
group and attempt to justify affirmative action as a way of making
amends for, or compensating for, or rectifying those past wrongs.

There are several things connected with a past wrong that might require this kind of treatment. There is first the past bad action or injustice itself. If there is a loss of some kind sustained, that loss may have to be made good, or compensated. (This may, of course, only be a part of what is required; just as more may be required of a thief than a return of the stolen goods.) Second, there is the suffering or pain, or other negative consequences, considered in themselves and not insofar as they give rise to or are part of, an enduring injury. Third, there are enduring injuries or states which interfere in some way with one's life and are a handicap of some kind. These may include injuries or states which do not continue all the way to the present but which have persisted in the past for some time, as well as ones which do continue to the present. Among these enduring injuries or debilitating states, there are those that are especially important, perhaps because of their severity, or because of the importance of that with which they interfere.

Forward-looking justifications are those which look to the future in a certain way and focus upon the consequences of the policy if put into effect. Of course, all three types of justification are concerned about future effects of the policy in some way.[7] What then distinguishes future-looking justifications? The answer seems to be that the "future-looking" justifications rely solely on future consequences and features of future consequences without essentially adverting to past circumstances.[8]

Perhaps the most familiar forward-looking type of justification is the utilitarian one. Strictly speaking, the ultimate justifying factor from a utilitarian perspective is the overall improvement of the general welfare of society. An improvement in the welfare of a particular group within society as a whole cannot suffice as a utilitarian justification unless it can be maintained that there will be an improvement in the general welfare as well. Of course, any improvement in the welfare of a group in society will *prima facie* be an improvement in the general welfare; but if there is a cost to this improvement in welfare, either to others not in the group, or to themselves at a later date, or in another connection, then there may not be an overall improvement in the general welfare.

Another kind of forward-looking justification is the egalitarian one. This proceeds from an equality-based deontological view that holds that a society that is more equal is, to that extent, more just, and thus that equality is something that ought to be striven for in itself. It is important to note that this justification is not strictly speaking a utilitarian one, even though utilitarian ones may sometimes argue for more equality. The difference here is that equality is regarded as an intrinsic value, whereas in a strict utilitarian view equality would only be striven for as an instrumental good, conducive to the general welfare.

In fact, an egalitarian argument of the kind just described is only one of a broader category of forward-looking arguments to be distinguished from the pure utilitarian one. This broad category can be called that of *ideal* arguments. These arguments are ideal in the sense that they judge the comparative worth of policies on the basis of whether or not they make society better in some ideal sense, i.e., whether or not they make society more like an ideal society, regardless of whether there is an overall improvement in the general welfare of society in the sense of its members having more of what they want. Since equality may be held to be at least one dimension of ideality, the egalitarian argument described above qualifies as an ideal argument.[9]

HOW THESE ARGUMENTS APPLY
TO THE TRADITIONAL CASES

Arguments of the above kinds have been applied to justify affirmative action in the cases of blacks, women, Hispanics, and Native Americans. Instrumental arguments have been made to justify affirmative action in hiring, citing the difficulty in enforcing anti-discrimination laws, because there is little in the way of tangible evidence in most cases of hiring discrimination, and because wherever there is a possibly determining subjective factor in hiring decisions, that subjective factor may be influenced, consciously or unconsciously, by prejudice in a way that is very difficult to identify.

Compensatory arguments for affirmative action in the case of blacks, say, have stressed the overwhelming history of injustice that they have suffered starting (in this country) with the shameful period of slavery. Since the concern to compensate focuses on present individuals, the past pain and injustice suffered under the era of slavery cannot be directly compensated for since those who should be compensated no longer exist. But the legacy of that period stays with contemporary blacks who have grown up with the knowledge that their race was once considered such a sign of inferiority that it could deprive one of the protection of law. And of course the discriminatory attitudes on the part of non-blacks that descend from the slave holder mentality operate even to the present day to cause difficulty for contemporary black Americans. Until relatively recently it was illegal in some states for blacks to associate with whites in schools, in the workplace, and in society. Equal treatment for blacks in housing, employment, and education was hardly more than a hope until the advent of anti-discrimination laws. And even after their institution, it has been argued that blacks are on an unfair playing field since the damage to their self-esteem caused from an early age by the still operative racial prejudice and presumption of inferiority in much of society robs them of an important motive or enabling force in the attainment of their life's aims. The fact that blacks see, within their own race, so comparatively few instances of success and so many examples of failure reinforces the feeling among them that efforts to succeed are futile and will be frustrated either by the overt hostility of whites or by the fact that in a sort of cosmic sense the deck is stacked against them. The mere fact, too, of the enormous differential of advantages apparently bestowed graciously upon whites and denied them makes the gulf that they would have to cross simply to catch up seem unmanageable, and the ability to compete beyond their powers. These disadvantages have all been thrust upon them by prejudice and bigotry of the past and of the present and are harms that therefore ought to be compensated for by some type of affirmative action.

Utilitarian arguments for affirmative action have been made which point to racially discriminatory attitudes as fostering racial divisions which cause problems for society as a whole,[10] and it has been argued that racist attitudes do harm even to racists themselves. And, of course, one need only observe that in the case of blacks over ten percent, and in the case of women over fifty percent of the population is underutilized in terms of their potential, which allows for massive inefficiency in society as a whole. As for other forward-looking justifications, ideal arguments for affirmative action in the case of blacks and women and other groups have been given which hold such programs to be necessary in order to promote equal ability to compete and equality of concern and respect.[11]

HOW THESE ARGUMENTS APPLY TO THE GAY CASE

Compensatory Arguments: Injustice and Suffering

A backward-looking argument for affirmative action in the gay case can be made on the basis of a need for compensation for injustice and suffering due to abuse by law, scientific and medical abuse, and abuse caused by social attitudes.

Abuse by law. One very important observation to make about the gay case for affirmative action is that unlike the black case one needn't go back to the distant past to find instances of the most heinous institutional mistreatment of individuals and the group as a whole. In the sense of liberation from statutory abuse by law, there has as yet been no general Emancipation Proclamation for gay people. Gay people have, of course, never in this country been subject to the horrors of slavery but they have been subject to legalized murder, torture, and the most horrendous "medical" experimentation forced upon them against their will. Nor is this mistreatment, especially the "medical" variety, enshrouded in the mists of centuries past, for it was happening as recently as the 1950s. And even today in half the states in the United States, a gay man can be legally imprisoned for making love to his life-partner.[12]

The history of legal abuse of gay people extends back to the earliest colonial days, in which the punishment for homosexual acts was death. Thomas Jefferson, a man noted for liberality and reason, whose founding principle of "life, liberty, and the pursuit of happiness" is loftily enshrined in the Declaration of Independence, was among the "liberals" who, in 1777, suggested that sodomy be punished by castration rather than death.[13] As recently as the 1940s, a man was convicted of sodomy, sentenced to 20 years imprisonment, and forced to serve the term in full, being released in 1963 at the age of 78.[14] Only in 1962 did the American Law Institute issue its Model Penal Code recommending that consensual same-sex activities between adults in private be decriminalized; and even today, despite that recommendation, half the states still have laws against same-sex sexual activities on the books.[15] As recently as the 1970s, well into the era of the "sexual revolution," in five states homosexual acts were punishable by life imprisonment, and in thirty-two others, the sentence could be as high as ten years.[16] Today, gay men and women are in danger of dismissal from their positions in the military, with all the hardship and loss of honor that entails, merely for homosexual orientation—for their status, and not for any behavior.[17] In some localities, the state of Colorado among them,[18] laws have been enacted or proposed which prohibit even anti-discrimination laws in favor of gay people from being passed, effectively legitimizing discrimination against a group with a long history of suffering from intense bigotry and vicious, unreasoning hostility. Indeed, given the intensely negative symbolism of such legislation in the context of this history, one might expect ordinary human decency to prevent its appearance. But the truth is that ordinary human decency is seldom in evidence when the engine of anti-gay bigotry is engaged. This was chillingly apparent in the transition between the horrors of Nazi Germany and the government set up by the liberating allied forces at the end of the Second World War in Europe. Under the Third Reich, gay people were put into concentration camps and forced to wear the pink triangle as a symbol of their sexual orientation and apparently were consigned to the lowest caste of the camp system, their lot destined to be an especially terrible one.[19] They faced extermination, or torture and death through horrendous "medical" experimentation, and their rate of survival was low. Nonetheless, when the allied forces liberated the concentration camps like angels of mercy, there was little mercy, or indeed, human decency shown to the gay prisoners. Instead,

> some American and British jurists of the liberation armies, on learning that an inmate had been jailed and then put into camp for homosexual activities, ruled that, judicially, a camp did not constitute a prison. If, therefore, someone had been sentenced to eight years in prison, had spent five of these in jail and three in a camp, he still had to finish three years in jail after libera-

tion. In at least one instance, a homosexual camp detainee was given a stern lecture by an American colonel, informing him that the United States also considered what he had done criminally offensive. For homosexuals, the Third Reich did not fully end with its defeat.[20]

This less than complete break with Nazi policy on gay people is also unnervingly apparent in the fact that the infamous Nazi version of the very legislation that made homosexual acts criminal was not voided until 1967 in East Germany, and 1969 in West Germany.[21]

Today in the United States, gay people suffer job discrimination, discrimination in child custody and adoption, and economic and legal discrimination in their domestic partnership arrangements. And as of 1986 and the Supreme Court decision in *Bowers v. Hardwick*, they have been deprived of a constitutional right to privacy governing private consensual sexual conduct, even within their own homes.

There is much in the way of injustices suffered by gay people if we only consider that which is due to the institutions of government, its laws, and its agencies. Now the percentage of all gay people who have actually suffered the full injustice of having these unjust laws applied against them, though hard to determine, is probably relatively small. When one adds, however, the powers and advantages of which one is deprived by law, which are allowed to others, the percentage would no doubt increase dramatically. Consider the legal impossibility of gay marriage. *Any* gay person who has ever wanted to marry another has been unjustly deprived of this because of the discrimination against gay people inherent in the legal system. Also, if you consider the effect that fear of the law's sanctions has had on gay people who have refrained from living with someone they love or even spending much time in private together, the numbers affected likely approach or move well into the majority of gay people. And the injustice of suffering the great insult of having such laws in effect has affected most gay people.

Scientific and medical abuse. The iniquitous "medical" treatment of, and experimentation on, gay people, sanctioned by science and allowed by law, was by no means a uniquely Nazi phenomenon. As barbaric, inhuman, and entirely alien to American inclinations as we may be accustomed to think such things are, one should attend to the fact that as recently as 1953 it was suggested in the *Journal of Social Hygiene* that castration of homosexuals for therapeutic effects was a valid subject for research under a controlled study.[22] And as late as 1959, there was a study detailing the effects of lobotomies on homosexual behavior.[23]

In fact, these horrendous practices were merely the results of a period of gross scientific negligence in the treatment of homosexuality as an illness, when in fact the objective, scientific features of illness either were entirely lacking or could be explained as adaptations to, or results of, the extreme homophobia of the social context, and when the purported "scientific" conclusions were dictated by social and religious prejudice. Formally, this period came to an end in 1973 with the removal of homosexuality from the American Psychiatric Association's official list of psychiatric disorders. But there still remain practicing therapists (especially psychoanalysts) who to this day toe the old pseudo-scientific line, sometimes by way of much sleight of hand and unscientific viciousness.[24]

Abuse caused by social attitudes. Another type of injustice suffered besides the sanction of unjust laws is discrimination in jobs and housing. That there is this sort of discrimination can hardly be denied. The fact that in several areas in the country there have been moves to rescind or prevent statutes outlawing anti-gay discrimination is testimony to the fact that being able to act on discriminatory attitudes is viewed as very important by many people. Even if primary discrimination does not take place because the employee is not open about his life, secondary discrimination may occur especially in jobs where social interaction or "collegiality" is regarded as important. Unless gay employees engage in positive deception to a quite considerable degree, they may be regarded as non-social or uncollegial because they do not involve their partners in entertaining duties or exchange personal comments about a private life. Thus, the only gay people likely to be at all successful in these positions will be those who daily engage in an elaborate ruse about their private life, possibly to the exclusion of any real one, and certainly at great cost to themselves psychologically and emotionally. The vast majority of gay people will no doubt be excluded from such employment, either by the discrimination of others because they have not practiced the art of deception well enough, or by their own decision that the price of doing so would be too high to pay. Doubtless because of this there is great underrepresentation of gay people in corporate America in general and in other areas like politics and the military hierarchy.

In fact, the threat or expectation of discrimination if they are at all open about their lives means that gay people often feel forced to choose between quality of personal life and quality of job. This is so because outside of the large cities, there usually isn't anything like an open, identifiable, or public gay community which can provide a support network for them against the ravages of heterosexism and homophobia. And yet if the gay person needs to move to a big city to get the benefits of such a support system, he or she might have to give up a better job for a worse one or take the risk of finding no job at all. These are things that no heterosexual is forced to choose between simply because he or she is heterosexual.

One can get an indication of how widespread and intense are discriminatory attitudes toward gays if one looks at one of the most "enlightened" of employment communities, that of higher education. According to a very revealing study of the attitudes of department chairpersons in universities, sixty-three percent reported that hiring a known homosexual would create serious problems or could not be done at all, while eighty-four percent said the same about hiring an advocate of gay rights. As for promotions, forty-eight percent said there would be barriers for known homosexuals, and sixty-five percent said there would be for gay activists. Fifty-five percent of the members of recruitment and promotion committees disapproved of homosexuals, as did sixty-three percent of the higher administration personnel and seventy-four percent of the trustees.[25] If such discriminatory attitudes exist at the very sources of the light of reason in our society, there is no doubt things are worse in places where that light seldom shines, or goes unnoticed when it does. The effect of these attitudes, even when mainly unspoken and not productive of dismissals or refusals to hire,[26] is chilling: frightened about the consequences of openness, the great majority of gay academics are in the closet, and even non-gay scholars are inhibited from engaging openly in research on gay issues.[27]

These discriminatory attitudes pervade even the institutions of justice in our society. The very criminal justice system itself, whose purpose is to protect and defend the rights of its citizens, often seems to condone assaults on those rights, when they are the rights of gay and lesbian citizens. Because of the intensity of homophobic attitudes among law enforcement officials and because of a wish not to have the homophobia of society in general come crashing down upon them, gay people often refuse to report crimes that occur against them, even if the crimes themselves have nothing to do with their sexuality. If the crimes do involve their sexuality, either as hate crimes or simple vandalism of their cars when parked near a gay bar, the reluctance is intensified. Studies suggest that upward of seventy percent of anti-gay hate crimes go unreported by their victims.[28] Why should this be? Why should gay people have such suspicion about the system intended to protect the innocent? The answer lies in the fact that they are often portrayed as guilty, regardless of the crime against them, simply for being gay. Even judges, with all the symbolism of judiciousness and fairness attached to their office, are capable of the most appalling judicial behavior in respect to gay people.[29]

A second form of the criminal justice system's complicity in the victimization of gay people is the effectiveness, especially in jury trials, of the "homosexual panic" defense. The principle underlying this defense seems to be that the mere fact that one man makes a sexual overture to another (no violence or intimidation or coercion need be involved—a mere invitation may be enough) is justification for a violent response of "self-defense" from the man approached, even if that "self-defense" amounts to the brutal murder of the other man. This sort of legal defense has actually resulted in leniency and even acquittals for murderers.[30] With attitudes and conduct like this in the domain of the arbiters of justice itself, it is not surprising that gay people are reluctant to appeal to the system for redress of grievances. To be prevented from appealing effectively for redress of grievances through the criminal justice system is a most appalling injustice in itself.

Compensatory Arguments: Enduring Harms

A backward-looking argument for affirmative action can also be made on the basis of a need for compensation for enduring harm done to gay people by the heterosexism and anti-gay bigotry of society, which includes damage to self-esteem, harm to self-development, harm to the ability to flourish, and the creation of a servility of temperament, especially in connection with their own sexual identity.

Damage to self-esteem. One of the most touching advertisements to appear on television in recent years is the one showing a little girl with large eyes looking directly into the camera as an adult voice (presumably that of one of her parents) heaps abuse on her. Her eyes progressively widen as the tirade continues until the final blow is landed: "I wish you had never been born." At this there is a piercing look of sorrow and anguish while the narrator stirringly cautions parents to listen to what they are saying because words can hurt. No doubt the intended message is conveyed to the viewer: beyond the emotional trauma created at the time, a child so abused will grow up with a damaged self-concept and low self-esteem and that will have an impact on her later life.

This is an evocative representation of precisely what happens to gay people throughout most of their lives, if in a somewhat less direct manner in most cases. It starts at a very early age, indeed in the very formative stages of the development of the self-image. Gay people are from early childhood recipients of the worst kind of verbal abuse imaginable, directed at the very possibility of homosexuality. Often the abuse begins before they have even the merest hint that it is at people like them that the abuse is aimed. And the first hints of this realization may come in the form of sexual fantasies and attractions over which they have no control and which quite take them by surprise. In the context of homophobic abuse generally, these thoughts and fantasies become something to be hidden lest one lose social acceptance. The results are feelings of guilt, shame and isolation, and a kind of internecine battle within one's psyche for the preservation, or development, of self-esteem.[31]

The protection of self-esteem is one of the central developmental tasks of childhood. . . . In the child's eyes his sense of self-worth is essential to his survival. The child who does not experience his value in the eyes of his parents will fear their abandonment and its attendant dangers to his existence. The older child and adolescent may even contemplate suicide. The maintenance of positive self-esteem is so fundamental a task that all of the structures of the personality contribute to its organization.[32]

This damage to self-esteem is serious and lasting, but it is particularly grievous in its severity and effects during adolescence when the hatred and contempt directed at homosexuality from the peer group is especially great. Add to that the fact that at that stage the gay person may be completely unaware of even a single instance of a gay person in history, recent or remote, who projected a positive rather than negative image of gay people, and you have a recipe for the descent of self-esteem to levels which become intolerable to some individuals. According to a recent report of the federal government, gay youth suicide attempts are up to six times more common than among their heterosexual counterparts.[33] The period of greatest risk seems to be the period of "coming out"–the period in which the adolescent begins to deal with the fact that homosexuality is a part of his or her makeup and not something that will go away, or is so insignificant that it can be hidden from oneself or others.[34]

The gravity of the psychological wound in this period makes it hard to believe that its effects do not linger in later life. Also, given the fact that the cause of the earlier wound (pervasive social disapproval and bigotry) continues unabated even after one has come out, it would seem to take an extraordinary psychological defense system to prevent the wound from being re-opened to one degree or another. But the psychological defense systems of most gay people are by no means impervious to assault; in fact, in perhaps the majority of cases the gay person's defense system is hamstrung because it is not allowed to be deployed. This happens to the extent that one is self-oppressed or remains in the closet as a gay person, when one does not come to the defense of gay rights, or attack the projection of false images of gay people, or simply does not reveal that one is gay because of the fear of the disapproval of others. If the disapproval of others is based on a grossly false, indeed ethically insidious, evaluation of the worth of something, then their disapproval is baseless and should not be avoided out of respect. If, of course, one is inclined to avoid it not out of respect but out of a wish to escape the potentially great ill effects of this admittedly groundless disapproval, that is another matter which raises additional issues that must be addressed. But unless one can with confidence maintain that one is keeping one's sexuality hidden solely because it is, according exclusively to the dictates of prudence, the only way to avoid physical harm or loss of livelihood or some such thing, it seems as if one is allowing the old feelings of lack of self-worth for being gay to influence one's actions. This is but one of the ways that the enduring harm to self-esteem, reinforced by the daily messages of disapproval and rejection that a gay person receives in a heterosexist society, can continue to have bad effects. The effects, which can be both in the realm of feeling and of acting, continue because the psychological wounds are deep.[35]

Strong indication that the wounds to a gay person's self-esteem run deep and last long is provided by the fact that even the rich and powerful remain in the closet. Gay people who are in positions of wealth and power are virtually immune to loss through discrimination and yet in the main still refrain from being open about their sexuality. This seems to indicate that there must be something internalized at work; both a fear of what people will think, or how they will act, *and* a feeling that somehow those thoughts and acts are justifiable. This inner feeling that one really is, at some level, as base as people may think if they know one is gay seems to be an essential component in the explanation of such closeted behavior. For if it weren't involved, defiance (being open about one's sexuality) would seem to be the most likely response to the disapproval of others, if it is unjustified and one cannot be hurt by it and conforming to it has negative personal consequences for one's life. As a scholar of gay and anti-gay symbolism in film says:

> What all this boils down to is that people aren't afraid to come out because of career considerations, economic reasons, or even a desire for privacy. They don't want to come out because they've been taught on the most basic level that it's disgusting and dirty to be gay, and they believe it.[36]

Harm to self-development. Another enduring harm that gay people suffer is a deficit in powers, skills, and abilities usually developed in the stage of adolescence. From puberty to the end of adolescence, non-gay young people are helped along the road to emotional, sexual, and social development by their family and friends, by their schools, by organizations public and private, by the news and entertainment media, and by the society at large. They are taught how to value one another as human beings and objects of love, as sources of aesthetic, psychological, and physical joy, as partners in a shared life plan, and as fellow students in the search for the fulfillment of a good life. Their sexuality is anticipated, embraced, and admired; it is cultivated like a precious bud expected to bloom into a beautiful flower. For gay young people, on the other hand, there is no careful husbandry tending to the growth and development of their sexuality; at best there is neglect, at worst, a policy of defoliation. Remember for a moment how much care and concern are put into the admiration, encouragement, and guidance of emerging heterosexual romantic feelings, of flirting, and of dating. This all helps the young people to work out the proper way to interact with those to whom they are attracted in a way that promotes well-being and respect for themselves and their partners, and to integrate their needs and aims in this regard into the general structure of the social community at large. All this is denied to gay youth; indeed, far from encouragement and admiration, if there are any signs of romanticism or flirtation, they are discouraged and suppressed—so much for the prospect of developing the skillful use and management of these tender feelings and an integration of them into one's own life plan and the life of the community.[37]

Harm to the ability to flourish. Other enduring harm is done to gay people by the distorting or obscuring or tainting of their conception of what is the good for them. Consequently, their development of the virtues is interfered with, and also their ability to advance toward the rational pursuit of what is the good for them. As a result, many are severely impaired in the ability to flourish. Not only are they robbed of the proper account of how they might flourish, they may also be robbed of any substantial idea of what flourishing would be like for them; perhaps they even are led to think that they are incapable of flourishing. Given that the pursuit of one's own good is what one ought to be allowed to do (consistent with being in the context of society), to be rendered handicapped in doing so by society would seem to argue for redress quite apart from any utilitarian considerations of the good this would do for oneself or one's society in the future. Also, in alienating gay people both from their potential life-partners and from society, the homophobic society deprives them of the material for the achievement of what is the good for them—even of that part of it which they can identify as such.

Indeed, as a result of the stultifying influence of homophobia in society, so distorted may be gay people's image of what is the good for them that they may see the components of it in themselves and in others as *bad,* and thus may be unwittingly enlisted in the frustration of their own and each other's rational ends. There are many examples of this, but a deeply tragic one would be this. Suppose that it is in fact part of the good for a certain gay man that he raise children. It is something he would find very fulfilling, and something he would do very well—he would be an excellent father. Suppose also that the kind of man who would be a perfect partner for him, with whom he would flourish in an enduring and loving relationship, is one who would also make an excellent father. Now suppose this man doesn't realize how fulfilling being a father would be for him; suppose that instead he has developed an aversion to the idea because he is afraid to be around children. He has, as it were, internalized somehow the ugly slander about gay men that they are inclined to be child molesters. He is, therefore, not only himself afraid to be in the presence of children, but also suspicious of those gay men who like children, or who have jobs dealing with them, or who wish to adopt them. Such an unfortunate man would not only fail to pursue the kind of life that would bring him the most happiness and fulfillment; he would sabotage any chances he had to live such a life by avoiding children and the kind of man who would be the ideal life-partner for him.

Servility of temperament. Internalized self-oppression produces a certain servility of temperament among gay people which causes them to accept living under constraints that would be unthinkable even for other historically oppressed groups and inconceivable for the dominant majority.[38] Imagine blacks being required not to show affection publicly to one another in couples because of some legal or social prohibition. It would be racist, appalling, and an invitation to revolt–indeed, it's hard to imagine that blacks would allow it ever to be an effective prohibition, regardless of what the law said. Now, observe that this is the very sort of thing that is done to gay people (especially gay men, because of the general pressure against the showing of inter-male affection, whether clearly sexual and romantic or not). Why is it that gay people stand for this type of appalling prohibition, indeed, even go out of their way to abide by it? Is it because to do so means nothing to them in the way of personal loss? Certainly not; it can and does have grave psychic effects, even at the deep levels of one's conception of oneself, and behaviorally, even when one is acting in private. Why then? Well, of course, there is the element of fearing reprisals. But if that is the only concern, why do they not then only abide by the prohibitions with regret, always on protest, always clamoring for a removal of the pressures that they submit to and deeply resenting what they are forced to do? Resentment would seem to be the appropriate feeling here, and not just a wistful longing for better days in the future. Yet gay people allow this; and it is in general because they have developed a certain kind of servility to the heterosexist culture around them: they have developed a slave's mentality. This is damage that needs repair; and since the society's mistreatment is the cause of the damage, it is the society that should set into operation the repairing mechanism.

The Utilitarian Argument

A utilitarian argument can be made for affirmative action in the gay case based on the fact that (1) the whole cycle will happen again and again unless the vicious homophobia and bigotry that has caused it is reduced and eliminated, and this cannot be done by the enactment of anti-discrimination laws alone (as we have seen in the case of women and blacks); and (2) the social fabric itself will be strengthened by the expanded inclusiveness because social friction will be reduced; and (3) even heterosexuals will benefit personally from the reduction of bigotry, since it will make them less prone to irrational behavior that may well be against their own interests (think of a businessman who dissolves a joint venture with a gay business partner who is very talented and whose abilities complement his own very well, simply because of his own intense bigotry), and it may well enrich their emotional life. It is a commonplace that American men are quite inhibited about expressing emotion in general and certainly toward other men. One significant factor in this reluctance is the fear of being thought to be, or of feeling oneself in some manner to be, homosexual. And yet a common lament is that it is just this emotional inexpressiveness that causes deep problems in relationships between heterosexual men and women. No doubt it also impoverishes the emotional life and happiness of men themselves both in their relationships to women and to other men, and it may heighten the aggressiveness between men even when they are supposed to be engaged in social cooperation.

The Instrumental Argument

That vicious anti-gay attitudes still exist in the country at large, and especially among some official governmental agencies is shown by the near hysteria that the proposed lifting of the ban on homosexuals in the military has caused in some quarters. One Sergeant Major wrote in the *Marine Corps Gazette* that "the Bible has a very clear and specific message towards homosexuals–'Those that practice such things are worthy of death.'"[39] That the attitudes at even the highest levels of the military run far deeper than the much rehearsed concern about privacy of living quarters comes across in the report that the Marine Corps Commandant, Gen. Carl E. Mundy, Jr., is "particularly concerned that the proud 217-year Marine tradition would be irreparably damaged by allowing gay men and lesbians to serve in uniform."[40]

In the face of attitudes of this kind of virulence and seeming implacability, it is hard to believe that even if there were anti-discrimination laws of the best sort in effect there wouldn't be many attempts, and many successful ones, to circumvent the laws. Since the intensity of the negative attitudes is so much greater than in the case even of blacks, and many, perhaps a majority of Americans, still hold the benighted view that homosexuality is gravely immoral, you have negative attitudes of a force and pervasiveness that occur in no other case. Therefore, the instrumental argument would seem to apply in the gay case with even greater force than in the case of blacks.

The Ideal Argument

An ideal argument for affirmative action for gay people could be based on at least two grounds. First, under the aegis of the principle of equality of concern and respect for all citizens, it could be argued that given such a history of legal contempt and abuse, no mere enactment of non-discrimination laws could reasonably be taken as an indication of the system's equal concern and respect for gay people. If anything, such a tepid move could be taken as a sign of lack of appreciation of the great value of equal concern and respect and what it means to be deprived of them. And second, one could argue that all are entitled to an equal chance at having a good life and without affirmative steps to correct the deficit in self-esteem and self-development, gay people would be disadvantaged in this venture.

ARE THERE SIGNIFICANT DIFFERENCES BETWEEN THE TRADITIONAL CASES AND THE GAY CASE?

One very important aspect of the losses to be compensated for in the traditional cases is that some are economic. Blacks are economically deprived and face an uphill battle on their own to achieve economic equality, or even equal ability to compete economically. The same can be said for women. But the above observations about the injuries suffered by gay people do not mention a class-wide economic deficit of this kind. What is mentioned, among other things, is a deficit in self-esteem. Should the government, whose concern, on at least one view, is with economic distribution, be concerned with improving the self-esteem of its citizens?

The intrinsic importance of self-esteem is fairly obvious at one level. But furthermore, it is interesting that it often lies at the basis of arguments for the critical nature of the need to make other compensations, especially economic ones. This suggests that it is, instead of being unimportant, rather the central good to be concerned about.

Rawls accords a principal place to self-esteem or self-respect in the hierarchy of goods:

> It is clearly rational for men to secure their self-respect. A sense of their own worth is necessary if they are to pursue their conception of the good with zest and to delight in its fulfillment. Self-respect is not so much a part of any rational plan of life as the sense that one's plan is worth carrying out. Now our self-respect normally depends upon the respect of others. Unless we feel that our endeavors are honored by them, it is difficult if not impossible for us to maintain the conviction that our ends are worth advancing.[41]

For Rawls self-esteem is the main primary good.[42] The proper distribution of self-respect, i.e., in equal amounts for all, is supposed to be effected by the affirmation by law that all are equal citizens. Only after this equality is secured does the question of economic distribution come into play:

> In a well-ordered society then self-respect is secured by the public affirmation of the status of equal citizenship for all; the distribution of material means is left to take care of itself in accordance with the idea of pure procedural justice.[43]

There seems a clear ranking here between the two with the distribution of self-respect having priority. It isn't as if Rawls thinks that self-respect is a good that a society should not be concerned to help distribute; it is rather that he thinks it can be distributed to the right extent by the public affirmation of equal citizenship for all. But what happens in a case in which we do not start from zero and build self-respect by such equal affirmation, nor even start from a deficit that accrues merely from the lack of such affirmation, but start with a group of people who have been made to think for all their lives that there is something about them that makes them disgusting, disgraceful, unspeakable, and fit only for elimination? Such a terrible deficit in self-respect is hardly something that could be expected to be redressed by mere affirmation of equal status under the law, especially if the law were to be followed only by a grudging public compliance, if that—especially, that is, if strong feelings of contempt still lodged in the hearts of others, to be confronted at every turn. And if you add to the lot that the characteristic so despised were something one might hide, though with effort, then the deficit would be even harder to make up by mere legal affirmation of equal status. For many would hide the characteristic, not wanting to face the unofficial public hostility and ridicule. And in doing so, not only would they lose the opportunity to come to take pride in and feel good about that characteristic, and so add to their self-respect, they would also by hiding it come to feel worse about it, since they would be hiding it out of a sense of unregenerate or unconverted shame.

The deficit, however, is one which has to be made up on Rawls's view, because it is the key to making the system of "distribution of material means" part of an overall system of justice that self-respect be secured, at least to the level where it would be if citizens were to live their entire lives under a system which legally affirmed their equal status:

> Thus the best solution is to support the primary good of self-respect as far as possible by the assignment of the basic liberties that can indeed be made equal, defining the same status for all. At the same time, distributive justice as frequently understood, justice in the relative shares of material means, is relegated to a subordinate place. Thus we arrive at another reason for factoring the social order into two parts as indicated by the principles of justice. While these principles permit inequalities in return for contributions that are for the benefit of all, the precedence of liberty entails equality in the social bases of esteem.[44]

Far from being something whose distribution the government should not be concerned with because the more important job of economic distribution renders it insignificant, self-respect is something so important that its equal distribution has precedence over other equalities, among them those of economic distribution. In fact, it would seem that if self-respect is indeed the basic primary good, as Rawls affirms, then a life deprived of self-respect is a life which is to that extent deprived of all goods, since it is a life deprived of the ability to enjoy those other goods, or at least to enjoy them as true goods and not mere trivial baubles, trinkets, and insignificant diversions.[45]

Another difference with the traditional cases might be thought to be the very fact that gay people can hide their membership in the group and pass as members of the majority and thus avoid the ravages of discrimination. Does this make the harm done to gays any less demanding of compensation?

First of all, it must be noted that some members of the traditional groups can pass for the majority also. Some blacks can and have, as have no doubt many Hispanics and Native Americans. Second, and more important, there are significant negative effects that gay people suffer even if they do pass for the majority, among them the above-discussed injuries to self-esteem, deprivation of powers and abilities that others have by law (marriage and child custody and adoption, etc.), harm to self-development, the production of a kind of servility of temperament, and harm to the ability to flourish. Only discrimination in jobs and housing may be reduced somewhat in impact by the ability of some to pass for the majority. But this may well be at the additional great personal expense of not having a private life, or of acting always as if one did not. And in any case, being forced to hide one's personal life, which is something no one would desire to do, is itself a loss that needs to figure into the compensation.

OTHER REASONS FOR AFFIRMATIVE ACTION

The Nature of the Factors Involved in the Production and Continuance of Anti-Gay Discriminatory Attitudes

There are other elements in the case of gay people that further justify a policy of affirmative action. Among these are the factors that otherwise would remain at work to continue to bring hardship to gay people in the future. Some of these factors do not exist at all in the other cases; some of them exist there, but to a lesser extent than in the gay case; and some, though they exist there, are more easily neutralized in their ill effects in the case of other groups than in the case of gays.

The intensity of negative attitudes and their social sanction. One of the most significant factors is the great intensity of the bigotry in the gay case. While the traditional groups still suffer greatly from bigotry, anti-gay bigotry is of a particularly brutal and ferocious kind. Studies suggest that the rate of violence (even excluding merely verbal violence) against gay people is four times the average of the rate of violence against all people.[46] An exploratory report to this effect was actually suppressed by the Reagan Justice Department after news reports of its conclusion that gays and lesbians are probably the most frequent victims of hate-motivated violence in America today.[47] And this violence often seems sanctioned, and expected by the perpetrators to be sanctioned, by the society at large. In one incident, three sixteen- and seventeen-year-old males caused a twenty-three-year-old gay man to drown by throwing him off a bridge even after he pleaded that he couldn't swim. Afterward, they went to a party and laughed and bragged about what they had done. Eventually, they were apprehended and sentenced to time in a youth center; but clearly they were not like, and did not regard themselves as like, most of the others in the center.[48] An aspect of the anti-gay violence here seems to be expressive of the social values and social solidarity of the group. To get anything like this sort of thing in such an intense form in the case of the traditional groups, one would have to go back to the days of KKK prominence in the South, when violence against blacks and even murder was used in a similar way.

Pervasiveness of secondary bigotry. So pervasive is secondary heterosexism, that often the most obviously appropriate extensions of discussions to include a gay element are simply ignored, as if the very idea of them never occurs to one. One case in point is a recent "Anatomy of Hate" conference sponsored by the Elie Wiesel Foundation for Humanity which focused on how children learn hatred. The panelists spoke of hatred based on ethnicity, class, religion, and national origin, but omitted any reference to hatred based on sexual orientation. When asked about this omission, panelist John Silber, President of Boston University, evidently thought not only that anti-gay hatred was unimportant, but that it was an affront to have brought up the question:

"Most of us consider sexuality a private concern," Silber replied indignantly, as though it were in bad taste for Dobbs [the man who raised the question about anti-gay hatred] even to have brought up the subject. Silber said he was sick of "so-called gay people trying to force their sexual lifestyles down everybody's throats, insisting on turning every meeting into a testimonial on sexual preference." He added that homosexuality "has no place in a discussion concerning children, for whom homosexual orientation is not an issue," and denied that gays have a place in a multicultural curriculum because "gayness is not a culture. If you make it a culture you've got to have a culture of hamburger eaters and pastrami eaters, too." As to the issue of whether children learn from their parents to hate gays, that's simply not a problem, said Silber, because "decent parents don't even discuss the possibility that there are homosexuals." Dobbs, he said, had made a "very bad choice with regard to where to bring up the subject."

None of the panelists took issue with Silber's remarks.[49] Apparently anti-gay hatred is not hatred, and it doesn't exist among children.

Another instance of secondary heterosexism is that in all the nearly five-hundred pages of a recent book which purports to be a study of the history and sociology of genocide, not once is serious consideration given to the question of whether the systematic use of the most heinous methods of execution and torture for "sodomites" throughout the Christian era constitutes genocide even though the case seems clearly to fit the definition used and the slaughter of heretics and witches *is* treated as genocide.[50] Apparently the state-sponsored slaughter of gay people is not genocide even when it happens in Nazi concentration camps.

Origin in and sanction by religion. Anti-gay bigotry is further distinguished by its origins and sources. There is no question that anti-gay attitudes originate in, or at least for the past several hundred years have been fostered by, religion, especially Christianity, in the West.[51] Religion has been the single most powerful ideological weapon used to keep gay people under oppression in this country whenever there has been a move toward the liberalization of laws and attitudes. Church leaders often enter the political fray in opposition to proposed gay rights legislation, and can at times seem even to condone or exonerate violence against gay people.[52] Television "evangelists" like Jerry Falwell and Pat Robertson, in their syndicated television programs, under the guise of spreading the "gospel of love" stir up and add fuel to the fire of hatred against gay people. While continuing to use the slogan "the wages of sin is death" as a code while making reference to AIDS, they reinforce anti-gay bigotry in the most reprehensible way, by forging a kind of metaphysical link between homosexuality and the disease (without ever mentioning the fact that in other countries AIDS is predominantly a disease among heterosexuals, or that it is virtually unknown among lesbians) and reverberating to the heinous mythology that homosexuality itself is a disease. They thus effectively add "self-defense" to the list of rationalizations that bigotry can use to motivate and justify anti-gay attitudes and even violence. A recent study found that in thirty-nine percent of the cases of verbal harassment of gay people, explicit references were made to God, religion, or the Bible.[53] The Bible, a religious text, has been drawn upon to support legal decisions with negative impact on gay people.[54] The most famous and egregious example of this is the U.S. Supreme Court's split decision holding that anti-sodomy laws applied to consenting adults in private did not infringe the constitutional right to privacy, where it was said that "condemnation of those practices is firmly rooted in Judeo-Christian moral and ethical standards."[55]

The fact that organized religion in this country galvanizes and stimulates anti-gay attitudes means that gays must have a champion in the form of the government to balance that force. The operation of this kind of religious opposition in the case of gay people can only be compared with something like a religious-based and supported caste system. Imagine the caste of the untouchables in India, or a country in which a great many of the people subscribed to a religion which held this caste system to be inviolable. Only then would you have a situation like the present one with religious inspired passions militating against the fair and equitable treatment, or even the most basic civil rights, of a certain group of people. By seeming to make homosexual love "the worst sin in the calendar," some religious groups make visceral rejection of it part of their very religious identity. This adds a note of near hysteria and fanaticism to their opposition to civil rights for gay people, which eclipses the more moderate sentiments of liberalism on the part of most of those in favor and often wins the day.

Besides the external effect of the religious basis of much of the anti-gay oppression in the form of the great intensity, pervasiveness, and durability of homophobic attitudes in others, there is also an effect on the internal side. That the divine being, the very font–one is taught–of goodness, love, value, and meaning, rejects you for what you are, for the feelings you have that are the core of your being and of the very thing, intimate personal affection, that gives meaning to your life, is an idea with which gay youngsters under the influence of a homophobic religion must somehow come to terms. If the rejection one imagines from one's parents for being gay is painful, how much more riven with trauma are the feelings one has about being rejected by, and ashamed before, a god who can see into one's inmost thoughts and emotions, and from whom one cannot hide one's erotic and romantic feelings. The effects of such a sense of rejection and shame upon the vulnerable, developing young psyche may well be incalculable. Yet it is the great misfortune of most gay people to have suffered under early training in a homophobic religion and not to have had the benefit of more enlightened religious instruction or instruction in an enlightened humanism.

Homophobia as a constituent in sexual identity. Another important factor in the production of much anti-gay feeling is the fact that one's gender role identity is defined in large part in terms of sexual object choice, and this involves a rejection of same-sex object choice as tantamount to defection to the other side, and an embrace of all the gender role characteristics of that side. People are raised in such a way as to have a strong part of their identity defined in terms of anti-gay hatred and the demonization of homosexuality. This is particularly true of males in our culture.[56] Boys early on in their development are taught to define themselves as males insofar as they are not girls, and not girl-like. Their anatomy early on convinces them they are not 'in danger of' being girls, but to be girl-like is a constant threat since that depends on how one acts, and on one's temperament and desires, not on one's body. And, at the stereotypical level of most early gender role instruction, to be homosexual and male is to be girl-like, to be weak, to be unmasculine. The threat of losing one's masculinity is especially vivid where there is a homosexual element in the make-up of the male, or there is something else which might be taken for such, as in the case of many young males who recognize the male bonding inclination in themselves. It is interesting that in the Native American cultures which include the berdache, who bears some of the traits of men and some of women in those cultures (as an alien observer might put it), there is no fear or hatred of the berdache on the part of the heterosexual men, who, indeed, freely engage the berdaches sexually. In those cultures the berdache is revered and is, in a sense, regarded as an independent third sexual category.[57] It would seem that since there is no fear of slippage into another category by one's behavior, there is no need to reinforce one's identity by rejection of the other. However, within the dominant cultural myths of this society, where the demonization of homosexuality is a means of continuing to define oneself as male (in particular), anti-gay prejudice especially among heterosexual males is particularly virulent and hard to defuse.

The suppression of gay history and culture. Another factor operative in the gay case is the informational vacuum that has resulted from the long-term, systematic suppression or elimination of virtually all historical facts about the homosexual aspects of the lives of the famous or notable, and about how homosexuality fit into the ordinary life of the various eras. In excising any reference to the fact of gay sexuality for so long, in refusing to mention actual cases, and failing even to consider possible cases, among historical figures in art, literature, politics, science, and other realms of human endeavor, Western society has through the ages been guilty of the cultural equivalent of genocide against gay people. That such figures as Leonardo and Michelangelo, Erasmus, Caravaggio, Alexander the Great, Frederick the Great, Whitman, Marlowe, Shakespeare, and even Plato and the Greeks, should go for so long without any serious treatment of, or investigation into that aspect of their lives is a scandal to academia and to a civilization committed to enlightenment and the pursuit of truth. The effect down to the present day is the prevalence of an almost complete ignorance about the reality of gay people, how common they have been, and how outstanding have been many in the annals of human excellence. This ignorance has allowed, and continues to allow, the grossest of false images to be projected about gay people, because there is no background of reality against which to judge them and find them fraudulent.

The lack of a support system in the heterosexist family. A final factor contributing to harm for gay people is the systematic hetero-sexism of the family in general in the present society, and, concomitantly, the lack of a familial support system for the developing gay child. Few families raise their children to believe that whatever their sexual orientation, they are to share in the love, support, and pride of the family for being good individuals of equal worth.

In the case of most oppressed groups, the young have some solace in their family. There they will find support and affection, and instruction as to how to cope with oppression. Gay youth, however, generally have no such solace in the family; consequently, they don't have the kind of protection from external abuse at an early age that gives them an inner strength to reject such abuse as misguided and the result of misconception and bigotry. This is a role that must be filled, for the benefit of gay youth, and later gay adults, if there is ever to be a solution to the problem of horrific damage to the self-concept culminating in suicide attempts in gay adolescence and having untold negative effects in later life.

The Ramifying Political Effects of Discriminatory Attitudes on Gay People

Gay people in general have the "option" of passing for hetero-sexual, and avoiding some of the worst direct consequences of anti-gay hatred. The vast majority "choose" to do this, and not be open about their sexuality. But that is not the end of the bargain, or of the effect the bargain has on gay people. Given the "option" of having one's hand cut off and being tossed into a ditch or being killed, one may "choose" to lose one's hand and be thrown into the ditch. But the further ramifications of this forced choice are even greater if one needs two hands to get oneself out of the ditch and back to a semblance of a normal life.

A very important result of the lack of openness about being gay is that it deprives gay people of even the most rudimentary kind of political access to the mechanisms of the state in determining the most important aspects of their lives. Only voting itself is accessible, and without any real power to influence the political agenda which determines what is to be voted on or to influence others in their voting considerations on matters of paramount interest to gay people, that is largely a power without effect in terms of significant participation, much less participation as equals, in the affairs of the state. While there have been gay political groups in existence since the 1970s and even before,[58] they have seldom had much power to influence politics, except in certain regions under certain circumstances, and very recently. The vast majority of gay people don't involve themselves with these groups even to the extent of sending money to them, or getting on their mailing lists. And the reason is their fear of coming out publicly, either individually or in a group. Actively to support or foster such an organization would mean getting on a mailing list, or sending a check with your name on it, and that would be making a public demonstration of your identity which would endanger your cover; even merely having such organizations in existence would bring attention to gay issues and with it a possible backlash where even what one has by virtue of one's cover might well be lost. The U.S. Supreme Court, in a 1938 decision, acknowledged that "Prejudice against discrete and insular minorities may be a special condition, which tends seriously to curtail the operation of those political processes ordinarily to be relied upon to protect minorities."[59] Now one might think that if non-discrimination legislation were brought into effect, that would solve this problem,[60] but even if that would ameliorate the difficulty, it would hardly deal effectively with the cause of the problem, unless the enactment of such laws were enough by itself to bring people out into the open about their sexuality by reducing dramatically the prejudice they fear. Indeed, gay people may be too intimidated by virulent homophobia even to make use of their rights under such laws since it would require coming out to do so. One might compare such a situation with that of blacks in the American South after Reconstruction, when the KKK exerted effective authority by intimidation even though the laws were for a time on the other side. In fact, there is evidence that even the most liberal anti-discrimination laws may not be enough to induce gay people to come out of the closet, given a history of oppression and underlying attitudes of disapproval that afflict one from the earliest years. Norway, for example, with its very progressive civil rights protections for gay people, nonetheless may have the most closeted gay people in Western Europe.[61] In the Netherlands, there is the 1990 testimony of a Dutch admiral that "most of the homosexuals [in the military] make a secret of their sexual orientation out of fear for reactions," even though the Dutch stopped official military discrimination against gay people as early as 1973.[62] Mere homophobic attitudes, so long as they keep people in the closet, can be seen clearly as a force to restrict political activity. The California Supreme Court recognized this in its ruling that firing people who said openly that they were gay violated political freedom that was guaranteed under the California Labor Code.[63] If indeed concealment is a principal barrier to political equality and the exercise of political rights toward that end, then failure to take steps to eliminate that barrier would seem to constitute a willing acceptance of effective political inequality. It would be a failure to accept that gays, as citizens, are entitled to equal concern and respect under the law.

THE AFFIRMATIVE ACTION SOLUTION

Various instruments have been proposed as affirmative action solutions in the case of the more traditional groups. In hiring and admissions to universities, quotas have been proposed as well as the less stringent goals. The distinction between quotas and goals is often lost in the context of political demagoguery, but it does exist. A quota-based system is not successful unless the quotas for the protected groups are met; while a goal-based system is successful if the goal is properly aimed at, whether or not it is achieved. It is true that a frequently used indicator of success of "proper aim" in goal-based systems is whether *eventually* the goal is achieved over the course of some extended period of time. Some opponents of such a system maintain that this makes it a "quota system" with a certain number of slots that must be filled. But that is simply false. Under natural assumptions about the availability and admissible competence of members in the protected groups, it seems sensible to hold that the burden of proof of "no discrimination" should be on the employer who after a significant period has not succeeded in hiring a certain reasonable number of people in the protected group, if that is the aim. And that is part of such goal-based policies. If the employer can give adequate reason for non-compliance, he will not be held to be in violation of the system.

Another kind of affirmative action policy would be one that merely makes a good faith effort to recruit employees from the protected group. This would not even be as stringent as a goal-based policy because there would not in general be any specific number or percentage in mind as the goal at which one should aim. Here, instead, what is intended is that certain steps should be taken to recruit, perhaps by means of an "outreach" program that directs recruitment energies towards the communities whose members one is trying to recruit. That these steps are taken is something that could be verified independent of the number of people eventually recruited.[64]

Besides programs that distribute job benefits and positions in connection with higher education, there are programs that focus upon satisfying a particular need of the groups. Thus there are special education programs like Head Start. There is also a concern for the distribution of other benefits which may result from but go beyond direct job benefits. Thus the concern to provide role models for members of the oppressed groups is aimed particularly at motivations to the achievement of excellence and happiness and the full exercise of talents, by the improvement of self-esteem. The actual mechanism employed may involve job benefits to the role models themselves but the intended benefits reach far beyond this.

Now a standard interpretation of the role model argument, which justifies affirmative action policies as a way of providing role models for members of the oppressed groups, holds it to be forward-looking and utilitarian in nature insofar as it attempts to improve the welfare of the as yet unformed, or not yet fully formed, members of oppressed groups in the future. The idea is that having role models benefits those who have not yet got to the stage of suffering from job discrimination and other forms of discrimination directed at adults and alters the social conditions that would perpetuate the problems. But the role model argument can also be viewed as a backward-looking one, and a justice-based forward-looking one. One can see it as (1) helping to equalize the otherwise unfair playing field, and (2) removing handicaps which were put there by bigotry but which may only come into operation later in one's life. As to the first point, the movement toward equalization is clearly needed, since members of the non-oppressed groups are going to have their own role models by virtue of their dominant status. And as to the second point, the handicaps would seem as much a matter for compensation as does the setting up of obstacles around a person which interfere with his freedom of movement or endanger him (an example of this would be the mining of Kuwait by the retreating Iraqi forces, or indeed, the mining of public areas by anyone). It's true that there is something future-connected here: the untoward events that cause actual harm (the setting off of a mine, say). But that does not mean that there is nothing that has happened in the past for which just compensation or rectification is due–there is, viz., the increase in danger for those who walk the minefield whether literally of physical explosives or figuratively of psychological prejudice.

Now, what sort of benefits should be distributed to gay people via affirmative action? If we focus on job benefits in and of themselves as the aim of the program, and merely as a way of making up for job-related harms, narrowly conceived, then we shall perhaps need to study the dimension of job-related harms (narrowly conceived) against gay people–such as loss of job, failure to be hired, denial of promotion. At present, sufficient information of this sort is not at hand. Indeed, even if we had it and knew how many job-related benefits to distribute, the mere distribution of them would do little by itself to alleviate the cause of much of the problem–anti-gay bigotry itself. For, so long as these benefits are distributed without effecting openness about sexuality on the part of their recipients (other than that which is minimally required to claim the benefit from the distributor), it neither significantly helps to improve their self-esteem nor to reduce the bigotry of those around them.

Clearly, effecting openness would do great benefit for gay people. One could even argue that it would be the single greatest benefit in the long run. For one thing, the most effective way of reducing anti-gay bigotry is by increasing personal interaction with openly gay people.[65] Such openness would thus have the twin benefits of reducing bigotry in others and of improving self-esteem, both in those who were open and in others who were not yet open but who saw the new openness of others. These two benefits in turn might combine to induce even more people to come out. And certainly, for those who are just developing an awareness of their gay identity, it would reduce the likelihood of severe injury to their self-esteem or disruptive interference with their self-development, and it would increase the likelihood of their being open about being gay.

These considerations can be put together in the form of a role-model argument, but one that is even more inclusive than the usual one in the case of other oppressed groups. When one realizes that, in the matter of openness about being gay, almost all gay people are in need of role models or good examples, not just the very young, it becomes clear that the role model strategy will be almost all-inclusive in its expectation of benefits. Gay people in general, and not just the very young, will benefit in increased self-esteem, in self-development, in their political development as free and equal citizens, and from the reduction of anti-gay bigotry. As gay people, with increased openness, learn how to integrate themselves honestly and completely into society and to divert to useful positive purposes the immense energies presently diverted into the frustrating strategies of deception and concealment, they will begin to savor the benefits of full and equal citizenship in the state, and of equal opportunity in the pursuit of a good life.

Affirmative action policies effecting openness would also have an aspect of "repayment in kind" for at least one of the harms suffered by gay people. For it is certainly true that the one harm suffered by almost all gay people is forced concealment of their sexual identity—with all the losses which that brings in its train. And bringing about openness would be a way of giving back what had been taken away.

An affirmative action program for gay people should therefore include inducements, even by higher pay, to openness on the job and in general. This type of affirmative action program could involve the recruitment of openly gay people for new positions, as well as incentives for already employed people to come out. The former may actually be at first easier than the latter because people who are already closeted in their jobs tend to have built such a structure of constraints around themselves having to do with their present environment and work associates that it may be very difficult for them to break free from it.

Since there are so very few openly gay people in most types of employment,[66] there should be no dearth of highly qualified candidates to draw upon in order to make moves in this direction. But although qualifications may be no problem, incentives may be needed to get gay people to be open, beyond the mere symbolic show of support contained in such gestures of recruitment, and these may have to involve extra money and some kind of support system connected with work that would address their special needs and concerns in coming out on the job. The extra incentives may be necessary to entice them to be open, when they know they may suffer emotionally from others for it; and they can be thought of as partial compensation for, or fortification against, incurring this cost, as well as remuneration for providing the service to the program of being openly gay, interacting with their work associates, and essentially giving them practical instruction to help dispel their ignorance about gay people.

It is interesting that for such an affirmative action policy for gay people, some of the criticisms lodged against affirmative action in the more traditional cases seem to lapse. The claim that the policy would injure the self-esteem of the oppressed group would not apply, first, because increased openness itself improves self-esteem in the gay case, and second, because what is indicated as the cause of the purported drop in self-esteem, the lowering of standards in order to make more members of the oppressed groups successful in the final selection process, would not be involved in the gay case. Also, the criticism that affirmative action programs in the traditional cases produce resentment does not seem as significant in the gay case, first, because, again, the cause of the resentment, i.e., having someone less qualified than you preferred to you for a job, would not be involved; and second, because it will be clear that those who do reveal their sexuality openly are taking upon themselves a special hardship that others are not, and this extra hardship can be seen as justifying extra compensation. A further traditional criticism related to justice would also be inapplicable. The policy of affirmative action in the gay case would not involve even a *prima facie* injustice to majority candidates, if the person chosen were the most qualified, either on ordinary job-content qualifications, or those extra qualifications involving the extra duties of being openly gay and combating prejudice. And even if there were any *prima facie* injustice done to the majority candidates, it could more reasonably than in other cases be held that it was justified because they had in fact benefited from the oppression of gays, especially in the case of heterosexual males–since they win a large quantity of self-esteem and esteem by others merely on the basis of not being or appearing gay, especially in youth.[67]

In addition to this kind of inducement to openness in order to provide role models for gay people in general, there ought to be some steps taken in the area of support for those who do become open and in the area of education to alleviate the ignorance that is the basis of much anti-gay bigotry. And this should take place at the very early stages of education.[68] Since there clearly would be resistance to this in many of the school districts across the country, it may have to be enforced from the federal level, in much the same way as was school desegregation in the 1950s. One might even see this in similar fashion as a prerequisite to equality of education for gay children. For just as it was found in *Brown v. the Board of Education* that separate is inherently unequal in the education of black children, so too it could be argued that secret is inherently unequal in the education of gay children.[69] And it is no argument against this that some people may oppose this sort of instruction for religious reasons. If religion is not allowed to decide what is taught in the schools on the nature of evolution, or to decide who one's classmates should be, why should it be allowed to decide what is taught about being gay?

The importance of the symbolic element in this kind of affirmative action program can hardly be underestimated. In the context of a history of the most appalling contempt and abuse, involving the depiction of gay people as abominable, as the lowest of the low and fit only for elimination, a mere legislative move to prevent further abuse can easily be read as a grudging compliance with scarcely the minimal requirements of civilized behavior. As such, it is hardly to be expected to increase self-esteem in this historically oppressed group. It might even reinforce a feeling of lower worth, since it might promote the feeling that gay people are not good enough to be entitled to compensation for hideous past treatment. It might thus be likely to prompt the same kind of feeling as would occur in a person whom another had habitually mistreated if he were merely told that the mistreatment would cease—and not given compensation for the mistreatment or even an apology for it. By comparison with what would be expected if the same thing had happened to members of the majority, gay people might well get the impression that they were not regarded as beings of equal moral worth. And it seems that society has a special obligation not to reinforce such a feeling when it has been responsible for producing it in the first place. Indeed, one might see as apt in the gay case words similar to those the Supreme Court used about black children in the 1950s. To separate gay young people and, later, adults from others of similar age and qualifications solely because of their sexuality, by allowing or causing them to remain hidden, "generates a feeling of inferiority as to their status in the community that may affect their hearts and minds in a way unlikely ever to be undone."[70]

I shall not here offer an estimate of the numbers that would be needed to operate an affirmative action role model program for gay people such as I have suggested. Given their virtual invisibility, even a very few role models in places of high visibility and influence may well have a powerful effect against the greatest inertial mass of bigotry. After that first wave, others of larger number would have to follow. Only then or later, once people are sufficiently out of the closet to be surveyed in dependable studies, can we even begin to address the question of how much in the way of further compensation should be given for society's appalling record of grievous abuse against gay people, which, shamefully, continues to the present day under the full authority of law.

NOTES

1. I shall leave this "affirmative aspect" requirement somewhat vague. I mean it to suggest that the point of the policy is in part to have a certain symbolic significance: that of representing a certain pro-attitude of encouragement, for ex-

ample, to members of that group. Now the pro-attitude may be directed at membership in that group pure and simple, or it may be directed at members of that group performing a certain role, or occupying a certain position (perhaps one which they have not much occupied in the past). This "message" or "symbolic" aspect of affirmative action is crucially important, I think, to an understanding of its moral significance; yet it is something that is often either neglected or relegated to the periphery in discussions of affirmative action. For an interesting discussion of this aspect of affirmative action, see Thomas E. Hill, Jr., "The Message of Affirmative Action," in his *Autonomy and Self-Respect* (Cambridge: Cambridge University Press, 1991), pp. 189-211.

2. The most familiar type of job benefit is probably that involved in preferential hiring. But there are other types of benefits that even now are used in affirmative action programs. These range from preferential admissions into educational institutions, to things less standardly recognized as instances of affirmative action, such as remedial schooling or training and "outreach" programs that attempt to offer help to victims of discrimination. See Irving Thalberg, "Themes in the Reverse Discrimination Debate," *Ethics* 91 (1980): 144.

3. See Michael Ruse, *Homosexuality: A Philosophical Inquiry* (Oxford: Basil Blackwell, 1988), p. 267: "I conclude, therefore, that although justice requires us not to discriminate against homosexuals, justice forbids us to discriminate in their favour. If, in employment, we treat homosexuals like normal people, then perhaps to our surprise we shall find that they are normal people."

4. I shall not here address myself to any of the criticisms which have been made in general against affirmative action in principle, except where I think these criticisms lapse in the particular instance of the gay case. My only aim here is to show that one can argue for affirmative action in the gay case just as one can (and many have) for affirmative action in the case of blacks, women, Hispanics, and Native Americans.

5. See Gertrude Ezorsky, *Racism & Justice: The Case for Affirmative Action* (Ithaca: Cornell University Press, 1991), pp. 3-4.

6. On one variety of this secondary kind of prejudice, see Mary Anne Warren, "Secondary Sexism and Quota Hiring," *Philosophy and Public Affairs* 6 (1977): 240-261.

7. In the "backward-looking" case, e.g., in order to ensure that the effects will provide some kind of compensation or rectification, and in the "instrumental" case, e.g., in order to ensure that the effects will actually help to implement the non-discrimination policy.

8. They may refer to present circumstances perhaps for purposes of comparison, as in the utilitarian justifications one must compare the future situation with the present one in order to determine whether it is better.

9. See Ronald Dworkin, *Taking Rights Seriously* (Cambridge, MA: Harvard University Press, 1977), pp. 232, 274, for the distinction between ideal and utilitarian arguments. Of course, equality may be only one of several characteristics thought to inhere in an ideal society and make it ideal; so, depending on the base of ideal characteristics there may be more than one type of ideal argument. The

distinction between ideal and utilitarian arguments might be confused by the tendency of some to describe what I have called ideal arguments as proceeding from a view of "ideal utilitarianism." This usage derives, I believe, from G. E. Moore.

10. See Ronald Dworkin, *A Matter of Principle* (Cambridge, MA: Harvard University Press, 1985), p. 294, for what seems to be an argument of this sort.

11. This latter is connected with what Dworkin speaks of as the principle that "no one in our society should suffer because he is a member of a group thought less worthy of respect, as a group, than other groups" (in Dworkin, *Matter of Principle*, pp. 210-211, 302, and Dworkin, *Taking Rights Seriously*, pp. 180f., 272ff.) and with one's entitlement to treatment as an equal (in Dworkin, *Taking Rights Seriously*, p. 227).

12. This is also true, though to a lesser extent, for lesbian women. An oddity in the history of the legal persecution of gay people has been the often complete concentration upon men to the exclusion of women. Those aware of the general invisibility of women in history will perhaps not find this surprising.

13. See Jonathan Ned Katz, *Gay American History* (New York: Meridian, 1992), p. 24.

14. Katz, *Gay American History*, p. 581, n. 96.

15. The Editors of the Harvard Law Review, *Sexual Orientation and the Law* (Cambridge, MA: Harvard University Press, 1989), pp. 6-7.

16. Dennis Altman, *Homosexual Oppression and Liberation* (New York: Avon, 1971), p. 44.

17. President Bill Clinton has promised to lift the ban, but under threat of right-wing Congressional resistance and military opposition, he has postponed signing an executive order to that effect until July 1993. Under what is described by some as a compromise plan, people presently involved in legal proceedings may be separated from active duty and put on standby reserve pending the final settlement of the issue.

18. As of the elections of November 1992.

19. See Richard Plant, *The Pink Triangle: The Nazi War against Homosexuals* (New York: Henry Holt & Co., 1986), pp. 167-168.

20. Plant, *Pink Triangle*, p. 181.

21. Plant, *Pink Triangle*, p. 181.

22. Katz, *Gay American History*, pp. 182-3. In this piece, according to Katz, the authors "summarize the generally ineffective attempts to treat homosexuality with electro- and pharmacological shock." Nor were such treatments limited to obscure or nameless victims. In the 1950s, Alan Turing, the brilliant British logician and mathematician, and one of the pioneering minds of computer science, arrested after naively telling police about a homosexual relationship, was given hormone "therapy" involving female hormones which caused him temporarily to grow breasts. Sometime afterward he fell into a depression and committed suicide. See Alan Hodges, *Alan Turing: The Enigma* (New York: Simon and Schuster, 1983).

23. Katz, *Gay American History*, pp. 191-3. While the patients were supposed to have been aggressive and "assaultive," the case reports, according to Katz, "do

not detail much 'aggressive, assaultive, destructive' behavior, the main justification for the lobotomies. Homosexual and autoerotic activity appear, in these reports, to constitute the 'management problem' for which lobotomy was performed."

24. See Kenneth Lewes, *The Psychoanalytic Theory of Male Homosexuality* (New York: New American Library, 1988), pp. 230-241.

25. Richard D. Mohr, *Gays/Justice: A Study of Ethics, Society, and Law* (New York: Columbia University Press, 1988), p. 146, n. 17.

26. It is hard to determine the exact effect of these attitudes in some hiring cases, even when there is clear evidence that they exist. Recently a high-ranking member of a department in one university was reported as commenting on a job candidate with excellent credentials that he was "a little too light in the loafers." The candidate was not, in the end, offered the job, but what exactly was the effect on others of this homophobic remark in the formation of their choice to offer the job to someone else is a difficult question.

27. See Mohr, *Gays/Justice*, p. 147.

28. See Kevin T. Berrill and Gregory M. Herek, "Primary and Secondary Victimization in Anti-Gay Hate Crimes: Official Response and Public Policy," in Gregory M. Herek and Kevin T. Berrill, *Hate Crimes: Confronting Violence Against Lesbians and Gay Men* (Newbury Park, CA: Sage Publications, 1992), p. 293. See also Gary David Comstock, *Violence Against Lesbians and Gay Men* (New York: Columbia University Press, 1991).

29. Herek and Berrill, *Hate Crimes*, pp. 294-295.

30. Herek and Berrill, *Hate Crimes*, p. 295.

31. Richard C. Friedman, *Male Homosexuality* (New Haven: Yale University Press, 1988), p. 197.

32. J. E. Mack, "Self-Esteem and Its Development: An Overview," in J. E. Mack and S. L. Ablon, eds., *The Development and Sustaining of Self-Esteem in Childhood* (New York: International Universities Press, 1983), p. 12; quoted in Friedman, *Male Homosexuality*, p. 197.

33. See pp. 2-136 of Alcohol, Drug Abuse, and Mental Health Administration, *Report of Secretary's Task Force on Youth Suicide, Volume 2: Risk Factors for Youth Suicide*, D.H.H.S. Pub. No. (ADM)89-1622 (Washington, DC: Supt. of Docs., U.S. Govt. Print. Off., 1989).

34. Joseph Harry, "Sexual Identity Issues," *Report of Secretary's Task Force*, pp. 2-132.

35. See Michael W. Ross, "Actual and Anticipated Societal Reaction to Homosexuality and Adjustment in Two Societies," *Journal of Sex Research* 21 (1985): 40-55.

36. Vito Russo, author of *The Celluloid Closet*, quoted in Richard D. Mohr, *Gay Ideas: Outing and Other Controversies* (Boston: Beacon Press, 1992), p. 26.

37. See John C. Gonsiorek and James R. Rudolph, "Homosexual Identity: Coming Out and Other Developmental Events," in John C. Gonsiorek and James D. Weinrich, eds., *Homosexuality: Research Implications for Public Policy* (Newbury Park, CA: Sage Publications, 1991). On the consequences of hiding one's

orientation, or being isolated from a gay community, see Linda Garnets, Gregory Herek, and Barrie Levy, "Violence and Victimization of Lesbians and Gay Men: Mental Health Consequences," in *Hate Crimes*, p. 211.

38. Internalized self-oppression and some degree of servility seem to be a general effect of social oppression of minorities (see Gordon W. Allport, *The Nature of Prejudice* [New York: Doubleday Anchor, 1958], pp. 143-144, 147ff). But what is so very distinctive about the gay case which makes this self-oppression apt to produce such abject servility is the complete absence of a social support system in the early years of one's life, and thus any sympathetic guidance in developing ways of coping with social oppression which preserve at least a modicum of dignity. Unlike blacks, for example, gay youngsters do not have gay families to teach them how to cope, and to nurture at least a central core of respect for themselves as members of the group.

39. Reported in the article "Armed Services Cite a Wide Range of Reasons for Ban on Homosexuality," *New York Times*, Jan. 27, 1993, p. A14.

40. "Armed Services," pp. A1, A14. The article continues: "Some Marines have gone so far as to suggest that the corps be disbanded rather than accept avowed homosexuals. 'It is better to wear proudly the uniform of another service than to see the Globe and Anchor progressively defamed,' Maj. Arthur J. Corbett, a Marine officer at the Naval War College, wrote in the current issue of the *Marine Corps Gazette*, a monthly journal." It is clear that the concern here is about dishonor and not discomfort–the mere presence of openly gay people is considered so deeply dishonorable as to make annihilation of the Corps the only worthy alternative.

41. John Rawls, *A Theory of Justice* (Cambridge, MA: Harvard University Press, 1971), p. 178.

42. Rawls, *Theory of Justice*, p. 534.

43. Rawls, *Theory of Justice*, p. 545.

44. Rawls, *Theory of Justice*, p. 546.

45. In offering an explanation of the exceptional injustice of racial and sexual discrimination, and why affirmative action may be justified, Thomas Nagel writes: "It has no social advantages, and it attaches a sense of reduced worth to a feature with which people are born. A psychological consequence of the systematic attachment of social disadvantages to a certain inborn feature is that both the possessors of the feature and others begin to regard it as an essential and important characteristic, and one which reduces the esteem in which its possessor can be held. Concomitantly, those who do not possess the characteristic gain a certain amount of free esteem by comparison, and the arrangement thus constitutes a gross sacrifice of the most basic personal interests of some for the interests of others, with those sacrificed being on the bottom." Nagel speaks of inborn characteristics, but it is clear from a footnote that what is important is that the feature in question be part of the person's self-image, a component of what is regarded as one's essence. This seems clearly to apply to gay people, regardless of what view one takes about the etiology of sexuality or about the nature of the category "homosexual" (whether, i.e., one views it as do the social constructionists or the es-

sentialists). See Thomas Nagel, "Equal Treatment and Compensatory Discrimination," in Marshall Cohen, Thomas Nagel, and Thomas Scanlon, eds., *Equality and Preferential Treatment* (Princeton: Princeton University Press, 1977), p. 15.

46. Comstock, *Violence*, p. 55.

47. Kevin T. Berrill and Gregory M. Herek, "Primary and Secondary Victimization in Anti-Gay Hate Crimes: Official Response and Public Policy," in Herek and Berrill, *Hate Crimes*, p. 292.

48. Comstock, *Violence*, p. 92.

49. Gabriel Rotello, "John Silber Rides Again: BU president explodes at gay activist at NYC anti-bias forum," *Bay Windows* [Boston], Dec. 3, 1992, pp. 3, 16, 18. This article originally appeared in *New York Newsday*.

50. Frank Chalk and Kurt Jonassohn, *The History and Sociology of Genocide: Analyses and Case Studies* (New Haven: Yale University Press, 1990). The definition given on p. 23 is: "*Genocide* is a form of one-sided mass killing in which a state or other authority intends to destroy a group, as that group and membership in it are defined by the perpetrator."

51. See John Boswell, *Christianity, Social Tolerance, and Homosexuality* (Chicago: University of Chicago Press, 1980). Boswell argues that the prevalence of anti-gay attitudes did not coincide with the rise of Christianity. Rather, he thinks that they arose sometime in the Middle Ages, long after Christianity had been established in the West, and then became identified with certain passages in the Bible that had been largely ignored, or not attended to, or interpreted in a different way until then.

52. The Catholic Church's Congregation for the Doctrine of Faith expressed the view that violence against gay people is "deplorable" but seemed to blame it on the moves for gay civil rights: "When civil legislation is introduced to protect behavior to which no one has any conceivable right, neither the Church nor society at large should be surprised when other distorted notions and practices gain ground, and irrational and violent reactions increase." This view was approved by Pope John Paul II and included in a 1986 letter entitled, of all things, "Letter to the Bishops of the Catholic Church on the Pastoral Care of Homosexual Persons." See Comstock, *Violence*, pp. 122-123, and Gregory Herek, "Cultural Heterosexism," in *Hate Crimes*, pp. 90-91.

53. Comstock, *Violence*, p. 142.

54. E.g., against the decriminalization of anal-genital and oral-genital contacts between consenting adults in private in California in 1971, and in a Virginia Supreme Court decision with similar effect in 1976 (allowing a "crime-against-nature" statute to be applied to private homosexual relations between consenting adults). See Comstock, *Violence*, p. 259.

55. Comstock, *Violence*, p. 123.

56. But it is by no means true of all cultures even now. This is brought out clearly in Gilbert Herdt's work on the Sambia, a people who regard homosexual activity as essential to the proper development of masculinity. See especially *Guardians of the Flutes* (New York: McGraw-Hill, 1981).

57. See Walter L. Williams, *The Spirit and the Flesh: Sexual Diversity in American Indian Culture* (Boston: Beacon Press, 1986).

58. See John D'Emilio, *Sexual Politics, Sexual Communities* (Chicago: University of Chicago Press, 1983), especially pp. 108ff.

59. *United States v. Carolene Products Co.*, 304 U.S. 144, 152 n.4 (1938).

60. As, e.g., Mohr seems to suggest in discussing this very court case. See Mohr, *Gays/Justice*, pp. 169-170.

61. Mohr, *Gays/Justice*, p. 161.

62. Quoted in Richard A. Posner, *Sex and Reason* (Cambridge, MA: Harvard University Press, 1992), p. 307.

63. *Gay Law Students Assoc. v. PT&T Co.*, 24 Cal. 3d at 488 (1979). Quoted in Mohr, *Gays/Justice*, p. 178.

64. In each of these types of programs, the quota-based, goal-based, and recruitment-based, one can further distinguish different criteria for actual employment of members of the protected groups. There may be protected group preference among equally qualified candidates, or when other candidates are better qualified by a certain increment, or when other candidates are better qualified by any increment so long as members of the protected group are at least minimally qualified.

65. See Mohr, *Gays/Justice*, p. 176, note 23. An Oregon state study found a close link between positive attitudes towards gay people and firsthand experience with them. State of Oregon, Department of Human Resources, *Final Report of the Task Force on Sexual Preference* (Portland: State of Oregon, Department of Human Resources, 1978), pp. 73-87.

66. And even in the few professions stereotyped as substantially gay like fashion designing, there are very few indeed who are open beyond their immediate circle.

67. Thus the usual rejoinder to the claim that the majority are paying for their complicity in past injustices, viz., that very few of the majority today have ever been involved in past injustices, would not apply here. It would be an unusual heterosexual male indeed in today's American society who did not win some measure of esteem from himself or from others for not "being a fag."

68. The evidence suggests that prejudice can appear as early as age three. See Frances Aboud, *Children and Prejudice* (Oxford: Basil Blackwell, 1988), pp. 29ff.

69. The decision in *Brown*, 347 U.S. 493, included this conclusion: "We come to the question presented: Does segregation of children in public schools solely on the basis of race, even though the physical facilities and other 'tangible' factors may be equal, deprive the children of the minority group of equal educational opportunities? We believe that it does." This reasoning would seem to apply to gay people who are closeted because of homophobia as youngsters in schools. The "tangible" factors are indeed the same because they are identical–there is no actual, official segregation of these gay youngsters into separate schools. But certainly the opportunities are not the same because their needs as gay people are not even acknowledged, much less addressed, in the way the counterpart needs of heterosexual youngsters are. Among these are the social needs of learning how to

interact with others as a gay person in the sense of just dealing with others who know one's identity as a gay person, of learning how to interact with others as a gay person in the sense of dealing with others as potentially intimate (including sexually, emotionally, and romantically intimate) partners, and of learning how to integrate into one's own identity certain features of oneself with those of others and with preferences for and expectations of developments in the future (the sort of thing which sets one on the road to a life plan for the future in terms of one's own personal pursuit of happiness).

70. Original at 347 U.S. 494.

PART IV.
THE MORAL MEANINGS OF SCIENCE

Explaining Homosexuality: Philosophical Issues, and Who Cares Anyhow?

Frederick Suppe, PhD

University of Maryland, College Park

SUMMARY. Standard behavioral and biological attempts to explain the etiology of homosexuality are surveyed. These include genetic, physiological (e.g., hormonal), constitutional (e.g., wrong pubic hair configurations), childhood experience, parenting, and psychoanalytic accounts. These are criticized from a number of perspectives,

Frederick Suppe is Professor in Philosophy and in History and Philosophy of Science at the University of Maryland at College Park, and Professor in the School of Nursing Doctoral Program on the Baltimore campus.

Correspondence may be addressed to the author at the CHPS/Department of Philosophy, 1102 Skinner Building, University of Maryland, College Park, MD 20742-7615.

[Haworth co-indexing entry note]: "Explaining Homosexuality: Philosophical Issues, and Who Cares Anyhow?" Suppe, Frederick. Co-published simultaneously in the *Journal of Homosexuality* (The Haworth Press, Inc.) Vol. 27, No. 3/4, 1994, pp. 223-268; and: *Gay Ethics: Controversies in Outing, Civil Rights, and Sexual Science* (ed: Timothy F. Murphy) The Haworth Press, Inc., 1994, pp. 223-268. Multiple copies of this article/chapter may be purchased from The Haworth Document Delivery Center [1-800-3-HAWORTH; 9:00 a.m. - 5:00 p.m. (EST)].

223

including inadequate conceptualization of homosexuality and heterosexuality. The use of path analysis to assess etiological accounts is examined, with particular attention being paid to the Kinsey Institute's *Sexual Preference* efforts. Drawing from the sociology of science, recent philosophical work on the growth of scientific knowledge, and historical considerations, the legitimacy of homosexual etiology as a scientific research question is examined. It is argued that homosexual etiology is a degenerative research program. The research program's conceptual crudity with respect to sexual identity and sexual orientation precludes it from making any scientific contribution. Thus the claim that homosexual etiology is a legitimate scientific issue is plausible only against the background of a set of late Victorian normative assumptions about "normal love," some surrogate thereof, or a political agenda. Implications of the homosexuality etiology case study for more general philosophical treatments of explanation are considered briefly.

Science has indeed discovered that, amid the lowest forms of bestiality and sensuousness exhibited by debased men, there are phenomena which are truly pathological and which deserve the considerate attention and help of the physician.

George F. Shrady
"Editorial: Perverted Sexual Instinct" (1884)[1]

In this century, sex research and medico-psychiatric opinion about variant sexual behaviors have been dominated by a late Victorian "Theory of Normal Love" wherein the sexually normal is procreative, and nonprocreative sexuality is abnormal.[2] Thus a central focus of sex research has been on deviant sexual behavior, with especial attention paid to the causes of such abnormal behaviors. Both biological and social-learning explanations of homosexuality have been offered. In this paper I explore a number of philosophical and methodological issues raised by the homosexual etiology literature.

SCIENTIFIC STUDIES OF HOMOSEXUAL ETIOLOGY

Rather than attempt any comprehensive survey of the homosexual etiology literature, I will content myself with merely summarizing the main sorts of explanations that have been attempted and commenting on some of the difficulties they have encountered and their underlying premises.[3]

Genetic Theories

It has been hypothesized that homosexuality is genetically caused. Since the early part of this century there have been standard plant and animal breeding techniques for determining not only the heritability of traits but also whether heritable traits are under the control of single genes or more elaborate interactive combinations. Such techniques are virtually precluded for human homosexuality on the basis of ethical considerations and long generational periods.[4] Studies of lower animal homosexuality are of questionable relevance to human homosexuality since the hormonally controlled mounting behavior of, e.g., rodents is quite unlike cortico-controlled human sexual behavior, and the fact that homosexual behavior and homosexual orientations are distinct components of sexual identity in humans but not rats.

Thus indirect means of assessing genetic makeups for homosexuality have been attempted: chromosomes of homosexuals vs. heterosexuals have been compared. Correlations between Klinefelter's syndrome patients and sexual offenses have been undertaken. On the ground that older parents are more likely to produce children with genetic abnormalities, a number of researchers have attempted to see if the parents of homosexuals were older at conception than were heterosexual controls.

Using Munich and Hamburg police records of homosexuals in Nazi Germany, Lang compared the sibling sex ratios of listed male homosexuals (121.1:100) to ratios established for a completely different population (106:100) and a control group (107.2:100).[5] He then invoked Goldschmidt's discovery of butterflies which are genetically female but morphologically male and concluded by analogy that some of the male homosexuals were morphologically transformed females who elevated the sibling sex ratios. A comparison with U.S. census data makes his 106:100 normal sex ratio suspect. In his study no direct examination of chromosomes was undertaken. Incredibly, a number of researchers have felt it worthwhile to attempt replications of his work.

A number of studies involving monozygotic and dizygotic twins reared together and apart have been done on the hypothesis that if homosexuality is genetic, then monozygotic twins should share some sexual orientation regardless whether reared together or apart. The 1952 Kallman early confirmatory results (in which he found 100% concordance for homosexuality in monozygotic twins but only 8% in dizygotic twins) generally have not been supported by replicative studies.[6] The fact that most of his twins were reared together provides little control for environmental causes, and thus renders questionable the attribution of a genetic basis. Twins raised together have unusually strong environmental influences on each other and enjoy a closeness other siblings do not. Thus, it is especially difficult to control for environmental effects, and so the preferred heritability research practice is to study twins reared apart.

More recently, in 1991, Bailey and Pillard found 52% of monozygotic co-twins and 22% of dizygotic co-twins were homosexual.[7] They calculated heritability of homosexuality using a genetic model. All of there subjects were reared together and thus treated by the model as having complete sharing of environmental parameters. They tout this as an advantage of their study, but in fact it is simply the perpetuation of one of the more serious flaws in Kallman's earlier study: failure to control for environmental influences on sexual orientation. Indeed, whereas in Kallman's study most of the twins "developed their homosexual behavior independently of each other" we have no indication this was so in Bailey and Pillard's study where 121 out of 127 knew their twin's sexual orientation.[8]

If homosexuality is hereditary, then on the assumption that homosexuals reproduce less than heterosexuals, some explanation for the persistence of homosexual genes in the population is required. Sociobiologists have provided four different models that account for this, but have put forth no convincing evidence that homosexuality is hereditary. Ruse provides useful philosophical and scientific evaluations of those models (chaps. 6-7).[9]

Hormonal Studies

A number of researchers, most notably John Money and various associates, have studied hormonally abnormal individuals, *inter alia*, attempting to discern if the syndromes correlate with homosexuality. Persons studied include masculinized females, hermaphrodites, and those experiencing delayed puberty, androgen insensitivity, and precocious puberty. Typically, few or no cases of homosexuality are reported, although in some cases this reflects more an absence of data than anything else.[10]

Many studies have been done attempting to find differences in various hormonal levels of homosexuals as opposed to controls–apparently on the theory that male homosexuals are less masculine than heterosexuals, and thus should have lower levels of male hormones such as testosterone, and that lesbians similarly should be hormonally more masculinized. A variety of measurement techniques have been used, and generally inconsistent and unconvincing results are reported in the literature.

In large part this is due to methodological problems such as failure to control for the use of narcotics, alcohol, and other substances that affect hormonal levels. Ricketts summarizes the problems:

> Since these studies reflect a decade's worth of biological thinking about adult hormone levels and homosexuality, it is well to attend with some care to the particulars of their methodology. To begin with, the vast majority of studies of plasma hormones involved only one blood sample. Single sample measures of hormones are notoriously suspect, due to secretion of hormones episodically or according to circadian or diurnal rhythms [reference omitted]. Parks et al. [reference omitted] measured LH, FSH, and testosterone in 12 adolescents (ages 16-19) and found major variations that would have made it difficult 'to properly evaluate the hormonal status of a subject from only one hormone determination.'[11]

Further, testosterone flows in 6-7 short secretory spikes per day that affect LH and FSH levels and is suppressed by psychological stress, physical stress, and exercise of long (but not short) duration. The percentage of testosterone binding increases with age (75-76).

Ricketts continues:

> Another major problem with a number of hormone studies is the lack of proper control groups. Several researchers used

no controls at all [references omitted]; several co-opted controls from other studies going on in their laboratories [references omitted]. Occasionally, homosexuals, were matched with blatantly inappropriate controls; Pillard et al. [reference omitted], for instance, compared volunteers from homophile organizations with soldiers in an officers training school who had been recruited for another study. . . .

But more frustrating than any of this is the utter gravity with which investigators have contemplated any statistically significant finding. . . . Some biological researchers appear to have forgotten that cardinal rule of statistical analysis: Correlation does not prove causality. (76)

Birke,[12] Gartrell,[13] and Ruse (sects. 5.2-5.4) provide additional methodological criticisms of this research.

Given the failure to find any replicable evidence that provides compelling grounds for a hormonal difference etiology for homosexuality, researchers now have turned to the development of prenatal theories. Hypothesizing that there are masculinized and feminized brains, Dörner et al. theorized that an androgen deficiency in males during a critical hypothalamic organization period would produce a feminized brain.[14] They have attempted to test this by differential LH level responses to the administration of estrogen, hormonal studies on rats under various stress levels, the claimed discovery of a higher frequency of homosexual births between 1940-45 when pregnant women were under greater stress due to W.W. II, and so on.[15] In their 1976 report, Dörner et al. offer the same account for transsexualism—which they view as an extreme form of homosexuality.

Birke has argued that Dörner's assumptions about the mounting behaviors of the rats evidencing homosexual or heterosexual orientations and the legitimacy of the rat as a model for human sexual behavior are inappropriate, and that the research is rooted in popular stereotypical conceptions of gender-appropriate behaviors.[16] Ricketts also criticizes Dörner's work:

Unfortunately there are major difficulties. . . . First [reference omitted], the Hohlweg effect [a positive estrogen feedback effect in response to LH injections] was not demonstrated in the bisexual men, who would have been expected to show a weaker estrogen feedback than the homosexuals but a stronger one than the heterosexuals. In fact the LH response of bisexuals was more negative than that of the heterosexuals. Moreover, seven of the 20 heterosexual men did show the response by the 96-hour point [footnote deleted]. Second, Dörner's et al. [reference omitted] insistence on conflating homosexuality and transsexualism is more willful than theoretically or empirically sound; under such circumstances serious consideration of this work is difficult. Finally, Kulin and Reiter [reference omitted] demonstrated that estrogen feedback can be present in normal adult men. The effect may be blocked by testosterone and is apparently maturational; that is, it does not appear until late in, or after, puberty.

More damaging evidence against Dörner's hypothesis of a female-differentiated brain in male homosexuals comes from studies of the estrogen feedback in XY males with the testicular feminization syndrome. . . . In two studies [reference omitted] genetic males with testicular feminization were tested; none of the seven subjects in the two samples showed the Hohlweg effect typical of some male homosexuals in the 1975 study of Dörner et al. (78)

While Ruse acknowledges the force of many of these objections, he argues there is no objection in principle to isolating certain forms of behavior as "male" or "female" and defends defining "heterosexual and homosexual behavior in terms of male and female behavior–a homosexual animal being one which shows sexual behavior more normally associated with the sex other than that to which it belongs. . . . After all, what is homosexual behavior if it is not this?" (120). This latter defense figures centrally in his conclusion that "Dörner's use of rat models is not conceptually inappropriate. What we need, having established the legitimacy of using animal models, is some good studies on animals close to us–like chimpanzees" (122).

Ruse does raise (123-124) a number of methodological objections similar to those of Rickets (above) but is encouraged by the fact that a methodologically stronger study done later by Gladue et al. replicates some of Dörner's key findings.[17] Unfortunately, Dörner's and Gladue's work has not been supported by subsequent studies.[18] This line of research has disappeared from more recent literature and appears to be moribund.

Recently there has been quite a stir over LeVay's 1991 announcement that a particular cell group, interstitial nuclei of the anterior hypothalamus (INAH-3) was found in postmortem studies of AIDS patients and various controls to be on average twice as large in heterosexual as in homosexual males and the latter closer to the size in females.[19] This is viewed as significant since these differences occur in a region of the brain known to be a regulator of "male-typical" sexual behavior. Further, an earlier study had shown the same region to be larger in men than in women.

Levay's interpretation of his findings is cautious, claiming only to have established that "INAH [3] is dimorphic with sexual orientation, at least in men, and suggests that sexual orientation has a biological substrate" (ibid., p. 1043). Even this may be too strong. The samples were small (6 females, 16 presumed heterosexual males, 19 homosexual males). Since the borders of the nuclei are not well defined, there is a fair degree of subjectivity in demarcating the borders of these groups, hence determining their volume. To control for this, the identifications were done "blind." No attempt was made to measure the number of cells in the region or cell density. Thus we have at best an indirect estimate of neural density or connectivity. A fair degree of methodological sophistication is displayed in the study: ANOVAs ("analyses of variance" which determine how much of the result is attributable to various sources) were used to look for possible confounding effects of other variables (e.g., AIDS patient or not) in the population, and Monte Carlo simulations were used to evaluate sensitivity of their findings to probability distribution assumptions.

In evaluating this and other studies, two issues need to be distinguished: the physiological findings and the interpretations put upon them. The bulk of the write-up in a scientific paper is the crafting of an interpretative argument designed to promote a favored interpretation by impeaching competing ones. The veracity of the physiological findings can be settled by replication. However, the very conception of the study and the interpretation of the findings rests primarily on the assumption that male homosexuals more resemble females than males, and so one expects to find a female's brain in a male homosexual. To the extent that assumption is not sustainable, the findings fail even to support the weak interpretative claims LeVay makes.

And the fact is that for all its methodological sophistication LeVay's research is conceptually crude. The binary labeling of regions of the brain or behaviors as "male-typical" or "female-typical" is unwarranted when the phenomena are known to exhibit considerable diversity [what LeVay calls "'exceptions' in the present sample (that is presumed heterosexual men with small INAH 3 nuclei, and homosexual men with large ones)"]–being akin to trying to describe a population by a measure of central tendency without regard for spread.[20] Similarly, Ruse's comments notwithstanding, the assumption that male homosexual orientation is to be equated with, or even strongly correlates with, female behavior is conceptually confused. When the confusions are sorted out, the weight of evidence is against the assumption. We will return to this issue below.

Morphological Studies

In 1934, Henry and Galbraith published a study in which they examined 123 males and 105 female patients for constitutional and physical characteristics usually associated with maleness and femaleness via some procedures of precise measurement but mostly by "direct impressionistic observations."[21] Measurements included torso-leg ratios; carrying angle of the male and female arms ("angle in males was sometimes as great as 178° while in females the angle may be only 15°"); width of shoulders to hips; pelvic development; consistency and distribution of fat; muscular development; firmness or softness of muscles; presence, distribution, and amount of hair on face, trunk, and extremities with especial attention paid to the masculine or feminine distribution of pubic hair and shaving; pitch and quality of voice; degree of genital development including presence or absence of a "scrotal fold."

Thirty-three patients (17 males, 16 females) who had conspicuous homosexual experience (defined as pleasure deriving from repeated homosexual relationships, failure to make an adequate heterosexual adaptation, and illness manifesting overt homosexual desires or compensatory strivings against them [p. 1249n]) were compared with 15 patients (5 males, 10 females) with good heterosexual adaptation on the above standards. Although their data often does not support or else disconfirms, they conclude that homosexual males are characterized by feminine characteristics and homosexual females by masculine characteristics.

Baharal,[22] Evans,[23] Kenyon,[24] and others have done similar studies. Sampling biases, failures of control (e.g., for comparable degree of exercise and concern over weight and physical shape), treating statistically significant but minor differences as important, and conflicting findings make drawing any conclusions from this data extremely risky.

The motivations underlying this sort of research are unclear. In some cases one suspects mean-spiritedness or maliciousness. For example, using no controls and providing no hard data–just anecdotal evidence–M. D. Gioscia claims to have examined 1,404 patients in a neuropsychiatric military hospital in 1944.[25] Manipulating a tongue depressor around the uvula, soft palate, and pharyngeal vault, he claims that 12% were found to have no gag reflex, and of those 89% were judged to suffer from "constitutional psychopathic state: Sexual psychopathology fellatio." He goes on to suggest that jabbing tongue depressors down throats is an effective way of detecting malingerers attempting military discharge by feigning homosexuality and that the test be used as a screening device in Selective Service pre-induction physicals.

G. W. Henry went on to publish a book version of his and Galbraith's earlier work, the research having been sponsored by the Committee for the Study of Sex Variants, Inc.[26] Henry was on the Executive Committee, but not its Chairman. The Eugenics leader Lewis Terman of Stanford was a member of the Committee. I suspect but have not been able to confirm that this Committee has connections with, or was strongly influenced by, the Eugenics movement. If this is correct, then the rationale behind the morphological studies would be clear–to attempt to establish that homosexuals deviated from an eugenically approved norm and then to discourage homosexuality by selectively breeding against it–much as the "Better Family" competitions encouraged breeding for superior "normal" characteristics. Lurking here is a very large question, on which I have seen little written–viz., the influence of the Eugenics movement on homosexuality research this century.

Social Learning Studies

A huge body of literature assumes that homosexuality is learned behavior and attempts to explain its etiology by discovering correlations between homosexuality and various childhood experiences or parenting situations. A number of studies have investigated the birth-order of homosexuals with inconclusive results, explaining their findings with suppositions such as that first born are overly protected (hence become sissies). Other studies investigate whether male homosexuals were the favorites of their mothers or the least favorites of their fathers, childhood play patterns (with same or other sex, doing stereotypically masculine or feminine activities), degree of athletic participation, amount of fighting, age of first sexual experiences, and so on. Underlying most of these studies is an erroneously presumed connection between male homosexuality and effeminacy, or lesbianism and masculinity–and the attendant search for parental or situational factors that teach males to be effeminate and females to reject the stereotypical feminine role.

Related studies attempt to correlate male homosexuality with loss of father (and attendant lack of live-in male role model) or degree of identification with father vs. mother and ethnic background. Opler claims overt homosexuality is much more common among Italian-Americans whereas latent homosexuality is much more common among Irish-Americans, attributing these findings to differences in traditional Irish and Italian family interaction patterns and sex roles.[27]

A huge number of studies attempt to explain the etiology of homosexuality in terms of the personality characteristics of the parents of homosexuals. E.g., Bieber et al.–which will be discussed at length in a later section–claimed homosexuals had close-binding, intimate, seductive, less often controlling, and remarkable mothers; and distant, detached fathers. Among such studies there is surprising agreement that the fathers of male homosexuals are detached, hostile, and rejecting. However, the very important Kinsey Institute large sample study that we will discuss in a later section fails to duplicate these findings. Bieber et al., Evans,[28] and Nash and Hayes[29] attempted to correlate parental characteristics with homosexuals being inserters vs. insertees (conveniently ignoring the fact that most pre-AIDS U. S. white male homosexuals performed both roles with regularity, often in the same episode). No adequate explanation is given for how the same parents can produce mostly heterosexual children with only a single homosexual one.

Components of Sexual Identity

One pervasive problem in the literature surveyed is a high level of conceptual confusion as to what counts as a homosexual and a heterosexual. Members of control groups often are merely presumed to be heterosexual when there is reason to believe this is not the case. (In fact, for example, a control group randomly selected from an introductory psychology class can be *expected* to have some homosexuals in it.)

The following components of *sexual identity* can be distinguished: *biological sex, gender identity, social sex role,* and *sexual orientation* (comprised of *sexual behavior, fantasy structure, patterns of affectional preference, arousal cue response patterns,* and *self-labeling*). All of these (singly or in combination) have been used as the basis for labeling persons as homosexual or heterosexual, although only the components of sexual orientation are appropriate for doing so and one may be homosexual in some components and heterosexual in others.[30] I have shown elsewhere[31] that these confusions ultimately are rooted in the Victorian "Theory of Normal Love." Confusion over what counts as a homosexual makes interpretation and comparison of studies difficult and in some cases makes contrasts between subjects and controls meaningless.

McIntosh[32] identified what she called the homosexual role and argued that it does not occur in all societies, emerging only in seventeenth-century England. Her view of the homosexual role has obvious affinities with closely related views of symbolic interactionism, labeling theory, and societal reaction theory in sociology. Weinberg and Williams summarize the latter approaches as follows:

> Taking into account the social context in which the homosexual lives leads to a fundamental change in the conception of

research. Instead of talking about homosexuality as a condition (which a person has to a greater or lesser degree) and seeking the causes of the condition, primary attention is directed to the ways in which the homosexual is affected by his social situation, for example, how the connotations and expectations surrounding homosexuality affect the homosexual's behavior and self concept.

. . . For example, what makes homosexuality "deviant," according to reaction theory, is not anything about the behavior per se but rather the fact that people differentiate, stigmatize, and penalize alleged homosexuals.

Other people's reactions involve assigning someone a deviant status which overrides his other statuses. This can influence him to identify and associate with other "deviants" and affect the view he has of himself and the world.[33]

Weinberg and Williams allowed societal reaction theory to guide the design of their study (8) which was a tri-cultural one (8). Their findings generally did not support the predictions of societal reaction theory for homosexuals (chap. 22), though they do conclude by recommending "that homosexuality be conceptualized in terms of social statuses and roles rather then as a condition" (274).

The various authors in Plummer strongly support this recommendation and attempt to support the approach with historical evidence and argument.[34] Most of the persons writing in De Cecco and Shively support the idea that the various components of sexual orientation identified above should be abandoned in favor of purely self-labeling notions.[35] While they are correct in stressing the self-labeling component of sexual orientation, a purely self-labeling approach cannot make sense, of e.g., persons who have a homosexual orientation but deny to themselves that they are and refuse to label themselves as homosexuals (the "Gee, was I drunk last night" syndrome). For these and other reasons I have raised[36] as well as the failure of Weinberg and Williams and Bell, Weinberg, and Hammersmith[37] to support the predictions of symbolic interactionism, labeling theory, and societal reaction theory approaches, I think we must continue to use the multi-dimensional approach to sexual orientation sketched above.[38]

236 Gay Ethics: Controversies in Outing, Civil Rights, and Sexual Science

The fact that sexual identity and sexual orientation are so multi-dimensional has serious implications for how sexual orientation research is conceptualized. First, we see that gender, gender identity, sex-role conformity, and the five components of sexual orientation are distinct dimensions. How strongly or loosely these correlate with each other is an empirical, not a conceptual matter. And the empirical evidence is that virtually every combination occurs among humans. This means that it is fundamentally inappropriate to label individuals as heterosexual, bisexual, or homosexual *simpliciter*. Minimally one would need to use separate labels for each of these eight dimensions. And for some of these, the appropriate labels will be such as "homosexual sadomasochistic–bondage–with leather fetish," or "heterosexual infantile scatological" with respect to, say, fantasy structure.[39] Thus, there are literally hundreds of sexual identities that get conflated with simplistic "heterosexual" and "homosexual" labels.

It follows, that within the gross "heterosexual" and "homosexual labels" there will be a great deal of diversity with respect to masculinity and femininity in its various dimensions. (Recall, here, that the Bem Androgyny Scale views masculinity and femininity as orthogonal, and so an androgynous person will be strongly masculine and strongly feminine.) In particular, no matter how many homosexual males were sissy boys or are effeminate, a substantial proportion of homosexual men were hypermasculine as boys[40] and are hypermasculine adults. Indeed, the available evidence is that homosexual men involved in SM activities are, and conceive themselves as, hypermasculine regardless which role is played. Indeed, in the "Leather" subculture the "slave" role often is viewed as the most masculine of all ("taking it like a man").[41]

Not only is it a mistake to identify male homosexuality with femininity and male heterosexuality with masculinity, it also is a mistake to lump all homosexual behavior into who mounts whom (as Dörner and Ruse are wont to do). Ruse writes: "one can go on to define heterosexual behavior in terms of male and female sexual behavior—a homosexual animal being one which shows sexual behavior more normally associated with the sex of the other than that to which it belongs" (120). Assuming "more normally associated" is a statistical, not a normative, condition, then the fact is that being the recipient in anal intercourse is a distinctively male role. Moreover, since males inevitably are the inserter in non-prosthetic anal intercourse, to play the inserter role is a male role. Thus, by Ruse's account, it is a heterosexual act to be the recipient in anal intercourse, just as it is to be the inserter.

Similarly, regardless whether the statistical incidence of fellatio in male or female mouths is greater, males always are the inserters and so that role is a heterosexual act regardless of the receiving mouth's gender. And for the insertee:

> Yet, twisting roles again, here [in a gloryhole], as at many a gay blowjob site, it is the sucker who is in control calling the shots. He attends in the first instance to his own pleasure, not giving in to the demands of his hole-piercing boothmates, not assuming a self-conception of servicer of and for others, a concept that would diminish his own agency. Indeed, in his studied 'passivity' he has even induced desire for him as agent in the manhandler on the right, while putting the cool on the assertive guy on the left, whose posture–stiff dick wholly pressed through the hole and twitching in open air–is difficult to maintain for any length of time unattended. The gloryhole neutralizes the insertor as dominator. There is cocksucking, but no facefucking, in traditional gloryhole sex. Thus, the geography of the gloryhole site, with its occluding of the traditionally active posture of the penetrator, allows our stud, despite his glazed-over mind and intense oral-fixation, to maintain a comprehensive sense of his own agency and to see himself completely on a par with those who would seek his services. Here, tropes of domination are taken up and reinscribed into a whole that asserts equality of persons. Raunch and sleaze–solvents of hierarchy–are two of life's great equalizers.[42]

No rat is capable of such conceptualization. The complexities of cocksucking cannot be reduced down to the rat-like mentality of who mounts whom–not even to that incarnation in humans who would study and dissect homosexuality.

And what *are* the "male" and "female" roles in "69," mutual masturbation, analingus, or felching? Clearly, no simple-minded equation of who mounts whom is an adequate conceptualization of sexual orientation.[43]

In short, any reasonable attempt to study the etiology of sexual identities or orientations will have to conceptualize them multivariately, and the components of sexual orientation will have to include a much richer variety of sexual activities than just vanilla male-male, female-female, male-female, and female-male couplings. Even if one limits oneself to standard variations, there are literally hundreds of different sexual identities and sexual orientations. Any simplistic heterosexual or homosexual classification does too much violence to the diversity of human sexuality to have a place in scientifically credible account of the etiology of sexual identity or orientation. For what it studies is an artifact of crude conceptualization, and thus is a non-existent phenomenon. This fact, probably more than any other, explains why so little sexual variation in fact is explained by past etiological studies.

SOME PHILOSOPHICAL OBSERVATIONS

Virtually all the research summarized above takes a group of presumed homosexuals, measures them for something, possibly compares these measures with a control group, and then does some sort of rudimentary statistical analysis. In many cases just percentage differences are noted. Others test for statistically significant mean differences or attempt to determine the extent of statistical correlation between homosexuality and other measured characteristics (with a minority of these attempting to assess the statistical significance of the differences in correlational strengths). The studies are almost always retrospective. Samples inevitably are highly biased in ways that preclude legitimately projecting any generalizations from the sample to the general population of homosexuals (or heterosexuals).

In short, one rarely finds any of the techniques employed that philosophers of science claim are appropriate for determining causality (hence etiology): no Mill's methods of agreement *and* difference,[44] no randomized experimental designs or prospective designs. Rather one mostly finds methods known by philosophers to be incapable of determining causal connections: retrospective studies that only demonstrate correlations are incapable of establishing causality, Giere[45] and others tell us.

When we realize that in these respects the homosexuality literature surveyed is quite representative of social and behavioral science research in general, we should be concerned. Is it that social scientists generally ignore or forget our philosophical claims despite periodic pious pronouncements such as:

> of course, these correlation studies do not indicate cause and effect. We fall too easily into the error of assuming that the parent causes the child's behavior. We must remember that there is evidence that the infant's behavior has been shown to affect the parent's behavior too.[46]

While this sometimes surely is the case, we must examine the issue more closely.

In my survey I attempted to sketch some of the underlying assumptions or theories that inform the various research approaches. Under the positivistic version of the *hypothetico-deductive (H-D) method*, one can develop a full blown etiological theory on slim or less evidence, then attempt to test it. Wherever a causal connection is postulated, the theory implies analogous correlations will be found. By doing correlational studies one can thus put one's theory to hard tests, where the absence of correlation falsifies the theory (subject to appropriate Duhemian caveats which can be ignored here). Thus those social and behavioral scientists who have listened to philosophers espousing the H-D method have good grounds for using correlational studies to test their etiological theories. Unfortunately the less-Popperian among us have stressed with insufficient effect the limited ability of such tests to *establish* etiological hypotheses and the need to look at difference cases and not just enumerate supporting instances of the theory. In a similar fashion, tests of statistical significance and frequency differences can be used to test etiological theories.

A crucial difference between correlation and causality stressed by philosophers is symmetry of the former and the temporal asymmetry of the later. To the extent that one has background or other information that can be used to determine the direction of presumed causal influence, one can then use correlational studies to assess causality or etiology. To the extent one's background knowledge is on solid ground, doing so is relatively unproblematic–the primary dangers being those of "causal forks" and "linked effects" which typically plague philosophical accounts of explanation.

Note also that solid background knowledge can be used as a surrogate for experimental controls in such a way as to give retrospective studies the probative strengths of prospective studies (Grünbaum 1984, p. 259). Unfortunately the background information invoked in homosexuality research typically is supplied by the very theories whose sole evidential basis at best is the failure to falsify under the H-D method just discussed–augmented, perhaps, by the inductive principle that repeating a theory often enough makes it true. Most of these background theories ultimately depend upon what in a later section we will call the "Victorian Theory of Normal Love" which was a late Victorian middle-class American social more–having huge normative force but enjoying virtually no evidential basis other then persuasive definition.

Finally, I should note that in cases where one suspects causal connections but where well-controlled randomized experimental designs or prospective studies are expensive, long lasting, and extremely difficult, it is a good practice to do a correlational pilot study to determine whether the larger study merits doing. And where the larger studies are morally repugnant or involve longitudinally tracking unmanageably huge numbers of subjects for many years with very expensive testing procedures to obtain reliable data (as would be the case for most studies of homosexual etiology) suggestive correlational pilot studies may be the closest you can come to an adequate empirical investigation of etiology.

From the above discussion we can begin to understand various reasons why social and behavioral scientists who choose to investigate homosexual etiology do so using research methods that ultimately are inadequate to the task. Understanding these practices adds to our appreciation of the realities of research although it does nothing to enhance the probative merit of the resulting etiological studies.

A large majority of the homosexuality etiology literature is most charitably interpreted as employing a statistical sense of causality, despite considerable evidence that a more deterministic notion often conceptually underlies particular studies. The sense in which statistical etiological accounts are intended to "explain" homosexuality is "accounting for dependent variable variance": how much of the variance in homosexual orientation can be attributed to, e.g., having a close-binding, intimate mother?

One important philosophical account of scientific explanation is Hempel's *Inductive Statistical (IS) Model*, where one explains events by deriving their likelihood from statistical laws such as: $P(E, C) = r$,[47] or else statements of such form as can be derived from them.[48] One might think that the social science determinations of the amount of variance in E that is attributable to C might qualify as an IS explanation. However, despite Hempel's (1965) failure to supply an analysis of statistical laws in his account of IS explanations, the variance allocation statements found in the homosexuality etiology literature surveyed almost without exception are likely not to qualify as statistical laws of the above form.

The other main statistical analyses of why explanation are Salmon's, which involve showing that C is statistically relevant to the incidence of E. The typical social science variance partitions will typically fail to provide fundamental enough factors to satisfy the screening-off rule requirements of Salmon's old S-R analysis and will certainly lack the causal markers added in his new account.[49] They even less resemble the accounts of explaining why by Bromberger, Toulmin, or even Suppe.[50] In short, the sorts of explanations supplied by the correlational and other statistical data reported in the literature surveyed above fail to satisfy any of the standard philosophical accounts of explanation.

In my estimation this is more a failure of philosophy of science then it is of the social and behavioral sciences: our philosophical theories of explanation have been developed in ignorance of the details of actual behavioral science research and the explanations based on it. An adequate philosophical theory of statistical explanation must be able to handle in fine detail the sorts of explanations afforded by multivariate and factor analysis, and facilitate understanding, e.g., the peculiar explanatory difficulties raised by high correlations in regression analyses (see Kerlinger as in note 79, pp. 177-178, for a summary of the problems)–difficulties which on Hempel's IS model should not occur.

In summary, then, I do not find in the philosophy of science literature much basis for impeaching these general social science research strategies embodied in the studies previously surveyed. The generally unsatisfactory state of such work does not reflect some fundamental impoverishment of science. Rather it reflects the fact that the science isn't very good–judged by precisely the standards prevailing in the social and biological sciences. In particular, the conceptual crudity with which the etiological problem is conceived and the inadequate research designs which follow are unacceptable under standards routinely achieved elsewhere in the social and biological sciences.

PSYCHOANALYTIC THEORIES OF ETIOLOGY

Psychoanalytic theories of homosexual etiology much more closely resemble philosophical accounts of explanation–especially those of Bromberger (1966) and Toulmin (1963) which place the locus of explanation on deviations from some general rule or an ideal of natural order.[51] Psychoanalytic theories typically postulate a standard developmental sequence (e.g., Freud's progression from the oral receptive to oral sadistic, anal sadistic, anal retentive, phallic, and Oedipal stages in infancy and early childhood and resulting later adolescent and adulthood behaviors)[52] coupled with the attempt to identify causes for specific patterns of deviation from the standard developmental sequence.

Psychoanalysis postulates three main accounts of male homosexual etiology: (1) *Faulty identifications* consisting of either a positive identification with women due to the father being absent or the presence of an overwhelming female (typically the mother) or else a failure to identify with men due to a strong feeling of fear or hatred of an overpowering or sadistic father. (2) *Unusual infantile fixations* due either to an exaggerated exclusive libidinal investment on the father in the mother's absence or an excessive genital attachment to the father if overt sexual behavior occurs between father and son. (3) *Homosexuality as a defense or adaptive mechanism* against castration anxiety rooted in penis envy exacerbated by the Oedipal conflict or incestuous attachment to the mother; or it may be a way of appeasing a mother who does not want her son to be aggressive and masculine, overcompensating for the son's hatred and destructive wishes for his father or other important male figure, or an attempt to appease a father by assuming a noncompetitive feminine role.[53]

Lester notes that "although most psychoanalytic views pertain to males, much of the hypothesizing can be transposed to females quite easily" (75). Doing so is, however, risky since there is little reason to suppose that male homosexuality and lesbianism are the same phenomenon, hence little reason to expect they should share a common etiology.

As is the wont of psychoanalysts, these etiological theories are evidenced largely on clinical data obtained by free association in the psychoanalytic session. Bieber et al., in a study sponsored by the Society of Medical Psychoanalysts, attempted to bolster that evidential base with a study of 106 male homosexuals and 100 male heterosexuals in psychiatric treatment with members of the Society. The subjects' psychotherapists filled out long questionnaires (up to 450 questions) about their patients' formative years, relations with parents, play activities, etc. Mean scores on the individual questions and a few cumulative score scales were calculated for homosexuals and heterosexual controls, and mean differences were tested for statistical significance at the 5% and 1% levels. The study's findings tended to support the suppositions of the main psychoanalytic theories of male homosexuality etiology surveyed above, especially as they related to close-binding intimate mothers, distant detached fathers, and childhood effeminacy. The Society of Medical Psychoanalysts also did a study of 24 female homosexuals and 24 female heterosexuals using essentially the same methodology.[54]

These studies are seriously flawed for a number of reasons including highly biased samples of psychoanalytic patients and the use of statistics inappropriate for supporting the conclusions drawn.[55] The statistical problems are roughly as follows: the Bieber et al. statistics almost exclusively involve assessing the statistical significance of differences in mean scores on homosexual and control responses to particular questions, or else aggregate mean differences on a collection of questions combined into a scale (e.g., their "Developmental Six Score," "Excessive Fearfulness of Physical Injury in Childhood Score," and "Twenty Questions Score"–see Table 1). Yet their conclusions from these statistics involve such

TABLE 1. Special Cumulative Scores/Scales from Bieber et al., *Homosexuality: A Psychoanalytic Study*

Parent Feminizing:

Did mother [father] discourage masculine activities?
Did mother [father] encourage feminine attitudes and activities?
Did mother [father] want patient to grow up to be like some particular person?
  (Who . . .)
Did patient ever want to be a woman?
Mother [father] was less or not encouraging of masculine traits compared
  to their siblings.

Parent Minimizing:

By mother [father] was patient least favored sibling?
Did mother [father] express affection for patient?
    in physical acts such as kissing and hugging?
Did mother [father] express contempt for patient?
Did mother [father] humiliate patient?
Did mother not show respect for patient?
Does patient feel mother [father] babied him?
Currently does patient feel respected by his mother [father] as an adult?

Developmental Six Score:

Was patient excessively fearful of physical injury in childhood?
Did patient avoid physical fights?
Was play activity before puberty predominantly with girls?
Was patient "lone wolf" in childhood?
Did patient participate in group games?
Did patient play baseball?

Excessive Fear of Physical Injury in Childhood:

In childhood was patient's mother unduly concerned about his health?
Was she unduly concerned with protecting him from physical injury?
Did mother's concern about health or injury cause her to interfere with or
  restrict his play, social or other activities?
In childhood was the patient excessively fearful that his assertiveness or
  nonconformity might anger mother?
    lose mother's love?
Does patient feel his mother "babied" him?
Did father humiliate patient?
Was father knowingly hated by patient?
Was father knowingly feared by patient?

20 Questions:

1. Relations between parents

   How much time did mother spend with father?
   Did mother and father share same interest?

2. Relation between patient and mother

   Did mother demand she be prime center of patient's attention?
   Does the analyst consider that the mother was seductive in her activi-
      ties with the patient? (Was there . . .)
   Did mother encourage masculine attitudes and activities?
   Did mother encourage feminine attitudes and activities?
   Was mother considered puritanical? Was mother considered sexually
      frigid?
   Did mother try to ally with son against father?
   Did mother openly prefer patient to husband?
   Did patient believe mother interfered with heterosexual activity during
      adolescence?
   Was patient mother's confidant?

3. Relation between patient and father

   Was patient father's favorite?
   Did patient feel accepted by father?
   Amount of time spent between father and patient?
   Did father encourage masculine attitudes and activities?
      Was father knowingly hated by patient?
   Did patient consciously fear physical injury from father?
      Did patient accept father?
      Did patient respect father?

Notes:

1. There are parallel versions of the "Parent Feminizing" and "Parent Minimizing" scales for mothers and fathers.

2. The above questions/scales are "inferential assessment" sub-scales
drawn from the questionnaire in Appendix A in accordance with directions
given in Appendix B.

claims as that "a picture emerged of a woman who was overly close to this particular [homosexual] son, spent a great deal of time with him and preferred him to his siblings. More often than not, she openly preferred him to his father. . . . there was an exaggerated concern about the son's health and possible injury, but . . . these mothers interfered with the son's assertiveness and they tended to dislocate his relationship with the father, siblings, and peers."[56] This, their *close-binding intimate mother* portrait, purports to be established for about 80% of mothers in the homosexual sample[57] on the basis of finding statistically significant differences in homosexuals and control means in 27 questions, where only one of the questions had over 66% positive sample response for the homosexuals and only twelve above a 60% sample response.[58] These statistics are totally incapable of establishing such claims. Correlation coefficients minimally are necessary but non-existent in Bieber et al. (1962); and *adequate* statistical substantiation would require the techniques of multivariate analysis.

Gonsiorek discusses a number of other serious methodological problems:

> But perhaps the most disturbing factor about the study was the fact that all data consists of judgments by the subjects' analysts. . . . The final form of the questionnaire was arrived at after a series of earlier questionnaires, which were tested on the analysts who later were raters. All of the researchers and rating analysts were members of one particular psychoanalytic society and many of the members had considerable input into, and knowledge of, the study. Finally, the findings of the Bieber group are in agreement with many aspects of psychoanalytic theorizing about homosexuality, and specifically are in clear accordance with theorizing about the role of Oedipal conflicts in homosexuality. Simply stated, the Bieber groups may have inadvertently designed and executed a study which would guarantee results in agreement with what the raters and researchers already believed they knew about homosexuality. The study may be nothing more than a measure of consensus among psychoanalysts about homosexuality; rather than an exploration of it. There are too many sources of possible con-

tamination in having many of the same analysts, who are already theoretically similar on the subject of homosexuality, design a study, rate the subjects and psychoanalyze the subjects.[59]

Just as psychiatric prejudices potentially contaminate the single case clinical data obtained via free association on the couch, via patient suggestibility, so too they compromise the Bieber et al. and Kaye et al. studies.

Although Gonsiorek's criticisms suggest these studies would have been improved had the patients filled out the questionnaires themselves or the subjects not been homosexuals undergoing psychoanalysis,[60] psychoanalysts generally would be opposed to such alleged improvements.[61] In 1970, Charles Socarides put the psychoanalytic case as follows:

> Only in the consultation room does the homosexual reveal himself and his world. No other data, statistics, or statements can be accepted as setting forth the true nature of homosexuality. All other sources may be heavily weighted by face-saving devices or rationalizations or, if they issue from lay bodies, lack the scientific and medical background to support their view. The best that can be said for the well-intentioned but unqualified observer is that he is misguided because he does not have and can not apply those techniques which would make it possible to discern the deep underlying clinical disorder or to evaluate the emotional patterns and interpersonal events in the life of a homosexual.[62]

Socarides offers no defense of the claimed epistemic superiority of psychoanalytic over other forms of data.

While Freud based his theory on "free association" clinical data, he was sensitive to the charge of client suggestibility contaminating clinical data, and he offered what Grünbaum terms the "Tally Argument" in defense of the probative value of free association data. In this argument Freud assumes two causally necessary conditions:

> (1) only the psychoanalytic method of interpretation and treatment can yield or mediate to the patient correct insight into the unconscious pathogens of his psychoneurosis, and

(2) the analysand's correct insight into the etiology of his affliction and into the unconscious dynamics of his character is, in turn, causally necessary for the therapeutic conquest of his neurosis.[63]

From these, Freud draws two conclusions:

Conclusion 1: The psychoanalytic interpretations of the hidden causes of P's behavior given to him by his analyst are indeed correct, and thus—as Freud put it—these interpretations "tally with what is real" in P.

Conclusion 2: Only analytic treatment could have wrought the conquest of P's psychoneurosis. (140)

Commenting on the argument, Grünbaum goes on:

It is of capital importance to appreciate that Freud is at pains to employ the Tally Argument in order to justify the following epistemological claim: actual *durable* therapeutic success guarantees *not only* that the pertinent analytic interpretations *ring* true or credible to the analysand *but also* that they *are* indeed veridical, or at least quite close to the mark. Freud then relies on this bold intermediate contention to conclude nothing less then the following: collectively, the successful outcomes of analyses do constitute *cogent* evidence for all that general psychoanalytic theory tells us about the influences of the unconscious dynamics of the mind on our lives. In short, psychoanalytic treatment successes as a whole vouch for the truth of the Freudian theory of personality, including its specific aetiologies of the psychoneuroses and even its general theory of psycho-sexual development. (140-141; emphasis in original)

The Tally Argument, if successful, vindicates Socarides's position and the corollary dismissal of nonclinical data. Further, as Crews has observed, "what Grünbaum calls the Tally Argument, [is] the only substantial reply to the charge of epistemic contamination that psychoanalysis has ever bothered to propose."[64] Socarides's position is thus no better than the Tally Argument.

In a powerful critique, Grünbaum argues that the Tally Argument is untenable. Freud himself later rejected or weakened each premise of the argument (chap. 2). Even if the premises were true "it would need the existential premise of documented cures in order to vouch for the etiologies inferred by means of free association" (160). And psychoanalysis has been unable to differentiate its claimed cures from those due to the placebo effect (chap. 2-C).[65]

Even if the Tally Argument were successful it would be unavailing for defending Socarides. For invoking it depends essentially on documented cures (140; chap. 2 passim). Despite claims of such cures of homosexuality,[66] these claims are so conceptually confused and questionable[67] as to be worthless in legitimizing the invocation of the Tally Argument. Thus we may conclude that Socarides's attempted defense fails, psychoanalytic clinical data is hopelessly contaminated, and Gonsiorek's criticisms of Bieber et al. (and by implication, of Kaye et al.) are telling ones indeed. To the extent that psychoanalytic theories of homosexual etiology are scientifically credible it will be on the basis of extra-clinical evidence.

CORRELATIONS, CAUSALITY, AND PATH ANALYSIS

Correlation coefficients were first introduced by Bravis (1846)[68] but were rediscovered by Francis Galton (1888),[69] who used them as a means of analyzing hereditary regression phenomena. His coefficient of correlation is essentially what is today called the sample correlation coefficient. Later, Pearson (1905) refined the idea into his correlation ratio [of the standard deviation of the mean values of x for each value of y to the standard deviation of x] and put correlational analysis on a firm mathematical footing.[70]

Sewell Wright (1921) was aware of the limitations of correlation analysis:

In all the preceding [correlational] results no account is taken of the nature of the relationship between the variables. The calculations thus neglect a very important part of the knowledge which we often possess. There are usually a priori or experimental grounds for believing that certain factors are

> direct causes of variation in others or that other pairs are re-
> lated as effects of a common cause. . . . Just because it involves
> no assumptions in regard to the nature of the relationship, a
> coefficient of correlation may be looked upon as a fact per-
> taining to the description of a particular population only to be
> questioned on the grounds of inaccuracy in computation. But it
> would often be desirable to use a method of analysis by which
> the knowledge that we have in regard to causal relations may
> be combined with the knowledge of the degree of relationship
> furnished by the coefficients of correlation.[71]

To rectify this problem in the context of assessing the heritability of
traits in animal and plant breeding studies, in a series of papers,
Sewell Wright, who then was Senior Animal Husbandman in
Animal Genetics for the Bureau of Animal Industry in the U.S.
Department of Agriculture, developed what is known as the method
of *path analysis*.[72] By 1921, Wright was calling it the "Method of
Path Coefficients" and "Analysis by Path Coefficient."

Similar analyses were developed within econometrics, and from
these–aided by Wright's work–social scientists such as H. M. Bla-
lock, Jr., introduced the techniques into the social sciences in the
latter half of the 1960s.[73] Considerable confusion arose whether it
was a technique for discovering causal structures or for exploiting
antecedently known causal information. Today it is a status multivariate analysis method in social science research. Path analysis is
essentially a technique of multivariate regression analysis for parti-
tioning the amount of variance explained in outcome variables. Path
analysis also is known as "Causal Modeling" today.

Wright was very clear that path analysis presupposes knowledge
of causal connections and is not a method for establishing them
(except in very special cases): path analysis, he tells us, is:

> a method of measuring the direct influence along each sepa-
> rate path in such a system and thus of finding the degree to
> which variation of a given effect is determined by each partic-
> ular cause. The method depends on the combination of knowl-
> edge of the degrees of correlation among the variables in a
> system with such knowledge as may be possessed of the
> causal relations. In cases in which the causal relations are

uncertain the method can be used to find the logical consequences of any particular hypothesis in regard to them.[74]

Writing for social scientists, Asher makes it clear why the
method is inadequate for establishing causal relations:

> Causal modeling techniques do not allow one to determine the
> direction of causality between two variables nor do they allow
> one to conclude that a causal relationship exists, except under
> a restrictive set of conditions. . . . A number of writers . . .
> specify three conditions that must be met in order to infer the
> existence of a causal relationship between two variables X and
> Y. The first condition states that there must be concomitant
> variation or covariation between X and Y, while the second
> condition requires a temporal asymmetry or time ordering
> between the two. These two conditions are not very trouble-
> some for we can often measure covariation and observe or
> impose a temporal sequence between the two variables [refer-
> ence omitted]. The third condition is more problematic, re-
> quiring elimination of other possible causal factors that may
> be producing the observed relationship between X and Y. . . .
>   The third condition requires that we rule out all other pos-
> sible causal factors. On what grounds can we make this deci-
> sion with any degree of confidence? There is a potentially
> infinite universe of such variables and there is no statistical
> test or coefficient that can tell us whether we have made the
> correct decision.[75]

The problems here are just multivariate analysis reflections of the
fact that the joint methods of agreement and disagreement are necessary to determine causality, and the method of disagreement only
works against the questionable supposition that potential causal
influences are limited to a finite list the investigator has thought of.
Monte Carlo simulations indicate that standard multiple regression
packages such as LISREL and EQS used to do path analysis can
extract the correct causal structure less than 19% of the time.[76]
    While path analysis thus has limited potential for establishing the
causes of homosexuality, it has great potential for investigating the
direct and indirect influence of various interactive factors claimed

by various theories of homosexual etiology. This is precisely the use of path analysis by the Kinsey Institute in their large-sample, replicative testing of the standard etiological theories.[77] In 1969-1970, 979 homosexual and 477 heterosexual men and women in the San Francisco area were given a 528-question structured interview that *inter alia* contained many questions pertinent to standard theories of homosexual etiology. I have discussed various aspects of the study including the adequacy of their sample elsewhere.[78] Here it will suffice to point out that for the purposes of refuting other theories, highly biased samples are quite adequate so long as the types of subjects used in those other studies constitute a subsample of the replicative study's sample and the latter's population does not go beyond the claimed scope of the replicated studies. Not only does Bell, Weinberg, and Hammersmith's sample meet these conditions, it is the most diverse and representative sample of homosexuals ever surveyed.

Based on a comprehensive survey of the homosexuality research literature, they consolidated the various hypothesized paths of direct and indirect etiological influence on homosexuality into a composite model that contained virtually all paths advanced in the literature. The model resembled Figure 1 except for having many more paths and variables. Then using their heterosexual and homosexual comparison data, they eliminated many variables and paths until they "included only the ones in which the homosexuals actually differed from the heterosexuals. . . . In many cases variables proved not to have any significant connection to adult sexual preference when other variables in the same or earlier stages were taken into account [footnote omitted]. Such variables were dropped outright and not included in the path analysis" (33). After other similar deletions of variables not significant in their influence and the development of certain composite measures summarizing a number of questions, the path diagram in Figure 1 was obtained.

Multivariate analysis determined the path coefficients shown on the various paths. The procedure is essentially a regression analysis which determines what distribution of path coefficients accounts for or explains the maximum amount of variance in the sexual orientation dependent variable.[79] The path coefficients indicate "how strong the effect of the 'upstream' variable is on the 'downstream'

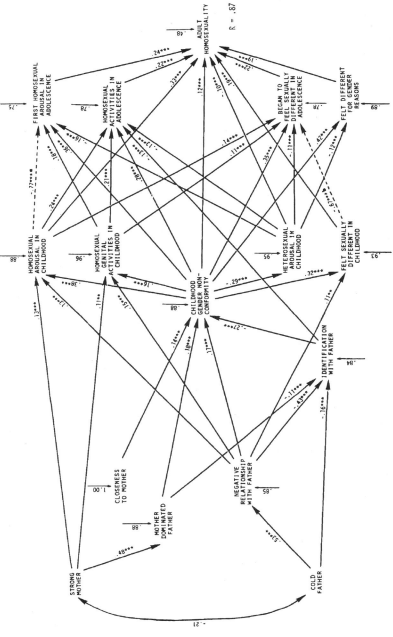

FIGURE 1. Path Diagram from Bell, Weinberg, and Hammersmith, *Sexual Preference: Its Development in Men and Women* (Bloomington, IN: Indiana University Press, 1981), pp. 224-225.

variable. The path coefficients can range from .00 to ± 1.00, and the larger the absolute value of the path coefficients the stronger the effect. (Statistically, the path coefficient tells us how much change in the 'downstream' variable, in standard deviation units, is caused by one standard-deviation unit change in the 'upstream' variable.)" (25). Products of connected successive paths indicate the strength of the beginning variable on the terminus variable of the composite path (34).

As already noted, Bell, Weinberg, and Hammersmith's use of path analysis is thoroughly appropriate, and their procedures for developing their composite etiology model are quite legitimate. Their findings are that psychodynamic theories that consider homosexuality to be the outcome of types of parental relationships or traits (as, e.g., the 1962 Bieber et al. claim), those that attribute homosexuality to poor peer relationships, theories that homosexuality often results from fortuitous labeling by others, views that homosexuality is the result of atypical experience by persons of the opposite sex or children being seduced by an adult of the same sex–none of these were supported by their data (chap. 7):

> What our study does suggest is that these theoretically predicted patterns, although they may occur in some instances, are not norms nor are they significant in providing an overall picture of how sexual preference becomes differentiated as homosexual or heterosexual. Consequently, our analyses lead us to believe that such notions should be rejected, or at least held highly suspect, until further research can provide more definitive answers. (186)

The only plausible basis for denying that this Kinsey Institute study constitutes a definitive refutation of the various social learning theories of homosexual etiology is to challenge the adequacy of their models and the questions they use to measure the various variables. For example, Bieber et al., base most of their findings (e.g., those pertaining to close-binding intimate mothers and distant detached fathers) on the composite measures listed in Table 1. Bell, Weinberg, and Hammersmith do not employ either these specific questions or those composite measures. Yet their Interview Schedule displays a large number of questions directed at the same concerns.[80] For example, their questions 65 and 66 concern desire to be of the opposite sex, questions 170, 171, 180 concern play with girls vs. boys, being a "lone wolf" in childhood, and playing group games including specifically baseball and football. Question 73 concerns fear of physical injury from father, and so on. However their data pertaining to "negative feelings towards father, dislike-hatred, lack of closeness, and lack of esteem came from the same [open-ended] interview question as did the more general measure, Negative Relationship with Father ('How would you describe your relationship with your father, including your own feelings and reactions to him, during the time you were growing up?')" (55). Since these data are crucial to their refutation of Bieber et al., one would have preferred them to be based on structured-answer questions (as were Bieber's et al., 1962, data) rather than on a single, open-ended question.

Why didn't Bell, Weinberg, and Hammersmith just use the Bieber et al. questions? The latter's schedule contained 450 questions, and the scales in Table 1 contain several dozen questions. Bell, Weinberg, and Hammersmith were attempting to replicate not just the Bieber et al. study, but most social learning etiological theories. To include questions from every study would have resulted in an unusably long interview schedule. Instead, they opted to develop a manageably long schedule (528 questions, taking 3-5 hours to administer) with about 200 questions regarding the subjects' childhood and adolescence that tapped the main variables found in the various etiological theories in the literature. While reasonable, doing so complicates interpreting the strength with which their data refutes prior theories and studies.

To nail this down one needs to take the questions they used and those used in a particular study (e.g., the Bieber et al. questionnaire), give them both to a diverse sample of subjects, and then use factor analysis to see whether the respective composite measures of the two studies are asking the same thing. Doing so in such a manner for the entire literature would be a Herculean task. My impression is that such pair-wise comparisons would tend to vindicate strongly the replicative adequacy of their study. I conclude, then, that the Bell, Weinberg, and Hammersmith *Sexual Preference* study is about as definitive a refutation of the extant social learning theories of homosexual etiology as we reasonably can expect to find in the social and behavioral science literature. Given the results of our prior discussion of psychoanalytic theories, this conclusion applies to psychoanalytic theories as well despite the fact that the data is entirely extra-clinical. In no small part, the impressive success of this replicative study is due to the appropriate choice of path analysis as the means for data analysis. Given the fact that path analysis was originally developed for studying the heritability of traits, it is surprising it is nowhere used in evaluating various genetic or hormonal theories of etiology.

It is important to be clear exactly what the Bell, Weinberg, and Hammersmith path study establishes. They suggest that it strongly favors a biological explanation of sexual orientation (chap. 19). It does no such thing. It shows only that no simple-minded, crudely conceived social learning or conditioning explanation of the sort thus far propounded explains much variation in sexual preference, orientation, or identity.

There are a number of possibilities consistent with this explanation: first, we have raised questions whether homosexuality and heterosexuality *simpliciter* are real phenomena, hence whether there is any explanation to be found. Second, if an explanation is to be found—whether biological or social—it will need to be sensitive to the variation in human sexual identity.[81] More subtle outcome variables might prove more amenable to explanation. Third, today's massive computational methods of data analysis leave open the prospect that a highly complex social-learning account incorporating an adequate conceptualization of sexual orientation or identity might prove to be correct. Fourth, although conventional wisdom has it you cannot get causality out of statistics, that conclusion seems true only for conventional statistical methods such as regression analysis. For there is at least one artificial intelligence "edge-detection" method, TETRAD II, that under Monte Carlo simulation is able to extract the true causal structure out of statistical data up to 85% of the time under circumstances where, as mentioned earlier, LISREL and EQS only do so less than 19% of the time. It is conceivable that with today's massive computational capabilities, TETRAD might be able to extract a complex causal account out of data sets where regression fails, or even, possibly from the Bell, Weinberg, and Hammersmith data set.

WHO CARES ANYHOW?

The difficulties encountered by biological theories of homosexual etiology, the impressive refutation of extant social learning theories of etiology by the Bell, Weinberg, and Hammersmith study, and the manifest epistemic inadequacy of psychoanalytic theories means that after nearly 1,000 studies of homosexual etiology, we really haven't established much of anything positive about the causes of homosexuality. Two responses to this are possible. One is the "back to the drawing board" response that treats etiology as terribly important and calls for more sophisticated rethinking of the matter and improved theories and studies.[82] The other, which I favor, is, "Who cares anyhow?" Why, after all, should we be concerned about the etiology of homosexuality?

Sociology of science tells us that the basic work of science is done in small (typically 50-200) person *invisible colleges* which form stable scientific communities specializing on a class of problems, typically with common methodologies.[83] These invisible colleges aggregate into larger specialties, sub-disciplines, and disciplines. Invisible colleges establish their own standards of scientific quality, and those standards are monitored by the larger specialties, journal editorial boards, and the like. A complex process for credentialing scientific work thus exists.[84]

From different perspectives, post-positivistic philosophy of science characterizes the scientific research done in such invisible colleges in terms of such theoretical entities as paradigms, domains, research programs or traditions, etc. The research within an invisible college is typically not done in a vacuum but rather is done against its shared background of a body of received fact and theory, background knowledge, and a research agenda informed and conditioned by these. Shapere discusses the role of scientific domains and background knowledge in determining what questions a science investigates.[85] Laudan details the role of what he calls research traditions in a discipline's scientific research and has further explored issues over how a science sets its cognitive goals.[86] Lakatos[87] discusses his research programs, Kuhn[88] his paradigms (now disciplinary matrices), and Toulmin[89] his intellectual and explanatory ideals–all of which are claimed to condition strongly the problems a science chooses to investigate.

As research within an invisible college matures, we find a growing body of cumulative research output in its domain. We can characterize the health of an invisible college on the basis of the richness of its domain, the ability of later research to avoid the main weaknesses of earlier research, the growth of a literature that is getting somewhere (rather than a succession of failed attempts that lead nowhere), and the extent to which the research increasingly is driven by its growing body of findings rather than from extra-scientific assumptions or ones imported from other disciplines. To extend Lakatos's apt terminology, we can speak of the research in an invisible college as progressive or degenerating.[90]

It is useful to inquire as to the health of the various invisible colleges concerned with homosexual etiology. Since Bell, Weinberg, and Hammersmith, investigation into social causes of homosexuality has become moribund. When we turn to genetic accounts, we find highly discontinuous research. As Bailey and Pillard note, "very little work has been done in this area from a behavioral genetic perspective"[91]–or from any other genetic perspective for that matter. In the hormonal area, Dörner's work garnered a lot of attention, then fell by the wayside as it failed to be replicated. LeVay's work is by an outsider who did it as a "hobby project" diversion from his usual neuroscientific research. In short, what we find are scattered episodic forays into homosexual etiology, which typically lead nowhere.

It is unclear whether there are any stable invisible colleges today concerned with homosexual etiology. But it is clear that there is little cumulative growth of a body of literature that builds upon prior successes. Moreover we find the scattered efforts recapitulating the basic conceptual confusions that have undercut prior failed attempts at explaining homosexual etiology. If there are invisible colleges, they seem inept at learning from prior failures.

The lack of progressiveness in etiological research is reflected in the fact that the basic conceptualization of the research problems is based on extra-scientific considerations, not a growing body of successful science. To see this, let us ask: What are the presuppositions that make the etiology of homosexuality seem an important scientific research question? As an outgrowth of my earlier work on homosexuality research and a debate with Robert Spitzer before the Society for Health and Human Values, I did a detailed evaluation of the American Psychiatric Association's 1980 classification of sexual disorders in DSM-III.[92] As I discovered a near total lack of competent scientific evidence substantiating its classifications of the sexual paraphilias as mental disorders, and realized that precisely the same reasons used to justify the removal of homosexuality per se as a mental disorder also called for the removal of all the paraphilias as per se disorders,[93] I came to suspect that the earlier inclusion of homosexuality and the continued inclusion of the paraphilias as mental disorders were nothing more than the codification of social mores masquerading as scientific results.

Such a thesis, of course, is an historical one and to establish it requires historical analysis and evidence. Elsewhere[94] I supplied that historical evidence, arguing that medico-psychiatric treatments of homosexuality, the paraphilias, and transsexualism this century were and continue to be rooted in a late Victorian view that Katz calls "The Theory of Normal Love."[95] On this theory sex-love was thought all-pervasive, and so lack of erotic feeling and extreme continence were viewed as sexual aberrations. Closely allied was the idea that emotions had genders or sexes, and by the 1880s and 1890s the dominant medical meaning of sexual normality and abnormality was the procreative vs. the nonprocreative and conformity vs. non-conformity to sex-role stereotypes.

The result included the hopeless confusion of homosexuality, transsexualism, effeminacy in males and masculinity in females, and other non-procreative acts into an undifferentiated "sexual perversion" category that still is being untangled and sorted out.[96] This "Theory of Normal Love" informs and conditions medico-scientific research even today (witness the confusions of effeminacy and male homosexuality in the even recent etiology research surveyed at the beginning of this paper). Only with the work of Kinsey, Evelyn Hooker, and the many studies commissioned by the National Institutes of Health Task Force on Homosexuality–all appearing after W.W. II–do we find significant amounts of research on homosexuality being done outside the medico-psychiatric professions. This research tends to be either not concerned with etiology or attempts to replicate medico-scientific etiological research using non-clinical, non-criminal populations–in the process generally failing to confirm earlier medico-psychiatric findings.

Historically, then, the basis for viewing homosexuality as an abnormality requiring treatment or prophylactic measures has been the Victorian "Theory of Normal Love"–for which not a shred of unbiased empirical evidence has been produced, it being a codification of a late Victorian middle-class ethos (one, incidentally, that provided a welcome climate for the ready, uncritical, popular acceptance of Freud's views on polymorphous sexuality). No empirically-validated replacement theory or findings have been produced that propel one to view homosexuality as a condition of problematic etiology *while* viewing the etiology of heterosexuality as unproblematic. Thus we have in the homosexuality (and other sexual variation) research area an instance where the background theory/beliefs conditioning a scientific research program are extra-scientific normative values in contrast to the more legitimate *scientific* ones that, e.g., Shapere and Laudan stress.

In short, the available scientific evidence provides no basis for treating the etiology of homosexuality as a legitimate *scientific* research problem. The situation here is similar to that of left-handedness. Earlier this century it was widely held that right-handedness was normal and left-handedness was abnormal and inferior. Strident attempts were made in the public schools to force children all to be right-handed, and there was concern over what caused the "disease" of left-handedness. Once it was accepted that there was natural variation in which hand was one's dominant hand, the etiology of left-handedness ceased to be a serious *scientific* research problem.

Moreover, those who continue to insist that there is a problem of homosexual etiology rely on uncritical acceptance of a crude homosexual/heterosexual classification scheme that can be sustained only in ignorance of, or at the price of rejecting, the cumulative knowledge coming out of the more progressive portions of the sex-research area. In short, there is every indication that homosexual etiology is the province of a degenerated research agenda, and no longer represents credible science. This is reflected in the fact that much of the biological etiological research is published in psychiatric and other journals "inappropriate" to a progressive *biological* research area. Continuation of such research has little scientific merit.

Against the line I have been defending, some will argue that we need to do research on homosexual etiology to have data to use in, e.g., court cases which concern child custody by homosexuals, controversies surrounding homosexual teachers, to argue that since gays aren't responsible for their sexuality it shouldn't be held against them, for opening the military to homosexuals, and the like. Several responses are in order. First, there is ample data demonstrating that homosexual parents are as fit as heterosexual single parents, and that children raised by homosexuals are as likely to be heterosexual as those raised by heterosexuals,[97] but these data have little effect on judicial deliberations.

Second, a key reason for the limited efficacy of such research on judicial and legislative deliberations is that opponents can negate the effect of such competent research by pitting against it the hostile and incompetent "expert" pronouncements of authorities such as Socarides. Expert witnesses can only be impeached on the basis of inadequate credentials, not the scientific cogency of their views. Thus one piles a confusing welter of conflicting "expert opinion" on the hapless jury. In such circumstance of "divided opinion," the experts siding with more conservative and traditional homophobic prejudices tend to prevail. The continued status of homosexual etiology as a "legitimate scientific problem" tends to perpetuate such proceedings as well as the continued labeling of homosexuality as a sexual deviation meriting study.

Third, to persist in defending the research legitimacy of homosexuality etiology for reasons outlined above is just to admit that it *is* part of a political, not a scientific, agenda. The defense of the research project thus rests on grounds no more scientific than the Victorian origins of the project. To the extent the research is legitimized by the political goals of its proponents, it is as a piece of social engineering rather than dispassionate science.

Who cares what causes homosexuality? Only those who subscribe to the Victorian "Theory of Normal Love," its current day remnants, or some moral or political agenda. But insofar as we act qua scientists, not I nor, I would hope, anyone of serious scientific aspirations.

AUTHOR NOTE

Dr. Suppe has published widely in the philosophy of science, including *The Structure of Scientific Theories* (University of Illinois Press, 1977) and *Facts, Theories, and Scientific Realism* in two volumes (University of Illinois, 1994). He also edited a volume on science and Christianity, *Knowing God, Christ, and Nature,* forthcoming. His current research focus is on computationally-intensive science, and in 1993-1994, he served as an NSF Fellow at Princeton where he worked with the Magellan team on the geological structure of Venus.

NOTES

1. *Medical Record* 26 (1884): 70-71. Quoted in B. Hansen, "American physicians' earliest writings about homosexuals, 1880-1900," *Milbank Quarterly* 67 (suppl. 1) (1989): 92-108.

2. See F. Suppe, "Medical and Psychiatric Perspectives on Human Sexuality" (Vol. 1; pp. 17-37) and "The Diagnostic and Statistical Manual of the American Psychiatric Association: Classifying Sexual Disorders" (Vol. 2; pp. 111-136) in E. Shelp, ed., *Sexuality and Medicine* (Dordrecht: D. Reidel, 1987).

3. A helpful summary of the main etiological research from the late 1930s to the mid-1970s is given by D. Lester, *Unusual Sexual Behavior: The Standard Deviations* (Springfield, IL: Charles C Thomas, 1975). M. Weinberg and A. Bell also give a comprehensive selection of abstracts of research up through about 1970 in *Homosexuality: An Annotated Bibliography* (New York: Harper and Row, 1972). M. Ruse (*Homosexuality: A Philosophical Inquiry* [Oxford: Basil Blackwell, 1988]) critically evaluates much of the more recent research as well as some earlier studies. Where they are contextually clear, further references to this last title will be given in the text.

4. Conceivably, the Human Genome Project could eventually provide an alternative approach if we had comprehensive enough genetic maps for large numbers of subjects and adequate information as to their sexual identity.

5. T. Lang, "Studies in the Genetic Determination of Homosexuality," *Journal of Nervous and Mental Disorders* 92 (1940): 55-64.

6. F. J. Kallman, "Twin and Sibship Study of Overt Male Homosexuality," *American Journal of Human Genetics* 4 (1952): 136-146.

7. J. M. Bailey and R. Pillard, "A Genetic Study of Male Sexual Orientation," *Archives of General Psychiatry* 48 (1991): 1089-1991. Bailey and Pillard also published a similar study, with similar findings on women. See Natalie Angier, "Study Suggests Strong Genetic Role in Lesbianism," *New York Times,* Mar. 12, 1993, p. A8.

8. For additional philosophical critique of Bailey and Pillard's study, see Edward Stein, "Evidence for Queer Genes: An Interview with Richard Pillard," *GLQ* 1 (1993): 93-110.

9. See also M. Ruse, "Are There Gay Genes? Sociobiology and Homosexuality," *Journal of Homosexuality* 6(4) (1981): 5-34.

10. J. Money and D. Alexander, "Psychosexual Development and Absence of Homosexuality in Males with Precocious Puberty," *Journal of Nervous and Mental Disorders* 148 (1969): 111-123.

11. W. Ricketts, "Biological Research on Homosexuality: Anselm's Cow or Occam's Razor?" *Journal of Homosexuality* 9(4) (1984): 65-93; 75. Reprinted in J. De Cecco, ed., *Bisexual and Homosexual Identities: Critical Clinical Issues* (New York: The Haworth Press, Inc., 1984). Where they are contextually clear, further references to this work will be given in the text.

12. L. I. A. Birke, "Is Homosexuality Hormonally Determined?" *Journal of Homosexuality* 6(4) (1981): 35-49. Reprinted in N. Koertge, ed., *Nature and Causes of Homosexuality: A Philosophic and Scientific Inquiry* (New York: The Haworth Press, Inc., 1981).

13. N. R. Gartrell, "Hormones and Homosexuality," in W. Paul, J. Weinrich, J. S. Gonsiorek, and M. E. Hotvedt, eds., *Homosexuality: Social, Psychological, and Biological Issues* (Beverly Hills: Sage Publications, 1982), pp. 169-182.

14. G. Dörner, W. Rohde, F. Stahl, L. S. Krell, and W. G. Masius, "A Neuroendocrine Predisposition for Homosexuality in Men," *Archives of Sexual Behavior* 4 (1975): 1-8.

15. G. Dörner, W. Rohde, K. Seidel, W. Haas, and G. Schotl, "On the Evocability of a Positive Oestrogen Feedback Action on LH Secretion in Transsexual Men and Women," *Endokrinologie* 67 (1976): 365-368. See also G. Dörner, T. Greier, L. Ahrens, L. Krell, G. Münx, H. Sieler, E. Kittner, and H. Müller, "Prenatal Stress as a Possible Aetiogenetic Factor of Homosexuality in Human Males," *Endokrinologie* 75 (1980): 365-368.

16. Birke, "Is Homosexuality Hormonally Determined?"

17. B. A. Gladue, R. Green, and R.E. Hellman, "Neuroendocrine Response to Estrogen and Sexual Orientation," *Science* 225 (1984): 1496-1499.

18. S. E. Hendricks, B. Graber, and J. F. Rodriguez-Sierra, "Neuroendocrine Responses to Exogenous Estrogen: No Differences between Heterosexual and Homosexual Men," *Psychoneuroendocrinology* 14 (1989): 177-185; L. Gooren, "The Neuroendocrine Response of Luetinizing Hormone to Estrogen Administration in Heterosexual, Homosexual, and Transsexual Subjects," *Journal of Clinical Endocrinolgg and Metabolism* 63 (1986): 583-588; and L. Gooren, "The Neuroendocrine Response of Luetinizing Hormone to Estrogen Administration in Humans is not Sex Specific but Dependent upon the Hormonal Environment," *Journal of Clinical Endocrinolgg and Metabolism* 63 (1986): 589-593.

19. S. LeVay, "A Difference in Hypothalamic Structure between Heterosexual and Homosexual Men," *Science* 253 (1991): 1034-1037. For reaction to this report, see M. Baringa, "News & Comment: Is Homosexuality Biological?" *Science* 253 (1991): 956-957.

20. Of course, the ANOVA does take into account sample variance. My point here is not primarily a criticism of the statistical analysis of the data. Rather my claim is that the very classification of these regions as male or female is inappropriate. At best we have physiological features that correlate with gender to some degree, and an adequate classification would reflect that fact. Such a tax-

onomy would, of course, require altering the data analysis by making recourse to normalized size distributions of INAH 3 regions for males and females. For other philosophical critiques of LeVay's work see Stein, "Evidence for Queer Genes," and Timothy F. Murphy, "Homosex and the Limits of Research" (unpublished paper).

21. G. W. Henry and H. M. Galbraith, "Constitutional Factors in Homosexuality," *American Journal of Psychiatry* 90 (1934): 1249-1270.

22. H. S. Baharal, "Constitutional Factors in Male Homosexuals," *Psychiatric Quarterly* 13 (1939): 391-400.

23. R. B. Evans, "Physical and Biochemical Characteristics of Homosexual Men," *Journal of Consulting and Clinical Psychology* 39 (1972): 140-147.

24. F. Kenyon, "Physique and Physical Health of Female Homosexuals," *Journal of Neurological and Neurosurgical Psychiatry* 31 (1968): 487-489.

25. M. D. Gioscia, "The Gag Reflex and Fellatio," *American Journal of Psychiatry* 107 (1950): 380.

26. G. W. Henry, *Sexual Variants: A Study of Homosexual Patterns* (New York: Paul B. Hoeber, Inc., 1948 [originally published 1941]).

27. M. Opler, "Schizophrenia and Culture," *Scientific American* 197 (1957): 103-110.

28. R. Evans, "Childhood Parental Relationships of Homosexual Men," *Journal of Consulting and Clinical Psychology* 33 (1969): 129-135.

29. J. Nash and F. Hayes, "The Parental Relationships of Male Homosexuals," *Australian Journal of Psychology* 17 (1957): 35-43.

30. M. Shively and J. De Cecco, "Components of Sexual Identity," *Journal of Homosexuality* 2 (1976): 9-27. Also see F. Suppe, "Classifying Sexual Disorders: The Diagnostic and Statistical Manual of the American Psychiatric Association," *Journal of Homosexuality* 9(4) (1984): 9-28; F. Suppe, "Curing Homosexuality," in R. Baker and F. Elliston, eds., *Philosophy and Sex*, rev. ed. (Buffalo: Prometheus, 1984), pp. 391-420; and F. Suppe, "In Defense of a Multidimensional Approach to Sexual Identity," *Journal of Homosexuality* 10(3/4) (1984): 7-14.

31. Suppe, "Medical and Psychiatric Perspectives."

32. Mary McIntosh, "The Homosexual Role," *Social Problems* 2 (1968): 182-192.

33. M. Weinberg and C. J. Williams, *Homosexuals: Their Problems and Adaptations* (New York: Oxford University Press, 1974), pp. 7-8. Where they are contextually clear, further references to this title will be given in the text.

34. K. Plummer, ed., *The Making of the Modern Homosexual* (Totowa, NJ: Barnes and Noble, 1981).

35. J. De Cecco and M. Shively, eds., *Bisexual and Homosexual Identities: Critical Theoretical Issues* (New York: The Haworth Press, Inc., 1984).

36. Suppe, "In Defense of a Multidimensional Approach."

37. A. Bell, M. Weinberg, and S. K. Hammersmith, *Sexual Preference: Its Development in Men and Women* (Bloomington, IN: Indiana University Press, 1981); and A. Bell, M. Weinberg, and S. K. Hammersmith, *Sexual Preference: Its Development in Men and Women–Statistical Appendix* (Bloomington, IN: Indiana Uni-

versity Press, 1981). Where they are contextually clear, further references to this first title will be given in the text.

38. See also Richard Mohr, *Gay Ideas*, chap. 7; Edward Stein, "The Relevance of Scientific Research about Sexual Orientation to Lesbian and Gay Rights" in this volume; and Suppe, "Curing Homosexuality," pp. 408-410.

39. See Suppe, "Classifying Sexual Disorders" and "The Diagnostic and Statistical Manual."

40. Bell, Weinberg, and Hammersmith, *Homosexualities*, chap. 7.

41. See M. Jackson, *Sir! More Sir!: The Joy of S & M* (San Francisco: Leyland Publications, 1992), J. Ricardo, *Leathermen Speak Out: An Anthology on Leathersex* (San Francisco: Leyland Publications, 1991), M. Thompson, *Leatherfolk: Radical Sex, People, Politics, and Practice* (Boston: Alyson Publications, 1991), and L. Townsend, *The Leatherman's Handbook II*, 2nd ed. (New York: Carlyle Publications, 1989).

42. See Richard Mohr's brilliant " 'Knights, Young Men, Boys': Masculine Worlds and Democratic Values," in *Gay Ideas: Outing and Other Controversies* (Boston: Beacon Press, 1992), pp. 129-218; 179-180.

43. For further critique of identification of animal mounting behavior with *human* homosexuality and heterosexuality, see Stein, "Evidence for Queer Genes."

44. As Adolf Grünbaum points out, the method of agreement alone is insufficient to establish causality. See *The Foundations of Psychoanalysis: A Philosophical Critique* (Berkeley: University of California Press, 1984), p. 256.

45. R. Giere, *Understanding Scientific Reasoning* (New York: Holt, Rinehart, and Winston, 1979).

46. Lester, *Unusual Sexual Behavior*, p. 72.

47. In words: the probability of event E under condition C is the real number r, where r is between 0 and 1.

48. C. Hempel, "Aspects of Scientific Explanation," in *Aspects of Scientific Explanation and Other Essays in the Philosophy of Science* (New York: Free Press, 1965), pp. 331-496.

49. The former account is to be found in W. Salmon, *Scientific Explanation and the Causal Structure of the World* (Princeton: Princeton University Press, 1970); the latter account is in *Statistical Relevance* (Pittsburgh: University of Pittsburgh Press, 1984).

50. See S. Bromberger, "Why Questions" in R. Colodny, ed., *Mind and Cosmos: Explorations in the Philosophy of Science* (Pittsburgh: University of Pittsburgh Press, 1966), pp. 86ff.; S. Toulmin, *Foresight and Understanding* (New York: Harper and Row, 1963); and F. Suppe, "A Nondeductivist Approach to Theoretical Explanation," in A. Grünbaum and W. Salmon, eds., *The Limits of Deductivism* (Berkeley: University of California Press, 1988), pp. 128-166.

51. Indeed, Freudian psychoanalysis may be one of the few scientific cases satisfying Bromberger's restriction to a finite number of types of deviations from the general rules in the expansions to "abnormic laws." See S. Bromberger, "Why

Questions?" in R. Colodny, ed., *Mind and Cosmos: Explorations in the Philosophy of Science* (Pittsburgh: University of Pittsburgh Press, 1966), pp. 86-11.

52. Although consulting Freud's original works is preferable, a convenient summary of Freud's developmental model is found in D. H. Ford and H. B. Urban, *Systems of Psychotherapy: A Comparative Study* (New York: Wiley, 1963), pp. 132-148. Pages 148-161 discuss Freud's views of the developmental behavior disorders which are just standard patterns of deviation from his normal developmental model.

53. The foregoing summary is paraphrased from Lester, pp. 75-76. See also I. Bieber, H. J. Dain, P. R. Dince, M. G. Drellich, H. G. Grand, R. H. Grundlach, M. W. Kremer, A. H. Rifkin, C. B. Wilber, and T. Bieber, *Homosexuality: A Psychoanalytic Study* (New York: Basic Books, 1962), chap. 1. Where they are contextually clear, further references to this latter title will be given in the text.

54. H. E. Kaye, B. Soll, J. Clare, M. Eleston, B. S. Gershwin, P. Gershwin, L. Kogan, C. Torda, and C. Wilbur, "Homosexuality in Women," *Archives of General Psychiatry* 17 (1967): 626-634.

55. F. Suppe, "The Bell and Weinberg Study: Future Priorities for Research on Homosexuality," *Journal of Homosexuality* 6 (1981): 69-97; 72. Reprinted in *Nature and Causes of Homosexuality.*

56. I. Bieber, "On Arriving at the APA Decision" (working paper for the Hastings Center Closure Project, n.d.), p. 4. This is an accurate summary of the claims of Bieber et al., 1962, chap. III.

57. Bieber, "On Arriving," p. 4.

58. Bieber et al., Table III-1, pp. 45-46. Control response frequencies were lower with one exception where the higher control response percentage was 47% as opposed to 17% for the homosexual group.

59. J. Gonsiorek, "Psychological Adjustment and Homosexuality," *Catalog of Selected Documents in Psychology* 7(2) (1977): 45; and microfiche MS 1478 (available from the American Psychological Association).

60. A number of replicative studies were done which incorporated such methodological improvements. Their results are conflicting. These attempts are reviewed in M. Siegelman, "Parental Background of Male Homosexuals and Heterosexuals," *Archives of Sexual Behavior* 3 (1971): 31-38.

61. What follows is an expanded version of F. Suppe, "Grünbaum, Homosexuality, and Contemporary Psychoanalysis," *Behavioral and Brain Science* 9 (1986): 261-262.

62. C. Socarides, "Homosexuality and Medicine," *Journal of the American Medical Association* 212 (1970): 1199-1202; 1199.

63. A. Grünbaum, *The Foundations of Psychoanalysis: A Philosophical Critique* (Berkeley: University of California Press, 1984), p. 140. Where they are contextually clear, further references to this title will be given in the text.

64. F. Crews, "The Future or an Illusion: The False Premises and False Promises of Freud," *New Republic*, Jan., 21, 1985, pp. 28-33; 32.

65. Also see Grünbaum, "The Placebo Concept."

66. E.g., Bieber et al.; L. J. Hatterer, *Changing Homosexuality* (New York: McGraw-Hill, 1970); and C. Socarides, *Changing Homosexuality* (New York: Grune and Stratton, 1968).

67. Suppe, "Curing Homosexuality," pp. 397-399.

68. A. Bravis, "Analyse mathématique sur les probabilités des erreurs de situation d'un point," *Mémoires presentés par divers savants à l'Académie royale des sciences de l'Institut de France* 9 (1846): 255-332.

69. F. Galton, "Correlations and Their Measurement, Chiefly from Anthropometric Data," *Proceedings of the Royal Society of London* 45 (274) (1888): 135-145.

70. K. Pearson, "Mathematical Contributions to the Theory of Evolution-XIV. On the General Theory of Skew Correlation and Non-Linear Regression." *Draper's Co. Research Memoires* (1905), Biometric Series II. Reprinted in *Karl Pearson's Early Statistical Papers* (Cambridge: Cambridge University Press, 1948), pp. 477-528.

71. S. Wright, "Correlation and Causation," *Journal of Agricultural Research* 20 (1921): 557-585; 559.

72. S. Wright, "On the Nature of Size Factors," *Genetics* 3 (1917): 367-374; S. Wright, "Correlation and Causation;" and S. Wright, "Systems of Mating," *Genetics* 6 (1921): 111-178; 114-117

73. Herbert Costner, personal communication.

74. Wright, "Correlation and Causation," p. 557.

75. H. B. Asher, *Causal Modeling* [Number 3 in the Sage Series of University Papers on Quantitative Applications in the Social Sciences] (Beverly Hills: Sage Publications, 1976), pp. 11-12.

76. P. Spirtes, R. Scheines, and C. Glymour, "Simulation Studies of the Reliability of Computer-Aided Model Specification Using the TETRAD, EQS, and LISREL Programs," *Social Methods & Research* 19 (1990): 3-66.

77. Bell, Weinberg, and Hammersmith, *Sexual Preference* and *Statistical Appendix.*

78. Suppe, "Bell and Weinberg Study."

79. For a good heuristic account of multivariate analysis techniques, see F. Kerlinger, *Behavioral Research: A Conceptual Approach* (New York: Holt, Rinehart, and Winston, 1979), chaps. 11-13; path analysis is discussed on pp. 232-237.

80. Institute for Sex Research, "A Study of Socialization, 1969-1970." Unpublished confidential document, 1969-1970, Indiana University.

81. See T. F. Murphy, "Reproductive Controls and Sexual Destiny," *Bioethics* 4 (1990): 121-142.

82. For example, A. Bell, "Research on Homosexuality: Back to the Drawing Board," *Archives of Sexual Behavior* 4 (1975): 421-431.

83. D. Crane, *Invisible Colleges: Diffusion of Knowledge in Scientific Communities* (Chicago: University of Chicago Press, 1972).

84. F. Suppe, "Credentialing Scientific Claims," *Perspectives on Science* 1 (1993): forthcoming.

85. D. Shapere, *Reason and the Search for Knowledge* (Dordrecht: D. Reidel, 1984).

86. L. Laudan, *Progress and its Problems: Toward a Theory of Scientific Growth* (Berkeley: University of California Press, 1977) and *Science and Values: The Aims of Science and their Role in Scientific Debate* (Berkeley: University of California Press, 1984).

87. I. Lakatos, "Falsification and the Methodology of Scientific Research Programmes," in I. Lakatos and A. Musgrave, eds., *Criticism and the Growth of Scientific Knowledge* (Cambridge: Cambridge University Press, 1979), pp. 91-196.

88. T. Kuhn, *The Structure of Scientific Revolutions*, enlarged ed. (Chicago: University of Chicago Press, 1970).

89. S. Toulmin, *Human Understanding*, Vol. 1 (Princeton: Princeton University Press, 1972).

90. The foregoing extracts themes common to D. Shapere, S. Toulmin, I. Lakatos, L. Laudan, and T. S. Kuhn but ignores many of the idiosyncratic differences that distinguish their positions. Thus my use of "progressive" and "degenerating" research is more inclusive than Lakatos and divorced from his specific characterization of a research program.

91. Bailey and Pillard, p. 1090.

92. American Psychiatric Association, *Diagnostic and Statistical Manual of Mental Disorders*, 3rd ed. (Washington, DC: American Psychiatric Association), 1980.

93. Suppe, "Classifying Sexual Disorders" and "Diagnostic and Statistical Manual."

94. Suppe, "Medical and Psychiatric Perspectives."

95. J. Katz, *Gay/Lesbian Almanac: A New Documentary* (New York: Harper Colophon Books, 1983).

96. One of my main themes in this paper is that even the current classifications are grossly underdifferentiated and thus constitute pseudo-categories of little scientific merit.

97. E. Lewin and T. A. Lyons, "Everything in its Place: The Coexistence of Lesbianism and Motherhood" (pp. 249-274), and M. Hotvedt and J. B. Mandel, "Children of Lesbian Mothers" (275-286), in *Homosexuality: Social, Psychological, and Biological Issues.*

The Relevance of Scientific Research About Sexual Orientation to Lesbian and Gay Rights

Edward Stein, PhD

New York University

SUMMARY. This essay considers the way in which scientific research is relevant to questions of lesbian and gay rights. It is specifically argued that such research is not relevant to these kinds of arguments because its results about the origins of sexual orientation do not necessarily–and should not be taken to–imply conclusions about moral entitlements. Questions about the moral and civic entitlements of gay men and lesbians are not bolstered or advanced by reference to biological accounts of sexual orientation. This is not to suggest, however, that research into the origins of sexual orientation is objectionable, only that it does not have the significance for moral rights that some have claimed.

We are interested in obtaining rights for our respective minorities as Negroes, as Jews, and as Homosexuals. Why we are Negroes, Jews or Homosexuals is totally irrelevant, and

Edward Stein is Assistant Professor in the Department of Philosophy, New York University, 503 Main Building, Washington Square, New York, NY 10003. He specializes in epistemology, philosophy of mind, and philosophy of science. He is the editor of *Forms of Desire: Sexual Orientation and the Social Constructionist Controversy* (Routledge, 1992).

[Haworth co-indexing entry note]: "The Relevance of Scientific Research About Sexual Orientation to Lesbian and Gay Rights." Stein, Edward. Co-published simultaneously in the *Journal of Homosexuality* (The Haworth Press, Inc.) Vol. 27, No. 3/4, 1994, pp. 269-308; and: *Gay Ethics: Controversies in Outing, Civil Rights, and Sexual Science* (ed: Timothy F. Murphy) The Haworth Press, Inc., 1994, pp. 269-308. Multiple copies of this article/chapter may be purchased from The Haworth Document Delivery Center [1-800-3-HAWORTH; 9:00 a.m. - 5:00 p.m. (EST)].

whether we can be changed to Whites, Christians or heterosexuals is equally irrelevant.

Frank Kameny
"Speech to the New York Mattachine Society," July 1964.[1]

There is, these days, quite a bit of scientific research that attempts to answer the question why some people are gay or lesbian and others are not. In this paper, I am concerned with the ethical relevance (if any) of such research and particularly with whether this research is relevant to questions concerning lesbian and gay rights. I will argue that the case for lesbian and gay rights of any sort needs to be made independent of any theory of the causes of sexual orientation. I begin with a brief survey of the theoretical background of research concerning sexual orientations as well as with the details of two recent scientific studies. I then examine the arguments that people make (at least implicitly) for connecting this research with lesbian and gay rights and conclude that these arguments are not up to the task. Having argued that such scientific research is not relevant to lesbian and gay rights, I describe the sorts of considerations that I think *are* relevant. Finally, I discuss whether such research should be done at all. I argue that the reasons people give that it should *not* be done are weaker than they might seem in light of my preceding arguments.

The Categories of Sexual Desire

Most people have sexual desires. Different people have widely varying sexual desires. They differ in the sort of sex they want to have and the sort of people they want to have sex with. In twentieth-century North America, most people think that the sex of the people you want to have sex with is a deep and an important feature of your sexual desire, more deep and important, for example, than their age, race, or the sort of place in which you want to have sex. Our very sexual identities are built around the particular feature of our sexual interest that we call sexual orientation: some people are heterosexuals, some are gay men or lesbians, and some are bisexuals.

A central point of contention in lesbian and gay studies concerns the nature of these categories. "Social constructionists" think our categories of sexual orientation (that is, gay, straight, and bi) refer to merely (that is, artifactual) social kinds while "essentialists" think these categories group humans into natural divisions in the same way that the categories of blood types (A, B, AB, O) group humans into natural divisions (what I call "natural human kinds").[2] Social constructionists deny this; for them, the categories of sexual orientation only pick out people in virtue of social facts, in the way, say, the category "yuppie" does. It is important to note that the essentialist is not committed to nativism about sexual orientation; it is perfectly consistent with essentialism that people have the sexual orientations they do because of the psychoanalytic structures they might have in virtue of their relationship with their parents.[3]

Most scientists doing research concerning sexual desire assume that some version of essentialism is true. Such scientists are looking to discover what makes people have the sexual orientations that they do, and they are betting that the correct account is going to be cast in primarily natural kind terms, rather than merely social ones. I have elsewhere emphasized the point that the debate between essentialists and constructionists is an empirical question, not a purely conceptual one.[4] Essentialism and the project of giving a scientific account of why people have the sexual orientations they do are mutually supporting: if essentialism is true, then there must be some scientific explanation for why people have the sexual orientations they do; for a deep scientific explanation to be possible, some version of essentialism must be true.

Some of the most interesting work by social constructionists has shown the radically different ways other societies "construct" sexual desire and thus group people into quite different categories according to their sexual interests.[5] Some social constructionists have thought that this historical and anthropological evidence proves that essentialism is false: if folks in New Guinea, for example, divide people into quite different categories of sexual desire from those scientists use, then essentialism is thereby shown to be false. While this sort of evidence is suggestive, it does not count against essentialism as strongly as some have thought since the essentialist has two possible responses. First, she could say that the differences social constructionists point to are merely social ones;

the very same natural human kinds exist beneath such social differences. This would be analogous to the fact that even though New Guineans may not have the *categories* associated with blood type, they do *have* (that is, they instantiate) blood types and thus fit into the associated categories. Second, the essentialist could respond by admitting that it is unlikely that *our* categories of sexual orientation apply to people in socially quite different societies while saying that this does not count against there being *some* categories that apply to people in virtue of their sexual desires. This "sophisticated" essentialist could admit that the sex of the person I want to have sex with is perhaps no more a deep property about my sexual desires than the hair color of the people I want to have sex with, while allowing that some features of people's sexual desire are deep and support natural human kinds.

The debate between essentialists and social constructionists may seem tangential to the question of the connection between the science of sexual orientation and lesbian and gay rights, but the questions are connected in two ways. First, the nature of the categories of sexual orientation is connected to the outcome of scientific research on the origins of sexual orientation in particular and sexual desires more generally. Second, given this connection, *if* there is a connection between science and lesbian and gay rights, then there will likely also be a connection between the essentialism-social constructionism debate and lesbian and gay rights.[6] Since, however, I will be arguing that, properly understood, there is no genuine connection between lesbian and gay rights and the science of sex and sexual desire, I will also implicitly be arguing that there is no connection between the essentialism-social constructionism debate and lesbian and gay rights.

The Assumptions of Scientific Research

Scientific research concerning same-sex sexual desire has a very bad history. Many studies done in the past century made amazingly naive assumptions about lesbians and gay men and often did horrible things to them as part of such studies or based on the mistaken conclusions drawn from them. Examples include studies done on the amount of facial hair and the hip-size of lesbians and gay men compared to their heterosexual counterparts and studies that supported the practices of treating gay men and lesbians with hormones and giving them electric shocks to change their sexual desires.[7] These studies typically assume that homosexuality is a disease that needs to be cured, that homosexuality is a moral failing, that homosexuality is unnatural, and that same-sex sexual attraction is a symptom of more general sex inversion. For reasons I assume are well understood, these are mistaken assumptions. But these studies make a further (and still common) assumption that is not so easily undercut: they assume that all science needs to explain about sexual orientation is why some people are lesbians or gay men; heterosexuality, according to these studies, is not in need of any explanation.[8] This point warrants some discussion.

Given the different positions of power that lesbians and gay men (as opposed to heterosexuals) have in this and other cultures, there is an asymmetry in how the origins of sexual orientation are explored and there is a recurring pattern of who asks such questions and in what contexts they ask them. Lesbians and gay men often ask themselves why they are gay; parents often wonder what they did to "make" their children homosexual; and scientists, psychiatrists, and others study what causes homosexuality. In contrast, few heterosexuals worry about why they are heterosexual; few parents worry about what they did to "make" their children straight; and few scientists or psychiatrists study what causes heterosexuality. But, from the point of view of science, it is no less a mystery how people become heterosexual than it is how people become homosexual. Simply saying that heterosexuality is the norm does not explain how people become heterosexual. Why some people are attracted to people of the same sex is as much a mystery as why other people are attracted to people of the opposite sex. A robust science of sexual orientation needs to explain both phenomena, and it needs to do so as part of an explanation of sexual desire more generally. We lack an adequate explanation of, for example, why some people like anal sex and others do not, and why some people are attracted primarily to blondes, others to redheads, while others place little significance on the hair color of their object choice. Perhaps the reason why more research gets done on the cause of sexual orientation in particular but not sexual desires in general is because of the social significance attached to sexual orientation and because most people (naively) accept essentialism about sexual orientation but not, for the most part, about other sexual desires.[9] Whatever the explanation for the special interest in sexual orientation in particular, this should not overshadow scientific/psychological research about why people engage in particular sexual acts and have the various sexual desires that they do.

Some might object to part of what I have said in the preceding paragraph. They might say there is an explanation of heterosexuality that does not apply to homosexuality: we can give a biological explanation of why people are heterosexual because heterosexual acts can produce offspring while homosexual acts cannot. In the more precise terms of an evolutionary explanation, the idea is that the desire to have sex with people of the opposite sex has greater selective advantage than the desire to have sex with people of the same sex. In general, evolutionary explanations of this form are perfectly good explanations: one can explain why members of a species have one trait rather than an alternative if the trait they have enables them to leave a greater number of descendants than the alternative trait would (in other words, if the trait they have gives them greater selective advantage). For a couple of reasons, however, this straightforward sort of evolutionary explanation cannot be used to explain heterosexuality.

First, there is a general problem with extending evolutionary explanations for why organisms have certain physical traits to why organisms behave in certain ways. The connection between genes and physical traits is closer than the connection between genes and behavior.[10] In the case of sexual behavior in particular, the connection between genes and behavior is mediated by the mind. It cannot be the case that a woman has a gene that *is* a behavior, for example, the behavior of putting her vagina around penises. Rather, a woman could have a gene that in some way has the effect of disposing her to want to put her vagina around penises. This disposition needs to be cashed out in terms of some psychological structure she has. Psychological structures can be given genetic explanations; dispositions and behaviors can only be explained genetically *via* such psychological structures. The point is that an evolutionary account of heterosexuality requires an account of the psychological structures underlying heterosexual behavior, an account we are lacking;

without such an account, one cannot assert that there is an explanation for heterosexuality but not for homosexuality.

There is a further problem with this evolutionary explanation of heterosexuality. Even if we could give evolutionary explanations of behavior, it is not at all clear that *exclusive* heterosexuality is the most selectively advantageous sexual behavior. Some sort of bisexuality, for example, might be a better strategy. In addition to putting his penis in women's vaginas, it might be selectively advantageous for a man to occasionally put it in some men's anuses. Determining the selective advantageousness of various sexual behaviors is a well-established problem.[11] At first glance, it would seem that exclusive homosexuality would disappear from the gene pool, since such behavior is not at all conducive to producing descendants. But, homosexuality seems quite a robust phenomenon. This suggests that homosexual behavior has some indirect selective advantage and/or that the appropriate ways of thinking about sexual desire and selective advantage are not in terms of our commonsense categories of sexual orientation. Either way, even setting aside my first objection, the proposed evolutionary explanation for heterosexuality is undercut.

Two Studies

Before I turn to the main question of this paper, I want to get two examples on the table, namely two recent studies of sexual orientation, the first by Simon LeVay[12] and the second by J. Michael Bailey and Richard Pillard.[13] LeVay examined the brains of 41 people–nineteen of them from men identified as homosexual (or bisexual) in their medical records who died of complications due to AIDS; six of them from men of undetermined sexual orientation who also died of AIDS who LeVay presumed were heterosexual;[14] ten of them from men also of undetermined sexual orientation who died of other causes; and six women, all presumed to be heterosexual, one who died of AIDS and five who died from other causes–in order to measure the size of their interstitial nuclei of the anterior hypothalamus (INAH-3) regions.[15] LeVay found that the INAH-3 regions of the self-proclaimed homosexual men who died of AIDS were significantly smaller on average than those of the men of undetermined sexual orientation. On this basis, he concluded that there is a correlation between hypothalami and sexual orientation and, further, that this correlation suggests there is something neurological/biological about sexual orientation.

In Bailey and Pillard's study, gay men with a twin brother (either identical or merely fraternal) or an adopted brother were asked a series of questions about their sexual practices and desires, and then their brothers were asked the same sort of questions. They found that fifty percent of the identical twins of gay men were themselves gay, twenty percent of fraternal twins were gay, as were ten percent of adopted brothers. They supposed these results to show that there is a significant biological component to sexual orientation because if there were no such component, then, for example, the adopted brothers would be equally likely to turn out to have the same sexual orientation as the twins.

Especially interesting are the reactions to these results both by the "mainstream" media and by many gay people, particularly gay political figures. Not so surprisingly, I suppose, the mainstream media took a sensationalistic approach to these discoveries. In regard to LeVay's study, they reported that homosexuality is *caused* by having smaller-sized INAH-3 regions of the hypothalamus.[16] These reports oversimplified LeVay's results—he does not, for example, claim to have found a cause of homosexuality, only to have discovered a neurophysiological feature that is associated with it—and they failed even to express any skepticism about the results (when in fact much skepticism is warranted due to small sample sizes, the fact that the "gay brains" came from people who had been infected with HIV for substantial periods of time, and the fact that the so-called control group was actually of undetermined sexual orientation),[17] and completely failed to put the study in any historical context. To the extent that mainstream reports quoted lesbian and gay activists, the reactions were that the results of these studies were politically useful because they showed being gay is natural, determinate, not a choice, not a psychological disorder, not something that should be cured, not something that is immoral, not something that should be punished, and that lesbian and gay men are a genuine minority group deserving of equal rights and protection against discrimination.[18] Both Pillard and LeVay share this view of the political implications of their studies.[19] It is this view that I examine and criticize in the next section.

CAN SCIENTIFIC RESEARCH ADVANCE LESBIAN AND GAY RIGHTS?

People who think discovering a cause for homosexuality has good moral and political implications for lesbian and gay rights have various arguments in mind for their view. All of these arguments seem to have the same general structure. They begin with the claim that homosexuality has a genetic, biological, or hormonal basis. They then link this claim in a conditional to some fact they claim would follow, such as "If homosexuality is genetic, then being a lesbian or gay man is not a psychological disorder." They then make the consequent of this conditional the antecedent of a conditional that has the consequent that lesbians and gay men deserve rights, recognition, and protection against discrimination, such as "If being lesbian or gay is not a psychological disorder, then lesbians and gay men deserve rights, recognition, and protection against discrimination." In its schematic form, the argument is as follows:

(1) Homosexuality has a biological basis.[20]
(2) If homosexuality is biological, then _____.
(3) If _____, then lesbian and gay men deserve rights, recognition, and protection against discrimination.
(4) Therefore, lesbians and gay men deserve rights, recognition, and protection against discrimination.

The different versions of the argument result from different ways of filling in the blanks. I will consider various ways of doing so in the following subsections.

Protected Group Status

One way to fill in the blank in the above argument involves the notion of protected groups. In the United States, various categories of people are singled out as warranting special protection against discrimination. So, for example, race, sex, gender, religious affiliation, age, disability, nationality, and ethnic status are in various contexts singled out as protected categories. If sexual orientation deserves to be a "special status" category, then this might entail that lesbians and gay men deserve rights.[21] Some people have argued that establishing a genetic basis for homosexuality will entail that sexual orientation should count as a protected category. The specific argument is as follows:

(1)   Homosexuality has a biological basis.

(2a) If homosexuality has a biological basis, then sexual orientation should be a protected category.

(3a) If sexual orientation is a protected category, then lesbians and gay men deserve rights, recognition, and protection against discrimination.

(4)   Therefore, lesbians and gay men deserve rights, recognition, and protection against discrimination.

But why should we believe premise (2a)? There are, in fact, several reasons for doubting its truth. First, just because a category has a biological basis does not thereby entail that members of it deserve protected status; there are many categories with a biological basis that are not thought to be morally relevant categories, much less, to be categories that warrant protected status. For example, hair color has a biological basis but people with a particular hair color do not constitute a protected category. Being a biologically-based category is thus not a *sufficient* condition for being a category that deserves protected status. It is worth noting that being biologically based is not a *necessary* condition either. For example, being of a certain religious affiliation or nationality are not biologically based but they constitute protected categories.

A friend of the "protected group" argument for lesbian and gay rights might respond to the hair-color example by pointing out that *if* people were unjustifiably discriminated against on the basis of hair color, then hair color *should* be a protected category and it should be *because* it is genetically based. Behind this response is the notion that being biologically based is not enough to make a category a protected one; there must be some *further* requirement, perhaps that the category is the basis for unjustified discrimination. While there does seem to be something right about it, the further requirement that there be "unjustified discrimination" against members of a category for that category to warrant special protection is not necessarily connected to the "biologically based" requirement. Any category that is the basis for unjustified discrimination—whether biologically based or not—seems a plausible candidate for a protected category. This very fact—that whether or not the category is biologically based seems to have nothing to do with whether the category should be a protected one—suggests that there is no interesting connection between the causes of sexual orientation and whether sexual orientation should be a protected category. Premise (2a) is thereby undermined.

This consideration against (2a) aside, there is a further problem with the protected category argument for lesbian and gay rights. Even if being gay or lesbian is biologically based, so much of what is crucial about being a bisexual, a lesbian, or a gay man would not be biologically based, and hence would not be protected by the argument with premises (2a) and (3a). For example, even if homosexuality is biologically based, actually engaging in homosexual acts, actually identifying as lesbian or gay, and so on, are *choices,* choices that each lesbian or gay man might well not have made (that is, he or she could have decided to be abstinent and closeted). Someone who was convinced that lesbians and gay men deserve rights only because homosexuality is biologically based believes people should not be discriminated against on the basis of their biological features and on these alone. For example, if I were convinced by the protected-status argument, I would think that people who had homoerotic desires should not be discriminated against on the basis of their having these desires. This is perfectly compatible, however, with my thinking that people who engage in same-sex sexual acts *are* appropriate targets of discrimination, criminal penalties, and the like.[22] A friend of the biological argument for lesbian and gay rights might try to respond to this criticism by attempting to make a connection between being protected against discrimination because one's desire is biologically based and being protected against discrimination on the basis of behaviors that stem from biologically-based desire. Without a detailed story of how it could be made, this connection seems implausible. Even if premises (1) and (2a) of the protected-status argument are true (and I have given some reason to doubt (2a)), there are further reasons to doubt premise (3a); even if sexual orientation is a protected category, lesbian and gay rights (in any non-trivial sense of the term "rights") do not follow.

This objection to the protected status argument seems to constitute an objection to all versions of the general argument with the biological basis of homosexuality as a premise and with the claim that lesbians and gay men deserve rights as the conclusion. Arguments of this form seem limited to showing that gay men and lesbians deserve rights only with respect to those attributes lesbians and gay men have in virtue of their particular biological constitution. Whether this objection applies to the other versions of the biological argument for lesbian and gay rights will be considered below. The conclusion of this subsection is thus two-fold: (1) being biologically based is neither a necessary nor a sufficient condition for establishing protected group status, and (2) biology seems to be infertile ground on which to plant an argument for lesbian and gay rights because behaviors not just desires are relevant to lesbian and gay rights.

Determinism

Another argument for lesbian and gay rights of the same general structure as the one discussed above involves determinism, the thesis that sexual orientation is not a choice.[23] The idea behind this particular argument is that if homosexuality has a biological basis, then sexual orientation is not a choice; but if sexual orientation is not a choice, then one can hardly be punished for or discriminated against on the basis of sexual orientation. The argument goes as follows:

(1) Homosexuality has a biological basis.
(2b) If homosexuality has a biological basis, then sexual orientation is not a choice.
(3b) If sexual orientation is not a choice, then lesbians and gay men deserve rights, recognition, and protection against discrimination.

(4)   Therefore, lesbians and gay men deserve rights, recognition, and protection against discrimination.

This argument suffers from one of the problems I discussed above with respect to the protected status argument: the biological basis of homosexuality at most establishes that lesbians and gay men do not have a choice with respect to their homoerotic desires, but it leaves open that they have a choice with respect to their behavior, their public identification of their sexual orientation, and the like. If lesbians and gay men deserve rights with request to virtue of the truth of determinism about sexual orientation, then it would still be permissible to discriminate against people on the basis of things about which they *do* have a choice, such as sexual behavior and public sexual identity. In other words, it is consistent with determinism about sexual orientation that lesbians and gay men are discriminated against in virtue of, for example, engaging in same-sex sexual acts. This is to say that premise (3b) is false.

As an analogy, consider alcoholism. Suppose, as seems to be the case, that a predisposition for alcoholism is congenital.[24] The truth of this claim might make it morally unacceptable to discriminate against someone because she is disposed to become an alcoholic. This, however, would *not* make it morally unacceptable to discriminate against someone who actually is an "active" alcoholic, that is, who gets drunk on a regular basis. Regardless of the biological basis of alcoholism, it is morally acceptable to decide not to live with someone, or not to hire her, because she is frequently under the influence of alcohol, a fact that affects her ability to behave responsibly. The point of the analogy is that even if the *disposition* to engage in a behavior is not a choice, actually engaging in that behavior may be a choice and, thus, discrimination on the basis of whether someone actually engages in such a behavior might be acceptable. Further, even if (contrary to fact) being an "active" alcoholic were biologically determined, it would *still* be acceptable to discriminate on the basis of being an active alcoholic. If this were the case, it would be wrong to *blame* someone for being an active alcoholic (since nothing she could do would, by stipulation, prevent her from drinking to excess), but this does not make it wrong to discriminate on that basis. Just because I cannot be blamed for a

behavior does not mean that I get any rights in virtue of my behavior or that it is morally wrong to discriminate against me in
virtue of it. Even if an active alcoholic is not to be blamed for her
condition, she does not deserve special rights or protection on the
mere basis of her status as an alcoholic.

The analogy to alcoholism shows two things. First, it makes clear
that the lack of choice about falling into a natural human kind does
not guarantee that people who fit that kind deserve rights, protection against discrimination, and the like merely on the basis of
doing so. This objection counts against premise (3b) of the determinism argument for lesbian and gay rights. Second, the analogy
makes clear why (3b) seems appealing at first glance. If a person
has no choice whether or not she falls into a particular human kind,
then she should not be blamed for fitting that kind. Freedom from
blame does not, however, entail freedom from discrimination or the
receipt of special rights. Friends of the determinism argument for
lesbian and gay rights seem to miss this point. Premise (3b) seems
plausible only if you think that the absence of blame entails rights
beyond the right not to be punished. The absence of blame does not
have this implication. The lack of choice about one's sexual orientation does not provide grounds for lesbian and gay rights; (3b) is thus
false, and the determinism argument for lesbian and gay rights fails.

The objection to the determinism argument for lesbian and gay
rights is that the lack of choice about one's sexual orientation does
not in itself provide grounds for lesbian and gay rights, that is, (3b)
is false. First (3b) is false because the lack of choice about one's
sexual desires fails to include much of what should be protected
under the rubric of lesbian and gay rights. So, for example, even if
my desire to have sex with other men was determined biologically—and thus not a choice and thus the basis for lesbian and gay
rights, protection against discrimination, and the like—my decision
to actually engage in sexual acts with other men would still *not* be
determined biologically, and would be a choice, and thus would
not be the basis for lesbian and gay rights, protection against
discrimination, and the like. Second, even if (contrary to fact) all
facets of being lesbian or gay (that is, engaging in same-sex sexual
acts or identifying oneself as lesbian or gay) were biologically
determined (3b) would still be false. Determinism about all facets

of sexual orientation would show the absence of blame for all facets of sexual orientation, but this would not in turn entail lesbian and gay rights, since the lack of blame is not grounds for positive rights. The determinism argument for lesbian and gay rights thus fails.

Naturalness

Another argument for lesbian and gay rights of the same general structure as the arguments considered above has to do with the "naturalness" of homosexuality. Some people think that being lesbian, gay, or bisexual is in some way *un*natural and, on that basis, they have defended discrimination against lesbians and gay men. Some friends of the biological argument for lesbian and gay rights seem to think that if they can undermine this charge of "unnaturalness" by showing a biological basis for homosexuality, they can undercut the argument for discrimination and replace it with an argument for lesbian and gay rights. This argument proceeds as follows:

(1) Homosexuality has a biological basis.
(2c) If homosexuality has a biological basis, then homosexuality is natural.
(3c) If homosexuality is natural, then lesbians and gay men deserve rights, recognition, and protection against discrimination.
(4) Therefore, lesbians and gay men deserve rights, recognition, and protection against discrimination.

The first thing to note about this argument is its use of the notoriously tricky term "natural." When opponents of lesbian and gay rights claim that lesbian and gay men are unnatural, it is quite difficult to figure out what they mean by the term. The same is true when friends of lesbian and gay rights use the term "natural" as in (2c) and (3c). To clarify the notion of naturalness with respect to sexual orientation, I shall enumerate various often-used senses of the term. When people claim that homosexuality is unnatural, they are using the term in one of the following senses:

A (sexual) behavior is unnatural if it:
(i)   does not contribute to the perpetuation of the species.
(ii)   involves using an organ or the like for a function other than the function it was selected to perform.
(iii)   is not performed by (non-human) animals.
(iv)   is caused by humans, is caused artificially, is not "in nature."

All four of these senses of unnatural either (a) fail to apply to homosexuality or (b) apply to a whole range of "acceptable" behaviors (for example, marriage, masturbation, contraceptive sex, skiing); as such, they are inadequate for grounding a case for discrimination against lesbians and gay men. Showing in detail that homosexuality is not unnatural in any of these senses is not, however, the point here.[25] Rather, the point is to see whether (2c) and (3c) are true in any sense of the term "natural." I shall argue that there are no good reasons to believe (2c) is true on any but the last sense of "natural."

> *i. perpetuation of the species.* Consider first (2c) under the first interpretation of "natural":
> (2c-i) If homosexuality has a biological basis, then homosexuality contributes to the perpetuation of the species.

Problems arise at first glance because there are lots of traits that humans have in virtue of their biology that do not contribute to the survival of the species. Perhaps the most obvious example of this is genetically-based impotence: this sort of impotence by stipulation has a biological basis, but it cannot contribute to the perpetuation of the species. The mere genetic basis of a trait does not thereby establish that the trait contributes to the survival of the species; in fact, some genetic traits do just the opposite.

This is perhaps a bit too quick. The persistence of homosexuality in the human gene pool is a problem for sociobiologists since exclusive homosexuals are not known for their reproductive success. Some sociobiologists, as an attempt to solve this problem, have argued that a gene for homosexuality is evolutionary adaptive. Although an exclusively homosexual individual would not leave any offspring of her own, her homosexuality might still be adaptive in the sense of increasing the number of copies of her genes that get into subsequent generations. Sociobiologists have tried to spin out various stories of how this might work, from lesbians and gay men who help their siblings raise their children, to queers who devote their time to the arts and sciences (rather than to reproduction) and thereby make the world a better place for future generations.[26] If, implausible as they seem, one of these sociobiological stories is right and homosexuality is adaptive, then this might help to make the case for (2c-i). This success, however, is only apparent: (2c-i) is a conditional statement; it says *if* homosexuality has a biological basis, then homosexuality contributes to the perpetuation of the species. There are other biological theories of homosexuality on which homosexuality does not contribute to the perpetuation of the species; since one of these theories *could* be true, the conditional is false–a biological basis does not entail the perpetuation of the species although some (implausible) biological theories, if true, would. Thus (2c-i) is undermined.

> *ii. performing evolutionary selected function.* Consider next:
> (2c-ii) If homosexuality has a biological basis, then homo-
> sexuality involves using organs only for functions they were
> selected to perform.[27]

This is also false. A behavior can be biologically based but still involve using an organ in ways other than the way the particular organ was selected for. Suppose, for example, that the human throat was selected for the role it plays in digestion. This is perfectly consistent with the fact that the throat plays a role in speaking, a behavior that also has a biological basis, although the throat was not, by stipulation, selected for because of the role it plays in speaking. More generally, traits that are selected for are often called into play in a whole host of ways for which the trait was not originally selected, and, in fact, may be used in behaviors that are not themselves selectively advantageous.[28] Thus (2c-ii) is false.

> *iii. performed by animals.* Consider the third sense of "nat-
> ural" that might be used to make sense of (2c), namely that a
> behavior is natural if (non-human) animals do it.

Some people who say homosexuality is unnatural think they can support this claim by pointing to the supposed fact that no animals exhibit homosexual behavior.[29] The empirical facts are not at all clear on this matter. It is clear that various mammals and other animals engage in sexual acts with conspecifics of the same biological sex.[30] But should we call this homosexuality in the same sense that we talk of human homosexuality? More generally, there is a worry that any attempt to draw a parallel between same-sex sexual acts among animals and homosexuality in humans is mistaken. For example, many studies of animal "sexuality" count a male animal who is "mounted" (that is, anally penetrated) by another male as a homosexual, but do not count as homosexual the male who does the mounting.[31] In contrast, in the human case, scientists count both the male who penetrates and the male who is penetrated (as well as men who engage in or desire to engage in various acts that do not involve anal penetration at all) as gay.[32] These worries aside, consider:

> (2c-iii) If homosexuality has a biological basis, then homosexuality is performed by animals.

Whatever the results of studies of animals, the biological basis of homosexuality in humans does not establish that homosexuality is performed by animals any more than, say, the biological basis of language in humans establishes that animals have the capacity for language. So the biological basis of homosexuality does not show that lesbian and gay men are natural in sense (iii) of the term; (2c) is obviously false if natural is read as being performed by animals.

A friend of using the "naturalness" of homosexuality as a premise in an argument for lesbian and gay rights might still hold out hope of making something of the existence of homosexuality in animals. The existence of homosexuality in animals might be taken to show that homosexuality is natural. This conclusion might be combined with the conditional "if homosexuality is natural, then lesbians and gay men deserve rights," to make the case for lesbian and gay rights. The argument would proceed as follows:

> (1') There are animals who engage in homosexual behavior.
> (2') Therefore, homosexuality is natural.
> (3c) If homosexuality is natural, then lesbians and gay men deserve rights, recognition, and protection against discrimination.

(4)   Therefore, lesbians and gay men deserve rights, recognition, and protection against discrimination.

The first problem with this argument is that the move from the fact that there are animals who engage in homosexual behavior to the naturalness of homosexuality seems invalid. Animals eat conspecifics, kill each other in painful ways, and do many other things we do not think are natural for humans. On any reading of natural in (2′) that is supposed to suggest natural *for humans,* the argument from (1′) to (2′) is invalid–you cannot deduce "natural for humans" from "animals do it." The move from (1′) to (2′) might be valid if "natural" is read so as *not* to apply to humans. But then the move from (2′) and (3c) will not be valid, because "natural" in (3c) must apply to humans for the premise to be the least bit plausible. For the naturalness of homosexuality to buttress the case for lesbian and gay rights, homosexuality must be natural in the human sense of the term.

Even if there is homosexuality in the non-human realm, this does not establish grounds for lesbian and gay rights. And, as I pointed out above, it is not obvious whether we should count the same-sex sexual behaviors of animals as homosexual behavior. Human sexual activity involves a complex array of cognitive functions–some conscious, others not–for which most animals are probably not equipped. So, while there might be parallels between certain sexual acts (that is, physical acts involving genitals) in which humans and animals engage (for example, both engage in penis-anus and penis-vagina intercourse), we might want to count sexual acts as homosexual or heterosexual only insofar as they fit into a certain cognitive network. Developing this line of thought concerning non-human sex and sexuality is beyond the scope of this article. For my purposes at the moment, I shall just suppose this account is right, that is, that there are interesting senses of "homosexual," "heterosexual," and "bisexual" applicable *only* to humans. Given this supposition, the question is whether this would affect lesbian and gay rights.

Opponents of lesbian and gay rights have tried to use the *absence* of homosexuality in animals as grounds for claiming that homosexuals are unnatural and hence not deserving of rights. The argument they have in mind goes as follows:

(5) There is no homosexuality in animals.
(6) Therefore, homosexuality is unnatural.
(7) If homosexuality is unnatural, then lesbians and gay men do not deserve rights, recognition, and protection against discrimination.
(8) Therefore, lesbians and gay men do not deserve rights, recognition and protection against discrimination.

Typically, this argument has foundered on the empirical evidence against (5). I have suggested a line of reasoning that could be used to defend (5): even though there is same-sex activity among animals, there is no *homosexuality* among animals because homosexuality (in the sense I am allowing it to be used here) involves a complex array of cognitive functions that non-human animals lack. This line of argument still will not be useful to foes of lesbian and gay rights because the same argument can be used to show that *hetero*sexuality is unnatural and, hence, that heterosexuals do not deserve rights. The same reasons for thinking that there are no homosexual animals provide grounds for thinking there are no heterosexual (in the sense of the term I am using it here) animals either. If the lack of homosexual animals shows homosexuality is unnatural, then the lack of heterosexual animals shows heterosexuality is unnatural as well. Further, if the unnaturalness of homosexuality counts against lesbian and gay rights, then the unnaturalness of heterosexuality counts against "straight rights" as well. Clearly, this is a *reductio ad absurdum* of the argument from (5), (6), and (7) to (8).

My main conclusion in this subsection is that the argument from the biological basis of homosexuality to lesbian and gay rights fails when it involves a premise about the naturalness of homosexuality that is read as being about the sexual behavior of animals. I have further argued that the presence or absence of homosexuality in non-humans is not relevant to lesbian and gay rights.

iv. not artificial. Finally, consider:
(2c-iv). If homosexuality has a biological basis, then homo-

sexuality exists in nature, is not artificial, is not constructed by humans.

On this sense of "natural," a biological basis for homosexuality does show that homosexuality is natural: if homosexuality has a biological basis, then human homosexuality exists in nature and is not constructed by humans. So (2c-iv) is true. But will it, together with the other premises of the argument for lesbian and gay rights under consideration, suffice for such an argument? Consider this argument with reading (iv) of "natural" inserted in the relevant places:

(1)   Homosexuality has a biological basis.
(2c-iv) If homosexuality has a biological basis, then homosexuality is not caused or made by humans, is not artificial, and exists in nature.
(3c-iv) If homosexuality is not caused or made by humans, is not artificial, and does exist in nature, then lesbians and gay men deserve rights, recognition, and protection against discrimination.
(4)   Therefore, lesbians and gay men deserve rights, recognition, and protection against discrimination.

I am assuming (1) is true, and I have noted that (2c-iv) is true. Further, the argument for (1), (2c-iv), and (3c-iv) is valid. All that remains to evaluate is (3c-iv). For reasons similar to those that undermined (3a) and (3b), (3c-iv) is doubtful. First, there are lots of human kinds that are not artificial (that is, that exist "in nature") but that do not provide grounds for giving rights to people who fall into those kinds (for example, being an alcoholic or having Down's syndrome). The mere non-artificiality of a human kind does not ground claims for rights. Second, the aspects of homosexuality that are biologically based and thus are not caused by humans (and that exist in nature and are not artificial) include only the having of homoerotic desires, but do not include embracing a lesbian or gay identity or entering into a lesbian or gay relationship. Queer identities and relationships are (like *straight* identities and relationships) made by humans, do not exist in nature, and thus are not part of the lesbian and gay rights that come out of the argument involving

(3c-iv). For (3c-iv) to be true, we need to adopt a *narrow* reading of lesbian and gay rights, so narrow as to be unrecognizable as lesbian and gay rights. If we adopt a more robust sense of lesbian and gay rights, (3c-iv) is implausible: the non-artificiality that homosexuality inherits in virtue of its biological basis does not provide grounds for lesbian and gay rights.

On either of the first three readings, (2c)–the conditional claim that if homosexuality has a biological basis, then homosexuality is natural–is, at best, unsupported. On the fourth reading, (2c) is true, but applying this reading of "natural" to (3c) undermines its plausibility. In fact, on all four readings of "natural," (3c) is undermined for the same sort of reasons that (3c-iv) is.

The failure of arguments from the naturalness of homosexuality to establish lesbian and gay rights does not show that homosexuality is unnatural; it only shows that finding homosexuality has a biological basis does not establish its naturalness (in senses (i) through (iv)). In fact, on any plausible reading of "natural," homosexuality *is* natural (although not because of its biological basis, if such a basis exists).[33] If I am right that homosexuality is natural, then this fact might be combined with (3c)–if it were true, which it is not–to get (4), the conclusion that lesbians and gay men deserve rights. But this argument for lesbian and gay rights does not require a biological basis for homosexuality.

Summary of Biological Arguments for Lesbian and Gay Rights

Many friends of lesbian and gay rights have claimed that scientific evidence for a genetic, hormonal, or biological basis for sexual orientation would be good news for lesbian and gay rights. The general idea behind this argument is to connect the existence of a biological basis for sexual orientation to lesbian and gay rights through something like the following schematic argument:

(1) Homosexuality has a biological basis.
(2) If homosexuality is biological, then _____.
(3) If _____, then lesbians and gay men deserve rights, recognition, and protection against discrimination.
(4) Therefore, lesbians and gay men deserve rights, recognition, and protection against discrimination.

I have considered above several possible ways of filling in the blanks of this argument and found all of them inadequate with respect to producing valid arguments. The general problem is to find some claim that will bridge the gap between the empirical claim (homosexuality has a biological basis) and the normative one (lesbians and gay men deserve rights). If the blank is filled in with an empirical claim, then (2) might be plausible but (3) will not be (this was the case when the blank was filled in with "homosexuality is natural in the sense of not being man-made"). If the blank is filled in with a normative claim, then (3) might be plausible but (2) would not be. A related problem is that even if the premises are true, the attributes lesbians and gay men have and the behaviors (if any) in which they necessarily engage in virtue of the (supposed) biological basis of their sexual orientation are all that will be protected under this argument. At best, this will include homoerotic desires and dispositions to engage in same-sex sexual acts, a rather narrow range with respect to what we typically mean when we talk of lesbian and gay rights.

Pragmatic Argument

Some friends of lesbian and gay rights might argue that biological arguments should be embraced even in light of my discussion above since such arguments for lesbian and gay rights seem to persuade people.[34] The idea is a pragmatic one: embrace the theories that help to establish lesbian and gay rights.[35]

I do not think this general line of argument is promising. Linking lesbian and gay rights to biology seems a bad strategy even on pragmatic or political grounds. First, a biological basis for homosexuality, even if it could persuade people to favor lesbian and gay rights in the short run, might at the same time spark a call for genetic engineering to prevent homosexuality and the development of amniocentesis techniques for the detection of homosexuality so as to enable the abortion of fetuses with the strongest potential to develop into homosexuals.[36]

Second, it just seems bad strategy to link lesbian and gay rights to the ups and downs of scientific research. Such research is, at best, still in its early stages and whatever suggestions that there is a biological explanation for sexual orientation might well turn out to be mistaken. Connecting lesbian and gay rights to science is too risky. People can be persuaded of various things by all sorts of bad arguments. That people are persuaded by biological arguments for lesbian and gay rights may suggest a public relations strategy that will be successful in the short-term, but it does not suggest a strategy suited for grounding a set of rights that are deeply important and that profoundly impact the lives of many men and women. Biological sophistry is still sophistry.

Third, the pragmatic argument for lesbian and gay right is committed to a picture of science that is potentially self-undermining. Friends of the pragmatic argument for lesbian and gay rights defend a particular scientific theory (the theory that homosexuality has a biological basis) because of its political effects. But if it becomes known that this is the justification for favoring one scientific theory over another, the persuasiveness of scientific theories in general–the very persuasiveness on which the pragmatic argument is based–will be undermined. In other words, although such arguments depend on the distinction between science and mere propaganda, these very arguments, if widespread, would erase this distinction.

As an example of the risks of connecting particular empirical theories with lesbian and gay politics, consider the relationship of the lesbian and gay movement in America to American psychiatry.[37] In the "pre-Stonewall" stage of the gay rights movement (from World War II to the late sixties), many gay rights activists embraced psychiatry and its language, partly on political grounds. The idea was that psychiatry could help legitimate lesbians and gay men and their organizations.[38] But as the gay movement grew, it came to reject psychiatry, ultimately protesting the American Psychiatric Association's classification of homosexuality as a psychological disorder. The point of the example is that science is a tricky political weapon; at best, it is a double-edged sword.

For the three reasons I have given above, I do not think that the pragmatic version of the biological argument for lesbian and gay rights fares any better than its non-pragmatic counterparts. Scientific research concerning sexual orientation is irrelevant to lesbian and gay rights. Attempts to link the science of sexual orientation to the case for lesbian and gay rights are misguided.

THE BASIS OF LESBIAN AND GAY RIGHTS

I have argued so far that scientific explanations of sexual orientations and desires will not be relevant to lesbian and gay rights. If this conclusion is right, one might wonder what sort of evidence and what kinds of arguments, are relevant to this issue. My answer, once it is stated, seems obvious: the arguments and evidence that should be given are *moral* and *political* in nature.[39] Consider, for example, the sorts of arguments that get made for equal rights for racial or religious minorities. Rather than appealing to any facts about the constitution of these types of people, these arguments involve theories of justice, rights, privacy, equality, and liberty. The arguments are moral and/or political in nature. The same is true for arguments for lesbian and gay rights, protection for lesbian and gay men against discrimination, respect for queer relationships, and so on; these issues are moral in nature and arguments for them should be cast in terms of justice, rights, privacy, equality, and liberty.[40]

This is not to say that empirical considerations are *never* relevant to moral issues. For example, if you have the view that it is wrong to cause wanton pain and suffering to any animal that can feel pain and be conscious of it, then the empirical discovery that pigs feel pain and are conscious of it would be relevant to the issue of whether the factory farming of pigs is morally acceptable. Sometimes empirical evidence is relevant to moral issues. In the particular case of lesbian and gay rights, evidence for any scientific explanation of why people have the sexual orientations and desires they do is not relevant. Despite this, empirical evidence may be of interest to some of the political goals many lesbians, gay men, and their political allies share. For example, showing that a person's sexual orientation is determined at birth might help to convince people that it is perfectly acceptable for lesbians and gay men to teach elementary school. Or showing determinism about sexual orientation is true might convince people of the futility of attempting to change queer people's sexual orientations. I do not mean to trivialize these possibilities and the extent to which they might be able to help forward parts of a gay-positive political agenda. My arguments above have, however, given us good reason to think empirical arguments for lesbian and gay rights in general are not forthcoming. Further, I am concerned about linking even more specific political aims to scientific research. Lesbians and gay men should be able to teach elementary school *even if* a person's sexual orientation is not fixed until puberty.

THE FUTURE OF SEXUAL ORIENTATION RESEARCH

Having argued that scientific evidence about sexual orientation does not bear on lesbian and gay rights, one might wonder whether this general research program ought to be pursued. As I have already mentioned, the history of the scientific study of sexual orientations and desires is checkered at best.[41] Even when such studies are undertaken with the explicit purpose of helping lesbians and gay men–either by hoping to buttress the case for lesbian and gay rights or to help lesbian and gay men understand, accept, or "cure" their homosexuality–they often begin with (implicitly) homophobic[42] assumptions and subsequently have the effect of hurting lesbians and gay men–either physically (through experimental techniques to cure them) or socially (for example, by perpetuating negative stereotypes about them). Given this history, it is no wonder that many lesbians and gay men are, at a minimum, skeptical about scientific research concerning sexual orientation. But does this history tell us anything about how we should view current and future scientific research about sexual orientation? Does it, as some have argued, suggest that such research should be abandoned altogether?

Consider several comments on scientific research on homosexuality that have been made by contemporary thinkers. The first is from Eve Kosofsky Sedgwick, a literary theorist. Sedgwick is skeptical of such scientific research because

> the presentation, often in ostensibly or authentically gay-affirming contexts, of biologically-based "explanations" for deviant behavior . . . [is] absolutely invariably couched in terms of "excess," "deficiency," or "imbalance"–whether in hormones, in the genetic material, or . . . in the fetal endocrine environment. If I had ever, in any medium, seen any researcher or popularizer refer even once to any supposed gay-

producing circumstance as the *proper* hormone balance, or the conducive endocrine environment, for gay generation, I would be less chilled by the breezes of all this technological confidence.[43]

The second quotation is from Fred Suppe, a philosopher of science:

> [T]he available scientific evidence provides no basis for treating the etiology of homosexuality as a legitimate *scientific* research problem. . . . [When] it was accepted that there was natural variation in which hand was one's dominant hand, the etiology of left-handedness ceased to be a serious *scientific* research problem. . . . [In light of these considerations] who cares what causes homosexuality? . . . [I]nsofar as we act *qua* scientist, not I, nor, I would hope, anyone of serious scientific aspirations.[44]

The third is from Gunter Schmidt, a sexologist:

> As long as society has not made peace with the homosexuals, research into the possible causes [of homosexuality is] . . . potentially a public danger to . . . [lesbians and gay men]. Seen in this light, it is good that we know so little about what causes heterosexuality and homosexuality.[45]

And, the fourth is from David Halperin, a classicist and cultural theorist:

> [The] search for a 'scientific' etiology of sexual orientation is itself a homophobic project, and needs to be more clearly seen as such.[46]

With these remarks as background, I turn to assessing the ethical merits of the (actual and possible) project of developing a science of sexual orientations and desires. I also briefly discuss research in other disciplines (for example, history and sociology).

To begin, almost all of the research in the past and much being done at present is, by its own characterization, concerned with the etiology of homosexuality. There are two serious problems with this way of framing the research. The first has to do with the word "etiology." "Etiology" has a general and a specific meaning: the general meaning is "cause or origin" while the specific meaning is the "cause(s) of a disease or abnormal condition." Even when "etiology" is used in the *general* sense (especially when the subject is same-sex desire), it brings with it the connotation of the *specific* sense. This is a problem because, simply put, homosexuality is not a disease, and scientific research should not begin with the assumption that it is. (This might be Halperin's point if we read his quotation as emphasizing "etiology," rather than scientific research on sexual orientation, including research not cast in terms of etiology.[47] It also might be part of Suppe's point.) The second problem with the science of sexual orientation characterized as studying the etiology of homosexuality is that this research is focused on explaining homosexuality but not heterosexuality. As I argued above in the opening section, homosexuality and heterosexuality are equally in need of explanation, and further, the origins of all sexual desires, not just sexual orientations, are not well understood. Properly described, then, this sort of scientific research, if it should be done at all, should be done on the causes of people having the various sexual desires that they do.

But simply changing the words (Sedgwick's focus) is not enough. The *assumptions* that go along with the typical way of describing such research are problematic as well. The assumption that homosexuality is abnormal and that heterosexuality does not need to be explained is what undergirds the ways of talking about homosexuality that Sedgwick discusses in her remarks quoted above. Talk, for example, of a *deficiency* in the number of INAH-3 cells in the hypothalami of gay men suggests that being gay is abnormal and demands an explanation in a way that being straight does not. These sorts of assumptions, not just the language that often goes along with them, need to be rooted out. Sedgwick's point needs to be heeded by scientists, not just with respect to their language but with respect to their assumptions, especially their implicit ones.

In the last two paragraphs, I have drawn *normative* conclusions: roughly, scientists should not (implicitly or explicitly) assume that homosexuality is abnormal or that they can explain homosexuality but not heterosexuality. Are these supposed to be moral norms or scientific norms? The "shoulds" in the above paragraphs are meant to have *both* moral and scientific force. They have scientific force because they tell scientists to avoid various undefended assumptions, some of which are hidden in their language. They have moral force because these assumptions and the language in which they are embedded have the effect of reinforcing and legitimating homophobia and the oppression of lesbians and gay men. To the extent that critics of the science of sexual orientation can be interpreted as I have suggested in the previous two paragraphs, they are making both scientific and moral criticisms.

Schmidt and perhaps also Halperin and Suppe seem to have a deeper worry than Sedgwick. The suggestion they make is that in a homophobic society like ours, scientific research about sexual orientation is *irreparably bad* for lesbians and gay men, even if assumptions like those I have discussed above are removed. The point here is similar to one made several years ago by Noam Chomsky with respect to research on possible correlations between race and intelligence. Richard Herrnstein argued for the existence of a genetic component to intelligence that is responsible for the differential performance by blacks and whites on IQ tests.[48] In response, Chomsky argued that the results of such an investigation (whatever they turn out to be), as well as *the very undertaking* of such an inquiry, would reinforce racism and other despicable attitudes.[49] That such experiments are being performed will, he claims, perpetuate the assumption that black people are less intelligent than white people and, further, the results of the studies will be used by racists to justify their favored public policies (such as the elimination of "head start" programs). He offers the analogy of "a psychologist in Hitler's Germany who thought he could show that Jews had a genetically determined tendency towards usury (like squirrels bred to collect too many nuts)."[50] Chomsky notes that:

there is the likelihood that even opening this question and regarding it as a subject for scientific inquiry would provide ammunition for Goebbels and Rosenberg and their henchmen. Were this hypothetical psychologist to disregard the likely social consequences of his research (or even his undertaking of research under existing social conditions), he would fully deserve the contempt of decent people.[51]

Chomsky thinks that the same attitude is appropriate with respect to research on race and intelligence. I read Schmidt and other critics of scientific research concerning sexual orientation as making a similar claim with respect to such research.

What Chomsky has to say about research on race and intelligence in particular and about how scientists should weigh the social implications of their work in general seems right. The relevant question is how much of what he says applies to the science of sexual orientation and desire. First, when there is obvious and imminent potential for morally problematic use of the results of scientific research (such as hormone treatments to "cure" homosexuality), scientists doing research on sexual orientation are morally required to attempt to prevent such use. This entails that *if* such research has obvious negative social effects greater than the positive effects of the increase in scientific knowledge that might come from such research, then such research ought not to be done. This is the crucial question for assessing the ethical status of a science of sexual orientation and desire: what are the effects (positive and negative) of such scientific research?[52] Precisely determining these effects is a complex matter, and I am not at all sure how one would go about it. Several points can, however, be made about this question.

First, note that the same sorts of ethical worries that can be raised with respect to scientific research about sexual orientation can also be raised with respect to historical, sociological,[53] anthropological, and literary research (for example). Just as scientific research can be based on homophobic assumptions and can be used against lesbians and gay men, so can *social* scientific research (broadly construed). Scientific research can perpetuate unsubstantiated nativist, nurturist, essentialist, and/or constructionist sentiments that lead to morally problematic social policies but so can social scientific research. Some historical, sociological, and anthropological research has found broad continuities in the way sexual orientation has been and is organized,[54] but other work in such fields emphasizes *dis*continuities.[55] Insofar as there are general worries about doing scientific research about sexual orientation, there are parallel worries about doing social scientific research. To the extent that scientists need to worry about the effects of their research, so do social scientists. And, as is the case with scientists, *well-intentioned* research does not entail *good* research (in either the ethical or the scientific sense). Social scientists and humanists who criticize the ethical problems with scientific research about sexual orientations should turn the same critical eye towards their own disciplines and their inquiries concerning sexual orientations and sexual desires more generally.

The second point to note about the ethics of research on sexual orientation is that even if the social effects of doing this research are bad at this time and place, such research is not bad in *all* times and places; just about any research has bad implications for *some* society. To use Suppe's example, research on the cause of right- versus left-handedness did, at one time, have bad social effects since left-handed people were thought to be diseased and/or cursed. At present, such research is ethically fairly neutral and may be (*contra* Suppe) of some scientific interest (perhaps because it can be used in exploring differences between the two hemispheres of the brain). The point is that in some future society, where prejudice, discrimination, and legal asymmetries on the basis of sexual orientation have disappeared, research on the origins of sexual orientation and desire would not have the negative social effects it has had in the past. So, if, in the (perhaps all too distant) future, such a non-prejudicial society were to emerge, scientific research on sexual orientations and desires would be morally acceptable.

Critics of scientific research concerning sexual orientations might respond, however, that the only motivation for such research in the first place is fear, hatred, and ignorance of lesbian and gay men; in an enlightened society such as the one I described, why people have the sexual orientations that they do will be uninteresting and irrelevant (as Suppe seems to suggest), or the differences in people's sexual orientations that currently exist will disappear and be replaced with a polymorphous sexuality. In such a society, the social interest and importance of differences in people's sexual orientations and desires will change compared to our present society. I do not, however, think that its interest and importance will disappear completely. Why people have the sexual desires they do involves the intersection of two deeply interesting and important questions about humans: (1) how do people develop widely divergent preferences, tastes, and desires, and (2) how should sex be understood as part of the human condition? Both of these questions span many disciplines–from biology to history, from cognitive science to sociology–and cut to the heart of our understanding of ourselves. It is unlikely that changes in attitudes toward lesbians and gay men will entail either the resolution of these questions or the dissolution of our interest in them.

A third point relevant to the ethical assessment of research on sexual orientation and desire is that, all else being equal, it is better to believe things that are *true* than things that are false. Truth has a certain stability to it; arguments based on truths fare better than those based on falsehoods. When attempting to evaluate the social consequences of scientific and social scientific research, one needs to consider the value in knowing the truth. Since there are an infinite number of truths about the world, it is a bad idea to try to gather all possible truths; still, this does not undermine the value, all else being equal, of knowing the truth about such an interesting and important question as why people have the sexual desires they do.

CONCLUSIONS

How do people develop sexual orientations and desires? This is an interesting question, but not for the reasons many people think. In particular, if my arguments in this paper are correct, the answer to this question is *not* relevant to the moral and political issue of lesbian and gay rights. Rather, the question is important as a part of our understanding of ourselves. Sex and sexual desire are basic and central to human nature; unlocking their mysteries through science and social science is a worthwhile project on its own merits. This research project, however, should not be pursued in a vacuum; its social implications should be considered. But the results of such research will not entail that lesbian and gay men deserve rights, privileges, or recognition. Such conclusions need to be established through moral and political arguments, not scientific ones.

AUTHOR NOTE

This essay is *for* David Eppel and Chris Seger. Thanks to Michael Bronski, David Halperin, Tracy Isaacs, Frances Kamm, Morris Kaplan, Gary Marcus, Bonnie McElhinny, Richard Mohr, Timothy Murphy, Eugene Rice, Bill Ruddick, and William Snyder.

NOTES

1. As quoted by John D'Emilio, *Sexual Politics, Sexual Communities: The Making of a Homosexual Minority in the United States, 1940-1970* (Chicago: University of Chicago Press, 1983), p. 153.

2. Ian Hacking has discussed this idea of natural human kinds in various places. See, for example, Ian Hacking, "Making Up People," in Thomas Heller, Morton Sosna, and David Wellbery, eds., *Reconstructing Individualism: Autonomy, Individuality, and the Self in Western Thought* (Stanford: Stanford University Press, 1986), pp. 222-236 (reprinted in Edward Stein, ed. *Forms of Desire: Sexual Orientation and the Social Constructionist Controversy* [New York: Routledge, 1992], pp. 69-88); "The Invention of Split Personalities," in Alan Donagan, Anthony Perovich, Jr., and Michael Wedin, eds., *Human Nature and Natural Knowledge* (Dordrecht: D. Reidel, 1986), pp. 63-85; and "A Tradition of Natural Kinds," *Philosophical Studies* 61 (1991): 109-126.

3. For some classic essays in the essentialist and social constructionist debate, as well as some more contemporary essays on the topic, see Stein, *Forms of Desire*. For my views, see my conclusion in that volume, "The Essentials of Constructionism and the Construction of Essentialism" (pp. 325-354); and my "Reframing Essentialism and Social Constructionism about Sexual Orientation" (work in progress).

4. Stein, "Essentials of Constructionism."

5. See, for example, Michel Foucault, *The History of Sexuality, Volume I: An Introduction*, Robert Hurley, trans. (New York: Pantheon, 1978); David Greenberg, *The Construction of Homosexuality* (Chicago: University of Chicago Press, 1988); and David Halperin, *One Hundred Years of Homosexuality and Other Essays on Greek Love* (New York: Routledge, 1990).

6. Many have thought that there is a connection between lesbian and gay rights and the essentialism-social constructionism debate but mostly *not* for the reasons I sketch here. For a discussion of some of these views, see Steven Epstein, "Gay Politics, Ethnic Identity: The Limits of Social Constructionism," *Socialist Review* 93/94 (1972): 9-54 (reprinted in *Forms of Desire*, pp. 239-294), and Diana Fuss, *Essentially Speaking: Feminism, Nature and Difference* (New York: Routledge, 1989), especially chap. 6, pp. 97-112. I discuss some of these ideas below in the section, "Basis of Lesbian and Gay Rights."

7. Among the silliest studies to find biological differences between homosexuals and heterosexuals are R. B. Evans, "Physical and Biochemical Character-

istics of Homosexual Men," *Journal of Consulting and Clinical Psychology* 39 (1972): 140-147; G. W. Henry and H. M. Galbraith, "Constitutional Factors in Homosexuality," *American Journal of Psychiatry* 90 (1934): 1249-1270; F. E. Kenyon, "Physique and Physical Health of Female Homosexuals," *Journal of Neurology, Neurosurgery and Psychiatry* 31 (1968): 487-489; and Muriel Perkins, "Female Homosexuality and Body Build," *Archives of Sexual Behavior* 19 (1981): 337-345. The correlations between these factors and sexual orientation that these studies found (to the limited extent that they found them) failed to be replicated though they are still cited. For a wealth of interesting historical documents surrounding such studies and an introduction to them, see Jonathan Katz, *Gay American History* (New York: Thomas Crowell, 1976), part II, "Treatment: 1884-1974," pp. 197-316, and part III, "Passing Women: 1782-1920," pp. 317-422, as well as the bibliographic data on pp. 901-905 and 917-922. For a discussion of shock treatment, see William Faustman, "Aversive Control of Maladaptive Sexual Behavior: Past Developments and Future Trends," *Psychology* 13 (1976): 53-60. For general surveys and discussion, see Peter Conrad and Joseph Schneider, *Deviants and Medicalization: From Badness to Sickness* (St. Louis: C. V. Mosley, 1980), especially chap. 7, pp. 172-214; G. J. Benfield, *The Horrors of the Half-Known Life: Male Attitudes Toward Women and Sexuality in Nineteenth-Century America* (New York: Harper and Row, 1976); Frederick Suppe, "Explaining Homosexuality: Philosophical Issues, and Who Cares Anyhow?" in this volume; and Timothy F. Murphy, "Redirecting Sexual Orientation: Techniques and Justifications," *Journal of Sex Research* 29 (1992): 501-523.

8. One noteworthy exception to this is Freud. In *Three Essays on the Theory of Sexuality*, James Strachey, trans. (New York: Basic Books, 1962), he says, "[F]rom the point of view of psycho-analysis the exclusive sexual interest felt by men for women is also [that is, in addition to homosexual sexual interest] a problem that needs elucidating and is not a self-evident fact . . . " (p. 12). This passage is from footnote 1, p. 10, which was added by Freud in 1915.

9. Richard Pillard disagrees. He says that "aside from a very general identity as 'homosexual' [which is almost definitely genetic], how gender atypical you are, whether you like to suck or fuck, whether you're top or bottom, etc., is probably determined more environmentally." See Edward Stein, "Evidence for Queer Genes: An Interview with Richard Pillard," *GLQ* 1 (1993): 93-110, here p. 102.

10. On this point, see Leda Cosmides and John Tooby, "From Evolution to Behavior: Evolutionary Psychology as the Missing Link," in John Dupré, ed., *The Latest on the Best: Essays on Evolution and Optimality* (Cambridge, MA: MIT Press, 1987), pp. 277-306.

11. For the classic statement of the problem, see Edward O. Wilson, *Sociobiology: The New Synthesis* (Cambridge, MA: Harvard University Press, 1975), p. 555; also Edward O. Wilson, *On Human Nature* (Cambridge, MA: Harvard University Press, 1978), pp. 142-147. For a summary and a sympathetic discussion of sociobiology's attempts to deal with homosexuality, see Michael Ruse, *Homosexuality: A Philosophical Inquiry* (New York: Basil Blackwell, 1988), especially chap. 6. For a careful (and damning) critique of the general program of

sociobiology, see Philip Kitcher, *Vaulting Ambition: Sociobiology and the Quest for Human Nature* (Cambridge, MA: MIT Press, 1985). For critiques of sociobiological theories of homosexuality, see Douglas Futuyma and Stephen Risch, "Sexual Orientation, Sociobiology and Evolution," *Journal of Homosexuality* 9(2/3) (1983-84): 157-168, reprinted in John De Cecco and Michael Shively, eds., *Origins of Sexuality and Homosexuality* (New York: Harrington Park Press, 1985); and Paul Bloom and Edward Stein, "Reasoning Why," *American Scholar* 60 (1990): 315-320.

12. Simon LeVay, "A Difference in the Hypothalamic Structure Between Heterosexual and Homosexual Men," *Science* 253 (1991): 1034-1037.

13. J. Michael Bailey and Richard Pillard, "A Genetic Study of Male Sexual Orientation," *Archives of General Psychiatry* 38 (1991): 1089-1096.

14. Suppe, "Explaining Homosexuality," criticizes the general tendency of scientists studying sexual orientation to presume that members of control groups are all heterosexual. In this case, the assumption is particularly problematic. LeVay thinks he can use Kinsey's data (A. C. Kinsey, W. B. Pomeroy, and C. E. Martin, *Sexual Behavior in the Human Male* [Philadelphia: W. B. Saunders, 1948]) about the "numerical preponderance of heterosexual men in the population" ("A Difference in the Hypothalamic Structure," p. 1036 n. 7) to justify assuming that *all* of the men who died of AIDS and who did not identify themselves as gay were heterosexual. But given the fact that only *thirty* percent of the men who have AIDS are straight (Centers for Disease Control, *HIV/AIDS Surveillance Report*, Oct. 1992, p. 8), this assumption seems unjustified. LeVay would have made a better case for presuming the heterosexuality of the six men involved if he had referred to the fact that these men had become infected through IV-drug use and then cited the statistic that about *seventy-five* percent of the men with AIDS who become infected with HIV through IV drug use are straight (ibid.). Jason Bromberg helped me find and make sense of these statistics.

15. LeVay looked to the hypothalamus because other studies seem to suggest that this part of the brain has something to do with "sex drive." While it is well-confirmed that the hypothalamus is involved in the unconscious aspects of human sex drive, some of the studies that connect the hypothalamus to sexual orientation present divergent conclusions and have typically not been confirmed by subsequent studies. See, for example, Christine de Lacoste-Utamsing and Ralph Holloway, "Sexual Dimorphism in the Human Corpus Callosum," *Science* 216 (1982): 1431-1432; Brian Gladue, Richard Green, and Ronald Hellman, "Neuroendocrine Response to Estrogen and Sexual Orientation," *Science* 225 (1984): 1496-1499; and D. F. Swaab and E. Fliers, "A Sexual Dimorphic Nucleus in the Human Brain," *Science* 228 (1985): 1112-1114.

16. Suppe, "Explaining Homosexuality," discusses the general tendency to confuse causality and correlation in the study of sexual orientation.

17. See Timothy F. Murphy, "Homosex and the Limits of Research," unpublished manuscript, pp. 4-10, for a more extended critique (somewhat along the lines I sketch here) of LeVay's study. See my commentary in "Evidence for Queer Genes" (pp. 105-108) for a brief critique of Bailey and Pillard's study.

18. For example, Andrew J. Humm, a commissioner on the Human Rights Commission of New York City and a gay rights activist said: "The fact that [LeVay's] report talks about homosexual orientation as something innate is good, because that's what most of us experience. Homosexuality used to be viewed as a character or moral defect, so if you want to look at it as hypothalamic in nature, that's probably a step toward looking at it for what it is" (Natalie Angier, "The Biology of What It Means to Be Gay," *New York Times*, Sept. 1, 1991, sect. 4, p. E1). For representative articles that say most lesbian and gay activists think the discovery of a genetic, biological, and/or hormonal cause of homosexuality would be good for the lesbian and gay movement, see Sharon Begley, "What Causes People to Be Homosexual?" *Newsweek*, Sept. 9, 1991, p. 52; Christine Gorman, "Are Gay Men Born That Way?" *Time*, Sept. 9, 1991, pp. 60-61; Dolores King, "Researcher Finds Clue in Brains of Gay Men," *Boston Globe*, Aug. 30, 1991, "Metro" section, p. 3; and Natalie Anger, "Zone of Brain Linked to Men's Sexual Orientation," *New York Times*, Aug. 30, 1991, pp. A1 and D18.

19. For Pillard's views, see Michael Bailey and Richard Pillard, "Are Some People Born Gay?" *New York Times*, Dec. 17, 1992, p. 21; "Evidence for Queer Genes"; and David Gelman, "Born or Bred," *Newsweek*, Feb. 24, 1992, pp. 46-53. For LeVay's views, see, for example, "Born or Bred," p. 49; and Denise Grady, "The Brains of Gay Men," *Discover*, Jan. 1992, p. 29.

20. Here "biological" is meant to include hormonal, genetic, neurophysiological, and all such disciplinary accounts in the life sciences.

21. I do not here mean to be engaging in constitutional analysis of the equal protection clause of the fourteenth amendment or legal analysis of federal civil rights legislation. At issue here is the more abstract ethical and political question of whether a biological basis for homosexuality entails that lesbians and gay men deserve special rights and protection against discrimination. For discussion of the legal issues, see Richard Mohr, *Gays/Justice: A Study in Society, Ethics, and Law* (New York: Columbia University Press, 1990), especially chaps. 5-7; Editors, *Harvard Law Review: Sexual Orientation and the Law* (Cambridge, MA: Harvard University Press, 1990); Morris Kaplan, "Autonomy, Equality, Community: The Question of Lesbian and Gay Rights," *Praxis International* 11 (1991): 195-213; and Cass Sunstein, "Sexual Orientation and the Constitution: A Note on the Relation Between Due Process and Equal Protection," *University of Chicago Law Review* 55 (1988): 1161-1179.

22. The distinction here is between a person's *status* and her *behavior*; this distinction has been emphasized by President Clinton in early discussion of lesbians and gay men in the military.

23. Some critics of essentialism and of scientific research concerning sexual orientation have mistakenly equated these views with determinism. See Stein, "The Essentials of Constructionism," for a discussion.

24. A comment about the examples I have chosen to illustrate some of my points: some of the analogies I offer for having a particular sexual orientation—for example, being an alcoholic, having tuberculosis, being a yuppie(?)–may seem to suggest that I think having a particular sexual orientation, in particular, being a

lesbian or gay man, is a bad thing. Nothing could be further from my intentions. The examples are not used to convey a negative attitude towards a particular sexual orientation but rather to make an illustrative analogy and to give the benefit of the doubt to the arguments I want to criticize. In this case, the analogy is to show that determinism with respect to a given trait is not enough to guarantee protection against discrimination based on the having of that trait.

25. For good critiques of the idea that homosexuality is "unnatural," see *Gays/ Justice*, pp. 34-38; and *Homosexuality*, pp. 188-192. Both Mohr and Ruse conclude that biology will not tell us what is "natural" in any *morally* interesting sense. Mohr says, "The search in nature for people's purpose, far from finding models for action, is likely to leave people morally rudderless" (p. 38). Ruse says, "[O]ne cannot tease out the moral status of human homosexual behavior on the grounds of biological naturalness" (p. 192). I more or less concur with what both Mohr and Ruse have to say on this topic.

26. See the references in note 11 above.

27. Something like this premise is defended by Michael Levin, "Why Homosexuality Is Abnormal," *Monist* 67 (1984), pp. 251-283. For a response to Levin, see Timothy F. Murphy, "Homosexuality and Nature: Happiness and the Law at Stake," *Journal of Applied Philosophy* 4 (1987), pp. 195-204. I will not even begin to criticize Levin's article which is so horrible that the most interesting philosophical question it gives rise to is: "Why was this article ever published by a respectable philosophy journal?"

28. See Elliott Sober, *The Nature of Selection* (Cambridge, MA: MIT Press, 1984), especially pp. 97-102, for his discussion of the selection *of*/selection *for* distinction. Also, Stephen J. Gould and Richard Lewontin, "The Spandrels of San Marcos and the Panglossian Program: A Critique of the Adaptationist Programme," *Proceedings of the Royal Society of London* 205 (1978): 281-288.

29. This argument was made by Plato in *Laws*, Book 8.

30. See, for example, Frank Beach, "Animal Models for Human Sexuality," in Ruth Porter and Julie Whelan, eds., *Sex Hormones and Behavior* (Amsterdam: Excerpta Medica, 1979), pp. 113-143; R. H. Denniston, "Ambisexuality in Animals," in Judd Marmor, ed., *Homosexual Behavior: A Modern Reappraisal* (New York: Basic Books, 1980), pp. 25-40; G. L. Hunt and M. W. Hunt, "Female Pairing in Western Gulls (*Larus occidentalis*) in Southern California," *Science* 196 (1977): 1466-1467; Ralph Noble, "Male Hamsters Display Female Sexual Responses," *Hormones and Behavior* 12 (1979): 293-298; R. G. W. Prescott, "Mounting Behavior in the Female Cat," *Nature* 228 (1970): 1106-1107; James Weinrich, "Is Homosexuality Biologically Normal?" in William Paul, ed., *Homosexuality: Social, Psychological, and Biological Issues* (Beverly Hills: Sage, 1982), pp. 197-208.

31. The same sorts of problems exist for homosexuality in female animals. Female animals that try to mount female conspecifics are thought of as engaging in homosexual behavior but not the females who allow themselves to be mounted by other females. In the human case, scientists count both sorts of behaviors—as well

as lots of other behaviors between women that do not involve "mounting" at all–as homosexual behavior.

32. Who counts as homosexual is, however, highly variable from time to time and culture to culture. For example, some cultures consider males who were penetrated by other males to be homosexuals but *not* men who penetrated other men. George Chauncey, Jr., "Christian Brotherhood or Sexual Perversion? Homosexual Identities and the Construction of Sexual Boundaries in the World War I Era," *Journal of Social History* 19 (1985): 189-212 (reprinted in Martin Duberman, Martha Vicinus, and George Chauncey, Jr., eds., *Hidden from History: Reclaiming the Gay and Lesbian Past* [New York: New American Library, 1989], pp. 294-317), shows that the distinction between penetrated and penetrator was common in the early twentieth century in North America. Today, in some Latin American, Islamic, and Mediterranean cultures as well as in some North American subcultures (e.g., prisons), the penetrated is considered "the woman" or "half a man" while the penetrator is considered "the man" or "doubly a man."

33. Fairly recently, a philosophical cottage industry has developed around coming up with an account of the distinction between natural and unnatural (or perverted) sex. The founding essay is Thomas Nagel, "Sexual Perversion," *Journal of Philosophy* 66 (1969): 5-17, reprinted with slight revisions in *Mortal Questions* (Cambridge: Cambridge University Press, 1979), pp. 39-52. Important subsequent essays on this topic include Robert Solomon, "Sexual Paradigms," *Journal of Philosophy* 71 (1974): 336-345 (reprinted in Alan Soble, ed., *The Philosophy of Sex*, 2nd edition [Savage, MD: Rowman and Littlefield, 1991], pp. 53-62); and Alan Goldman, "Plain Sex," *Philosophy and Public Affairs* 6 (1977): 267-287 (reprinted in *Philosophy of Sex*, pp. 73-92). None of these three accounts appeal to biological evidence to ground the notion of natural sex. On all three of these accounts, homosexual sex is *not* unnatural sex (although see Sara Ruddick, "Better Sex," in Robert Baker and Frederick Elliston, eds., *Philosophy and Sex*, 2nd ed. [Buffalo, NY: Prometheus Books, 1984], pp. 280-299). This is not to say that I agree with any of these accounts of what natural sex is. Insofar as I think there is a coherent sense of "natural" here, I agree with Nagel that it will be a *psychological* notion. I hope to explore the distinction between natural and unnatural sex in a future essay.

34. A recent poll showed that people who think that homosexuality is biologically-based are more likely to favor lesbian and gay rights than those who do not.

35. Fuss, "Essentially Speaking," and Epstein, "Gay Politics, Ethnic Identity," discuss the connections between the essentialism-social constructionism controversy and lesbian and gay politics. Given the connection between essentialism and scientific research on sexual orientation, many of the arguments that they consider might be relevant here. For example, one might argue for essentialism on pragmatic grounds: if people believe in essentialism, then they will be more likely to favor lesbian and gay rights. It is arguments of this form that my discussion is meant to address.

36. For a suggestive early discussion of this question, see Lawrence Crocker, "Meddling with the Sexual Orientation of Children," in Onora O'Neill and Wil-

liam Ruddick, eds., *Having Children* (Oxford: Oxford University Press, 1979), pp. 145-154. For a more recent discussion, see Timothy F. Murphy, "Reproductive Controls and Sexual Destiny," *Bioethics* 4 (1990): 121-142.

37. See Ronald Bayer, *Homosexuality and American Psychiatry*, 2nd. ed. (Princeton: Princeton University Press, 1987).

38. See *Sexual Politics*, pp. 116-117.

39. To appreciate the distinction between moral and political that I invoke here, consider New York Governor Mario Cuomo's position on abortion: while he thinks abortion is morally wrong, he thinks that there are political reasons for letting individuals make their own moral decisions about abortion.

40. Such moral arguments can be found, for example, in Mohr, *Gays/Justice* (Parts Two, Three, and Four) and Ruse, *Homosexuality*, chaps. 8-10.

41. See note 7 above.

42. The word "homophobia" was coined by George Weinberg, *Society and the Healthy Homosexual* (New York: St. Martin's Press, 1972), to describe a psychological disorder involving fear of homosexuals and homosexuality (as manifested in people of all sexual orientations). More recently, the word has taken on broader meaning referring to fear and hatred of homosexuals regardless of its causes and manifestations. I follow that broader, more current usage of the term. By doing so, I mean to subsume the more recently coined word "homo-hatred" under the concept "homophobia."

43. Eve Kosofsky Sedgwick, *Epistemology of the Closet* (Berkeley: University of California Press, 1990), p. 43; emphasis in original. See also her "How to Bring Your Kids Up Gay," *Social Text* 29 (1991): 18-27.

44. Frederick Suppe, "Explaining Homosexuality," this volume; emphasis in the original.

45. Gunter Schmidt, "Allies and Persecutors: Science and Medicine in the Homosexuality Issue," *Journal of Homosexuality* 10(3/4) (1984): 139.

46. Halperin, *One Hundred Years of Homosexuality*, p. 49.

47. In a personal communication, Halperin discouraged this narrow reading of his thoughts on the matter.

48. The most well-publicized of his articles is Richard Herrnstein, "I. Q.," *Atlantic Monthly*, Sept., 1971, pp. 43-64. This article is excerpted from his *I.Q. in the Meritocracy* (Boston: Little, Brown and Co., 1971).

49. Noam Chomsky, "Psychology and Ideology," *Cognition* 1 (1973): 11-46. The relevant sections are reprinted as "The Fallacy of Richard Herrnstein's I. Q.," in Ned Block and Gerald Dworkin, eds., *The IQ Controversy* (New York: Random House, 1976), pp. 285-298, see especially pp. 294-297, and "Comments on Herrnstein's Response," *Cognition* 1 (1973): 407-418 (reprinted in *The IQ Controversy*, pp. 310-324; see especially, pp. 320-321). For Herrnstein's response, see Richard Herrnstein, "Whatever Happened to Vaudeville? A Reply to Professor Chomsky," *Cognition* 1 (1973): 301-310 (reprinted in *The IQ Controversy*, pp. 299-309; see especially pp. 307-309).

50. Chomsky, "The Fallacy of Richard Herrnstein's I. Q.," p. 294. All references to this title are to the reprinted version.

51. Ibid., p. 295.

52. With this much, LeVay and Pillard agree, as their attempts to justify their research through claims that it has positive effects for lesbian and gay rights demonstrate. See note 19 above and the associated discussion of their views.

53. Schmidt, "Allies and Persecutors," especially p. 138, includes sociology among those disciplines with which he is concerned.

54. See, respectively, John Boswell, *Christianity, Social Tolerance, and Homosexuality* (Chicago: University of Chicago Press, 1980); "Revolutions, Universals and Sexual Categories," *Salmagundi* 58-59 (1982-83): 89-114; and "Concepts, Experience and Sexuality," in *Forms of Desire*, pp. 133-174; Frederick Whitam and Robin Mathy, *Male Homosexuality in Four Societies: Brazil, Guatemala, the Philippines, and the United States* (New York: Praeger Scientific, 1986); and Stephen O. Murray, *Social Theory, Homosexual Reality* (New York: Gay Academic Union, 1984).

55. See, respectively, Foucault, *History of Sexuality*, especially, part two, chap. 2, "The Perverse Implantation" (reprinted in *Forms of Desire*, pp. 11-24); Mary McIntosh, "The Homosexual Role," *Social Problems* 16 (1968): 182-1931 (reprinted in *Forms of Desire*, pp. 25-42, and reprinted with postscript in Kenneth Plummer, ed., *The Making of the Modern Homosexual* [Totowa, NJ: Barnes and Noble, 1981], pp. 30-49); Halperin, *One Hundred Years of Homosexuality*; and Greenberg, *The Construction of Homosexuality*.

Fixation and Regression in the Psychoanalytic Theory of Homosexuality— A Critical Evaluation

Michael Ferguson, PhD

San Francisco, California

SUMMARY. This essay evaluates the notions of fixation and regression in the psychoanalytic theoretical conceptualization of homosexuality. Charles Socarides has had a central role in formulating the most prominent and influential psychoanalytic metapsychological understanding of homosexuality in recent years and for that reason this essay focuses principally on him. The concepts of fixation and regression are central to his understanding and I argue that the evolution of these concepts in contemporary usage renders them irrelevant to formulating the current psychoanalytic understanding of homosexuality and that their continued use by analysts reflects a negative attitude toward homosexual behavior on the part of Socarides and many other analysts that stems from an extremely narrow and idealized conception of human development.

The debate over homosexuality is not only a debate over scientific conceptualizations; it is a debate over values and a vision of

Michael Ferguson received his doctorate in philosophy from the University of Illinois at Chicago in 1982. He has authored numerous articles on topics in psychoanalytic theory and sexuality. Correspondence may be addressed to him at 721 Arguello Blvd. #101, San Francisco, CA 94118.

[Haworth co-indexing entry note]: "Fixation and Regression in the Psychoanalytic Theory of Homosexuality–A Critical Evaluation." Ferguson, Michael. Co-published simultaneously in the *Journal of Homosexuality* (The Haworth Press, Inc.) Vol. 27, No. 3/4, 1994, pp. 309-327; and: *Gay Ethics: Controversies in Outing, Civil Rights, and Sexual Science* (ed: Timothy F. Murphy) The Haworth Press, Inc., 1994, pp. 309-327. Multiple copies of this article/chapter may be purchased from The Haworth Document Delivery Center [1-800-3-HAWORTH; 9:00 a.m. - 5:00 p.m. (EST)].

society and the kind of life deemed good and desirable for people to live. These are not scientific issues; they are philosophical issues. But insofar as the results of scientific research are brought to bear upon these issues, the validity of that research is of the highest importance. Obviously attitudes toward homosexuality are shaped not only by scientific considerations, but also by moral, social, religious, cultural, and personal psychological influences. While it is quite arguable that scientific considerations deserve no more weight than non-scientific factors in shaping attitudes toward this issue, it must also be clear that an attitude toward a particular subject that is essentially moral, cultural, or personal in nature not be permitted to guise itself as having an exclusively scientific foundation, and thus pretend to a general validity beyond the personal and cultural boundaries within which it arises and to which it is necessarily confined.

It is my view that the attitude of Charles Socarides as well as that of most present-day psychoanalytic writers toward homosexual behavior embodies this difficulty,[1] and I intend here to dismantle the aura of scientific validity surrounding these attitudes and leave them exposed for the cultural and personal biases that they truly are. Irving Bieber once noted that "All *psychoanalytic* theories assume that adult homosexuality is psychopathologic and assign differing weights to constitutional and experiential determinants."[2] Socarides, moreover, has offered a justification for his continued use of the term "perversion" in referring to a wide variety of sexual behaviors, including homosexuality. He notes Freud's dislike of the term but claims that Freud continued to use it "free from its pejorative meaning and in a scientific sense."[3] He concedes that the term "sexual variation" would eliminate any tenor of moral or social disapproval, but he rejects this term because it "obscured the nature of these conditions as true disorders" (*Preoedipal*, p. 21). In my view Socarides has not abandoned a bias against homosexuality, and I intend to show here that this bias is not well-founded on *scientific grounds*, contrary to his insistence.

It would be easy and pointless to cite many examples of prejudice against homosexuality in the clinical judgements of analysts, but one can easily perceive a negative bias against homosexuality in the work of Cornelia Wilbur, Masud R. Khan, Adam Limentani,

Lionel Ovesey, Sandor Rado, Abram Kardiner, Mervin Glasser, Jacob Arlow, and many others. The bias consists in their view of homosexuality as "disordered sexual behavior," "deviant," or "pathological" and therefore inconsistent with healthy psychological well-being. Gay people should be the object of "treatment," and the disappearance of their homosexual behavior would be seen as an indication of "improvement." This is a bias. They believe it is a bias that is *scientifically* well-founded. But it is not. It is a reflection of their personal prejudices, the prejudices of the times in which they lived, and their own misunderstanding regarding the scientific foundations of their attitude.

This critique will concentrate on the normative biases inherent in two theoretical concepts that undergird many analysts', and particularly Socarides's, understanding of homosexuality: namely, fixation and regression. I hope to show that these concepts as they are applied today to understanding homosexuality contain a bias that is founded on a particular social and developmental ideal. This ideal of human development is not a conclusion forced by rational scientific inquiry. Rather, it is based on an ultra-conservative conception of acceptable human psychosexual development, and this conservatism is rooted in the cultural background and temperament of the analysts themselves, not in the results of scientific research. I have no illusions that this behemoth of disapprobation can be dispelled by rational arguments. Prejudice cannot be overcome by argument alone, but it can be stripped of its intellectual legitimization. An alternative theoretical framework can be created for understanding homosexuality that does not incorporate the currently entrenched partiality. These are the objectives toward which this presentation will strive.

THE CONCEPT OF FIXATION

In 1915, Sigmund Freud understood fixation as the result of an ideational representation of an instinctual striving being denied entry into consciousness. Fixation of the libido meant the *attachment* of an instinctual striving to an ideational representation which is not admitted into consciousness.[4] The libido as Freud came to use it was an abbreviation for the instinctual urges, which in turn were the psychological manifestation of biological processes that occur continuously within an organism.[5] This is the concept of fixation which remained with Freud for the rest of his life and which prevailed within psychoanalysis for many years after.

A significant alteration of this concept began with Rene Spitz. Spitz continued to define fixation in terms of the drives and their overgratification: "the point of fixation marks the point at which either the drive (the partial drive) or the object relations, or both, have reached the maximum gratification available to them."[6] But Spitz sets this conception down within a far-reaching innovation, which has resulted in a modification of the original understanding of the concept itself. That innovation is his theory of ego development and the means by which fixation points become incorporated into that development and influence the subsequent course of that development.

The modification that occurs is twofold. First, fixations are no longer conceptually isolated psychic phenomena. They occur in conjunction within a much broader field of psychological developments occurring over the first several years of life in which they play an interdependent, but not necessarily preeminent, role. This contextualizing of fixations has the effect of diminishing the psychological importance of fixations *in themselves*. Their importance becomes related to the way in which they influence the subsequent development of compensating and defensive structures in the psychological landscape. The second change that crept into the understanding of fixation is a linkage with the concept of adaptation to the environment into the *retrospective understanding* of fixation points and their role within the psychic apparatus. Spitz understood psychological development in terms of a temporally laid down hierarchy of psychic organization levels, with each dependent on the previous ones. Each "layer," so to speak, is deposited on top of the previous one and to a large extent takes its form and shape from the earlier foundation upon which it is dependent. He likened development to an "epigenetic landscape" consisting of an "inclined plain, with valleys, and confluences of valleys and with branchings of valleys" (*Genetic Field*, p. 53). Fixation points, to carry the analogy further, are like the mountains and hills that give shape to the landscape and determine which areas will be passable or impassable (*Genetic Field*, pp. 88, 99). Fixation points are now seen as the anchor points of compensating defensive processes, which in turn are measured in their adequacy by how well they achieve satisfactory adaptation to the environment. Inadequacy of adaptation is the measure of "psychiatric disease" by virtue of this relationship to psychic fixation points. In other words, the child whose behavior is seen as maladaptive to school or the adult whose behavior is seen as maladaptive to society becomes the object of psychiatry *by virtue of the relationship between his maladaptive behavior and his psychic fixation points* (*Genetic Field*, p. 88). This is the beginning of a linkage between the concept of fixation and the notion of adaptation. This understanding of fixation points seems to be very close to the way in which Socarides uses the concept of fixation points.[7] He draws upon Spitz's notions of maturation and adaptation to justify his conception of homosexual development as one that is the result of a failure to negotiate the maturational process properly (*Homosexuality*, p. 76).

Socarides's use of this concept refers fixation not only to the anchor points of developmental distortions but also to the developmental pattern itself. He often refers to "developmental fixations"– as distinct from "libidinal fixations"–and speaks as if it is the whole phase of development which is fixated. "The preoedipal period, especially the years between one and a half and three, is crucial to the genesis of a sexual perversion. In this period, a preoedipal fixation occurs and is primary; a regression may occur to this early fixation point under conditions of stress" (*Preoedipal Origin*, pp. 41 ff.). At certain points in the course of his patient Roger's treatment he says, "when regression became too intense the analyst asked him to sit up for most of the session. This was a true fixation at the preoedipal period and did not represent a regression from the oedipal conflict" (*Homosexuality*, p. 290; also see p. 484).

Here, fixation refers to the whole "period" of development, not to isolated libidinal experiences. Mervin Glasser also attributes "perversion" to "*fixation* at this [early developmental] *phase.*"[8] This version of the concept of fixation jettisons its correlation with the classical libido theory of Freud and can only find justification for its use in a judgment on the course of the patient's psychological development that is based on a preconception of normality rather than an analysis of libidinal attachments. Socarides does continue to use fixation in its older sense when he speaks of "libidinal fixations," but his understanding of homosexuality depends predominantly on this broader concept of developmental fixation rather than on fixation as a sticking point of the libido. Under such a usage, the libido theory, at least in its classical form, is being quietly abandoned, without articulating the current reformulations. The focus of attention is not on the development of the libido and its fixation points, but rather libidinal orientation is being seen as the outcome of a whole configuration of psychological developments that occur as a result of the relationship between the infant and its mother and are more or less independent of specific sexual experiences.[9]

This shift in the referent of fixation to developmental phases instead of experiences of sexual overgratification is further underscored by Socarides's list of the observations which to him indicate preoedipal fixation: (1) a primary identification with the mother accompanied by severe gender confusion, (2) intense anxiety upon attempting separation from the mother, (3) general behavior markedly childish (this is elaborated to mean that acting out replaces remembering, and oral and anal fantasies and practices), (4) moderate to severe disturbance in the sense of ego boundaries and body image, (5) the presence of oral incorporative, oral aggressive complexes which dominate the person's life and may be accompanied by semi-delusional oral anxieties, dreams of internal persecuting objects, fears of poisoning, or fears of being swallowed (*Homosexuality*, p. 81).

This list of phenomena could not describe a libidinal fixation in the sense of Freud and Hermann Nunberg. Clearly, they might represent psychological issues that originate in the earliest years of life in response to disturbances that might have occurred during that time, but it is not at all clear that the term "fixation" describes or explains either the origin of this constellation of psychological issues or their continuation into the present. All that can be said is that a certain pattern of development has taken place with a certain array of symptoms and behaviors derived therefrom which trace their origin back to various experiences or patterns of infant-maternal interaction in the first years of life. But where is the "fixation," and what is it that is "fixated?"

Robert Stolorow and Frank M. Lachmann, perhaps sensitive to this theoretical problem, move away from the use of the term "fixation" in reference to explaining the origins of "perversions" and instead advocate the concept of "developmental arrest" to refer to interferences with selfobject differentiation and representational integration, for which "perversions" act as a compensatory psychological adjustment.[10] They say, for example, " . . . the function of sexual perversion is, in part, to compensate for a structural impairment in selfobject-boundaries, a remnant of a developmental arrest."[11]

But "developmental arrest" does no better than "fixation" at being psychologically descriptive, and carries with it the same denigrating connotations as does "fixation." There is no evidence that development has been "arrested." Development has indeed occurred, but there is no evidence of any "arrest." The individual faced certain conditions in early life that shaped his or her psychological development. Development indeed went forward and reached certain well-established psychosexual results. Compensatory and defensive structures, including sexual preferences, arose to compensate for deficiencies in the nurturing environment. But where is the *arrest*? A large part of Stolorow and Lachmann's effort is aimed at explaining the course of development that has in fact taken place. If instead it had been arrested, it should be obvious and not require conceptualization, rather like a plant that has not grown to its full size because of a lack of nutriments. But what Stolorow and Lachmann are describing is not akin to this, it is more akin to the development of a dwarf, whose size and body features are not the product of any "arrest" but are rather the natural and appropriate outcome of his or her development, based on his or her genetic endowment. In the case of dwarfism the determining factors are genetic, in the case of psychological development, and particularly of sexual orientation, the determinants are predominantly environmental, and especially significant are the parents or important selfobjects. But from the point of view of the growing child, constitutional and environmental influences are equally unavoidable, and psychological development must accept them as a given and proceed in a way that is natural under those given conditions.

When the word "fixation" is used to hearken back to the origin of a group of symptoms it creates a dual distortion. First, it creates the impression, inherent in the term itself, that something is still trying somehow to move in some way, but is being prevented by some sort of knot or barrier, and that the solution to the problem must therefore lie in untying this knot that has somehow been tied. But this is a misleading picture because, secondly, it plays down the significance of the subsequent development of defensive and compensatory psychological resources that grew up in response to the originating situation. And it is not enough to uncover the original experiences that began the course of development and "undo" them, but elaborate psychological defensive structures built up and reinforced over many years must be systematically dismantled. In Socarides's case reports, most of the effort is expended on dismantling the defensive structures; the fixations (in the libidinal sense) are never discussed. In terms of development it is not clear from Socarides's case reports that developmental arrests have been resolved or that "progress" has been made apart from the claim that the defensive system which formerly included homosexuality as a mainstay has been dismantled and another set of defenses which include heterosexuality has been established in its place. The idea that this represents progress is essentially a value judgement and not an inference drawn from any scientific conceptual framework. Certainly the idea that "fixations"–of any form–have been resolved does not lend any credence to this claim because the fixations are never described in any specificity.

In the case of his patient, Sumner, Socarides says that a major aim of the first two years of the analysis was to "promote empathic responses and shared experiences, thereby enabling him to reach a stage where his representational world could be structured in such a way that structural conflicts belonging to the oedipal period could be defined and analyzed" (*Homosexuality*, p. 316). I will not presume that these structural conflicts are equivalent to fixation points, but it can be observed that Socarides is never specific about what fixation points there are in this case. In a lengthy discussion, Socarides analyzes Sumner's homosexual behavior in terms of its defensive functions, particularly warding off ambivalences, the narcissistic satisfactions sought and gained in homosexual encounters, for example, the desire for a "perfect experience," merging with ideal-ized masculine figures, and experiences of grandiosity.

I will not attempt to evaluate the accuracy or the clarity of any of Socarides's analysis, but I will point out that there is nothing in any of Socarides's presentation of this case that is remotely akin to anything resembling the concept of "fixation." He does describe intense psychological needs that trace their origin back to infantile developmental conditions involving Sumner and his mother. This may indeed be accurate. But the point to be made here is that the concept of fixation does not describe the situation or play a role in enhancing our understanding of Sumner's homosexual behavior. Indeed, Socarides does not make use of this concept in his clinical description, although he does draw on it for his general theory. One of the major flaws in Socarides's theoretical position on homosexu-ality is this: he continues to depend for theoretical and explanatory purposes on a concept that has no tangible clinical referent.

THE CONCEPT OF REGRESSION

The importance of the concept of fixation is reinforced by its relationship to the concept of regression in Socarides's theory of homosexuality. Libido regresses, and the places to which it re-gresses are the fixation points:

> What disturbs genital primacy? It is, of course, castration anx-iety and guilt feelings directed toward the oedipus complex. After genital enjoyment has become impossible because of castration anxiety and oedipal fears an individual regresses to that part of his infantile sexuality to which he is fixated. (*Ho-mosexuality*, p. 106)

Or again:

> The homosexual, disturbed in his genital sexuality by castra-tion fear, regresses to that component of his infantile sexuality which once in childhood gave him security or at least reassur-ance against his many fears. (*Homosexuality*, pp. 107-108)

Since these statements imply that homosexuality ism almost by its very definition, "regressive" on Socarides's theoretical viewpoint, it is necessary to examine this concept in order to illuminate its role in his theory and to lay bare how it conveys the attitude of the clinician more than it describes the psychological reality of the patient.

Freud delineated three different senses of regression in *The Interpretation of Dreams*.[12] The first he called topographical regression. This understanding of regression was based on a belief that the psychic apparatus is organized into systems or agencies that process excitations from internal or external stimulation and that this processing followed a temporal sequence as the excitation moved through the psychic apparatus. Thus one could speak of a direction to the normal movement of excitation through the mental apparatus. Regression becomes a reversal in the direction of this processing of mental excitation (*Interpretation*, pp. 537 ff.) Dreams were, for Freud, an example of this first kind of regression. Mental excitation in dreams, instead of moving progressively toward the motor end of the apparatus, moves backward toward the sensory apparatus (*Interpretation*, p. 542).

The second sense of regression he called temporal regression, and it referred to a hearkening back to older psychic structures. Although he does not use it in exactly this way in *Interpretation of Dreams*, this notion of regression played an important part in his theory of sexuality. Regression became synonymous with a return to an earlier phase of sexual development.[13] In his later work regression is used to refer to the retreat of the libidinal organization under pressure from the superego,[14] this is the second form of regression: temporal regression.

The third form of regression was what Freud called formal regression. This referred to primitive methods of expression and representation taking the place of the normal ones. Hallucinations are an example of this type of regression, which Freud understood as "thoughts transformed into images" (*Interpretation*, p. 544). This form of regression is sharply distinguished from the topographical because Freud noted with respect to hallucinations that they occurred "in spite of a sensory current flowing without interruption in a forward direction" (*Interpretation*, p. 544). Regression in this sense became synonymous with archaic modes of expression, meaning picture language (in reference to dreams), symbolic connotations, "conditions which perhaps existed before our thought language had developed."[15]

One can see a relationship between the second and third forms of regression in that both make reference to a return to things that are older, whether it is an older phase of mental development, or an older mode of representing thought. The topographical understanding of regression is the most distinct because it refers to the mechanical workings of the mental apparatus in processing excitation. I think it is fair to say that this topographical understanding of regression has not survived in contemporary usage and that when contemporary psychoanalysts use the term regression, they are using it in a sense that derives from Freud's second or third conceptions of regression, rather than the first. I will expand on this point in a moment, but I would like to make one observation that I think is significant: when Freud used regression in connection with "the perversions," he was using it primarily, if not exclusively, in the topographical sense and not in the temporal or formal sense.

In *Three Essays on the Theory of Sexuality*, he uses regression to describe the cause of perversions as the result of "other channels of the sexual current being blocked" (232n). A few pages later he speaks of perversion as a regression of sexual current to a fixation point (237n). Still again, in discussing the preponderance of perverse sexuality in the psychoneuroses he likens the libido to "a stream whose main bed has become blocked" (170). My point is that where regression is used in conjunction with the concept of fixation, the sense in which Freud is using it is the topographical sense and not the temporal or formal sense.

The concept of regression has undergone an evolution since Freud, but not as dramatic a one as the concept of fixation. Hermann Nunberg (1955) used the concept of regression in the topographical sense recalling the "flowing" metaphor of Freud and also in the temporal sense in that once the libido settles on the fixation point, the older libidinal organization revives and becomes active.[16]

The important transformation of this concept began with Ernst Kris (1952). For Kris regression means the "primitivization of ego functions,"[17] which is closest in continuity to Freud's formal sense of regression. Merton Gill and Margaret Brennan (1959) reformulated the concept of regression in terms of an elaborate theory of ego autonomy–autonomy being defined in terms of the balance of power and control between the ego and the id, on the one hand, and the environment, on the other.[18] Regression represented a disturbance in the balance of this relation. David Rapporport (1967) used regression to refer to hypnotic states where "images, ideas, fantasies, representing id contents rise to consciousness, and the sense of voluntariness disappears."[19] Otto Kernberg does not offer a definition or discussion of the concept of regression itself, but understands regression to mean extreme distortions and explosions of affect, projections, violent behavior, etc.[20] Still, this concept of regression is akin to Freud's formal sense in that it refers to the ascendancy of more primitive thought processes and modes of expression and representation. This use of the term regression, derived from Freud's formal sense, is the one that has become the most common in contemporary usage.

To characterize Socarides's use of this concept and its application to homosexuality, we must begin with the characteristics of regression enumerated in Edward Weinshel's 1966 summary of a panel discussion on severe regressive states during analysis held at the American Psychoanalytic Association meeting in New York in December of 1965.[21] Socarides himself summarizes from this panel report at length, and in it the concept of regression is characterized this way: (1) There is a pointed intactness in the ego's relations with reality, but reality testing is consciously and/or unconsciously temporarily ignored (to save the pleasure principle). (2) Moreover, object relations are impaired to the point of dedifferentiation and disruption in the boundaries of the various psychic structures. (3) More archaic ego states, functions, and defense mechanisms make their appearance. (4) The nature of the anxiety seems related to problems of preservation of self and identity rather than oedipal conflict, not unlike that seen in psychotic states.[22]

This conceptualization of "regression" is in line with Freud's formal sense, but again it bears no resemblance to the topographical sense of regression, which is the retreat of the libido to fixation points. Socarides uses regression in a number of ways, and I will enumerate some of them here. For the most part he uses it in the sense of the Weinshel report (see the cases of Campbell (pp. 265-270) and Roger (pp. 289-290, 458-463) in *Homosexuality* and the case of Willard (pp. 237-240) in *Preoedipal*), but he also speaks of homosexuality as a "regressive adaptation through identification with the mother" (*Homosexuality*, p. 110).

Socarides uses regression in the temporal sense on several occasions (*Homosexuality*, p. 183). In one place he cites Freud's *Three Essays* in describing perversion as a reaction to sexual frustrations, "with a regression to infantile sexuality secondary to arrested development" (*Homosexuality*, p. 105). Castration anxiety is also seen as instigating regressions from genital sexuality to components of infantile sexuality wherein the homosexual person felt reassured and at the same time found some satisfaction (*Homosexuality*, pp. 107-108).

Socarides describes how as the analysis of Roger progressed the homosexual behavior became less and less ego-syntonic (due no doubt to transference), but this placed the patient in danger of a "regressive pull to the preoedipal fixation point where there was a desire for and dread of merging with his mother" (*Homosexuality*, p. 460). In this instance there seems to be the implication that homosexuality actually prevents regression (in the formal sense of the Weinshel report), and the receding homosexual behavior due to the "progress" of the analysis created the danger of regression.

There are several conclusions to be drawn from this discussion. (1) Regression, when it is used to refer to homosexuality or to characterize homosexual behavior, is used in only one sense of the several described here, and that is what Freud called the topographical sense, that is, a return of the libido to a fixation point. (2) Regression in the temporal sense cannot refer to homosexuality, because homosexuality does not represent a stage of libidinal organization such as the oral or anal or phallic, but rather, homosexuality is compatible with all of the temporal stages of sexual development, and, insofar as this form of regression is related to homosexuality, it merely describes the psychological function that homosexuality serves and the form it takes under these different libidinal organizations. Homosexuality itself is not the object of the regression. (3) The most widely used concept of regression today, what corresponds most closely to Freud's formal sense of regression and the concept detailed in the Weinshel report, does not even remotely apply to homosexuality. Homosexuality is not an archaic mental process; it is not a disordered or psychotic process; in fact, it may serve an important defensive function in preventing regressions of this sort (see *Preoedipal*, esp. p. 240). In short, the term "regression," or "regressive," as applied to homosexuality can only be descriptive when it is used in the sense of a turning back of the libido to fixation points in the early senses used by Freud and Nunberg. But this conceptualization no longer reflects the psychoanalytic understanding of homosexuality, which understands it as a component of a broadly configured defensive structure formed and shaped over many developmental phases. Therefore the conclusion that I draw is that "regression" or "regressive" are terms whose use in psychoanalytic references to homosexuality has become an archaism; it no longer reflects the current theoretical understanding of homosexuality, and I will argue that its continued use in reference to homosexuality represents the deprecatory attitude of psychoanalysts toward homosexuals and homosexuality.

VALUATIVE CONNOTATIONS

The term "regression" carries disparaging connotations when it is applied to homosexuality because its primary sense has come to denote a deterioration in mental functioning and intrapsychic balance. While regression is an inevitable and ultimately beneficial part of the therapeutic process, it would not be considered a desirable end state, nor would it be seen as a satisfactory condition in which a person should live. In this sense there is a depreciatory import to the term in that regressive states in and of themselves are not desirable conditions for normal life. These negative connotations are carried over to homosexuality when regression is used to refer to homosexual behavior itself or to homosexuality as a regressed form of sexuality. Homosexuality, insofar as it is seen as "regressive," is thus imbued with a certain inferiority; there is at least condescension attached to viewing homosexuality as a regressive behavior pattern and in some it amounts to distaste as well.

The topographical sense of regression, meaning a flowing back of instinctual energy, does not carry these valuative connotations with it. This may partly explain, or reflect, the fact that Freud's attitude toward homosexuality was so benign, since this was the sense in which he used it to refer to homosexuality. But as I argued above, that sense of regression is not descriptive of the current psychoanalytic understanding of homosexuality. The continued use of this term in reference to homosexuality is an archaism and preserves a pejorative judgment on homosexuality still endorsed by many contemporary psychoanalysts. Psychoanalytic "acceptance" of homosexuality is like the acceptance of bad weather. It carries recognition of necessity, but not approval.

The valuative connotations implied by the concept of "fixation" (or "developmental arrest") derive from the shift in its referent from the instinctual energy seeking discharge to entire phases of infantile development. For this concept of fixation to retain any of the connotations natural to the use of such a term, it must imply that the whole process of psychological development is now the thing that is fixated, rather than libido that has been stuck to an overgratifying experience. This is the point where normative connotations and the idealism of the analytic enterprise begin to fasten on to the meaning of the term. For in order to perceive a pattern of development as being fixated, one must presuppose a preferred course or outcome of that developmental process. Spitz explicitly states this and even offers an entire theory of "normal," or "healthy"–or, as I would suggest, *preferred* development (*Genetic Field*, esp. pp. 199-207).

Socarides has carried this same kind of valuative bias into his understanding of homosexuality stating that in the perversions (including homosexuality), genital sexuality has been replaced by one component of infantile sexuality (*Homosexuality*, p. 167). Socarides defines "standard sexual performance" as "sexual relations occurring between adult male and female pairs in which penetration is desired and possible" (*Homosexuality*, p. 23). Any and all of the many modifications of this are classified as "disordered sexual behaviors," and this includes the "perversions," such as homosexuality. But Socarides has mistaken an evaluative conceptualization for a scientific description. This normative bias, based on an extremely narrow concept of "health" or "normality" is not peculiar to Socarides. It is quite common to psychoanalytic writers of many theoretical allegiances. I have singled out Socarides only because he is one of the more prominent psychoanalytic writers on the subject of homosexuality.

The point I wish to emphasize is that normality is not a scientific concept; it is, like adaptation, and as Spitz himself admits, a construct inferred from the study of gross distortions in the developmental process. It is not something one actually encounters in real life, it is an idealized model that has been inferred or hypothesized. It represents what the analyst regards as valuable and desirable in human life, which, in turn, reflects, perhaps, the values of the culture in which he or she lives.[23]

Still today leading analysts refer to homosexuals as "perverts" and even write entire papers devoted to discussing "the perversions." Jacob A. Arlow, for example, admits that the term "perversion" does connote an adverse judgement, but claims that its essential meaning is a "turning away from the ordinary course." Then he says, "The phenomenology of perversion should be approached from a natural science point of view, divorced from any judgmental implications."[24] But the judgmental implications were already made when it was decided what "the ordinary course of development" is, and furthermore, when it was decided that "the ordinary course of development" leads to the most desirable outcome. But psychologically speaking, the tendency toward homosexuality is a positive, growth-promoting adjustment, albeit to circumstances that did not favor heterosexual adjustment, but it is certainly not the case that homosexuals are generally worse off in their intrapsychic balance than heterosexuals. The overwhelming majority of psychotherapy patients are heterosexual, and many of these people have serious problems with their heterosexual adjustment. Yet clinicians do not see their *heterosexuality* as problematic. On the other hand a homosexual who is content with his sexual adjustment is seen by many as an unpromising candidate for treatment because he is unlikely to see his "maladaptive" sexual adjustment as something that ought to be changed.

From a scientific point of view, from a theoretical point of view, there is no basis for viewing homosexuality as necessarily "maladaptive," or "pathological," or "perverse." It is a condition that arises naturally in certain selfobject environments. These selfobject relations, while often containing many destructive features, are not, generally speaking, any less wholesome than many heterosexual environments. From an intrapsychic point of view, homosexuality serves defensive, growth-promoting, and self-esteem regulating functions. Socarides himself details this. It is the core of the psychological organization for individuals who are exclusively homosexual. The association of homosexuality with pathology is essentially a moralistic one that derives from an extremely narrow ideal of development on the one hand and religious and social intolerance on the other. The latter point has not been an object of this inquiry; the interest here is in exposing the valuative bias in purportedly "scientific" formulations. It is true that many psychoanalysts claim to have abandoned the pejorative attitudes implicit in the terminology discussed here. But the fact that they continue to use a language which is depreciatory and condescending toward this class of people belies their protest in that the implication remains that the lives of "perverts" are less desirable, less fulfilling, and less appropriate as a social role model than heterosexual lives, and it reflects a commitment to an extremely narrow model of human development: one that I would say reflects years, if not centuries, of outright social intolerance.

No parental couple could be perfectly suited to every twist and turn of a child's psychological development. No marriage between two adults could be perfectly attuned at all times to the psychological needs of a growing child. There are inevitable deficiencies and vulnerabilities in every human being's development and sexual behavior does play a compensatory and defensive and self-actualizing role in every person. Human life is very rich and very diverse in its environmental and social possibilities under which children are nurtured and developed. To call every deviation from one prescribed ideal pathway "perverted" or "disordered" or "distorted" is unworthy of educated people. It is a blemish on psychoanalysis that most analysts persist in these attitudes, but they should not be allowed to delude themselves into thinking that these prejudices are founded on sound scientific research and are therefore perfectly rational and devoid of all bias. The biases are built into the purportedly scientific concepts. The object of this study has been to point that out. It is hoped that the exposure of this currently steadfast value-laden conceptual framework will be a stimulus for developing a fresh conceptual approach that will promote a more enlightened and sympathetic scientific understanding of homosexuality and all sexual behavior.

NOTES

1. There is one person that I want to exempt from this remark, and that is Richard A. Isay. Isay's views on the development of homosexuality differ markedly from those of Socarides. See his "The Development of Sexual Identity in Homosexual Men," *Psychoanalytic Study of the Child* 41 (1986): 467-489; and "Fathers and their Homosexually Inclined Sons in Childhood," *Psychoanalytic Study of the Child* 42 (1987): 275-294. Isay places much more emphasis on the ways in which social factors interact with, shape, and modify intrapsychic forces based on early development. Isay has a much longer view of psychosexual development, and his conception of development seems to be much more plastic and flexible than Socarides's emphasis on the first few years of life. Isay believes homosexuality can be integrated into a healthy, well-adjusted, and productive lifestyle in many people and does not view homosexual behavior as inherently pathological. He believes that efforts to change homosexual behavior are usually injurious to the patient's self-esteem and are in any case very likely to fail. Isay, however, does not develop an alternative model of metapsychological development with the scope and depth of Socarides's, and I believe his views, while enlightened and positive, represent a minority position within psychoanalysis.

2. Irving Bieber, *Homosexuality: A Psychoanalytic Study* (Northvale, NJ, and London: Jason Aronson, 1988), p. 18; emphasis in original.

3. Charles W. Socarides, *The Preoedipal Origin and Psychoanalytic Therapy of Sexual Perversions* (Madison, CT: International Universities Press, 1988), p. 21. Where they are contextually clear, further references to this work will be given in the text.

4. Sigmund Freud, "Instincts and Their Vicissitudes," in *The Standard Edition of the Complete Psychological Works of Sigmund Freud*, Vol. 14 (London: Hogarth Press, 1915), p. 123. See also Sigmund Freud, "Repression," in *Standard Edition*, Vol. 14, pp. 146-158; 148.

5. Freud, "Instincts and their Vicissitudes," esp. pp. 121-122, 123.

6. Rene Spitz, *A Genetic Field Theory of Ego Formation* (New York: International Universities Press, 1959), p. 87. Where they are contextually clear, further references to this work will be given in the text.

7. Charles W. Socarides, *Homosexuality: Psychoanalytic Theory* (Northgate, NJ, and London: Jason Aronson, 1989), pp. 103, 334. This title was originally published in 1978 as *Homosexuality*. Where they are contextually clear, further references to this work will be given in the text.

8. Mervin Glasser, "Identification and Its Vicissitudes as Observed in the Perversions," *International Journal of Psychoanalysis* 67 (1986): 11; second emphasis mine.

9. See also Otto Kernberg, "Developmental Theory, Structural Organization and Psychoanalytic Technique," in Ruth F. Lax, Sheldon Bach, and J. Alexis Burland, eds., *Rapprochement: The Critical Subphase of Separation-Individuation* (New York: Jason Aronson, 1980), p. 28; and Otto Kernberg, *Internal World and External Reality* (New York: Jason Aronson, 1980), Chap. 2.

10. Robert Stolorow and Frank M. Lachman, *Psychoanalysis of Developmental Arrests: Theory and Treatment* (New York: International Universities Press, 1980), p. 94.

11. Stolorow and Lachman, p. 150.

12. Sigmund Freud, *The Interpretation of Dreams*, in *Standard Edition*, Vols. 4-5 (Originally published 1900), p. 548. Where they are contextually clear, all further references to this work will be given in the text.

13. Freud, *Three Essays on the Theory of Sexuality*, in *Standard Edition*, Vol. 7 (Originally published, 1905), p. 240.

14. Sigmund Freud, *Inhibitions, Symptoms, and Anxiety*, in *Standard Edition*, Vol. 20 (Originally published 1926), pp. 113ff.

15. Freud, *Introductory Lectures on Psychoanalysis* in *Standard Edition*, Vols. 15-16 (Originally published 1916-1917), p. 199.

16. Hermann Nunberg, *Principles of Psychoanalysis* (New York: International Universities Press, 1955), pp. 102 and 237 respectively.

17. Ernst Kris, *Psychoanalytic Explorations in Art* (New York: Schocken Books and International Universities Press, 1952), p. 312.

18. Merton M. Gill and Margaret Brennan, *Hypnosis and Related States: Psychoanalytic Studies in Regression* (New York: International Universities Press), 1959.

19. David Rapoport, "The Theory of Ego Autonomy," in Merton M. Gill, ed., *The Collected Papers of David Rapoport* (New York: Basic Books, 1967), pp. 722-744; p. 728.

20. See Otto Kernberg, *Severe Personality Disorders* (New Haven: Yale University Press, 1984), pp. 266-274.

21. Edward M. Weinshel, "Severe Regressive States During Analysis," *Journal of the American Psychoanalytic Association* 14 (1966): 538-568.

22. See Weinshel, p. 538; quoted in *Homosexuality*, p. 464.

23. Cf. Rene Spitz, *The First Year of Life* (New York: International Universities Press, 1965), pp. 199ff., 299ff.

24. Jacob A. Arlow, "Discussion of papers by J. McDougall and M. Glasser. Panel on Identification in the Perversions," *International Journal of Psychoanalysis* 67 (1986): 245-250; 249.

Homophobia and the Moral Authority
of Medicine

Abby Wilkerson, MA
Silver Spring, Maryland

SUMMARY. This essay identifies ways in which medicine expresses and legitimizes homophobic values. Examples of such homophobia are identified in the treatment of people with HIV, moralistic interpretations of people with AIDS, certain conceptions about ways in which HIV is transmitted, media representations of AIDS, and even in the way in which medicine's "objectivity" reinforces a moral view inimical to gay men, lesbians, and bisexuals. It is concluded that the notion of medical objectivity and traditional conceptions of the ethics of health care hinder an appreciation of the ways in which medicine presumes and perpetuates homophobic values.

Lesbians, gays, and bisexuals are not easily seduced by the romantic myth of modern medicine as the entirely benevolent, healing face of technology. It was, after all, medical science which recast the sin (or, alternatively, crime) of homosexuality as "moral contagion," insanity, or sickness and called for compassion even while devising treatments such as castration, hypnotherapy, psychoanalysis, drugs, and aversion therapy.[1] Thus one of the first targets of

Abby Wilkerson lives in Silver Spring, Maryland, and is a doctoral candidate in the Department of Philosophy at the University of Illinois at Chicago. Correspondence may be directed to her at the Department of Philosophy m/c 267, University of Illinois at Chicago, Chicago, IL 60607-7115.

[Haworth co-indexing entry note]: "Homphobia and the Moral Authority of Medicine." Wilkerson, Abby. Co-published simultaneously in the *Journal of Homosexuality* (The Haworth Press, Inc.) Vol. 27, No. 3/4, 1994, pp. 329-347; and: *Gay Ethics: Controversies in Outing, Civil Rights, and Sexual Science* (ed: Timothy F. Murphy) The Haworth Press, Inc., 1994, pp. 329-347. Multiple copies of this article/chapter may be purchased from The Haworth Document Delivery Center [1-800-3-HAWORTH; 9:00 a.m. - 5:00 p.m. (EST)].

the post-Stonewall liberation movement was challenging the medical/psychiatric construction of homosexuality, just as the women's health movement was beginning to resist medical constructions of femaleness. Both movements recognized that medicine and its construction of knowledge were a medium for both the expression and the legitimation of political values–that medicine could harm people, control them, by calling them sick.

After women and gay and bisexual men had engaged in these struggles for a dozen or more years, the AIDS epidemic, which in the United States initially affected mostly gay males, became a new arena for activism and advocacy. Grassroots groups began providing the counseling, health care, and support services which they could not find elsewhere and went on to address civil rights concerns as well as broader social and political issues. Groups such as AIDS Coalition to Unleash Power (ACT UP) focused on standard health concerns as well as relationships between cultural values and representations, HIV transmission, and the medical and social treatment of people with AIDS (hereafter PWAs).

Participants in all of these movements–gay liberation, women's health, AIDS–connect their health concerns as members of oppressed groups not only to their economic position but to their sociocultural or political status as well and see medicine as helping to perpetuate this diminished status, due to the privileged form of moral–hence political–authority which it wields. Despite the fact that the cultural authority of medicine resides largely in the presumed objectivity of medical science, value judgments against members of oppressed groups continue to be expressed in the practice of medicine as well as in the broader social uses of medical discourse. For example, as Timothy F. Murphy points out, certain formal medical claims about homoeroticism may have been retracted, yet continued interest in practices such as conversion therapy suggests that there are still judgments of inferiority to be found in the theory and practice of medicine.[2] If medicine plays a significant role in the perpetuation of oppression, as activists claim, then the institution of medicine itself must be evaluated according to principles of justice, particularly in terms of its moral and political authority–a concept which has significant implications for both bioethics and social philosophy.

There seem to be obstacles to recognizing these implications, however. Analytic philosophers tend to construe the relation between health and justice in terms of the allocation of resources and the distribution of access to health care,[3] yet many of the concerns of activists cannot readily be addressed within these constraints. Iris Young refers to this framework (which she sees as characteristic of mainstream liberal philosophy in general) as the "distributive paradigm" of justice, arguing that it functions to obscure significant and widespread harms experienced by some disadvantaged groups in society, such as homophobia,[4] which are particularly difficult to address within the constraints of the distributive paradigm.[5] Young recognizes oppression as a key aspect of injustice, widening the scope of analysis beyond distributive concerns to include aspects of oppression such as cultural imperialism,[6] exploitation, marginalization, violence, and powerlessness. Although access to health care is indeed an agonizingly important issue, now more than ever before,[7] Young's recommendation to look beyond issues of allocation and distribution can be fruitfully applied to an examination of medical constructions of the relationship between sexual identity and HIV transmission, and more broadly the role of medicine in the perpetuation and legitimation of homophobia. This examination will also suggest interesting connections between medicine and the cultural conceptualization of justice, two discourses which are usually perceived as distinct and autonomous.

On the face of it, medical discourse and mainstream conceptualizations of social justice serve quite different purposes, yet both are used as instruments of just and beneficial public policy. The discourse of social justice (which I take to encompass a broad political spectrum and to include popular discourse as well as social/political philosophy) is used in the moral evaluation of public policy. Is this course of action compatible with the requirements of justice? Medical discourse in the form of concepts, values, and "facts" shapes questions such as: Is this course of action medically sound? How will it affect public health?

Despite the attempt to employ each discourse in the service of just and beneficial public policy, however, their influence has not always been egalitarian. This is most obvious in the realm of medicine, which is presumed to be value-free; yet not only has it been used as an instrument of oppression against lesbians, gays, and bisexuals, it has also served as an ideological support for other forms of oppression.[8]

Inegalitarian influences can also be found in the discourse of justice. Iris Young argues that the prevailing distributive formulation (despite great concern for objectivity) obscures significant harms which systematically accrue to members of disadvantaged groups such as gay people (a claim I will support below in the context of AIDS). Obscuring such harms may even reinforce social callousness toward the suffering of these groups and a lack of will to remedy these harms in the name of justice. Significantly, both discourses share the central epistemic principle of objectivity, a value hotly contested in recent and influential work in feminist theory, epistemology, and philosophy of science.[9] I will argue that lesbian and gay experiences with medicine also raise questions about the value of this principle, at least as it is typically construed and employed, and that these questions are an important concern for bioethics.

ASPECTS OF MEDICINE AND THEIR MANIFESTATIONS IN THE CONTEXT OF AIDS

Iris Young recommends a broader approach to justice than the distributive framework, adding oppression as a central concern. Taking this argument as my point of departure, I will distinguish several aspects of the institution of medicine in order to illustrate the ways in which medicine is not only invested with the authority of an expert discourse to which laypersons do not have access, but also holds moral authority which often functions to perpetuate oppression against those who are already disadvantaged. In my view, certain philosophical and cultural aspects of medicine have important implications for justice which are often overlooked in traditional philosophical accounts, and even more importantly, the ways in which these aspects reinforce one another go largely unrecognized in biomedical ethics. I believe this examination will indicate not only the systematic influence of homophobic practices and beliefs, both subtle and overt, throughout all of these aspects, but also that the role of medicine in helping to perpetuate an oppressive social structure is largely independent of distributive concerns such as access to health care.

The relevant aspects of medicine may be defined as follows:

1. The practices of individual providers and the rules and systems of specific medical institutions.

2. The cultural transmission of technical and nontechnical medical information through various channels; expert discourse as it is filtered through mainstream media and popular culture.

3. Biomedical theory and specific conceptualizations of organs, systems, diseases, and pathology forms; medical discourse on its own terms. A vital recognition of feminist and AIDS activism is that biomedical understandings are frequently mediated through ideology.

4. Medicine as cultural myth–based in large part on its actual or perceived relation to science, which is accorded the epistemic status of indisputable "Truth." (As a character exhorted in *Flatliners*, a recent horror movie, "Philosophy has failed. Religion has failed. Now it's up to physical science!")

PRACTICES OF PROVIDERS AND INSTITUTIONS

Despite the cultural myth of medicine as a sacred calling or mission of mercy, there has been often widespread reluctance or refusal on the part of health-care providers to treat HIV-positive people. In Minnesota, for example, despite the existence of a Human Rights Act which outlaws discrimination on the basis of disability, a Health Department study found that "21 percent of 241 HIV-infected respondents could not find a dentist willing to treat them."[10] This is not a purely Midwestern phenomenon: forty-eight percent of physicians responding to a recent Los Angeles County survey will not treat HIV-positive patients.[11]

Such unwillingness can in many cases be directly attributed to bias. Rose Weitz cites studies which "have found that up to 76 percent of doctors would prefer not to treat persons with HIV disease because they either fear infection or believe such persons do not deserve their services." She notes, "Another study concluded that nursing, medical, and chiropractic students . . . all considered persons with AIDS less competent and less morally worthy than persons with cancer, diabetes, or heart disease."[12] PWAs interviewed by Weitz report physicians' mistreatment of them in the following ways:

> (A)dopting unnecessary precautions against contagion such as donning gowns and masks, informing people who are infected with HIV but have yet to develop any opportunistic infections that they will die within a few months, speaking rudely or abruptly, and [as late as 1989] warning persons with HIV disease that they can infect their families if they hug them, cook their meals, or wash their clothes.[13]

Another issue in PWAs' treatment by individual practitioners or at specific sites is the role of partners and other chosen family members in decisions about health care.[14] Visitation rights and decision-making powers are frequently denied to gays and lesbians (and to companions from gay and lesbian support organizations) when lovers or friends are hospitalized,[15] as in the famous case of Sharon Kowalski, a lesbian who was partially paralyzed in an accident, and her partner Karen Thompson. Kowalski's parents obtained guardianship and denied Thompson visitation or any other role in Kowalski's recovery, forcing Thompson to endure a lengthy legal battle in order to be with her partner and support her in recovery.[16] The HIV epidemic drastically increased the number of those facing this problem, and as a result, the "Patient's Bill of Rights" of the PWA Coalition affirms "The right to the choice of 'immediate family member' status for those the patient may designate."[17]

MEDICAL INFORMATION IN MASS MEDIA AND POPULAR CULTURE

Oppressive ideological influences can readily be detected in popular health and medical discourses. What is presented as medical advice in these domains may actually be based on moralistic assumptions which are neither made explicit nor defended, a point which is particularly salient with respect to AIDS. Right-wing discussions of the epidemic, for example, frequently conflate the language of medical pathology with the moral language of sin and blame, lending a scientific air to moral and political pronouncements. A conservative organization in Texas, seeking the reinstatement of an anti-sodomy law which had been declared unconstitutional in that state, invokes the moral and rhetorical authority of medicine by calling itself "Dallas Doctors Against AIDS."[18] Conservatives have gone so far as to claim medical grounds for art censorship, such as the "link between art and disease . . . drawn by the president of the Massachusetts chapter of Morality in Media, who was reported to have said, 'People looking at these kinds of pictures become addicts and spread AIDS,'"[19] or Senator Jesse Helms's call for "the National Endowment for the Arts to censor art with lesbian/gay or sexual themes" due to the fear that such "promotion" of homosexuality would foster HIV transmission.[20]

It is no surprise that conservatives already appalled by the movement whose slogan was "gay pride" would find in the AIDS epidemic reason to condemn not only sexual practices associated with gay men, but gay identity itself. For example, conservative commentator Gene Antonio invokes scientific authority to justify a pronouncement of homosexuality "per se" as wrong:

> Homosexuality per se must be taught as an unhealthy, unsafe and lethal sexual alternative. "It's a very major risk to enter these communities," warns June Osborn, Dean of Public Health at the University of Michigan and a professor of epidemiology. "So tell the fifteen or sixteen-year-old kid who's going to declare his same-sex preference that there's a serious chance of infection that can truly be a matter of life and death."[21]

"Entering a community," "declaring a preference" are thus conflated with unsafe sexual practices, all of which are assigned moral blame. Antonio's emphasis on the deadliness of homosexuality underscores the danger of gay identity, desire, and preference, even as it obscures the fact that it is specific practices, by no means confined to those who define themselves as gay, which put one at risk of HIV transmission–practices which are moreover not biologically determined by ineluctable sexual essences but are social creations.

Interestingly, Antonio chooses to omit part of Osborn's original statement, which appears in an article by John Langone. It continues in the following way:

> The false hope of a vaccine or a cure prevents people from examining their sexual options. False hopes keep people from having to face up to the fact that prevention is the most rational thing, and it is possible–not easy, but possible.[22]

Unhealthy, unsafe, lethal; options, rational, prevention, possible. The tone has changed from Antonio's moral apocalypse to a call for prudence–a significant difference. Invoking scientific verification in the use of the epidemiologist's statement and her professional stature, Antonio implies that responsibility in sexual choices is a contradiction in terms for gay men; yet such responsibility is *exactly* what the omitted portion of Osborn's statement emphasizes. Moreover, Osborn raises a new point, undercutting an unreflective faith in medicine at the expense of prevention and education.

An important question to pose at this point is whether conservative attitudes toward homoeroticism are oppressive, yet remediable by greater medical sophistication. After all, the objection may be made that medicine "itself" is in no way implicated by political (mis)uses of medical information. Moreover, the brief comment by the epidemiologist Osborn is not reducible to political diatribe and even offers the useful (if basic) advice to weigh one's options; it does not offer plain condemnation. However, it is not only the case that right-wing condemnations of gay sexual identity and of PWAs invoke medical authority; but, as I will argue in the next section, both mainstream media representations of AIDS and medical conceptualizations, which are ostensibly politically neutral or value-free, can also be seen to tacitly reproduce these same right-wing attitudes. Thus both popular and expert medical discourses are not only frequently difficult to separate but may even share a susceptibility to ideological influence and an availability for tacit political service.

BIOMEDICAL THEORY AND SPECIFIC CONCEPTUALIZATIONS

The connection between popular and expert medical discourses does not merely involve the use of scientific data to shore up moral/

political judgments, which are then presented in the form of medical information for the masses. Pathologization can take forms that are *simultaneously* medical and moral. I will argue that homophobia significantly influences many scientific conceptualizations of HIV transmission. Furthermore, even in the absence of overtly homophobic attitudes on the part of researchers, the marginalized status of lesbians, gays, and bisexuals means that there is a lack of knowledge about gay sexuality already (frequently so much so that researchers are not even aware of their ignorance). This situation in turn exacerbates drastically the difficulty of obtaining HIV transmission information, and functions to reinforce homophobia and gay oppression by failing to challenge "medical" claims that are actually based on tacit moral assumptions.

A construction of difference as Otherness shapes information regarding the transmission of HIV.[23] Not only do such perceptions of difference affect the way the "facts" are presented, but they affect the way the "facts" are *conceptualized.* In the early years of the epidemic, for example, transmission was discussed in terms of identities and "risk groups" rather than in terms of practices, imposing a dichotomy between a riskless Us and a jeopardized Them. Simon Watney, Cindy Patton, Jan Zita Grover,[24] Paula A. Treichler, and others have noted that the term "general population," often used in measuring the significance of the epidemic, is implicitly white, middle-class, and heterosexual, an identity perceived not as a social creation but codified somehow in nature itself, certified as safe, natural because outside so-called risk groups.

In this light, AIDS can be understood as a social crisis not only in the obvious epidemiological sense but in terms of the moral and political contradictions which it reveals. Homoeroticism is perceived as impossible—or, possible only in the realm of the Other. In ordinary times, social boundaries are both invisible and unconscious, and experienced as impermeable, inevitable, a fact of nature. Yet viruses follow their own logic, uninformed by a society's doctrines about gender and sexual orientation, about who is "supposed" to get sick and who is not. Viruses are immune to the cultural meanings of National Basketball Association championships and starring roles opposite Doris Day. Thus the epidemic reveals the effacement of boundaries, a transgression which is then cast as both the cause and the sign of inevitable social, psychological, and medical havoc. First perceived as a gay phenomenon, HIV has been discussed and represented in terms of its "spread," "containment," and "saturation," as if it had "natural" limits which are in danger of violation.[25] Thus a frequent result of such conceptualizations has been the call to reinforce social boundaries through such means as immigration controls and restrictions on homosexual content in government-funded art and educational materials.[26]

Many constructions of the "facts" of transmission have involved the pathologization of gay male sexuality, in the guise of stern warning about the "misuse" of organs. References abound in the critical literature to the 1985 *Discover* article which refers to the "fragile anus" and the "rugged vagina"–only one of which, in an apparently unconscious reversal of gender stereotype, can stand up to the really rugged penis.[27] It is vital to remember that the conceptualization of AIDS as a "gay disease" occurred despite the knowledge–in the first year of the epidemic–that "men and women, straights as well as gays," were affected.[28]

Not all of the medical misconceptualizations of HIV/AIDS can be directly attributed to homophobia, however. Some of them are due to plain ignorance. Cindy Patton identifies the assumption in much scientific research "that gay men represent a homogeneous population," and notes the irony in "basic [medical] ignorance about contemporary gay male sexual practice, identity, and community" despite the fact that scientists and physicians are "presumed to be the 'authority' on which forms of sex might be 'safe.'"[29]

And if medical science is ill-informed about gay male sexual practices and their relation to HIV transmission, it can be even more so about lesbian sexuality. Dr. Charles Schable of the Centers for Disease Control (CDC) made the now-infamous assessment that there was no need "to study lesbians because 'lesbians don't have much sex'"–this in a statement to the lesbian magazine *Visibilities*.[30] And in the data which the CDC did compile, the only women classified as lesbians were those who had not had sex with a man since 1977[31]–yet in "an ongoing Kinsey study, 46 percent of the self-identified lesbians surveyed reported having sex with a man since 1980."[32]

Moreover, when physicians do the reporting, it may be their own assumptions about a woman's sexual orientation which get recorded. Leonard notes, for example, that "It is very likely that most women will be assumed to be straight, and will never even be asked if they have had sex with other women. . . . the CDC found it impossible to categorize nearly 700 out of 5,000 women because they couldn't determine their sexual behaviors from the report forms." And if a woman has not been diagnosed accurately (not unlikely, given the lack of research on manifestations in women) then she will not be included in the statistics.[33]

Yet another statistical and conceptual problem is the CDC's use of hierarchically ranked categories of risk. For example, Leonard notes, "If you are a lesbian IVDU [intravenous drug-user] with an IVDU partner, the possibility of woman-to-woman transmission would be ignored and you would be counted solely as an IVDU, even if you never shared needles."[34] It seems unlikely that government agencies have a stated policy of neglecting lesbians and bisexual women in the epidemic—yet the end result is not altogether different than if there were such a policy.

What should one make of these examples of oppressive practices, attitudes, and misconceptions in various aspects of medicine: Do they indicate deep problems with the institution of "medicine itself," or are they mere, though unfortunate, aberrations from "good" medicine? "Science as usual," or "bad science?"[35] Is it not possible that providers' refusal to treat PWAs, their blame and fear of PWAs, and their failure to recognize the status of chosen family members can be rectified with *better* medicine, more attention to good medical science, a little more objectivity in dealing with patients, and better medical education? That moralistic "medical" pronouncements are a misuse of medical language for rhetorical purposes, and not a problem of medicine at all? That the pathologization of gay identity and ignorance of gay sexuality can be remedied simply by greater scientific accuracy, the rehabilitation of naturally unruly discourses and practices? A response to these questions should emerge in the following discussion of the cultural status of medicine.

MEDICINE AS CULTURAL MYTH

Embedded in a society's myths are its deepest values, those which structure the beliefs and practices of that society. Medical discourse embodies (a verb I use both literally and figuratively) a social mythology, and a crucial part of the story told in this mythology is the nature and meaning of social difference. Various social groups are differentiated from one another on the basis of traits which are thought to be biologically based or physiologically manifested, such as gender, sexual orientation, race, age, and physical ability level. Medical conceptualizations of such differences have an exalted status due to the association of medicine with science, which is perceived as detached, objective, inherently unbiased; yet not only do scientific "facts" regarding difference influence social practices, these conceptualizations (such as the "fragile anus/rugged vagina" doctrines) are frequently based on an implicit norm whose reference points include heterosexual maleness.

Thus, not only do medical science and practice convey implicit moral/political judgments, but these judgments often serve the interests of those who are most privileged in society, reassuring them of the rightness and inevitability of their social position, and doing so at the expense of those who already face social disadvantages. Medical discourse has been employed, for example, in arguments against gays in the military or against public school curricula sensitive to the needs of lesbian and gay youth. Political judgments using medical discourse can appear to be grounded in scientific objectivity, with its paramount epistemic authority, so that challenges to medical ideologies of difference may be seen as attempts to regulate science according to "interest group" politics.[36] Objecting to the implicit homophobia of the "fragile anus/rugged vagina" concept is thus made to seem roughly analogous to claiming discrimination against diabetics because their doctors do not allow them donuts.

Michel Foucault provides a historical overview of the developing ideological functions of medicine. The modern valorization of scientific objectivity fostered the "medicalization" of society, replacing the church as the repository of the value of social order, and re-mapping the moral domain from the soul onto the body. In the process of medicalization, complex social forces, as manifested in the health of individuals, were re-presented as discrete phenomena, the disconnected pathologies of individual organisms.

This ideological triumph, Foucault argues, was made possible by the epistemology of medicine. He summarizes its key epistemic principle in the following way: "That which is not on the scale of the gaze falls outside the domain of possible knowledge."[37] Objectivity is the central epistemic norm contained in this metaphor: an objectification achieved by a separation between knower and known, so that the object of study becomes the Other, literally made into an object; and a radical detachment from feeling, emotion, experience. Seeking liberation from bias, the gaze metaphor effaces any active participation, involvement, or vested interest in the construction of knowledge, and casts the body and its experiences and sensations into the realm of the (passive and insensate) Other.

Iris Young locates medical science in the context of the historical association of "despised groups with the body, setting them outside the homogeneity of the nation."[38] Medical discourse provided justification for this association, and the status of the profession itself also helped to justify the "normative dualist" valorization of a certain conception of intelligence as the paramount human value. This attribute, intelligence conceived as the capacity for reasoning, was then associated with those who were most privileged–white, heterosexual, middle- and upper-class males–in contrast to socially devalued groups whose existence was supposedly ruled by the body rather than the constraints of reason.

Nineteenth-century medical science codified the social norm of difference as pathology, "naturalizing" socially constructed differences (reading them as truths of nature) and "normalizing" them (classifying according to a hierarchical norm), thereby:

> (G)enerat(ing) theories of human physical, moral, and aesthetic superiority, which presumed the young, white bourgeois man as the norm. The unifying structure of that reason, which presumed a knowing subject purified of sensuous immersion in things, made possible the objectification of other groups, and their placement under a normalizing gaze.[39]

Young's indictment of the oppressive influences of medical authority is primarily historical. The treatment of gays, lesbians, and bisexuals in the AIDS epidemic, however, reveals that medicine's contribution to an oppressive social climate is not merely a matter of outmoded doctrines corrected by the progress of medical science. Medical theory and practice continue to harm those who are gay; and these harms as well as broader social manifestations of homophobia are sometimes made invisible, sometimes made to appear inevitable or even morally appropriate, by virtue of the cultural authority of medicine.

JUSTICE, MEDICINE, AND THE SCALE OF THE GAZE

Iris Young argues that medical discourse and traditional accounts of justice share epistemic principles which help to perpetuate injustice. Mainstream moral and political theory, as well as popular discourses of social justice, generally share medicine's epistemology of detachment, with its conception of objectivity as distance and neutrality. There is a sense that unbiased public policy, for example, requires giving all groups or individuals equal standing and weighing their interests accordingly. Differential treatment of any kind is felt to be "preferential treatment," which is understood as unfair, inherently wrong. Yet the problem remains that different social groups may have different needs or experience certain harms differentially as members of particular groups; if so, differential treatment may be required to redress these harms.

The epistemic standard of the discourse of social justice, like that of medicine, is "the scale of the gaze." Yet the detachment, which signifies objectivity, that is conveyed in this visual metaphor (as in Thomas Nagel's "view from nowhere"),[40] is in contradiction with the inherently perspectival character of vision.[41] Both medical discourse and the discourse of social justice have denied any epistemic role to experience and feeling (both sensory and emotive),[42] and their social locations. Attending to lesbians' and gay men's experiences with medical discourse (which I do not separate from medical practice) could foster a profound social conviction of the injustice of homophobia. Yet the "view from nowhere," which prescribes nonpreferential treatment for all, seems inadequate to dismantle the categories of social hierarchy imposed by the medical gaze–a task which is necessary to determine what justice requires of society in relation not only to health but also to the broader social status of gays, issues which activist movements have rightly claimed are connected.

Moreover, like the ideology of medicine, the mainstream conceptualization of justice upholds the enlightenment valorization of reason not only as the utmost human value but as the essence of agency itself, the chief resource for the pursuit of human needs. From this perspective, it is reason and argumentation which bring about social change and liberation. Yet as Iris Young points out, oppression persists despite a "discursive commitment to equality" in recent history.[43] She argues that the distributive paradigm of justice fails to address cultural imperialism, the overt and subtle devaluation of oppressed groups via cultural mythology. I would argue that it is not only the distributive focus of the mainstream concept of justice which obscures this phenomenon, but also its emphasis on reason and objectivity to the detriment of other human resources. Objectivity may help establish the impermissibility of overt discrimination, but does nothing to foster the knowledge of others' experience or the suspension of trust in the universality of one's own experience–achievements which may be particularly difficult for members of privileged groups. What María Lugones writes of ethnocentrism can be applied to homophobia (or perhaps heterocentrism) as well.

> You do not see me because you do not see yourself and you do not see yourself because you declare yourself outside culture . . . . dis-engagement is a radical form of passivity toward the ideology of the ethnocentric racial state which privileges the dominant culture as the only culture to 'see with' and conceives this seeing as to be done non-self-consciously.[44]

Lugones clarifies that moral and political questions are always also epistemic questions. Her argument also suggests that the central problem with "the scale of the gaze" is that the apparent freedom of the gaze to master all it surveys disguises its inherent confinement to surfaces, the expulsion not only of subjectivity, but of the seer's awareness of her own locatedness, from the realm of knowledge.

Furthermore, the mandate of objectivity seems beside the point when it comes to the vital task of untangling the psychologically complex issues in the making and promulgation, as well as the unmaking and remaking, of cultural mythology. The formulation and evaluation of social policy in accord with the requirements of justice are tasks which traditionally have been carried out separately from cultural analysis–a separation which obscures the ideological connections between the two realms. Finally, if cultural mythology is indeed the force behind the scenes which so often shapes social practices and relations, mythmaking itself is a central task in the pursuit of social justice, and one which will require far more than objectivity.

In order to overcome medical homophobia and create and implement policies which will foster health and restore the moral standing of lesbians, gays, and bisexuals, medical mistreatment of PWAs must be exposed; medical vilifications of homoeroticism and legitimation of an oppressive social structure must be opposed; and more generally the institution of medicine must be held to principles of justice. We can explore medicine's potential to inform a nonhierarchical understanding of social relations and pursue new epistemic models challenging the definition of expertise–and the separation between expert and layperson–in order to address the subjective aspects of medicine, which are not mere "side effects." Finally, many kinds of discursive interventions are needed, forays into the realm of mythmaking, which, it must be remembered, occurs in all discourses, not only those concerned with storytelling in the usual sense. In addition to a healthy suspicion of both medical authority and the merits of social hierarchy, lesbians, gays, and bisexuals offer the tremendous resource of their experiences, speaking as health-care workers and professionals, medical consumers, activists, parents, teachers, family members, and friends. But if this resource is to achieve its full value, heterosexuals will have to listen, to "see themselves," perhaps even to cultivate a healthy suspicion of much that is familiar and trusted.

AUTHOR NOTE

An earlier version of this paper was presented at the Second National Graduate Student Conference on Lesbian, Bisexual, and Gay Studies, 1992, in Urbana-Champaign. The author would like to thank Tim Murphy for his interest and for his insightful comments and questions, as well as useful references. Sandra

Bartky's responses were also extremely helpful, as were those of Lisa Heldke and Pat McGann, both of whom supplied encouragement as well as insight. She thanks Jenny Faust and the undergraduates in her AIDS course (especially Bob Blume and Carolyn Kotlarski) at the University of Illinois at Chicago in the spring of 1991. Finally, she is grateful to Carrie Brecke and Durrell Dew for providing comfort and cheer at the right time(s).

NOTES

1. See Jeffrey Weeks, *Coming Out* (London: Quartet, 1977), pp. 23, 28-30.
2. Timothy F. Murphy, "Redirecting Sexual Orientation: Techniques and Justifications," *Journal of Sex Research* 29 (1992): 503-523.
3. Examples of the distributive approach include Norman Daniels, *Just Health Care* (Cambridge: Cambridge University Press, 1985), and David Gauthier, "Unequal Need: A Problem of Equity in Access to Health Care," in President's Commission for the Study of Ethical Problems in Medicine and Biomedical and Behavioral Research, *Securing Access to Health Care: The Ethical Implications of Differences in the Availability of Health Services,* Vol. 2 (1983), pp. 179-205. Recent exceptions to this approach do not necessarily invoke the language of justice, yet to my mind their emphasis on the relation between sexist or heterosexist oppression and health care situates their analysis within this framework. See Susan Sherwin, *No Longer Patient* (Philadelphia: Temple University Press, 1992); Timothy F. Murphy, "Is AIDS a Just Punishment?" *Journal of Medical Ethics* 14 (1988): 154-160, "No Time for an AIDS Backlash," *Hastings Center Report* 21 (1991): 6-10; and many articles from *Hypatia* 4(2 and 3) (1989).
4. In this article, I use "homophobia" in the broad sense in which it is often employed, referring both to those beliefs and practices which together create a social climate hostile to gays, lesbians, and bisexuals, as well as to the mental states and actions of specific individuals. Neither intention to discriminate nor feelings of fear or hatred are necessary conditions for homophobia in this sense.
5. Iris Marion Young, *Justice and the Politics of Difference* (Princeton: Princeton University Press, 1990).
6. María C. Lugones and Elizabeth V. Spelman, "Have We Got a Theory for You! Feminist Theory, Cultural Imperialism and the Demand for 'The Woman's Voice,'" *Women's Studies International Forum* 6 (1983): 573-581.
7. This major concern of activists is shared in philosophical discussions of the epidemic. Richard Mohr's groundbreaking *Gays/Justice: A Study in Ethics, Society, and Law* (New York: Columbia University Press, 1988), for example, identifies access to health care as crucial in the age of AIDS.
8. See Weeks; Sherwin, pp. 213-216.
9. Representative examples include Linda Alcoff and Elizabeth Potter, *Feminist Epistemologies* (New York: Routledge, 1993); Sandra Harding, *The Science Question in Feminism* (Ithaca: Cornell University Press, 1986); and Alison Jaggar, *Feminist Politics and Human Nature* (Totowa, NJ: Rowman & Allanheld,

1983), "Love and Knowledge: Emotion in Feminist Epistemology," in Ann Garry and Marilyn Pearsall, eds. *Women, Knowledge, and Reality* (Boston: Unwin Hyman, 1989), pp. 129-155.

10. "Minnesota Dentist Fined for Denying Treatment to AIDS Patient," *Chicago Tribune*, Mar. 22, 1992.

11. "Doctors Balk at Treating AIDS Patients," *Chicago Tribune*, Mar. 22, 1992. See also Caryn Christensen, Ann King-Meltzer, and Barbara Fetzer, "Medical Students' Reactions to AIDS: The Influence of Patient Characteristics on Hypothetical Treatment Decisions," *Teaching and Learning in Medicine* 3 (1991): 138-142, and Michael D. Quam, "The Sick Role, Stigma, and Pollution: The Case of AIDS," in Douglas Feldman, ed., *Culture and AIDS* (New York: Praeger, 1990), pp. 29-44.

12. Rose Weitz, *Life with AIDS* (New Brunswick and London: Rutgers University Press, 1991), pp. 80 and 25, respectively.

13. Weitz, p. 64.

14. Kath Weston, *Families We Choose: Lesbians, Gays, Kinship* (New York: Columbia University Press, 1991).

15. Cindy Patton, *Sex and Germs* (Boston: South End Press, 1985), pp. 69-70.

16. Warren J. Blumenfeld and Diane Raymond, *Looking at Gay & Lesbian Life* (New York: Philosophical Library, 1988), pp. 257-258.

17. "PWA Coalition Portfolio," in Douglas Crimp, ed., *AIDS: Cultural Analysis, Cultural Activism* (Cambridge, MA: MIT Press, 1988), pp. 146-168; 160.

18. Dennis Altman, *AIDS in the Mind of America* (Garden City, NJ: Anchor, 1987), p. 69.

19. David Eberly, "Homophobia, Censorship, and the Arts," in Warren J. Blumenfeld, ed., *Homophobia: How We All Pay the Price* (Boston: Beacon Press, 1992), pp. 205-216; 207.

20. George M. Carter, *ACT UP, the AIDS War, and Activism* (Westfield, NJ: Open Magazine Pamphlet Series, 1992), p. 12.

21. Gene Antonio, "Legal Restrictions are Needed to Control AIDS," in Lynn Hall and Thomas Modl, eds., *AIDS: Opposing Viewpoints* (St. Paul, MN: Greenhaven, 1988), pp. 128-132; 133.

22. John Langone, "AIDS," *Discover*, Dec., 1985, pp. 25ff.; 53.

23. Paula A. Treichler, "AIDS, Gender, and Biomedical Discourse: Current Contests for Meaning," in Elizabeth Fee and Daniel M. Fox, eds., *AIDS: The Burdens of History* (Berkeley: University of California Press, 1988), pp. 190-266; Paula A. Treichler, in *AIDS: Cultural Analysis, Cultural Activism*, pp. 31-70; Peg Byron, "HIV: The National Scandal," *Ms.*, Jan./Feb., 1991, pp. 24-29; Simon Watney, "AIDS, Language, and the Third World," in Erica Carter and Simon Watney, eds., *Taking Liberties* (London: Serpents Tail, 1989), pp. 183-192.

24. Jan Zita Grover, "AIDS: Keywords" in *AIDS: Cultural Analysis, Cultural Activism*, pp. 17-30.

25. Treichler, "AIDS, Homophobia, and Biomedical Discourse," pp. 65-66; also see Grover.

26. Richard Mohr also argues that mandatory premarital screening for HIV serves a similar symbolic function. See *Gays/Justice*, pp. 252-256.

27. Treichler, "AIDS, Homophobia, and Biomedical Discourse," p. 37.

28. Charles Perrow and Mauro F. Guillén, *The AIDS Disaster* (New Haven: Yale University Press, 1990), p. 3; Gena Corea, *The Invisible Epidemic* (New York: HarperCollins, 1992).

29. Patton, pp. 26, 139.

30. Zoe Leonard, "Lesbians in the AIDS Crisis," in ACT UP/NY Women & AIDS Book Group, eds., *Women, AIDS, and Activism* (Boston: South End Press, 1990), p. 113.

31. Byron, p. 28.

32. Leonard, p. 114.

33. Leonard, pp. 115, 116.

34. Leonard, p. 115.

35. Sandra Harding, *The Science Question in Feminism* (Ithaca: Cornell University Press, 1986).

36. See Iris Young's argument that standard usage of the concept of "special interest groups" functions to obscure the appeal to justice in the demands of oppressed groups.

37. Michel Foucault, *The Birth of the Clinic* (New York: Vintage, 1975), p. 166.

38. Young, p. 111.

39. Young, p. 130.

40. Thomas Nagel, *The View from Nowhere* (Oxford: Oxford University Press, 1986).

41. Susan Bordo, "Feminism, Postmodernism, and Gender-Scepticism," in Linda J. Nicholson, ed., *Feminism/Postmodernism* (New York: Routledge, 1990), pp. 133-156.

42. Jaggar, "Love and Knowledge."

43. Young, p. 124.

44. María Lugones, "Hablando Cara a Cara/Speaking Face to Face: An Exploration of Ethnocentric Racism," in Gloria Anzaldúa, ed., *Making Face, Making Soul: Haciendo Caras* (San Francisco: Aunt Lute, 1990), pp. 46-54; 51.

Index

Ablemindism, 146*n*48
Ablon, S.L., 218*n*32
Aboud, Frances, 221*n*68
ACT UP, 33
Adam and Eve, 12
Affirmative action:
  backward-looking rationale for,
    181-18,211,216*n*7
  compensatory aspects of,
    183-184,185-196,212
  defined, 167,180,215*n*1
  distribution of benefits,
    180,200,211-212
  economic and employment
    inducements, 209,212-213
  extent of efforts required, 209-210
  forward-looking rationale for, 182
  gay entitlement to, 4,150,181
  groups entitled to, 167,183
  injury to self-esteem, 213
  instrumental rationale for, 181
  need for, 4,167,178*n*59,179-189,
    202*ff*.
  quotas discussed, 209-210,221*n*64
  reduction of harm, 180
  resentment about, 213-214
  self-esteem, 4,191-192,198,
    199-200,219*n*45,221*n*69
  social benefits of, 4,196-197,
    211-212
  utilitarian aspects of, 182
African-Americans, 183,184,
    195-196,197,201,208,215,
    216*n*4
AIDS, 5,18,23,74,79,88*n*7,90*n*25,
    93,114,174*n*13,204,230,
    303*n*14,330,332,333-334,
    337,342
  See also HIV, PWAs

Alcoff, Linda, 345*n*9
Alexander, D., 263*n*10
Allport, Gordon W., 219*n*38
Altman, Dennis, 97-98,109*n*1,
    110*n*11-12,217*n*16,346*n*18
American Law Institute, 185
American Psychiatric Association:
  judgments on
    homosexuality, 23,188,
    259,268*n*92,292
Animals: homosexuality in, 176*n*41,
    225,228-229,265*n*43,
    285-288,305*n*30,305*n*31
ANOVA, 230,263*n*20
Anti-discrimination education:
  benefits of, 214
  need for, 159
  techniques of, 214
Anti-discrimination laws:
  affectional behavior and, 148-149
  content of,161,163-165,172*n*
  deficits of,181,197,198,199,
    214-215
  effect against stereotypes, 159,195
  enforceability of, 4,168-169
  and exercise of religion, 138,
    167-168
  evidence of compliance, 165,166,
    168-169
  federal involvement, 148
  government interest in, 163*ff*.
  illegal in Colorado, 173,186
  justifications of, 4,170,216*n*3
  protecting people perceived gay
    or lesbian, 163-164
  proving violations, 169-171
  public and private sector, 164
  reasons justifying discrimination,
    149-150

349

Heterosexism, 120,189,193
Heterosexuality:
  compared with homosexuality,
    11-12,15
  compulsory, 19
  as essence of sexuality, 12,
  as narcissism, 16-17,19-20
  panorama of, 32-33,83,90*n*31
  privilege of, 24*n*6
  and the union of differences,
    13,15-17
  unresearched, 273,274,324
Hill, Thomas, E., Jr., 90*n*32,217*n*1
HIV, 74,276,333-334,337-338
Hoagland, Sarah Lucia, 145*n*39
Hodges, Alan, 217*n*22
Hoffman, Martin, 109*n*1
Holloway, Ralph, 303*n*15
Homophobia:
  and closeting, 3
  defined, 345*n*4
  diminishing, 221*n*65
  effects of, 181*ff.*,189,205
  internalized, 53,193,195,219*n*38
  in medicine, 5,187-188,
    217*n*22-23,329-330,
    332-333
  in military, 122*ff.*
  origin of term, 307*n*42
  political impediment, 209
  and religion, 23,25*n*19,138,
    151,197,203-205,
    220*n*51-52
  and sexual identity, 205-206,2
    21*n*67
  in universities, 189-190,218*n*26
  See also Health care theory,
    Medicine
"Homo-Narcissism" (*see* Michael
  Warner)
"Homosexual panic" defense, 190
Homosexuality:
  alleged disvalues of, 23
  analogies with language, 10,13,22
  in animals, 176*n*41

and brain structures, 230-231
challenges to received culture,
  22-23
compared with heterosexuality,
  1-2
as developmental arrest, 242,315
genetic theories of, 225-226,
  274-275
hormonal theories of, 226-231,
  263*n*15-18
meanings of, 2,11-12,14,21
and medicine, 187-188,217*n*22-23
and mental illness/perversion,
  310*ff.*,315,324
moral standards for, 20-23
morphological aspects of,
  231-233,272
and narcissism, 15
need of moral justification, 2
panic/phobic theory of, 15
in parental relationships, 17,
  177*n*49,261,268*n*97,325
pathological interpretations of,
  310,329-330,337
as perversion, 313
purposes of, 12
psychoanalytic theories of, 5,
  242-249,310*ff.*
as regressive, 317-322
social learning theories of,
  233-234,256-257
strengths of, 18-19
theories of origin, 4,5,148,
  161-162,173*n*6,177*n*46,
  219*n*45,225-234,272-274,
  296ff.
and the union of differences,
  15-17
value of, 2,22-23
Hooker, Evelyn, 259
Hotvedt, M.E., 263*n*13,268*n*97
Housing, 188
Howe, Florence, 146*n*47
Hudson, Rock, 48
Human Genome Project:

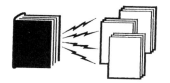

Haworth
DOCUMENT DELIVERY
SERVICE
and Local Photocopying Royalty Payment Form

This new service provides (a) a single-article order form for any article from a Haworth journal and (b) a convenient royalty payment form for local photocopying (not applicable to photocopies intended for resale).

- *Time Saving:* No running around from library to library to find a specific article.
- *Cost Effective:* All costs are kept down to a minimum.
- *Fast Delivery:* Choose from several options, including same-day FAX.
- *No Copyright Hassles:* You will be supplied by the original publisher.
- *Easy Payment:* Choose from several easy payment methods.

Open Accounts Welcome for ...
- Library Interlibrary Loan Departments
- Library Network/Consortia Wishing to Provide Single-Article Services
- Indexing/Abstracting Services with Single Article Provision Services
- Document Provision Brokers and Freelance Information Service Providers

MAIL or *FAX* THIS ENTIRE ORDER FORM TO:

Attn: **Marianne Arnold**
Haworth Document Delivery Service
The Haworth Press, Inc.
10 Alice Street
Binghamton, NY 13904-1580

or **FAX:** (607) 722-1424
or **CALL:** 1-800-3-HAWORTH
(1-800-342-9678; 9am-5pm EST)

PLEASE SEND ME PHOTOCOPIES OF THE FOLLOWING SINGLE ARTICLES:
1) Journal Title: _____

    Vol/Issue/Year: _____ Starting & Ending Pages: _____

Article Title: _____

---

2) Journal Title: _____

    Vol/Issue/Year: _____ Starting & Ending Pages: _____

Article Title: _____

---

3) Journal Title: _____

    Vol/Issue/Year: _____ Starting & Ending Pages: _____

Article Title: _____

---

4) Journal Title: _____

    Vol/Issue/Year: _____ Starting & Ending Pages: _____

Article Title: _____

(See other side for Costs and Payment Information)

COSTS: Please figure your cost to order quality copies of an article.

1. Set-up charge per article: $8.00
   ($8.00 × number of separate articles) _____

2. Photocopying charge for each article:
   - 1-10 pages: $1.00 _____
   - 11-19 pages: $3.00 _____
   - 20-29 pages: $5.00 _____
   - 30+ pages: $2.00/10 pages _____

3. Flexicover (optional): $2.00/article _____

4. Postage & Handling: US: $1.00 for the first article/
   $.50 each additional article _____
   Federal Express: $25.00 _____
   Outside US: $2.00 for first article/
   $.50 each additional article _____

5. Same-day FAX service: $.35 per page _____

6. Local Photocopying Royalty Payment: should you wish to copy the article yourself. Not intended for photocopies made for resale. $1.50 per article per copy
   (i.e. 10 articles x $1.50 each = $15.00) _____

GRAND TOTAL: _____

METHOD OF PAYMENT: (please check one)

❏ Check enclosed   ❏ Please ship and bill. PO # _____
(sorry we can ship and bill to bookstores only! All others must pre-pay)

❏ Charge to my credit card: ❏ Visa; ❏ MasterCard; ❏ American Express;

Account Number:_____ Expiration date:_____

Signature: X_____ Name: _____
Institution: _____ Address: _____
City: _____ State:_____ Zip:_____
Phone Number: _____ FAX Number: _____

MAIL or *FAX* THIS ENTIRE ORDER FORM TO:

Attn: **Marianne Arnold**
Haworth Document Delivery Service
The Haworth Press, Inc.
10 Alice Street
Binghamton, NY 13904-1580

or FAX: (607) 722-1424
or CALL: 1-800-3-HAWORTH
(1-800-342-9678; 9am-5pm EST)